ZERO COMMENTS

ZERO COMMENTS

BLOGGING AND CRITICAL INTERNET CULTURE

GEERT LOVINK

Routledge
Taylor & Francis Group
New York   London

Routledge
Taylor & Francis Group
270 Madison Avenue
New York, NY 10016

Routledge
Taylor & Francis Group
2 Park Square
Milton Park, Abingdon
Oxon OX14 4RN

© 2008 by Taylor & Francis Group, LLC
Routledge is an imprint of Taylor & Francis Group, an Informa business

International Standard Book Number-13: 978-0-415-97316-8 (Softcover) 978-0-415-97315-1 (Hardcover)

Library of Congress Cataloging-in-Publication Data

Lovink, Geert.
    Zero comments : blogging and critical Internet culture / Geert Lovink.
        p. cm.
    Includes bibliographical references.
    ISBN 0-415-97315-5 (hardback : alk. paper) -- ISBN 0-415-97316-3 (pbk. : alk. paper)
    1. Blogs--Social aspects. 2. Internet--Social aspects. I. Title.

HM851.L689 2007
303.48'33--dc22   2007005611

Visit the Taylor & Francis Web site at
http://www.taylorandfrancis.com

and the Routledge Web site at
http://www.routledge.com

Contents

Acknowledgments

Following *Dark Fiber* (2002) and *My First Recession* (2003), this book is the third in a series of studies into critical Internet culture conducted from 2003 to 2006. I should say, "we present" as, compared to my earlier publications, this work is even more a product of a network of collaborations. I tried as much as possible to mention and quote those with whom I share ideas and material. There is even a special chapter dedicated to the issue of "free cooperation" in which I look into the art of (online) collaboration.

I would like mention Trebor Scholz, with whom I organized the Free Cooperation conference in Buffalo, New York, April 2004; Anna Munster, who was the co-author and co-organizer of the Distributed Aesthetics workshop at the Wissenschaftskolleg, Berlin, May 2006; Florian Schneider, with whom I wrote several texts on Internet activism; Soenke Zehle, co-founder of the Incommunicado list and main contributor to the conference in June 2005; and last but not least, my dear friend Ned Rossiter, co-author of the Organized Networks essay who moved from Australia to Europe at around the same time as I did. The support of Ned in the making of this book has been phenomenal as he commented on first drafts of many chapters.

Early research and conceptual development for this book was done in 2003 at the Centre for Critical and Cultural Studies (CCCS), University of Brisbane, Australia, where I enjoyed working as a postdoctoral fellow. I would like to thank the director, Graeme Turner, and Andrea Mitchell for their generous support. At CCCS Gerard Goggin, Mark McLelland, and Graham St. John were wonderful colleagues.

Financial support came from the Araneum prize that the Ministerio de Industria de España and Fundacion ARCO awarded early in 2004 for the concept. Thanks to Tania Román and Vicente Matallana from LaAgencia who managed the prize.

The appointment in 2004 as a research professor at the Hogeschool of Amsterdam within the School of Interactive Media, and associate professor within the new media program of Media & Culture, University of Amsterdam was an honor. In particular, I wish to thank the director of Interactive Media, Emilie Randoe for her continuous support. Soon after we settled in, I was able to realize a dream, founding the Institute of Network Cultures (INC), which I built up with its energetic producer Sabine Niederer. With Sabine at the helm, the INC organized four conferences in one year and started a range of publishing, teaching, and research activities, many of which flowed into this book. I want to thank her for her ongoing, dedicated support and grace under pressure.

This book was partly written and then finished during my 2005–2006 fellowship at the Wissenschaftskolleg in Berlin, the Institute of Advanced Study. I am grateful for their support and wish to thank all staff at Wiko.

Respect to Toshiya Ueno and Natalie Magnan, thanks for the music.

Matthew Byrnie at Routledge took the book proposal on board at an early stage. I would like to thank him and Stan Spring at Routledge for making the book possible. Before submitting the manuscript, I worked with copy editor Henry Warwick and I wish to thank him for his insights and the elegant way he shaped the material.

Finally, my greatest debt is to Linda Wallace, love of my life, complicit agent in all matters, and here also main copy editor, to whom I dedicated this book.

Geert Lovink

Introduction: The Pride and Glory of Web 2.0

Blogging is a form of vanity publishing: You can dress it up in fancy terms, call it 'paradigm shifting' or a 'disruptive technology', the truth is that blogs consist of senseless teenage waffle. Adopting the blogger lifestyle is the literary equivalent of attaching tinselly-sprinkles to the handlebars of your bicycle. In the world of blogging '0 Comments' is an unambiguous statistic that means absolutely nobody cares. The awful truth about blogging is that there are far more people who write blogs than actually read blogs.

—Stodge.org, The Personal Memoirs of Randi Mooney, posted on
May 5, 2005, (14) comments

By 2005, the Internet had recovered from the dot-com crash and, in line with the global economic figures, reincarnated as Web 2.0.[1] Blogs, wikis and "social networks" such as Friendster, MySpace, Orkut, and Flickr were presented as the next wave of voluntary alliances that users seek online. Virtual communities had become a discredited term, "associated with discredited ideas about cyberspace as an independent polity, and failed dotcom ideas about assembling community in the shadow of a mass-market brand such as forums on the Coca Cola site."[2] Instead, there was talk of swarms, mobs, and crowds. Media had turned social. From collaborative content production such as Wikipedia, to social bookmarking on Digg, there was a new élan. The BBC designated 2005 as the "year of the digital citizen."

The Boxing Day tsunami of 2004, the July 7th London bombings, and Hurricane Katrina in the United States all demonstrated the fact that citizens now have an integral role in the production of news. The BBC received 6500 e-mailed mobile images and video clips showing the fires at the Buncefield oil depot, thousands more than the number received after the London bombings.[3] Media started to look more participatory and inclusive, concluded the BBC report. That is the perception management side of the story. The challenge here is to come up with "harsh meditations" that reflect on Internet discourses in real time, based on informed engagement.

Despite a new generation of applications, the spectacular rise of the Internet population, and increased user involvement, most of the topics facing the Internet remained much the same: corporate control, surveillance and censorship, intellectual property rights, filtering, economic sustainability, and governance. As I wrote in the introduction to *My First Recession*, it was important for me to stay on-topic and not leave the scene. Much of what I deal with in this book is "unfinished business." It is no doubt uncool to deal with unresolved issues and to celebrate the new or critique it is in much higher demand. We cannot merely map old power struggles onto new terrain. It is justified to share the enthusiasm around free wireless infrastructure, peer-to-peer networks, and social software. I nonetheless chose to look into ongoing issues such as the stagnant "new media arts" sector, the whereabouts of German media theory, the "nihilist" impulse of blogging, the way triumphant Dutch architecture avoids dealing with the Internet, the "ICT for Development" galaxy and its World Summit of the Information Society, the abyss of Internet Time, and the progress made at the Sarai New Media Initiative in Delhi, five years after its opening. Despite all the victories, the confusion whether new media are frontier technologies or liminal activities has not yet been resolved. Finally, together with others, I indulged myself in speculative thinking and elaborate on collaborative work done on three concepts that have emerged in recent years: free cooperation, organized networks, and distributed aesthetics. I also give an update of "tactical media," a meme that we designed during the roaring nineties.

In my work on Internet culture I distinguish three phases: First, the scientific, precommercial, text-only period before the World Wide Web. Second, the euphoric, speculative period in which the Internet opened up for the general audience, culminating in the late 1990s dotcom mania. Third, the post-dot-com crash/post-9/11 period, which is now coming to a close with the Web 2.0 mini-bubble. Blogs, or Weblogs, really began around 1996 and 1997, during the second euphoric phase, but remained off the radar because they had no e-commerce component. The significant change of the past several years has been the "massification" and further internationalization of the Internet. In 2005, the one billion user mark was passed. The globalization of the Internet has been mostly invisible for the dominant Anglo-American Internet culture due to organized willful ignorance and a deficit of foreign language skills. It is hard for some to realize what it means that English content on the Web has dropped well below the 30 percent mark. Growth has also led to further nationalization of cyberspace, mainly using national languages, in contrast to the presumed borderless Internet that perhaps never existed. The majority of Internet traffic these days is in Spanish, Mandarin, and Japanese, but little of this seems to flow into the dominant Anglo-western understanding of Internet culture. This picture becomes further complicated if you take into account the "cross-media" potential of the two billion mobile phone users, blogomania in Iran, South Korea possessing one of the densest broadband infrastructures, and the rise of the Internet in China.

In this introductory chapter I do not intend to synthesize all the concepts that I discuss in this book. Instead, I will highlight a few threads that, in my view, characterize the state of the arts between 2003 and 2006. Some of them deal with the darkening of the Internet after 9/11, whereas others address the economics of Internet culture. There is no doubt that technology such as the Internet lives on the principle of permanent change. There is no normalization in sight. The "tyranny of the new" rules, and it is this echo of the dot-com era that makes Web 2.0 look so tired right out of the gate. We can despise the relentless instability as a marketing trick, and ask ourselves why we, time and time again, get excited by the latest gadget or application. Instead of transcending the market noise and detaching ourselves, we may as well reconcile ourselves to the same old change and enjoy precisely selected and manufactured revolutions. A decade after its appearance and rapid growth in popularity, Internet culture is torn apart by contradictory forces that make it no longer possible to speak of general trends in either good or evil directions. Whereas permanent change takes command and massive control regimes have been introduced, the tens of millions of new users that are being added on a monthly basis give the medium unexpected twists as they accept the given and joyfully appropriate services in ways that market watchers could never have guessed.

Net critic Nicholas Carr asks if there is a counter-argument to be made to the Web 2.0 hype. "All the things Web 2.0 represents—participation, collectivism, virtual communities, amateurism—become unarguably good things, things to be nurtured and applauded, emblems of progress toward a more enlightened state. But is it really so?"[4] Web 2.0 promoters, says Carr, "venerate the amateur and distrust the professional. We see it in their praise of Wikipedia, and we see it in their worship of open-source software and their promotion of blogging as an alternative to 'mainstream media'." My answer to this differs from Carr, who is reluctant to undermine the good parts of the traditional professional model. The libertarian praise of the amateur grows out of a distrust of and resentment toward large organizations that are wary of the anarcho-capitalist recipes on how to innovate. Utilizing open networks threatens the closed IP-focused knowledge management systems. In the libertarian approach, the professional becomes an obstacle because of this trade-union-like behavior. The result of a lacking pluriformity of models is an unarticulated reluctance to think up economic models for (emerging) professionals that leave behind the copyright structure, yet are desperate to earn a living from their work. Carr defends the fact-checking journalists that are employed inside the media industry. "In his article *We Are the Web*, Kevin Kelly writes that 'because of the ease of creation and dissemination, online culture is *the culture*.' I hope he's wrong, but I fear he's right—or will come to be right."

The question I pose here is how the praise of the amateur can be undermined, not from the perspective of the endangered establishment but from that of the creative (under)class, the virtual intelligentsia, the precariat (the contemporary worker who faces more job uncertainty than her proletariat precursor), the multitude that seeks to professionalize its social position as new media workers. We need economic models that assist ambitious amateurs to make a living from their work. "Everyone is a professional." Related to this is the still outstanding debate of professional standards, certifications and codexes: what is Web design, who can do it, and how much does it cost? How do new tasks, related to computer networks, fit into existing institutions such as hospitals, trade unions, and museums? We cannot answer before we have codified the work practices, much in the same way guilds have done this in the past and professional organizations are doing right now. Is it the aim of professionalization of new media work to create new, separate sectors in society, or rather should we dissolve these tasks within existing professions? I will discuss this question further when I look at the example of new media arts in its relation to contemporary arts: is self-referentiality a sign of maturity or rather one of an unsustainable ghettoization? Can we argue in favor of radical transdisciplinarity while at the same time create an archipelago of micro-disciplines? Such issues can be tackled through fundamental practice-based research, which was my model in founding the Institute of Network Cultures in 2004.

Crusaders of the Free

Unreconstructed fragments of 1990s Internet ideology are still floating around. These are mostly facilitating concepts that appeal to freedom-loving, young users. Take blogger Ian Davis, for whom Web 2.0 "is an attitude, not a technology. It is about enabling and encouraging participation through open applications and services. By open I mean technically open but also, more importantly, socially open with rights granted to use the content in new and exciting contexts. Of course the Web has always been about participation and would be nothing without it. Its single greatest achievement, the networked hyperlink, encouraged participation from the start."[5] Read the catchy self-definition of Digg: "Digg is all about user powered content. Every article on Digg is submitted and voted on by the Digg community. Share, discover, bookmark, and promote the news that's important to you!" It is not enough to deconstruct the lure of such techno-libertarianism in an academic journal or on a mailing list. The rebel-business talk of change has nowhere near been taken apart. No dissidents have yet stood up to object to the hypocritical agenda behind "free" and "open" in broader public arenas. What, in fact, should be done is to demand from the Free gurus to come up with an innovative economic model every time they "free up" the next cultural or social activity.

On a more visionary scale, Wikipedia founder Jimmy Wales listed "Ten Things That Will Be Free." The list was inspired by David Hilbert's address to the International Congress of Mathematicians in Paris in 1900 where he proposed 23 critical unsolved problems in mathematics. Apart from the obvious free encyclopedia and free dictionary, there are standard curriculum schoolbooks, maps, communities, academic publishing, music and art, but also TV listings, product identifiers, search engines and file formats.[6] Richard Stallman, pioneer of the free software movement, never managed to eliminate the confusion that "free" in his view does not mean "free-of-cost" but instead expresses the freedom of possibility to change computer code. For me there is no immediate connection between free and freedom. Things that are simply free-of-cost (as in "free beer") may satisfy the millions only to obscure the fact that the promoters, and the virtual class in general, cash-in elsewhere in the chain. The emphasis of Lawrence Lessig, Tim O'Reilly, Joi Ito, and many others on the right to remix mainstream content is an important issue but not crucial as most aspiring artists produce their own work. It is a bad postmodern cliché to state that today's cultural production merely consists of quotations. The exclusive focus on young and innocent amateurs that just want to have fun, and the resentment against professionals is not accidental. Amateurs are less likely to stand up and claim a part of the fast increasing surplus value (both symbolic and in real money terms) that the Internet is creating. Professionals who have been around for a while would understand what the implications will be for content producers if one giant such as Google instead of book publishers ends up controlling money flows. What is important here is to envision sustainable income sources beyond the current copyright regimes.

The vices of Internet architecture must be known (and not left unquestioned) so that its virtues may prevail. The ideology of the free as one of its key components is part of the lubricious business language. In his essay *The Destruction of the Public Sphere*, Ross McKibben states that the most powerful weapon of market-managerialism has been its vocabulary. "We are familiar with the way this language has carried all before it. We must sit on the cusp, hope to be in a centre of excellence, dislike producer-dominated industries, wish for a multiplicity of providers, grovel to our line managers, even more to the senior management team, deliver outcomes downstream, provide choice. Our students are now clients, our patients and passengers customers."[7] According to McKibben, it is a language that was first devised in business schools, then broke into government, and now infests all institutions.

> It has no real historical predecessor and is peculiarly seductive. It purports to be neutral: thus all procedures must be "transparent" and "robust", everyone "accountable". It is hard-nosed but successful because the private sector on which it is based is hard-nosed and successful. It is efficient; it abhors waste; it provides all the answers. It drove Thatcher's enterprise culture. It is more powerful than the kind of language Flaubert satirized in the *Dictionnaire des idées reçues* since, however ridiculous it might be, it determines the way our political (and economic) elites think of the world.

"You shall give everything away free (free access, no copyright); just charge for the additional services, which will make you rich." This is the first of the "Ten Liberal Communist Commandments" that Olivier Malnuit published in the French magazine *Technikart*. The person who embodies these values like no one else is the Japanese venture capitalist, hacker, and activist Joi Ito. Slavoj Žižek quoted Malnuit's commandments and lists Bill Gates and George Soros as liberal communists. Žižek says,

> The signifier of liberal communist Newspeak is "smart". Being smart means being dynamic and nomadic, and against centralized bureaucracy; believing in dialogue and co-operation as against central authority; in flexibility as against routine; culture and knowledge as against industrial production; in spontaneous interaction and autopoiesis as against fixed hierarchy. Their dogma is a new, postmodern version of Adam Smith's invisible hand: the market and social responsibility are not opposites, but can be reunited for mutual benefit.[8]

Žižek goes on to say that liberal communists are pragmatic; they hate a doctrinaire approach. "There is no exploited working class today, only concrete problems to be solved: starvation in Africa, the plight of Muslim women, religious fundamentalist violence." Žižek's conclusion comes as no surprise: "We should have no illusions: liberal communists are the enemy of every true progressive struggle today." Liberal communists give away with one hand what they grab with the other. This goes to the core of the Internet ideology that makes us blind to what we actually pay, while overly happy to join the gift economy of the free.

Žižek mentions the necessity, in instances such as racism, sexism, and anti-Semitism, to build coalitions with the liberal communists. But what about the case of the Internet? Isn't it time to bail out from the shared agendas with the libertarians, call for the exodus and confront the libertarians with their double agendas? Felix Stalder and Konrad Becker from Vienna summarize the fight for media freedom in a neat way.

> The goal is to devise new ways in which information can flow freely from one place to another, from people to people. Instead of deepening fragmentation, information and cultures are held to be a resource produced and used collaboratively, rather than being controlled by particular owners. People should be free to appropriate information as they see fit, based on their own historical and personal needs and desire, rather than having to consume the standardized products of McWorld.[9]

My take here is that we can only continue to spread such calls for liberty if they also contain antagonistic statements about the "state of the free." We cannot continue to uncritically support creative commons, open source, and knowledge for all platforms such as Wikipedia if their ideological premises cannot be discussed.

Internet Jihad in the Netherlands

A major challenge during the research of this book concerned the murder of Dutch filmmaker Theo van Gogh by Muslim fundamentalist Mohammed Bouyeri on November 2, 2004, two blocks from our apartment in the Eastern part of Amsterdam. Several months earlier, van Gogh had shot a film with then Dutch member of parliament Ayaan Hirsi Ali about the position of women in Islam. The new media component of violent Islam fundamentalism posed a range of ethical questions for me that go way beyond the disputes with trolls that I described in my previous publications. List moderators, community sites, and providers constantly find themselves in the uncomfortable position of having to deal with an Internet culture gone out of control, something they would rather like to keep free and open. Mohammed B. (as he was referred to in the Dutch press until his conviction) and his friends made intensive use of the Internet to shape and propagate their views. They operated in several discussion forums and made their own Web pages. They had their own Web pages for jihad fighters, often with MSN groups, for example, under the name of "5434" and "twaheedwljihad."[10] van Gogh also was actively involved in the Dutch Internet with his Web site *De Gezonde Roker* (*The Healthy Smoker*). During 2004 Weblogs in the Netherlands were at the height of their popularity. The hype was in full swing and scores of celebrities, from ministers to crooners, maintained a personal blog. The conspiratorial chats, massive online hate speech and racism, and peer-to-peer sharing of beheading videos in the months leading up to van Gogh's murder mark the final realization of the democratization of the Internet. From then on, it was no longer legitimate to speak of new media's democratic potential. Internet and mobile phones had penetrated society to such an extent that it felt ridiculous to even ask about the impact technology had as if it were still outside. Internet and society, at least in the Netherlands, had completely merged. Why should one be surprised that "radical losers" (a term by Hans Magnus Enzensberger)[11] publish Web sites, transfer files, exchange messages via e-mail, discuss in Web forums and news groups, and talk to each other via chat, instant messaging, or video-conferencing?

In October 2005 University of Amsterdam researcher Albert Benschop published a report about the van Gogh case, in which he emphasized the new media aspect. For Benschop, the Internet is a free state and a refuge for awkward opinions. Theo van Gogh had learned, just like his killer, how to make use of it. As a columnist, van Gogh had been dumped by many newspapers and magazines for his extraordinarily insulting texts; writings that were legal under Dutch law in the name of tolerance and freedom of the individual; a tenet close to the heart of Holland. Following Benschop's analysis, we have to connect the move of Dutch politics toward right-wing politics under Pim Fortuyn (who was assassinated in 2002) with a specific reading of Internet freedom. Theo van Gogh considered the Internet to be the only medium on which he could speak freely. Benschop in his "chronicle of a political murder foretold:"

> The rise of populist Fortuynism in the Netherlands went hand in hand with a strong hardening of the political debate and a coarsening in the style of discussion. It was difficult not to notice that many people who make use of the Internet contributed to this polarized hardening. Many discussion forums have degenerated into refuges for people who deeply insult and slander each other, and even threaten each other with death.[12]

Polarization in society after 9/11 is further amplified by the libertarian Internet architecture that ensures an unconditional and absolutist freedom of speech.[13] Benschop says,

Communications via Internet do not have immediate repercussions on the local social life of the individual participants. Thus they feel free(r) to express themselves in a disinhibited way. This is precisely the reason why Internet communications are characterized by two extreme manifestations of social behavior: being excessively and unwontedly sweet to other people ("netslutting" or "flirting") and excessively insulting or even threatening people ("netshitting" or "flaming").

Dutch Muslim youth visited sites such as How to Prepare Myself for Jihad, with calls to fight in Chechnya. On the Moroccan site for youngsters mocros.nl, Theo van Gogh had been threatened with death for months. Already in April 2004 a picture of the filmmaker was posted on a forum page of mocros.nl, with the text "When is it Theo's turn?" In this poster, a target with seven bullet holes was projected over his throat, chest, and head. "Allah will quickly get rid of this literal and figurative swine." Mohammed B. used the Internet to find texts on radical Islam, which were then translated into Dutch.

Public reaction to the murder was equally extreme. On Moroccan Web sites and discussion forums—before they curbed themselves—many contributions from Islamists alleged the godless pig had finally got what he deserved, that Allah's will had triumphed and van Gogh had received a suitable dose of his own medicine. A vistor signed on to the maroc.nl site as Robrecht wrote "Praise the martyr who shot down Theo van Gogh! That's how the Zionists and their servants come to their bloody end!" Albert Benschop: "Many people transformed their sorrow over van Gogh's death into an exceptional aggressiveness towards everything experienced as 'culturally impure'. We were too weak and we should hit back." "We cannot even express our opinion in our own country anymore" (Angelica). Apart from huge outrage about infringement of freedom of speech and senseless violence, people cry out for revenge in the form of more violence. "Perhaps next time we should finish off an imam when he opens his trap about Dutch society" (anonymous). "Who sets fire to the first mosque? I hope many will go up in flames" (Dutch person). "Dutchmen wake up! It's about time we take the law into our own hands and start in the underprivileged areas" (Henk). "Throw that scum out of the country and close the doors!" (Leo). So much for the infamous Dutch tolerance.

Societies in turmoil, such as the Netherlands, produce more (digital) data than anyone can process. Few scholars are technically and linguistically up to the job of monitoring the multitude of fast-moving translocal chat rooms, blogs, and sites. The detailed empirical study of Albert Benschop cries out for a critical theoretical follow-up and a shift of Internet studies away from soft constructivism and *Ideologiekritik* toward a nonjudgmental approach that is ready to dig into the dirty everyday doings of the network society. We need to say farewell to theories that equate the Internet with democracy, empowerment of Identity and The Good. The Theo van Gogh case study is by no means the only one. *Smart Mobs* author, Howard Rheingold, had to revise his optimistic vision of how (mobile) technologies were empowering the swarms for the good. The Power of the Many can take us in any direction. During the Sydney beach riots of December 2005, thousands of protesters mobilized through SMS messages that called to clear the beaches of Lebanese men and others of Middle Eastern appearances.[14] In another instance, jailed members of the PCC gang in São Paolo, Brazil paralyzed the metropolis by orchestrating an intimidation campaign out of their prison cells, using SMS messaging and a TV network showing a cell phone interview with someone who presented himself as the PCC leader.[15] In response, the Brazilian government planned to submit a bill forcing mobile phone operators to install equipment that will block signals inside prisons.

"We Lost the War"

A deeper understanding of the Internet ideology has been hampered by the range of Homeland Security measures of the Bush administration, willingly copy-pasted by coalition governments. War-on-terror measures, worldwide, can be credited for the return of pure and worthy libertarian ideas such as being cool and, yet again, countercultural. Instead of displaying their usual optimism, in 2005 a leading hacker from the German Chaos Computer Club, Frank Rieger, wrote a Declaration of Capitulation. It was called "We Lost the War. Welcome to the World of Tomorrow."[16] This manifesto indicates that the hegemonic strategy of simply claiming a superior knowledge position as computer programmer against the powers that be no longer works. Rieger calls on his constituency to, again, investigate what, under the current circumstances, amounts to an underground attitude. The text starts with the mysterious sentence, "Losing a war is never a pretty situation." His picture of the victorious mood around 2000, just before the dotcom crash and 9/11 sounds accurate. "We had survived Y2K with barely a scratch. The world's outlook was mildly optimistic after all. The 'New Economy' bubble gave most of us fun things to do and the fleeting hope of plenty of cash not so far down the road. We had won the Clipper-Chip battle, and crypto-regulation, as we knew it was a thing of the past. The waves of technology development seemed to work in favor of freedom, most of the time."

These days, says Rieger, "democracy is already over". 9/11 is being used by the elite to push through repressive legislation that would normally be flat-out rejected, or at least resisted. In his manifesto, Rieger writes, "Cooking up the terrorist threat by apparently stupid foreign policy and senseless intelligence operations provides a convenient method to get through with the establishment of a democratically legitimized police state." Rieger points out that hackers now have to build the very tools they once detested. Because of massive investments in internal security, Internet culture is changing. He warns that anonymity will become a precious thing. "Closed user groups have already gained momentum in communities that have a heightened awareness and demand for privacy." Decentralized infrastructure is needed. But most of all fun! "Exposing surveillance in the most humiliating and degrading manner, giving people something to laugh about must be the goal. Also, this prevents us from becoming frustrated and tired. If there is no fun in beating the system, we will get tired of it and they will win. So let's be flexible, creative and funny, not angry, ideological and stiff-necked."

It is curious to see that these concerns, conspiracy-driven paranoia or not, fail to mention what people are actually doing on the Web. The gap between the code hacking class and the ten of millions who chat, skype, link, Google, message, and e-mail with each other is greater than ever. The millions of ordinary users simply do not exist. The fight over the Internet is portrayed as a heroic struggle between the hackers and the security forces. The user masses are not even considered a spectator audience. The hi-low distinction that once plagued the television discourse returns here, except that the one billion Internet users simply do not exist.

Debating Web 2.0

Please, God, just one more bubble!

–A bumper sticker

It is important to analyze the Web 2.0 hype and see how it differs from the late-1990s dotcom days. The days of empty portals have long gone by. Instead, bands and brands are running after the roaming hordes of users in an attempt to boost their popularity. What we gained compared to 1999 is the realization that people do not flock to the Web for e-commerce but for conversation.[17]Instead of the Web 2.0 term that Tim O'Reilly plugged, Trebor Scholz prefers to talk about "sociable web media." Trebor, posting on the iDC list: "The term Web 2.0 is yet another fraudulent bubble designed to trick investors with pretended newness. It's just like McDonald's re-stacking their greasy beef layers to sell an entirely new product every 6 months."[18] Nonetheless, the cluster of applications referred to as Web 2.0 are relatively new, as are the tens of millions of users who make use of social networks such as Digg and Facebook and sites like Wikipedia. And let's not forget the economic exchanges through eBay or Craigslist.

Writing in the same mailing list thread, what fascinates technologist Andreas Schiffler is how Web 2.0 presents a rediscovery of existing technologies such as RSS Netscape 1999, AJAX XML/HTTP Request IE5, and DHTML/CSS IE5. These were popular features with browser-based companies, which were then transformed into a social phenomenon. It seems besides the point to classify the 70 odd million MySpace users as mere victims of corporate media simply because Newscorp's Rupert Murdoch at some point acquired the site. It seems hard for corporate consultants, hackers, and media activists to move away from the broadcast model and fully accept, beyond good or evil, the massive uptake of user content production and related networks of friends. The disdain of AOLers locked up in their crappy Microsoft products sits deep, but in reality only shows that early adaptor elites have long lost their grip on the Internet.

Web 2.0 promoters have rightly been accused of hyping emerging sites so that they can be sold to venture capitalists who then replace the management and alienate users who then move on so a new cycle can start elsewhere. Yet this isn't the end of the story. Jon Ippolito: "To dismiss the innovations behind Web 2.0 simply because venture capitalists are using this silly term to squeeze cash out of investors is like dismissing the environmental movement because British politicians are suddenly waving green flags to court election-year voters. Let's not confuse the carpetbaggers with the communities." Saul Albert admits: "There is nothing wrong with the business proposition if you can maintain the delicate balance of my needs against the imperatives of funders and advertisers." He then gives the example of del.icio.us that had a chance to supersede (kill) Google with a bottom-up public knowledge infrastructure at some point immediately before it was bought. Juha Huuskonen of Pixelache in Helsinki reminds the list participants that it "seems essential for an organization/service/tool to maintain their image as the 'good guys', something that might become increasingly difficult for commercial services in future. One complex and important issue seems to be how to deal with monopolies, both in the case of commercial services like Google but also for projects like Wikipedia. The magic role of the 'benevolent dictators' like Jimbo Wales for Wikipedia or Linus Thorvalds for Linux does not seem like a lasting solution."

Sloganism for the Tagged:

- Last year she lost four days to flu, and seven days to spyware (ad)
- How to Connect Citizens to a Structure

- The Power of the Default (slogan)
- Blogging 'n Belonging
- Theory of the Surrounding Society
- Polluted talent pools
- Weaving what the network demands
- Pathologies of the Self-instructing Child (book title)
- The Tragedy of the Nomadic
- Expertocracy International
- Blogging for Tenure
- Critique of Capturing (subtitle)
- "Where are you?" replaced "How are you?"
- Google Blockage Syndrome
- Pioneering the Untaggable
- Visualize Whirled Peas
- Become a Filter
- I was an enemy of linearity
- Michel Serres and the necessity of parasites
- I shagged Tom from MySpace (t-shirt)
- NaKisha's blog theory is a brain fart that she cannot get out of her head. It's like she knows what to do but how can she when she feels like her life is standing still.
- These worlds were not made for me.
- You can't blog this (Danah Boyd)
- I fart in elevators (MySpace t-shirt)
- Just a bunch of assholes with cameras and some software
- Account deleted because it was not used for a long time or violated our terms of use. Please contact us if you want it back.

A Short-Lived Discordia

Juha Huuskonen, who organized festivals about the Dot Org Boom, mentions trust, security, credibility, and monopolies as the topics that connect different discussions. This is also what the following didactic story, or *Lehrstück* in the Brechtian sense, is all about. Toward the end of *My First Recession*, in a chapter on open publishing, I discussed the coming into being of a group blog called Discordia, which was launched in mid-2003.[19] Its aims were "social filtering, collaborative moderation and different styles of communication." Having gone through a long coding process (using Scoop software), with members having to deal with internal differences exclusively online, this "Slashdot of the Electronic Arts" surprisingly closed down 16 months after its launch. It is interesting to briefly discuss its failure as the issue of filtering, and moderation has by no means disappeared simply because we are in the age of Web 2.0. Discordia's original intention was to have a Web forum that would use ranking of postings and comments as a way to overcome the "enlightened dictatorship" of mailing list moderators. Discordia was a failed attempt to overcome rivalries between professional cultures such as criticism and theory, visual arts and computer programming. For some, the content was too academic to feel that they could make a valid contribution. Joseph Rabie: "I have always thought that Discordia suffered, and did not flourish, because of a propensity of many posters to be 'objective'—almost in a third person sort of way. Blogs are exciting when people put their own selves on the line."

As it often goes, users lost track and could not remember the URL, login name, and password. Others expected a much more visible presence of the founding collective that ran the project. Soon after its start, Discordia was caught in a downward spiral. Discordia programmer Peter Traub: "The general concept of the site was good but the nature of the content possibly drove people away or just intimidated them to the degree that they did not feel comfortable contributing. The lack of regular updates to the site causes users to check back less frequently. And when users check back less frequently, the number of new posts drops."[20] In the end, the chemistry between content producers and coders was frayed. The influence of programmers simply turned out to be too big, leaving the project in limbo once the coding job was done. Expectations to have the kind and number of responses *a la* Slashdot could not be fulfilled. It was time for a new project, but Discordia as a debating platform had barely begun and was just about to pick up some Web traffic. The Discordia saga proved that one cannot enforce a complex Web 2.0 platform on a community.

Apart from the group dynamics, the main reason for Discordia's failure was the lack of coherence within the global new media arts community to have public debates on the World Wide Web, away from the safety of cozy, inward looking lists. The critical mass simply wasn't there to start working with the ranking system. There was not enough of an interest to join an equal, open dialogue between critics, artists, and programmers. This problem can be extended to other fields such as humanities and social sciences, activism, contemporary, civil society, and the NGO-sector and autonomous social movements. The problem is not one of technophobia. Rather, it is caused by avant-gardism having adopted the Internet relatively early and not feeling the need to upgrade yet again. The excitement of tactical media geeks, NGO workers, community activists, and electronic artists, including their accompanying academics, curators, and critics toward Web 2.0 has been remarkably low.

Perhaps Discordia had placed too much emphasis on getting the network architecture right. The utopian spark within the new media arts community failed. People did not get enough out of posting. Facilitator Trebor Scholz, looking back: "For debates I chased people to post and chased yet others to respond to what was posted. I see no point in having a tool like Discordia just for those who built it. I saw our role in the creation of context, it should not be about us providing content as well." U.K. media artist and programmer Saul Albert: "The conversations had during its development ended up being the most valuable bit for me. When we'd finished making the tool, I didn't need it for anything. I think the idea of a collaborative Weblog was only an uncomfortable stepping stone on the way to something far more distributed and dissonant than we envisaged." Albert sums up insights he made while working on Discordia: "There needs to be regular interpersonal contact at the core of a project, in my opinion. *A priori* categorization doesn't work, even if it's playful. It just confuses people. Choices of technology should follow the needs of a group of people with a goal in mind."

Cynical Spirit of the Blogosphere

Instead of deconstructing the Web 2.0 as the blanket term referring to startups that generate more RSS than revenue and are driven by the same old Silicon Valley types, I spent most of my research time during the Berlin winter of 2005–2006 formulating a General Theory of Blogging.[21] It will remain an ontological question whether criticism of emerging phenomena is indeed possible. What I mean by critical inquiry is that I ignore the legitimate but, in my view, all too correct position that blogs can only be studied through their different genres (political, educational, research, narrative, and so on). Blogs are the proxy of our time. It is a techno-affect that cannot be reduced to the character of the individual blogger. There are possibly as many blogs as there are voices and topics. Rough estimates in early 2006 came close to 100 million.[22] How can you do research when your object is in a state of hyper-growth and permanent transformation? This is the case with the blogosphere. Instead of merely looking into the emancipatory potential of blogs, or emphasizing their counter-cultural folklore, I see blogs as part of an unfolding process of "massification" of what is still a new medium. What the dotcom medium after 2000 lost is the illusion of a rapid overhaul of society as such. The void thus created made way for large-scale interlinked conversations through automated social software systems, of which blogs are but one of many applications.

Chapter 2 of this book attempts to formulate a theory that moves away from the commonly held presumption that blogs would have an elective affinity with the news industry. With this I do not only mean the "citizen journalist" label but, more structurally, the built-in a priori that blogs should produce "feeds" and that the essence of blogging is ranking. Instead of focusing on the quality of the content, and the culture of writing, diary keeping, and reflection, blogs have become more of a rat race for maximum attention, measured in links and friends. Whereas blog software has facilitated the massification of the Internet, bringing easy-to-use publishing to tens of millions of users worldwide, by 2005 the blogosphere went into hysterical overdrive. A next wave of Internet chauvinism emerged. Blogs lost their slackness and first-movers started looking for the exit. The snarky undertone of much of the postings disappeared. Slick self-promotion began to take over, moving from collectively defining the news issues around 2003 during the days of the Howard Dean campaign to the precarious blogging of "How to Make Money with Your Blog." In that sense, the "sticky nihilism" of the blogosphere may already have become history as "truthfulness" often conflicts with the public image. The cynical take on blogs is that their sole purpose has been to create a talent pool for the publishing industry. Signing up these talents is not only benefiting the media business, it is threatening the positions of those journalists who do not deliver. They will be fired. In the end, it is not the blog world but the media industry that will be strengthened.

This Is Not an Economy 2.0

First build relationships, then revenues.

–Paul Szydlowski

On the business side there is a growing uncertainty, now that convergence has become a reality, if Web 2.0 is the beginning of the end. Finally, the technology sector bumps into the Content Question. Up until now this has only existed as a discourse without an object. The "content is king" slogan from the late 1990s remained an empty promise. "What will people watch, listen to, and do with these machines now that they are becoming interchangeable and interconnected?" Saul Hansell asks in *The New York Times*. Hansell lists three anxieties of old-line media: "Business-model anxiety. Will paid download services undercut TV networks' huge advertising revenue? Creative anxiety. McLuhan is out. The medium is no longer the message. Anyone who wants to tell a joke or spin a tale can produce any combination of video, text, sound and pictures for viewing on a 50-inch TV, a laptop computer or a cell phone screen. Control anxiety. Since the invention of the high-speed printing press, mass media have been created for the masses, not by them. Now we can all be DJs and film directors, distributing our podcasts and movies online without groveling before a studio executive. The career prospects for hit makers, gatekeepers and even fact checkers may well be in doubt."[23] But before getting all flustered and excited, let us research the actual incomes and labor conditions of the creative class.

Whereas user crowds move from social bookmarking to photo sharing and classification as the next thing, what remains unresolved is an equally decentralized and distributed Internet economy. For most users the Internet is not free; they pay considerable money for hardware and cables, external drives, connectivity, software and upgrades, design features, and subscriptions. Content producers pay to have their work shown.[24] The techno-libertarian model of the 1990s remains prevalent, which says that those who write software and provide the telco-infrastructure will make the money on the basis of the ignorant masses who are all too happy to hand over their content for free. How content producers are going to make a living is perceived as a personal problem that is rarely discussed. Most of them are amateurs and the few professionals generate their income through old media such as the printing press, film, television, and radio.

One of the few changes we witnessed over the past years has been the rise of tools such as Google's Adsense.[25] However, it remains to be seen exactly how much Web authors can actually earn through such services. Nicholas Carr, ranked number 689 on Technorati, reported a net loss of $1425 over the first year of his Rough Type blog.[26] Darren Rowse, a Melbourne-based professional who runs ProBlogger ("Helping Bloggers Make Money") advises use of Chitika's eMiniMalls that "selects the top products for your web page and displays interactive and robust information such as product ratings, descriptions, reviews and related blog content."[27] The economic rationale here is to "turn page views into profit." Online advertisements are no longer the manual placement of Web banners. Earnings can come through sponsoring, business blog writing, merchandising, online donations, and the old tricks such as consultancy and speaking engagements. In many such cases the blogger has to act as an independent representative of Big Business. As a corporate proxy, out in the field, the blogger-as-spy equals not so much the salesman (think Tupperware) but should be considered more as part of a civilian network of informants. Increasingly bloggers are drawn into corporate structures, getting involved in a complex economy of links, tags, traffic data, and, indeed, micro debits.

The list of tools that will give the blogger the impression of making money grows on a daily basis. Many such services will no longer exist in a few years. Take this example of two companies called Prosper and Zopa who are convinced that social networking along the lines of MySpace can be combined with borrowing and lending. "They're intent on using eBay as a model for listing and bidding on loans without the involvement of a bank. Call it peer-to-peer finance. There are already some 800 groups on

Prosper ready to loan money to specific causes, such as the Apple User Group, 'a lending group for those wishing to purchase either a Macintosh or Apple iPod'."[28]

"The Internet business path is about to split," says Seth Goldstein.[29] "One direction leads to an open approach to data, governed by the principles of transparency and publicity. The other direction leads to a closed approach to data, focused on privacy and opacity: the black box. Both directions have legitimate and consistent end-user benefits and economic rationales." Goldstein warns of the danger of being stuck in the middle: "Looking to increase your edge but not locking up the information it is based on; or promoting your open-ness but not sharing data back to the system." In this rather confusing picture, we're moving to a mixed economy, where a steadily increasing army of independent Web workers will try to make a living. In this outsourcing model, research and the manufacturing of consent further relaxes the borders that work inside and outside the corporate walls. Blog software increasingly speeds up the model of the firm as a networked organization in which business increasingly becomes a permanent regrouping of loose units. However, a great deal of this shift remains ideological and a redistribution of financial resources such as research budgets and profit fail to materialize. Whereas the network takes on more risks, the concentration of power in fewer hands further increases.

Translate this back to the Internet economy and we see that the most profitable businesses are playing an intermediary role. Nicholas Carr: "They've realized that, when it comes to making money on the Web, what matters is not controlling the ultimate exchange (of products or content or whatever) but controlling the clicks along the way. That's become even more true as advertising click-throughs have become the main engine of online profits. Who controls the most clicks wins."[30] According to *Long Tail* author Chris Anderson, venture capitalists openly admit that there is no money to be made in content, including blogs. The business plans that make sense are not so much content creators as aggregators and filters.[31] He quotes David Hornik, a venture capitalist at August Capital: "While different filtering technologies may make it slightly more likely that an end user finds his or her way to a piece of obscure content, it will not likely be sufficient to catapult an artist into the mainstream. The beneficiary of the filtering is the end user and the filterer, not the content owner per se." Oso, the Latin America Regional Editor at Global Voices put it this way: "Aggregators are better funded than content creators. Floating in a sea of noise, we become dependent on islands of aggregation (Digg, Google News, del. icio.us/popular, Newsvine, Boing Boing, Global Voices) to guide us to the gems. Our dependence on those sites ensures their funding (either by investment, grants, or ads). But the people who make the actual content, the heart of the artichoke, go unpaid."[32] Another reason could be the so-called 1% rule, which says that if you get a group of 100 people online then one will create content, 10 will interact with it (commenting or offering improvements), and the other 89 will just view it. Seen from this perspective, the content producer is just a tiny minority that can easily be overlooked. The question then becomes why this number of 1% is that low.[33]

Where social networking and blogging proves to be a hit among users, the underlying business model of such services remains shaky. Too much money is again pouring into too many unproven, unprofitable ideas. According to a report in the *Los Angeles Times*, MySpace and YouTube have yet to make money, "and some skeptical investors wonder what hope there is for all the copycats. 'There is a risk that we're going back to the marketing of eyeballs without a business model,' said Jim Lussier, a general partner with Norwest Venture Partners in Palo Alto. He has kicked the tires on nearly two dozen online video companies but said he couldn't find anything unique."[34] As long as innovative Internet startups depend on the 1990s model of venture capital, leading up to a takeover or IPO, the hope that a change in culture will occur will remain slim. It is only a matter of time until the development of Internet applications will no longer happen on the U.S. West Coast, for instance shifting toward the centers of mobile devices in Asia and Europe. At such a point, cultural differences have to be made productive, taking into account, for instance, that credit cards, the dominant e-commerce payment system right now, are full of social limitations and used only in a limited number of countries.[35]

In or Out?

This book will prove that, contrary to the "new new" hype, the position of new media in society is no closer to resolution than it was during the "old new" hype of the first Web bubble. Mass adaptation has lead to a "status anxiety"[36] of an emerging discipline that is polymorphously perverse in nature. The in-between position is increasingly becoming uncomfortable. There is a multitude of talent going nowhere. Shifts in the integration of technological networks into the everyday have proven no guarantee that institutional change will occur. Despite all the talk, the Internet has not delivered the revolution it promised. Societies adapt to Information and Communication Technologies (ICTs) but do not change in a fundamental way and prove remarkably flexible in staying as they are. Logically speaking, this means that the ideology, and not the world, will have to adjust. So far, this has not happened. How can libertarian techno-celebrities continue to sell dream worlds about freedom and leveling the fields without being scrutinized? There is little indication that they will shut up or even face serious opposition. There seems to be a never-ending demand among geeks and entrepreneurs for salvation. We can only repeat so often that the Web is not a place apart. So, how can young people be educated to resist the seductive calls of the Californian sirens? Would it suffice to design alternative memes? Are insider calls for reform useless in that only something entirely different can stop the spin? Should we believe in the power of the argument and continue the strategy of ideology criticism, knowing that such intellectual endeavors fail, time and again? *Zero Comments* was written in the firm belief that we have to work through issues. We have to study the patterns behind perpetual change. Besides its archeology, new media now has a history of its own, full of disruptions, anomalies, failed attempts, unnoticed remakes, comebacks, and rare instances of the new. I have seen it as the task of my ongoing critical Internet culture research to not only write such histories but to shape future understanding, in close collaboration with a network of friends and fellow thinkers.

CHAPTER 1

Blogging, the Nihilist Impulse

An der rationalen Tiefe erkennt man den Radikalen; im Verlust der rationalen Methode kündigt sich der Nihilismus an. Der Radikale besizt immer eine Theorie; aber der Nihilist setzt an ihre Stelle die Stimmung.

—Max Bense (1949)

This chapter proposes a general theory of blogging in which an analysis of user cultures is blended with a cultural critique of contemporary Web applications. I will first look into the merits of blog culture, then deal with the question of net cynicism, and finally, the nihilist condition of blogging. I circumvent both techno-determinism and cultural analysis Žižek-style. The aim here is neither to promote nor to deconstruct citizen journalism or to downplay the significance of participatory media. The empowering aspects of the hyped-up Web 2.0 applications are self-evident. Blogs have changed the world in various ways; the point, however, is to interpret them. What I am after is the nihilist structure of blogs as software and culture. The explicit aim is not to classify bloggers as digital nihilists. Instead, I am searching for a creative nihilism that openly questions the hegemony of mass media. Blogs zero out centralized meaning structures and focus on personal experiences, not, primarily, news media.[1]

So far, blogs have been discussed mainly in oppositional terms, as being a counter-voice to the dominant news industry. The leading blog culture, made from those who co-developed the technology and created early adaptor communities around these applications[2] is a mix of angry, confused, cynical, and engaged voices. The identity circus called the "blogosphere" is not exactly the place where progressive types set the tone. As a sign of the times, the blogging majority is conservative, and this was already noticeable in the responses to 9/11 and the U.S.-led invasion in Afghanistan and Iraq. Leaving the enabling rhetoric and democratization potential aside, blog culture is not, by definition, progressive and cannot be heralded as "anti-establishment."

Following Santa Barbara theorist Alan Liu, we could say: "I blog, but I am cool."[3] Blogs record our lives and prove to what extent people are formed by the media events into which they are drawn. Far from what most pioneers preach, blogs fit perfectly well into the concert of big media. Michael Massing, writing in the *New York Review of Books* in late 2005, states that the majority of U.S. blogs lean right and seamlessly fit into the talk radio and cable news landscape. Eight of the top ten blogs in the United States are conservative.

A list of the most visited blogs includes the following:

- InstaPundit, run by University of Tennessee law professor Glenn Reynolds
- Power Line (three lawyers)
- michellemalkin.com, a syndicated columnist who defended the internment of Japanese-Americans during World War II
- Free Republic (conservative activists)
- Captain's Quarters (run by a call-center manager)
- the Volokh Conspiracy (a UCLA law professor)
- Little Green Footballs, a commentary on foreign policy with a pro-Israel bias

The U.S. Army is giving "exclusive content" to pro-war bloggers.[4] Mitigating this, somewhat, is the number one center-left political blog, the Daily Kos, which owes its popularity in part to its community-style approach, where registered readers post their own comments as well as comment on the posts of others.[5]

Blogs fix the social in a specific manner. These techno-fixes are not neutral; they reflect the broader cultural atmosphere of our time. One could credibly say that early, e-mail–centered Internet culture was dominated by a counter-culture (from hippies to hackers), and the Web decadence of the 1990s was owned by second-generation yuppies and built by slackers and Generation X types. What they all had in common was, at least, a nominally libertarian mindset: conspiratorially anti-state and pro-market. Blog culture, on the other hand, is a post-9/11 beast. Blogs do not operate in some wild, open Internet out there (as one imagines newsgroups and lists do), but clearly create their own secluded social networks that consolidate their affiliations through link lists, blogchalking, RSS feeds, and the like. Blogs are always both private and public and are characterized by a culture of desired affiliation. The path to understanding blogs lies somewhere between an analysis of software functionalities and the early adopter culture that invented and shaped the blogosphere.

Some advice: Don't just think of the American pantheon of blog heroes, or the trashy, frivolous, and studiously non-serious MySpace.com if you want to get an insight into the specifics of this particular technology. Instead, you need to mix Clay Shirky and his powerlaws (which explain how the most influential bloggers—the so-called A-list—became so powerful) with Chris Anderson's Long Tail theory, which states that the true potential of blogs lies in the millions of blogs that only get a few page views per day.[6]

It is dangerous to "vitalize" Internet applications and their user cultures. There is a tendency to overcode. Because of the endless variety of the tens of millions of blogs out there, it is tempting to indulge the carnival of difference and ignore underlying communalities. My thesis here is that one must study undercurrents in techno-culture and avoid the seduction to just keep on surfing and kicking. We should not simply reduce blogs to their problematic relationship with the news industry. Mere empowerment does not automatically lead to worthy content. Blogging appeals to a wide register of emotions and affects as it mobilizes and legitimizes the personal. And to what effect are these affects mobilized?

Let's first try to answer the question of what blogging is. A Weblog or blog is commonly defined as a frequently updated Web-based chronological publication, a log of personal thoughts and Web links, a mixture of diary forms around what is happening in a person's life, and reports and comments on what is happening on the Web and the world out there. The blog allows for the easy creation of new pages: text and pictures are entered into an online template within the Web browser (usually tagged by title, category, and the body of the article) and this data is then submitted. Automated templates take care of adding the article to the home page, creating the new full article page (called a permalink), and adding the article to the appropriate date- or category-based archive. Because of the tags that the author puts onto each posting, blogs let us filter by date, category, author, or other attributes. It (usually) allows the administrator to invite and add other authors, whose permissions and access are easily managed.[7]

To Blog with Quality and Distinction

Laughin' and clownin', just to keep from crying.

—**Sam Cooke**

What makes a blog good, according to Glenn Reynolds, is a personal voice and a rapid response time. Microsoft's former in-house blogger Robert

Scoble lists five elements that made blogs hot. The first is "ease of publishing," the second he calls "discoverability," the third is "cross-site conversations," the fourth is perm linking (giving the entry a unique and stable URL), and the last is syndication (replication of content elsewhere).[8] Lyndon from Flockblog gives a few tips that help blog writing, showing how ideas, feelings, and experiences are compressed into the news format, and how dominant Microsoft PowerPoint has become: "Make your opinion known, link like crazy, write less, 250 words is enough, make headlines snappy, write with passion, include bullet point lists, edit your post, make your posts easy to scan, be consistent with your style, litter the post with keywords."[9] Whereas the e-mail–based list culture echoes a postal culture of writing letters and occasionally essays, the ideal blog post is defined by zippy public relations techniques.

Web services like blogs cannot be separated from their output. The politics and aesthetics defined by first users will characterize the medium for decades to come. Blogs appeared during the late 1990s, in the shadow of dotcom mania.[10] Blog culture was not developed enough to be dominated by venture capital with its hysterical demo-or-die, now-or-never mentality. Blogs first appeared as casual conversations that could not easily be commodified. Building a laidback parallel world made it possible for blogs to form the crystals (a term developed by Elias Canetti) from which millions of blogs grew year by year, until around 2003 they reached critical mass.

Blogging in the post 9/11 period closed the gap between Internet and society. Whereas the dotcom suits dreamt of mobbed customers flooding their e-commerce portals, blogs were the actual catalysts that realized democratization, worldwide, of the Internet. As much as democratization means engaged citizens, it also implies normalization (as in the setting of norms) and banalization. We can't separate these elements and only enjoy the interesting bits. According to Jean Baudrillard, we're living in the "Universe of Integral Reality." If there was in the past an upward transcendence, there is today a downward one. This is, in a sense, as Baudrillard says, "the second Fall of Man Heidegger speaks of: the fall into banality, but this time without any possible redemption."[11] If you can't cope with high degrees of irrelevance, blogs won't be your cup of tea.

The blogosphere has been shaped neither by dotcom entrepreneurs nor by techno-geeks. Basic computer knowledge does the job. Not even html skills are required. For business types there is no immediate money in it. The open character of blogs even forms a risk for those who are into branding and PR. The geeks feel protected in their Slashdot community and prefer the cleanliness of ASCII in e-mail versus the glossy personality-driven approach of blogs. For most academics, blogs are irrelevant as they don't count as publications. The same could be said of Internet activists who have not moved beyond the use of e-mail and their own content management system. A massive uptake of blogs, wikis, and podcasts among civil society organizations has yet to happen. Radical leftists and anti-globalists have their hands full with projects like Indymedia and usually do not look beyond their niche. We don't need to mention the new media arts scene here, as they are miraculously absent. The contemporary arts scene is not familiar with blogging. However, this is not the case with bands, their fans, and labels.

Are Blogs Vague? So Is Tuesday

The motor behind the expansion of the blogosphere is the move away from code toward content. There is no more need for empty demo design. Blogs are not a test or proposition. They actually exist. Early 2006 rough counts estimate approximately 100 million blogs worldwide.[12] From early on, blog culture has been the home of creative and social content producers. I hesitate to say journalists and academics because despite the fact that many have such a professional background, it would be false to locate pioneer bloggers inside institutional setups. Yet blog culture wasn't anti-institutional either. Much like the cyberculture of the 1990s, the first generation of bloggers possesses colorful biographies. However, a dominant culture, like the Californian techno-hippies, failed to emerge and if it exists, it is tricky to label. Blogging comes close to what Adilkno once described as "vague media."[13] The lack of direction is not a failure but its core asset. Blogging did not emerge out of a movement or an event. If anything, it is a special effect of software, as constitutional to it is the automation of links, a not-overly-complex technical interface design issue.

It was Brisbane Queensland University of Technology scholar Axel Bruns who came up with the theory of blogging as "gatewatching." At first, the term seemed too rigid and indifferent, too docile. It lacked sovereignty. Gatewatching implicitly positions blogs as passive and secondary compared to news sources (if we follow the analogy, the news gates on the East and West Coast of the United States, monitored from the Midwest). I warmed to the term when I saw that it was an accurate description of what blogs do, namely monitor the news media gatekeepers and colleague bloggers who are involved in what Bruns calls "participatory journalism."[14] Gatewatchers comment on the choices of those who control the news gates. Yet, this is no longer an activity of bystanders. Through, for instance, automated news syndications (RSS feeds) the process of annotation becomes news itself. Watching is incorporated into a system of notation and is then fit to be fed. Even though news agencies such as Reuters do not consider blog entries worth mentioning, opinion makers might take notice (at least, that's what some bloggers hope). In this way, the gatewatcher is placed inside a hermeneutic circle, in which news is taken as a given and then interpreted. Personal diary entries are complementary to news, yet do not change the exegetic nature of blogging. I blog, therefore I watch.

There is a widespread presumption that blogs have a symbiotic relationship with the news industry. This presumption is not uncontested. Hypertext scholars track blogs back to the 1980s and HyperCard and the 1990s online literature wave in which clicking from one document to the next was the central activity of the reader. For some reason, the hypertext subcurrent lost out in mainstream explanations of what blogging is all about. What remains is an almost self-evident equation between blogs and the news industry. To counter this, it would be important to dig into the rich history of literary criticism and see how blogging relates to diary keeping. It could be useful to formulate a theory of blogging as a "technology of the self," a concept developed by Michel Foucault. Blogs experiment with the public diary format, a term that expresses the productive contradiction between public and private in which bloggers find themselves. Until recently, most diaries have been private. They may have been written to be published at a later stage, often after the author passed away, but were nonetheless "offline" in the sense of not being accessible. Despite obvious differences, there are also communalities, as we can read in Thomas Mallon's *A Book of One's Own, People and Their Diaries*. Bloggers will recognize themselves in what Mallon writes: "I'm always behind. I try to write each night, but I often don't get around to writing up a day until several more days have gone by. But I manage to keep them all separate. I suppose it's a compulsion, but I hesitate to call it that, because it's gotten pretty easy. There comes a point when, like a marathon runner, you get through some sort of 'wall' and start running on automatic. Of course, there are days when I hate writing the thing. Who needs it? I'll ask myself; but I'll do it anyway."[15]

After reading hundreds of diaries, Mallon concludes that no one ever kept a diary for just himself. "In fact, I don't believe one can write to oneself for many words more than get used in a note tacked to the refrigerator, saying, 'buy bread'."[16] Keeping a diary provokes reflection about the activity itself. For Mallon, Virginia Woolf is the greatest critic of the genre: "The activity is, after all, so queer, so ad hoc, and supposedly so private, that it doesn't seem amiss for the diarist to stop every so often and ask himself just what he think he's doing." Woolf's fundamental motive is to "hold on to it all, to cheat the clock and death of all the things that she had lived." What intrigues me here are the "time folds" that we so often find in blogs as well. Many of Virginia Woolf's entries, says Mallon, are provoked by her neglect of regular dairy writing. "The journals are frequently interrupted by physical illness, madness, the press of work or social life. And sheer disinclination."[17] Sound familiar?

Situating blogging between online publishing and the intimate sphere of diary keeping brings into question the already disturbed separation between what is public and what is left of privacy. It is remarkable that many participants do not perceive blogs and social networking sites such as Orkut or MySpace as a part of public life. Online conversations between friends are so intense that the (mainly young and often naive) users do not realize, or care, that they are under constant observation. Yahoo! researcher Danah Boyd explains:

> Teens are growing up in a constant state of surveillance because parents, teachers, school administrators and others who hold direct power over youth are surveilling them. Governments and corporations are beyond their consideration because the people who directly affect their lives have created a more encompassing panopticon than any external structure could ever do. The personal panopticon they live in is far more menacing, far more direct, and far more traumatic. As a result, youth are pretty blasé about their privacy in relation to government and corporate.[18]

Boyd therefore advises: "Unless we figure out how to give youth privacy in their personal lives, they are not going to expect privacy in their public lives." Until further notice, the festive documentation of the private will continue, and it is up to family, social workers, and clergy to reconcile with this potlatch. Instead of raising concerns, one might better start harvesting human feelings from Weblogs, as wefeelfine.org has been doing.

Because of its public diary character, the question of whether blogs operate inside or outside the media is not easy to answer. To position the blog medium inside could be seen as opportunistic, whereas others see this as a clever move. There is also a tactical aspect. The blogger-equals-journalist might find protection under such a label in case of censorship and repression. Despite countless attempts to feature blogs as alternatives to the mainstream media, they are often more precisely described as feedback channels. The act of gatewatching mainstream media outlets does not necessarily result in reasonable comments that will then be taken into account by any internal review by the media. In the category "insensitive" we have a wide range, from hilarious to mad, sad, and sick. What CNN, newspapers, and radio stations the world over have failed to do, namely to integrate open and interactive messages from their constituencies, blogs do for them. To blog a news report doesn't mean that the blogger sits down and thoroughly analyzes the discourse and circumstances, let alone checks the facts. To blog merely means to quickly point to news facts through a link and a few sentences that explain why the blogger found this or that factoid interesting or remarkable or is in disagreement with it.

Blog entries are often hastily written personal musings, sculptured around a link or event. In most cases, bloggers simply do not have the time, skills, and the financial means to do proper research. There are collective research blogs, working on specific topics, but these are rare. What ordinary blogs create is a dense cloud of impressions around a topic. Blogs will tell you if your audience is still awake and receptive. Blogs test. In that sense, we could also say that blogs are the outsourced, privatized test beds, or rather the unit tests[19] of the big media.

Blogs without Frontiers

The boundaries between the mediasphere and the blogosphere are fluid. A detailed social analysis would, most likely, uncover a gray area of freelance media makers moving back and forth. From early on journalists working for old media ran blogs. So how do blogs relate to independent investigative journalism? At first glance, they look like oppositional or potentially supplementary practices. Whereas the investigative journalist works months, if not years, to uncover a story, bloggers look more like an army of ants contributing to the great hive called public opinion. Bloggers rarely add new facts to a news story. They find bugs in products and news reports, but rarely unmask spin, let alone come up with well-researched reports.

Cecile Landman, a Dutch investigative journalist and Iraqi blogger supporter with the Streamtime campaign, knows both worlds. "Journalists need to make a living. They can't put just anything on-line. Bloggers don't seem to bother too much about this, and that does create a conflict."[20] According to Landman, blogging is changing the existing formats of information. "People are getting bored with the given formats; they don't catch up with the news anymore, it no longer glues on their memory sticks. It is like a song that you have listened to too often, or a commercial advertisement; you hear it, you can even sing the words, but they are without meaning. Mainstream media start to grasp this. They have to search for new formats in order to attract readers (read: advertisers)" and blogs are but a small chapter in this transformation.

We cannot presume that blogs—by default—have a progressive-leftist attitude toward ruling politicians and large corporations. When I moved back to the Netherlands from Australia in 2004, I had to reconcile the fact that this once liberal, tolerant country was dominated by tough talking bloggers, whose non-conformist attitude was aimed at breaking the liberal consensus, and who openly expressed racist and anti-Semitic diatribes under the banner of free speech. When I supervised a Master's thesis of Sjoerd van der Helm on the Dutch blogosphere, it struck me how confrontational the shockblogs were that he discussed.[21] Just to mention a few of these Dutch shockblogs, they are Hersenscheet, Neukia, GeenStijl, Retecool, Volkomen-kut, Drijfzand, Skoften, and Jaggle. Here, trivial information is mixed with marketing and straight-out information warfare where bloggers perform personal attacks on public figures. Occasionally, shockblogs offer investiga-tive reports as the shockbloggers (who post anonymously and collaborate in groups) are eager to scoop news. "Specialized websites, in growing competi-tion with mainstream news outlets, need to break stories to generate a fan base. So those start-ups try to break news online whenever they can and on a moment's notice," Peter Johnson noted in *USA Today*.[22]

Some sites also offer users the possibility of "fotofucken" (manipulating news photos). Shockblogs are among the most visited blogs in the Neth-erlands. These sites, for instance, played a critical role in the ongoing saga around the murder of Dutch filmmaker Theo van Gogh, who ran a shock-blog called *De Gezonde Roker* (The Healthy Smoker). Shockblogs were the first to report the incident and then instantly turned into online stages where fierce discussions took place on how Dutch society should respond to migrant Islamic culture. What the shockblogs did was to set the tone of the discussion, thereby further fueling tensions between (ethnic) communi-ties. This was reflected in the Dutch–Moroccan Web forums, which played a pivotal role in the months before and after the van Gogh murder.[23]

Blogs are utilized by anyone, for any purpose. The PR industry discov-ered that if you pay them, they'll blog. This can be an effective weapon in case a product or company is being attacked. Fake blogs—a form of viral marketing[24] that are one PR or advertising agency's attempt to gen-erate interest in their client's product by creating a fictional character on the Internet—have drawn criticism from real bloggers.[25] O'Dwyer's PR Daily reported that PR giant Edelman hired RedState.org blogger Michael Krempasky "for his ability to connect with conservative audiences".[26] Krempasky, on his site, refers to the Edelman gig as his "day job" versus his blogging hobby. His first mission was to play up Wal-Mart stores' con-tribution to the Hurricane Katrina relief campaign (August 2005).[27] Some Straussian insights could be of importance for bloggers. Information is not always put out there to enlighten us, and blogs are no exception to this rule. The more popular blogs become, the less we can make the claim that blogs enlighten. To paraphrase Leo Strauss and his neo-con contraband, we could say that the blogger who whispers in the ear of the king is more important than the king. If you have talent, your blog postings will not be held accountable. Trivial training in these basic, if esoteric, Straussian principles can alert bloggers to the possibility that political life may be closely linked to deception. Deception, not truth, is the norm in political life. Bloggers are the tellers of noble lies, not only to people at large but also to powerful politicians.[28]

There are plenty of studies under way about the relationship between bloggers, the news industry, and the political class. Joe Trippi, who ran the online campaign for presidential candidate Howard Dean, in 2003 wrote, by now, a classic, heroic account in which blogging succeeded and exceeded political failure. During the Dean campaign blogs functioned as fund-raising vehicles, opinion research tools, and grassroots mobilizing tools. As Trippi said: "a candidate lost, but his campaign won." Blogs not only played a crucial part in the sudden rise of Dean, but, as Trippi admits, they also accelerated Dean's Iowa defeat. "Of course, the Internet played a big part in spreading the 'I Have a Scream' speech, proving in the most perverse way how powerful the medium has become."[29] It is odd to see how a defeat can turn into a powerful founding myth. Hopefully it will not be as catastrophic as the founding myth of the Serbian nation, the defeat of the Serbian army during the Battle of Kosovo Polje by Ottoman forces in 1389, or the formation of ANZAC in the annihilation of Australian troops under British command at Gallipoli during World War I, which formed the ANZAC legend, a tragedy that in recent years has been celebrated as the birth of the nation.

How do we analyze media of such an informal character? A Weblog is the voice of a person, as überblogger Dave Winer once defined it. It is a digital extension of oral traditions more than a new form of writing.[30] Through blogging, news is being transformed from a lecture into a conversation. Blogs echo rumor and gossip, conversations in cafes and bars, on squares and in corridors. They record "the events of the day".[31] With today's "recordability" of situations, we are no longer upset that computers "read" all of our moves and expressions (sound, image, text) and "write" them into strings of zeros and ones. In that sense, blogs fit into the wider trend where all our movements and activities are being monitored and stored. In the case of blogs, this is carried out not by some invisible and abstract authority but by the subjects themselves who record their everyday life. When people are still upset to find that they've been fired after having made critical remarks about their employers on their blogs, one realizes we are still in the early days for the spread of this insight. "Who reads my blog anyway?" Well, apparently your boss does.[32]

Techno-determinism has its merits but too often fails to see the social dynamics among users and is even worse when it comes to understanding the power politics of scientific disciplines and genres. Blogs ignore boundaries and rules, not because they are inherently subversive and defy determinism, but because they are social experiments; not out of a belief system, but simply because they are the state of the art. The antiquated spirits among us continue to scribble in our paper diaries—or push print once our blog entry is online—and will do so until it is time to move on.

Life is filled with change and adventure, and the attention given to blogs will, at some point, fade away. They will be replaced by the next feature in the same way that blogs themselves replaced the dominance of the Web site and homepage.

Truisms for the Blogged

- Deadly sin: laboriously detailed blow-by-blow transcripts of unsatisfactory telephone conversations with service suppliers (Big Blogger 2005)
- Dennis: "Why you should get to know me: Because I already know I'll hate you, and I'm daring you to prove me wrong."
- Read the weblog, wear the T-shirt, live the life.
- Starting Is Easy, Finishing is Hard.
- You don't need a sack of hammers to make a delicious fondue. (Dr. Phil)
- Interests: drinking wine (if I feel like being sophisticated), not working, handling remote controls.
- "I'm getting sick of my stepdad, he's such a dick. He always bitches about something, I think he looks for something to bitch about." Ernie
- My memory is a blog full of creative ideas but nothing to show for it.
- He died with an empty inbox.
- This is my blog, dammit, and I'll rant about six-month-old memes if I want. (waxy.org)
- Friday Night Cat Blogging
- Are you buzz compliant? Wear a Web 2.0 badge.
- Every day is a winding road. (Sheryl Crow)
- I was going to cut my hair, but now that Andy Samberg is hitting it big I will grow it out. (blog subtitle)

In their 2005 book *Blog!*, subtitled "How the Newest Media Revolution is Changing Politics, Business and Culture," American journalists David Kline and Dan Burnstein bring together interviews with key U.S. bloggers in politics, business, and culture. In between pages filled with forced optimism and pumped-up confessions of self-made blog celebrities, we find little that questions the rhetoric of never-ending growth and success. To once again critique this all too American attitude seems repetitive.

The blog hype cannot measure against the late-1990s dotcom hysteria. The economic and political landscape is simply too different. What interested me was the oft-heard remark that blogs were cynical and nihilistic. Instead of ignoring this accusation, I did a trial and ran both keywords through the systems to test if they were hardwired virtues, linked and consolidated inside the Blog Nation. Instead of portraying bloggers as "an army of Davids," as Instapundit blogger Glenn Reynolds' book title suggests,[33] it might be better to study the techno-mentality of users and not presume that bloggers are underdogs on a mission to beat Goliath. "We can fact-check your ass," Ken Layne once stated, but the everyday reality of bloggers is a different one. Most do not have the time and concentration to do thorough research work and would rather follow the herd, something for which bloggers are famous. What Reynolds presents as the end of the power of Big Media turns out to be a clever way for newspapers and other media outlets to integrate their customers in interactive ways. Even though traditional media should "beware of the people who are having fun competing with you," Reynolds warns that distrust in Big Media "can't be a good thing over time."[34]

A Critique of Internet Reason

Historically it makes sense to see Internet cynicism as a response to millennium madness. In January 2001, Greg Sherman and Amy Avila wrote in the dotcom magazine *Clickz*: "Among investors, consumers, and the media, there's a pervasive sense that all the promises about the Internet have amounted to one huge, boldfaced lie—and that we're now paying for the sins of yesterday's overexuberance."[35] In *My First Recession* (2003), I mapped the post-dotcom hangover. In this light, cynicism is nothing more than the discursive rubble of a collapsed belief system, cold turkey after the market rush. The Clinton years of globalization (1993–2000), so well described in Hardt and Negri's *Empire*, now in retrospect seem so optimistic and innocent. The long anticlimax that followed did not indulge in a collective sense of crisis. Post-2000 the ecstasy is still there (parties, drugs, technology); what fails is the synthetic glue that brings together all the orgasmic exercises. Blogging turns out to be an amputated experience. The everyday apocalypse came, and we blogged it. So, are we back in the slacker age of Douglas Coupland and his Generation X? Perhaps, but without even the space or time to slack anymore. Now, it seems, amputated body and brain parts are frantically scampering about, looking for streams of revenue, even as global finance is at a new peak and hungry for a new boom.

It would be misplaced to collectively denounce bloggers as cynics. Cynicism, in this context, is not a character trait but a techno-social condition. The argument is not that bloggers are predominantly cynics by nature or conviction, or vulgar exhibitionists who lack understatement. It is the general culture that has become cynical.[36] What is important to note is the Zeitgeist into which blogging as a mass practice emerged. Internet cynicism in this case would be a cultural spin-off from blogging software, hardwired in a specific era. This techno-attitude results from procedures such as login, link, edit, create, browse, read, submit, tag, and reply. Blogging and social networks have become the hegemonic modes of Internet use. Some would judge the mere use of the term *cynicism* in this context as blog bashing. So be it. Again, we're not talking about an attitude here, let alone a shared lifestyle. Internet cynicism no longer believes in cyberculture as an identity provider with its related entrepreneurial hallucinations. It is constituted by cold enlightenment as a post-political condition and by confession as described by Michel Foucault. "People are taught that their liberation requires them to 'tell the truth,' to confess it to someone (a priest, psychoanalyst, [or Weblog]), and this truth telling will somehow set them free."[37]

There is a quest for truth in blogging. But it is a truth with a question mark. Truth here has become an amateur project, not an absolute value, sanctioned by higher authorities. In a variation of a common definition we could say that cynicism is the unpleasant way of performing the truth.[38] The Internet is not a religion or a mission in itself. For some it turns into an addiction, but that can be healed like any other medical problem. The post-dotcom, post 9-11 condition borders on a "passionate conservatism," but in the end rejects the dotcom petit bourgeois morals and their double standards of cheating and hiding, cooking the books and then being rewarded big fat paychecks. The question is, therefore, how much truth can a medium bear? Knowledge is sorrow, and the knowledge society propagators have not yet taken this into account.

Internet cynicism is frank first and foremost about itself. The blog application is an online commodity with a clear use-by date. Spokker Jones: "Forty years from now when the Internet collapses in a giant implosion of stupidity I want to be able to say, 'I was there.'"[39] It is said that Internet cynicism gave rise to sites like the now defunct Netslaves.com, which was dedicated to horror stories of working the Web. It was a sounding board for those "burned by the incompetence, moronic planning, and hysterical management of New Media companies."[40] Exhibitionism equals empowerment. Saying aloud what you think or feel, in the legacy of de Sade, is not only an option—in the liberal sense of "choice"—but an obligation, an immediate impulse to respond in order to be out there, to exist with everybody else.

In the Internet context it is not evil, as one of Rüdiger Safranski's book titles suggested, but, instead, triviality which is the "drama of freedom." As Baudrillard states, "All of our values are simulated. What is freedom? We have a choice between buying one car or buying another car?"[41] And to follow Baudrillard, we could say that blogs are a gift to humankind that no one needs. This is the true shock. Did anyone order the development of blogs? There is no possibility of simply ignoring blogs and living the comfortable lifestyle of a 20th century "public intellectual." Like Michel Houellebecq, bloggers are trapped by their own inner contradictions in the Land of No Choice. The *London Times* noted that Houellebecq "writes from inside alienation. His bruised male heroes, neglected by their parents, cope by depriving themselves of loving interactions; they project their coldness and loneliness on to the world."[42] Blogs are perfect projection fields for such an undertaking. We can extract blogging philosophy from novelists such as Rainald Goetz, Irwine Welsh, Matias Faldbakken, or Brett Easton Ellis—or we may as well all become celebrities ourselves. That would be a blogging strategy. Gutenberg fiction is no longer a common reference, but a special effect of the media industries, kept alive by an ever-increasing amount of film adaptations, awards, and, indeed, the Internet.

Italian theorist Paulo Virno provides clues as to how we could use the term cynicism in a non-derogative manner. Virno sees cynicism connected to the "chronic instability of forms of life and linguistic games." At the base of contemporary cynicism, Virno sees the fact that men and women first of all experience rules, far more often than facts, and far earlier than they experience concrete events. Virno:

> But to experience rules directly means also to recognize their conventionality and groundlessness. Thus, one is no longer immersed in a predefined "game," participating therein with true allegiance. Instead, one catches a glimpse of oneself in individual "games" which are destitute of all seriousness and obviousness, having become nothing more than a place for immediate self-affirmation—a self-affirmation which is all the more brutal and arrogant, in short, cynical, the more it draws upon, without illusions but with perfect momentary allegiance, those same rules which characterize conventionality and mutability.[43]

How is the cynical reason connected to criticism? Is cynical media culture a critical practice? Thus far, it has not proven useful to interpret blogs as a new form of literary criticism. Such an undertaking is bound to fail. The "crisis of criticism" has been announced repeatedly and blog culture has simply ignored this dead-end street. There is no need for a new media clone of Terry Eagleton. We live long after the Fall of Theory. Criticism has become a conservative and affirmative activity, in which the critic alternates the losses of value while celebrating the spectacle of the marketplace. It would be interesting to investigate why criticism itself has not become popular and aligned itself with a new media practice such as blogging, as cultural studies popularized everything except theory itself. Let us not blame the "Blogging Other" for the moral bankruptcy of the postmodern critic. Instead of conceptual depth, we get broad associations, a people's hermeneutics of news events.[44] The computable comments of the millions can be made searchable and visually displayed, for instance, as buzz clouds. Whether these maps provide us with any knowledge is another matter. It is easy to judge the rise of comments as regressive compared to the clear-cut authority of the critic. Insularity and provincialism have taken their toll. The panic and obsession around the professional status of the critic has been such that the void created has now been filled by passionate amateur bloggers. One thing is sure: blogs do not shut down thought.

Wikipedia's amateur encyclopedians describe cynics as

those inclined to disbelieve in human sincerity, in virtue, or in altruism: individuals who maintain that only self-interest motivates human behavior. A modern cynic typically has a highly contemptuous attitude towards social norms, especially those which serve more of a ritualistic purpose than a practical one, and will tend to dismiss a substantial proportion of popular beliefs, conventional morality and accepted wisdom as irrelevant or obsolete nonsense.

In a networked environment, such a definition becomes problematic as it portrays the user as an isolated subject opposed to groups or society as a whole. Internet cynicism is a not a gateway to drugs or anything nasty. To talk about evil as an abstract category is irrelevant in this context. There is no immediate danger, it's all just fine. The idea is not to create a dialectical situation. There is only a feeling of stagnation amidst constant change. We could call it "romanticism of the open eyes." According to Peter Sloterdijk, cynicism is "enlightened false consciousness."[45] A cynic, so Sloterdijk says, is someone who is part of an institution, or group whose existence and values he himself can no longer see as absolute, necessary, and unconditional, and who is miserable due to this enlightenment because he or she sticks to principles in which he or she does not believe.

The only knowledge left for a cynic to trust in is Reason, which, however, cannot provide him or her with a firm basis for action, and this again is another reason for being miserable.[46] Following Sloterdijk, cynicism is a common problem. The question of whether it is universal or, rather, limited to Western societies, is too big to be discussed here, but most certainly we see it on a global scale in knowledge-intensive sectors. Stefan Lorenz Sorgner summarizes Sloterdijk:

We live from day to day, from vacation to vacation, from news show to news show, from problem to problem, from orgasm to orgasm, in private turbulences and medium-term affairs, tense, relaxed. With some things we feel dismay but with most things we can't really give a damn... We would still like to see a lot of the world and in general "to live a whole lot more."[47]

In the same spirit, we have to deal with another proposition, what Berlin-based writer, musician, and blogger iMomus called *moronic cynicism*. On July 14, 2005, iMomus posted a long list of what "moronic cynicism" could be. I made the following remix of his theory-proposal:

> Moronic cynicism is a form of naïveté turned inside out, naïveté with a sneer. Imagine a child smoking a cigarette. Passive aggression, self-destructiveness and negative capability are close cousins to moronic cynicism. The moronic cynic uses cynicism as a way to prepare for the worst. The worst consequently arrives. To be cynical is to be on the side of the worst, to think with its logic and to see with its eyes. Moronic cynicism is attacking both the consumers and the companies that supply their needs. "Wake up!" you scream to people who are already awake, thank you very much! Moronic cynicism is seeing the entire people, government and institutions of a nation as possessing some kind of "original sin." Moronic cynicism is joining the mosque and carrying the bomb in your backpack because the world is evil. Moronic cynicism is the narcissistic mindset of an individual in a fragmented culture where all individuals resemble one another, and everybody is secretly miserable. Moronic cynicism is thinking that "empowerment" is acting on your own behalf rather than on the behalf of others. Moronic cynicism wonders why the phone never rings. Moronic cynic, you will become the monster you claim to fight![48]

Moronic cynicism only tells us part of the story. Let's investigate the optimistic side. David Weinberger, co-author of *The Cluetrain Manifesto*, speaks of the "virtue of engineering cynicism, which comes out of, and is reflected in, the engineer's daily work experience."[49] Weinberger does not believe that the cynicism of the (computer) engineer is a character flaw. "It is key to their strength." Cynics are the better optimists because they do not shy away from human flaws. Weinberger: "Cynics believe that there is an ideal that humans choose not to live up to. For engineers, the ideals often are those of rationality: they like their work relationships characterized by the exchange of objective information unsullied by subjective, selfish motivations." Words of users or clients should not be taken at face value. The cynic responds positively to the straightforward truth. "That's why engineers will stand up in a sales call and painstakingly go over the list of bugs, flaws, weaknesses and dropped features: they are being straight in an environment that only tells half the story. Despite what the horrified sales folk think, the engineers are not trying to screw up the deal." What the cynic shows is a borderless trust in the idea that things can be improved. Long live the cynical optimist.

We are operating in a post-deconstructivist world in which blogs offer a never-ending stream of confessions, a cosmos of micro-opinions attempting to interpret events beyond the well-known 20th century categories. Blogged cynicism emerges as a response to the increasing levels of complexity within interconnected topics. There is little to say if all occurrences can be explained through post-colonialism, class analysis, and gender perspectives. However, blogging arises against this kind of political analysis, through which a lot can no longer be said. Let's look at what I call the nihilist impulse of blogging. Cornel West did not define nihilism as a philosophical doctrine but far more, "a lived experience of coping with a life of horrifying meaninglessness, hopelessness, and (most important) lovelessness."[50] Whereas cynicism refers to knowledge, nihilism relates to existence and nothingness.

Blogs bring on decay. Each new blog is supposed to add to the fall of the media system that once dominated the 20th century. This process is not one of a sudden explosion. The erosion of the mass media cannot be traced easily in figures of stagnant sales and the declining readership of newspapers. In many parts of the world television viewership is still on the rise. What is declining is the "Belief in the Message." That is the nihilist moment, and blogs facilitate this culture as no platform has ever done before. Sold by the positivists as citizen media commentary, blogs assist users in their crossing from truth to nothingness. The printed and broadcasted message has lost its aura. News is consumed as a commodity with entertainment value. Instead of lamenting the ideological color of the news, as previous generations have done, we blog as a sign of the regained power of the spirit. As a micro-heroic, Nietzschean act of the pajama people, blogging grows out of a nihilism of strength, not out of the weakness of pessimism. Instead of repeatedly presenting blog entries as self-promotion, we should interpret them as decadent artifacts that remotely dismantle the mighty and seductive power of the broadcast media.

Blogs express personal fear, insecurity, and disillusion—anxieties looking for partners-in-crime. We seldom find passion (except for the act of blogging itself). Often blogs unveil doubts and insecurity about what to feel, what to think, believe, and like. They carefully compare magazines and review traffic signs, nightclubs, and t-shirts. This stylized uncertainty circles around the general assumption that blogs ought to be biographical while simultaneously reporting about the world outside. Their emotional scope is much wider compared to other media due to the informal atmosphere of blogs. Mixing public and private is constitutional here. What blogs play with is the emotional register, varying from hate to boredom, passionate engagement, sexual outrage, and back to everyday boredom.

Open-Armed Resistance

Having learned a lesson or two from the cultivated madness of the dot-com era, the management book writers David Kline and Dan Burnstein have become cautious about promoting yet another hype (labeled Web 2.0). In *Blog!* they describe their "real-world futurism" as a way to balance their excitement about the potential of digital technology to change the world with the realization that "it would take time to suffuse its way into the deep fabric of business, economics, political life, education and entertainment."[51] The underlying economic premises of the dotcom era were all correct; the only mistake was the time factor. The same could be said about the hype surrounding blogs. Everything that has been written about blogs changing the media landscape is right, so Kline and Burnstein believe; the only mistake bloggers could make is to think that change will happen overnight. These patient revolutionaries refrain from a thorough deconstruction of blog architecture. In their thinking, blogs are a given and neither ontology nor appearance need discussion. The impact on society is measured in the form of a kaleidoscope of microscopic yet significant opinions within the U.S. blogosphere. Stating the obvious, Kline and Burstein see blogs as late materializations of 1990s promises. It is the killer application of our times, much like e-mail and instant messaging were ten years ago. While blogs coexist with other media, Kline and Burnstein predict increasing cross-fertilization.

Blogging is neither a project nor a proposal but rather a condition whose existence one must first fully recognize. "We blog," as Kline and Burnstein say. It is today's a priori. Australian cultural theorist Justin Clemens explains: "Nihilism is not just another epoch amongst a succession of others: it is the finally accomplished form of a disaster that happened a long time ago."[52] To translate this into new media terms, blogs are witnessing and documenting the diminishing power of the mainstream media, but they have consciously not replaced its ideology with an alternative. They zero out old structure but do not claim to be its predecessor. Users are tired of top-down communication and yet have nowhere else to go. "There is no other world" could be read as a response to the anti-globalization slogan "Another world is possible."

Caught in the daily grind of blogging, there is a sense that the network is the alternative. It is not correct to judge blogs merely on the basis of their content. Media theory has never done this and, in this case, should shy away from this method. Blogging is a nihilistic venture precisely because the ownership structure of mass media is questioned and then attacked. Blogging is a bleed-to-death strategy. Implosion is not the right word. Implosion implies a tragedy and spectacle that fails. Blogging is the opposite of the spectacle. It is flat, yet meaningful. Blogging is not a digital clone of the "Letter to the Editor." Instead of complaining and arguing, the blogger puts him or herself in the perversely pleasurable position of media observer.

In an interview with Brandan W. Joseph, Paulo Virno makes the connection between nihilism and the contemporary work conditions outside of the factory, known as post-Fordism. Virno:

> Post-Fordism takes advantage of abilities learned before and independently of entrance into the workplace: abilities brought forth by the uncertainty of metropolitan life, by uprootedness, by the preceptual shocks of technological mutations, even by video games and the use of cellular phones. All this is at the base of post-Fordist "flexibility." These experiences outside the workplace were taken into the production system and became known as "just in time" and were authentic and proper professional requirements. Great European thought, from Nietzsche to Heidegger, described the 'nihilism' that characterizes forms of life outside of the stringent rationality of the productive process: instability, disenchantment, anonymity, and so on. Well, with post-Fordism, the nihilistic mentality enters into production, constitutes in fact one of its precious ingredients. To work profitably today in offices and factories, it is necessary to have a great familiarity with the situation and the fragility of all states of things.[53]

The only missing step is how to integrate social software and network architectures—and their uses—into this argument.

The commenting on mainstream culture, its values and products, should be read as an open withdrawal of attention. The eyeballs that once patiently looked at the reports and ads have gone on strike. According to the Utopian blog philosophy, mass media are doomed. Their role will be taken over by participatory media. The terminal diagnosis has been made and it states: closed top-down organizations no longer work, knowledge cannot be managed, and today's work is collaborative and networked. However, despite continuous warning signs the system continues to successfully (dys)function. Is top-down really on its way out? Where does the Hegelian certainty come from that the old media paradigm will be overthrown? There is little factual evidence of this. And it is this state of ongoing affairs that causes nihilism, not revolution, to occur.

As Justin Clemens rightly states "Nihilism often goes unremarked, not because it is no longer an issue of contemporary philosophy and theory, but—on the contrary—because it is just so uncircumventable and domi-nating."[54] The term has dropped almost completely out of establishment political discourse. The reason for this could be the "banalization of nihil-ism."[55] Or to rephrase it, the absence of high art that can be labeled as such. This might have changed with the rise of writers such as Michel Houel-lebecq. Andre Gluckmann explained the 2005 migrant riots in the French suburbs as a "response to French nihilism." What the revolting youth did was an "imitation of negation."[56] The "problem of nihilism," as Clemens notes, is the complex, subtle, and self-reflexive nature of the term. To histo-ricize the concept is one way out, though I will leave that to others. Another way could be to occupy the term and reload it with surprising energies: cre-ative nihilism. French orientalist Burnouf, who coined the term nihilism, merely used it to point at the philosophical concept of nirvana, in this con-text, a state of supreme liberation, being no longer attached to Big Media. It was Turgenev who gave the term its negative meaning of terrorism and intellectual radicalism.[57] We need to go back to its original meaning and stress the "creative destruction," zeroing out outdated belief systems.

To clarify, not everyone has moved to the blogosphere. In a posting to the German Rohrpost list, Berlin-based new media theorist Florian Cra-mer asks why the e-mail–based mailing list culture did not transform into blogs.[58] Like e-mail–based mailing lists, blogs go back to a UNIX semantic (var/log). Unlike lists, the rule for blogs is to be subjective, individual, and private. One has to follow the dictates of subjectivity. Cramer sees a shift away from the discursive exchange between list subscribers toward a for-mal and technical way of networking through RSS and backtrack links. Instead of comments arriving as separate, equal e-mails, comments on blogs are treated as secondary pages, with smaller fonts. Cramer also points at a cultural difference between lists and blogs; where lists are often inter-national and tolerant of imperfect English, blogs are more often written in the native language of the owner and are seen as products of a subjective literary style, not as vehicles for international commerce and trade.

According to Cramer blogs reflect a "cocooning" tendency in society, in which the blogosphere has to be interpreted as a "monad" (as Leibniz described it), a closed and self-referential environment in which ranking and linking to other blogs becomes more important than page views. What makes Cramer's notes worth mentioning is the fact that the common body of literature on blogs does not deal with any of the mentioned concepts or ideas. The original posting of the blog owner is not equal to the answer of respondents. Users are guests, not equal partners, let alone antagonists. And, as noted earlier, most blogs are written in the writer's native language (German, Parsi, Mandarin, and the like). Glenn Reynolds, discussing the differences between lists and blogs, believes that the blog world will not succumb to the "tragedy of the commons" in the way e-mail has. People who post on blogs can't commandeer the time of others, says Reynolds. Nobody will read list postings except voluntarily. Blogs, says Reynolds, make it much easier to "route around idiots" as they are interlinked discussion forums, not one list.[59]

The following remark of venture capitalist and hacker Joi Ito fits into Cramer's argument about blogs.

> "I've had several online communities in the past," Ito told Kline and Burstein, "and I've usually named them something functional. The first mailing list that I ran featured cool Web sites and was called Netsurf Japan. But inevitably the community of users starts getting in fights over every little thing, so this time I just decided to call my Web site Joi Ito's Web. It's not necessarily a vanity thing, but more so I can say, 'You can do what you want but you're in my living room, so be respectful because I have to take care of this place.' I feel like I am a custodian of a community. I am happy to have people come but it really is kind of like a party in my living room".[60]

Blogs echo this sentiment. It is clear that blogs can perfectly direct and monitor discussions and filter out dissident voices. You will hardly find a critical voice on Ito's site. Blogs create communities of like-minded people. Debates happen within homogeneous Weblog clouds. The management of comments is deadly simple. Exclusion of dissent is no longer necessary, as adversaries will not post on each other's blogs. At best, they quote and link. Most bloggers would admit that it is not their aim to foster public debate. If you disagree with a fellow blogger, it is even unwise to write a comment. Instead, it is much safer to post the remark on your own blog. "I blogged you." The chance that someone like Ito might respond to it is almost zero. Herein is the limit of blogging. Many blogs completely switch off the possibility of response, in particular the celebrity diaries and CEO blogs written and maintained by professional editors.

Cramer also points to the close relation between the spread of ADSL broadband technology and blogging. The "always on" condition provokes an online writing style that feeds off surfing. Cramer discusses the social shift away from shared access spaces, both in the cultural sector and business, toward solitary work at home. This movement away from the public environment of dotcom offices and Web design firms toward private surroundings reflects the economic move from a collective entrepreneurial culture toward unemployed/freelance individuals. It also reflects the e-mail–based mailing list versus blog dynamic: the list as many to many, the blog as one to many. In the case of blogs you consciously have to go there (in particular, the first visit), whereas list traffic comes to you. The introduction of RSS-feeds that warn your Web site about the latest postings elsewhere has not changed this.

Nihilism? I'm too cynical to believe in nihilism...

—Stuart Studebaker, 2005, early-warning.blogspot.com

Bloggers are creative nihilists because they are "good for nothing." They post into Nirvana and have turned their futility into a productive force. They are the nothingists who celebrate the death of the centralized meaning structures and ignore the accusation that they would only produce noise. They are disillusionists whose conduct and opinions are regarded as worthless.[61] Clemens notes that in the public discourse the term nihilism has been replaced by such appellations as "anti-democratic," "terrorist," and "fundamentalist." However, over the past years there has been a noticeable renaissance of the term, though usually not more than in a passing remark. Significant theorization of the "condition" was done in the mid-20th century, which included reworking sources from the 19th century like Kierkegaard, Stirner, and Nietzsche. Existentialism after the two World Wars theorized the Gulag, Auschwitz, and Hiroshima as manifestations of Organized Evil that resulted in an overall crisis of existing belief systems. For those still interested in theory, Arthur Kroker's *The Will to Technology & The Culture of Nihilism* (2004) is a must-read as it puts Heidegger, Nietzsche, and Marx in a contemporary, techno-nihilist perspective.

We're faced with an "accomplished nihilism" in that bloggers have understood that the fulfillment of nihilism is a fact.[62] Gianni Vattimo argues that nihilism is not the absence of meaning but a recognition of the plurality of meanings; it is not the end of civilization but the beginning of new social paradigms, with blogging being one of them. Commonly associated with the pessimistic belief that all of existence is meaningless, nihilism would be an ethical doctrine where there are no moral absolutes or infallible natural laws, and truth is inescapably subjective. In media terms, we see this attitude translated into a growing distrust of the output of large commercial news organizations and the endless spin provided by politicians and their advisers. Questioning the message is no longer a subversive act of an engaged citizenry but an *a priori* attitude, even before the TV or PC has been switched on.

Nihilism designates the impossibility of opposition—a state of affairs that, unsurprisingly, generates a great deal of anxiety. Nihilism is not a monolithic belief system. We no longer "believe" in Nothing, as in 19th century Russia or post-war Paris. Nihilism is no longer a danger or problem, but the default postmodern condition. It is an unremarkable, even banal feature of life, as Karen Carr writes, and is no longer related to the Religious Question. Blogs are neither religious nor secular. They are post-virtue. The paradoxical temporality of nihilism today is that of a not-quite-already-Now. In the media context, this would be the moment when mass media lost their claim on the truth and could no longer speak as the voice of authority. Let us not specifically date this event in time, as such an insightful moment can be both personal and cultural–historical. It is the shift from the festive McLuhan to the nihilist Baudrillard that every media user is going through, found in the ungroundedness of networked discourse that users fool around with.

Translating Carr's insight to today's condition, we could say that the blogger is an individual "who lives in self-conscious confrontation with a meaningless world, refusing either to deny or succumb to its power."[63] Yet, this does not result in a heroic gesture. Blogging does not grow out of boredom, or emanate from some existential void. Carr rightly remarks "for many postmodernists, the presence of nihilism evokes not terror but a yawn."[64] Compared to previous centuries, its crisis value has diminished. If bloggers are classified nihilists, it merely means that they have stopped believing in the media.

The so-called global always-on, always-linked, always-immediate public conversation speeds up the fragmentation of the media landscape. Kline and Burnstein disagree here (they ain't no nihilists). "Rather than seeing the proliferation of specialty blogs as an indicator of the fragmentation of our society, we should see this trend as providing a way for citizen-experts to emerge and to bring together global constituencies in many disparate fields."[65] Seen from the political class perspective, handpicked bloggers can be instrumentalized as "opinion indicators."[66] However, they can as easily be dismissed the next day as "pajama journalists" and ignored as noise. As every hype necessarily has to crash, the wave of negative PR is pre-programmed. Bloggers might communicate what issues people tell the media they want to think about. But once the hotness has worn off, who cares? The nihilism starts there, after the fall of the blogs, the stolen laptop, crashed server, unreadable back-up files, disappeared online service provider, comments (0). That is when we can truly show off our Pathos des Umsonst, the gesture of Being in Vain.

David Kline writes, "Not everyone is pleased that the untrained rabble now dares to speak in public. 'One wonders for whom these hapless souls blog,' snipes Indiana University dean Blaise Cronin. 'Why do they choose to expose their unremarkable opinions, sententious drivel, and unedifying private lives to the potential gaze of total strangers?'"[67]

Criticism will also come from insiders. "Blogs are fun," Ezra Klein tells Burstein and Kline. "I like them. But they're a flawed and problematic medium. They encourage polarization and extremism rather than debate and understanding. They turn on snark and mockery more often than facts and agile argument."[68] Former Microsoft in-house blogger Robert Scoble points out the limitations of blogs if you are collaborating: "A blog is great at posting new stuff. But it's not great factoring in and working together with people on a single idea or project. I see wikis as complementary to blogs."[69]

Heightened activity on the invisible "long tail" of the media business is not contrary to its mobilizing capacity to reach large crowds. Joe Trippi points out that blogs can have their maximum influence in a time of a closely and evenly divided electorate. Like other media, their role is important but actually marginal. However, it is when marginal matters that blogs can be most influential. The point is not to scale-up to television levels but to set off avalanches. Trippi is still ecstatic:

> This was nothing less than the first shot in America's second revolution, nothing less than the people taking the first step to reclaiming a system that had long ago forgotten they existed. This was democracy bubbling to the surface, flooding the landscape, and raising all of us along with it.[70]

Trippi concludes:

> In the coming weeks and months and years, these hundreds of thousands will be followed by millions and this revolution will not be satisfied with overthrowing a corrupt and unresponsive political system. It won't stop at remaking politics. And it won't pay attention to national borders.[71]

Rough Type blogger Nicholas Carr once referred to theater director Richard Foreman and his use of the term "pancake people." The pancake personality lacks depth and shape. "We've been pounded into instantly-available pancakes, becoming the unpredictable but statistically critical synapses in the whole Gödel-to-Google net," Foreman once wrote on the Edge.org Web magazine. "Today, I see within us all (myself included) the replacement of complex inner density with a new kind of self-evolving under the pressure of information overload and the technology of the 'instantly available'. A new self that needs to contain less and less of an inner repertory of dense cultural inheritance—as we all become 'pancake people'—spread wide and thin as we connect with that vast network of information accessed by the mere touch of a button."[72] Bloggers are the ones cooking the pancakes, standing in the kitchen, chatting over the batter. It is an old complaint: we no longer need the knowledge, a link will do. "Just send me the link." Whereas in the act of searching, it is not just sufficient to find the link, the art of homemade rhetoric and the roughness of instant interpretation are what matter to bloggers. Jason Calacanis: "I always loved the 'unplugged' acoustics and live sets at rock shows. Like going to Carnegie Hall. You know, you can see an orchestra, or you can see Bob Dylan on the stage with just a guitar, harmonica, and his soul—no major production, you just focus on the music. To me blogs are like that, less produced, more soulful—more real."[73]

With the main growth of the Internet happening outside of the West, the nihilist question needs to be re-examined from various perspectives. For one of these I turn to Iran, a country that since 2003 has seen an incredible surge in blogs and blogging. Blogging has become so prominent that it is no longer considered marginal. Whereas the West is tired of so-called "virtual" identities, in countries like Iran there is an abundance of fake identities. Anonymity has been a crucial precondition for what Masserat Amir Ebrahimi calls the "indigenization of cyberspace."[74] Writing in one's own language and alphabet can be seen as a starting point. In an essay in *Pages* magazine entitled "Emergence of the Iranian Cyberspace and the Production of the Self in Weblogestan" Ebrahimi argues that blog software facilitates indigenization because it "creates social environments where the presence of different thoughts and mentalities form a space similar to their real living spaces. Weblogs become private homes situated in 'the global city' of the Internet and give a familiar taste to cyberspace." Similar to the "digital city" metaphor in Europe of the 1990s, blogs in Iran facilitate a home for newcomers. This process of appropriation is not created within the context of a public sphere, which, in the case of Iran and many other countries, is heavily guarded, but instead situates itself in a quasi-safe, protected zone, "for Iranian youth that want to preserve their freedom." The danger in such a situation for self-deception and isolation is imminent, says Ebrahimi. The failure to learn a language, in this case English, can cause a group to act as if they live within a ghetto or closed society. According to Ebrahimi, many Iranians engage in "Web-wandering" (surfing), looking at pictures, while restricting themselves to conversations with their fellow-countrymen. I would add here that such closure is further facilitated, and not discouraged, by the inward looking monad architecture of blogs.

The role of blogs in Iranian society, says Ebrahimi, is to define people's identity. "The most inexpensive and easiest way to rediscover themselves is to experience the transition from predefined and reactionary roles in real life to their 'real' or desired roles in the virtual space." Here, in "Weblogestan," personalities emerge that have high social potential but no possibility of existence in the real world. "The virtual identities give the writer a special authority that only pertains to the virtual space. In many objections, petitions or communications these people sign with their own Weblog names because their real names have no particular authority."

Weblogestan becomes a mirror for the revelation of the unknown personalities and faces of people who for years, or perhaps centuries, have been accustomed to hiding their inner worlds from the influence of external authority. In blogosphere, these people go public while still hiding their "real" identity.

Whereas the virtual world is a reaction to the "musts" and "must-nots" of a society that is still confused in its behavior and dispositions in the physical world, it is still considered a mirror. "One can see oneself as one wishes" and "one can improve oneself in the mirror." In Ebrahimi's *Pages* article, Harfhaye Alpar comments: "It is like a mirror because it is always open. I go and look what I have written every five minutes without reading it, just like a purposeless look that I throw at the mirror." And: "One looks for one's selves, even in others' Weblogs." Users create associations with the word Weblog in which they can recognize themselves. Whereas the mirror might be a poetic leitmotiv, Annabelle Sreberny writes, in the same issue of the *Pages* magazine, that the danger is "in an environment of instant access, when people are ready both to say anything and to do anything, the scope for delusion, rumor and rapid, violent response is high."[75] The identity struggle has replaced the fear of repression, the question of persecution, and the art of writing as Leo Strauss described it. What occupies the bloggers in this case is not what is written, that is, what meaning is hidden between the lines, but how I present myself.

From the perspective of Internet security, it is questionable how safe anonymous blogging in Iran really is. There are multiple Internet Service Providers (ISPs) in Iran that have their own international connections. In that sense, it is not centralized in the same way Internet traffic is managed in China, so any surveillance would have to occur at an ISP level. Given the amount of traffic and the lack of centralization, comprehensive monitoring of all traffic simply is not feasible in the case of Iran. However, if someone is already suspected or targeted, or if the authorities want to begin monitoring traffic between a limited number of IP addresses, then it is definitely possible to monitor and capture all Internet communications for these limited targets. In practice, there is little true anonymity in the blogosphere. This is largely due to a lack of information on how to secure online communications and because additional layers of security cause inconveniences that most users are unwilling to endure. These security facts make the massive role-playing in the case of the Iranian blogs an all the more interesting phenomenon.

A Spivakian mantra springs to mind: Can the subaltern blog? The question seems both absurd and serious. Why would the world's marginal, excluded poor even know about blogs? Don't they have more urgent matters on their mind? A possible answer could be that, of course, the subaltern blogs, and it is not up to moral Western do-gooders to decide if the subaltern should or should not (yet) blog. Perhaps the subaltern would rather gather under a tree or use SMS on their cell phones? Perhaps the global poor blog away and no one in the West notices. Perhaps they never will notice — and they have not missed a thing. Most likely they don't blog in English. Perhaps they understand the security risks? Of course, people would have to learn to read and write first. The next steps to use a computer and blog are minor steps compared to more immediate issues such as housing, water, electricity, and education. Japanese rave theorist and DJ Toshiya Ueno responds to the question of whether the subaltern blogs: "The subaltern that can reach the means of blogging, on their own or with the help of others, is not subaltern anymore. He or she then enters the side which can speak about the subaltern."[76]

Business writer David Kline just can't help but take up his New Age tone when he explains that despite all the real existing nihilism, blogging is not in vain.

> The truth is that these are not just the tiresome ramblings of the boring written to the bored. Though for the most part not professional writers, bloggers are often eloquent in the way that those who are not self-consciously polished often are—raw, uncensored, and energized by the sound of their newly awakened voices. And by keeping a daily record of their rites of passage, bloggers often give a shape and meaning to the stages and cycles of their lives that would otherwise be missed in the helter-skelter of modern existence.[77]

Foucault scholars would say something similar, namely that blogs are "technologies of the self,"[78] as discussed previously. But what if the self has run out of batteries? With Dominic Pettman we could say that blogging is a relentless pursuit in the age of exhaustion.[79] Blogs explore what happens once you have smashed the illusion that there is a persona behind the avalanche of similar lifestyle choices and pop identities within online social networks.

For some, nihilism kicks in when they realize that media freedom is undermining the very notion of listening. Liberal evangelist Carl Trueman notes that the whole blog phenomenon is "inherently ridiculous. The more serious it tries to be, the more absurd and pompous it becomes."[80] He struggles with free speech in the age of blogs. "Where everyone has a right to speak, everyone ends up thinking they have a right to be heard; and when everyone in general thinks they have a right to be heard, then you end up with a situation where nobody in particular is listened to." Trueman suggests a classic leftist strategy to overcome the state of relativism in order to save the very existence of the church that wants to be heard.

"Laugh at your own ridiculous complicity in this nonsense; expose the systemic contradictions for all they are worth; mock the blogworld for all of its inane self-importance; and in so doing try in some small way to subvert the system from the inside."

Snake Eyes and Boxcars

"Hi, I'm a reader. I've recently started a blog of my own at blogspot.com, and I wonder if you'd consider adding a link to me. I'll put up a reciprocal link." No matter how much talk there is of community and mobs, the fact remains that blogs are primarily used as a tool to manage the self. With management I refer here as much to the need to structure one's life, to clear up the mess, to master the immense flows of information, as to PR and promotion of the Ich AG (I Ltd.), as it is called in crisis-ridden Germany. Blogs are part of a wider culture that fabricates celebrity on every possible level. Some complain that blogs are too personal, even egocentric, whereas most blog readers indulge in exhibitionist insights and can't get enough if it. Claire E. Write advises writers who blog to not offer a possibility to leave comments. "A few bloggers maintain that blogs that don't allow reader comments are not 'real' blogs. Most bloggers don't follow that line of thinking and believe that reader comments turn a blog into a message board. The essence of a blog is not the interactivity of the medium: it is the sharing of the thoughts and opinions of the blogger. Adding comments to your blog opens up a host of problems: you will spend a great deal of time policing the posts, weeding out spam and trolls, and answering endless technical questions from registrants."[81] This advice obviously goes against the core values of the A-list bloggers. Isn't it interesting that blogging services offer the possibility to switch off comments? You then neither have to deal with the "(0) comments" nor with the hundreds of spam messages and the occasional annoying responses. *The Cluetrain Manifesto* guru David Weinberger states "blogs are not a new form of journalism nor primarily consist of teenagers whining about their teachers. Blogs are not even primarily a form of individual expression. They are better understood as conversations."[82] But what if most of that conversation mainly consists of messages posted by the irrelevant Other?

Consequently, could we qualify blogs as groupware? Back in 1978, groupware was defined by Peter and Trudy Johnson-Lenz as "intentional group processes plus software to support them."[83] As we have seen, blog functionality only partially facilitates "computer-mediated social interaction".[84] The debate that blogs are primarily a Web publicity platform, the next generation of the homepage, or belong to group of social interaction applications such as Usenet and Web forums is not an academic one.

In 2002, Clay Shirky introduced the follow-up of groupware. He called it "social software" and defined it as being "all software that supports social interaction."[85] Whether blogs really foster this social interaction should remain an open question. Most likely the social aspect of blogs will be phased out and developed elsewhere into other products, leaving the blogs to perform the introspective duty of the online diary. High traffic blogs will have to be generated from added functionalities that are being thrown onto the market on a daily basis, from Attention Trust Approved icons, scuttle, search this blog, furl archive, tag cloud, and skypecard to Poll of the Week, XML, podroll, and swikis. Blog pages are starting to look like the baroque e-commerce portals of the late-1990s—a bad omen. All of these buttons distract from reading and don't just point to other sites, but are mainly there to increase traffic and increase the status in the blogo-hierarchy.

Are bloggers risk-takers? Of course blog culture is different from the entrepreneurial risk cult embodied by management gurus such as Tom Peters. Much like Ulrich Beck defined risk, bloggers deal with hazards and insecurities induced by never-ending waves of modernization. What is blogged is the relentless uncertainty of the everyday. Whereas entrepreneurs colonize the future, energized by collective hallucinations, bloggers expose the present in which they find themselves caught. Blogging is the answer to "individualization of social inequality." It hits back, not so much with collective action, but with massive hyper-individual linking. This is the network paradox; there is simultaneous construction and destruction of the social at hand. The timid internalization ends and transforms into radical revelation. No Web site anticipated this practice better than the FuckedCompany.com website,[86] a predecessor of blog culture where employees of New Economy firms anonymously post rumors and complaints and, even more interesting, internal memos. Bloggers disrupt the disrupters. They override the constant talk about change. It is remarkably easy to attack the post-modern corporation as it solely depends on a hollow public image, developed by third-party consultants. Online diaries, rants, and comments so easily defy the manufactured harmony at which community engineering aims.

In *Democracy Matters*, Cornel West writes "the problems plaguing our democracy are not only ones of disaffection and disillusionment."[87] He sees the greatest threat coming from three dogmas: (1) free-market fundamentalism, (2) aggressive militarism, and (3) escalating authoritarianism. This has severely narrowed political dialogue. West: "The problem is not the vociferous shouting from one camp to the other; rather it is that we have given up being heard. We are losing the very value of dialogue—especially respectful communication—in the name of the sheer voice of naked power." It still remains an open question if blogs can open the space for such a dialogue. The danger of blogs, says West, is that "some go too far into crude advocacy the other way." As Florian Cramer indicated, from the perspective of a sophisticated 1990s online debating culture, blogs are a sign of regression, despite the fact that a few might cause extensive discussions. With the exception of the happy few A-list blogs, most sites either have "no comments" or closed down the possibility of responding altogether. After having conducted a few experiments, most editors of news organizations have by now closed down the possibility for online Letters to the Editor (as they are still called). The "other" is garbage. The online hooligans, previously known as plebes, do not generate additional value, so says the cynical judgment. A good many of the blog operators seem to agree.

Democracy Matters has a chapter called "Nihilism in America".[88] West distinguishes between the evangelical nihilism of the neo-conservatives around Bush and a paternalistic version practiced by Democrats like John Kerry and Hillary Clinton. A third form, the so-called "sentimental nihilism," prefers to remain on the surface of problems rather than pursue their substantive depth. It pays simplistic lip service to issues rather than portraying their complexity.[89] This tendency to remain on the surface, touch a topic, point to an article without even giving a proper opinion about it apart from it being worth mentioning, is widespread and is foundational to blogging. How many of the postings, we can ask with West, are Socratic questioning? Why is the blogosphere so obsessed with measuring, counting, and feeding, and so dismissive of rhetoric, aesthetics, and ethics? Let's not end with moral questions. The wish to overcome nihilism goes back to Nietzsche and is also relevant in the context of blogging. How to overcome meaninglessness without falling back into centralized meaning structures is the challenge that the blogging millions are posing.

It is interesting to see how West refers to Weblogs. In the chapter "The Necessary Engagement with Youth Culture," West paints a somber picture of personal depression and loneliness that fuel "media-influenced modes of escapism." These include the high use of drugs; the growing popularity of performing sex acts at incredibly young ages; and the way in which so many kids have become addicted to going online and instant messaging or creating Weblogs in which they assume an alternate personality. "This disgraceful numbing of the senses, dulling the mind, and confining to an eternal present—with a lack of connection to the past and no vision for a different future—is an insidious form of soul murder."[90] Like many of the lifestyle critics, West fails to see that it is the same Internet, the same blog culture, that is the organizational motor behind the democratic movements he so praises as "impassioned voices of dissent, often expressed with special fervor through the marvelously democratic medium of the Web."[91] It is drugs that initiate kids into Dionysian culture, yet the same drugs can result in a destructive addiction. Hip hop, praised by West as the solution, is judged by others as the ultimate form of macho cynicism. Thus, a guide to navigate such contradictions within cultural forms is needed.

West concludes: "We need a bloodstained Socratic love and tear-soaked prophetic love fueled by a hard-won tragicomic hope."[92] West makes a plea to out-Socratize Socrates by revealing the limits of the great Socratic tradition. "Must not the rigorous questioning and quest for wisdom of the Socratic be infused with the passionate fervor and quest for justice of the prophetic?" West asks and begs Socrates for more emotional intelligence. Blogging, commenting, and linking could be considered a start to overcome indifference, but could as well be classified as cold references. Blog content is usually emotional in some way, supportive and often melodramatic, but that cannot be said of the techno-networking act itself.

The prophetic has been corrupted to such an extent that it will take time before all traces of dotcom market fundamentalism have been overcome. No more gurus anymore? That will be hard to accomplish given the current celebrity-driven culture that is so deeply inscribed in our habitus. The world of blogs makes no difference here. But the scale and the depth of visionary nonsense certainly have. Blogs do not tell the story of freedom in the free software sense. Free software guru Richard Stallman's worthy but repetitive insistence on freedom to change code is irrelevant in the blog context because users have been given the option of not having to deal with (html) code so that they could finally focus on content creation and social networking. At the heart of the success of blogs lies its automated (but not necessarily proprietary) software. Users have been reasonably happy with the limitations of blogs. Stallman's freedom is only relevant for a tiny (yet crucial) workforce of software programmers that have the skills, time, and desire to write—and change—code.

Blogito Ergo Sum

So what form of (post)blogging cannot be extinguished or snuffed out? Blogging is already seductive and contagious; what it needs is positive examples to lead us away from the news spectacle so that it can position itself with a style of its own. The quest for insurgent software is on the table again. We do not need free/open source software to run a blog—that already exists (WordPress, bBlog, etc.). Where user desires lie when it comes to preferred ways of contacting, collaborating, and sharing needs to be studied before code hacking proceeds. How can a networked "democratic individuality" come into being if we want to avoid talking about communities and collective identities? How can software weave what the network demands?

A little phenomenology of posting is in order. The act of posting is constitutional in blogging. If we blog, we post. The philosophy of the blog posting could start with the difference between post and posting. Chris Garrett:

> Answer this, what is the basic unit of blogging? The blog post. Each post is like an individual worker in your workforce. Some posts might work harder than others. Some attract more attention than others. Each earns you a little revenue, together they are your means of gaining income. So common sense point number one; it makes sense that if you grow your work force, your body of work within your blog, that your income potential will grow.[93]

How do blog postings relate to the theory of the postal system, as developed by Jacques Derrida and Bernhard Siegert?[94] When Siegert writes "what is, is posted," this also counts for the Internet, and list culture and blogs in particular. The epistemological *a priori* here is the posting. "Everything that is being the case, is passed along," may as well be considered the motto of the blogosphere. In the process, we alter what is the case with our musings. Blogs arise in an environment in which useless bickering has become the rule and entropy has reached maximum levels. In that sense, the Shannon distinction between noise and signal has lost its critical significance as a metaphor because everything can be classified as noise. For machines, the signal-to-noise ratio is evident and is dealt with by utilizing increasingly fine filters.

What is significant for me is nonsense for you. This is the problem of meaningful search engines as much as surfable classification systems for the blogosphere that are neither based on popularity nor personal preferences such as RSS feeds. The question is no longer, as Shannon put it, how to communicate in the presence of noise. In the act of data creation we have become fully aware of its noise status. The fact that producing information (according to Flusser) means generating difference is not changing this techno-existential given. The question is no longer whether humans and their "redundant languages" are inferior to machine code (we are), but whether that code is open or closed and is stored and analyzed by states and corporations for security and commercial reasons. The Internet is full of relays, with traffic carefully monitored and filtered (by humans, mind you; think of the 50,000 Chinese employed to filter, monitor, and censor the Chinese Internet). We may send fewer and fewer letters, but we're still posting.

"Try to build up yourself and you build a ruin" (Augustine). This also goes for blogs. What seems to be a standard yet customized, user-friendly medium turns out to be unreliable if you are at it over a longer period of time. Blogs that have been untouched for three months are wiped from the server. The liquid self may have thought to find refuge in providers such as blogger.com or blogspot.com, but most blog services prove to be unstable when it comes to archiving the millions of blogs they host. The average age of a Web page is 6 months, and there is no reason to believe this is not case with blogs. As New York media theorist Alex Havias writes, "many Weblogs are short-lived, and in any event, we can assume that all Weblogs are likely to be kept in operation for a finite amount of time. These local archives need to be duplicated elsewhere. At present there is nothing as simple as RSS that allows for these archives to be duplicated."[95] The popular saying that the Internet will remember everything is turning into a myth. "If your Web site is not simple to update, you will not update it." That was a problem in the 1990s. The statement now is, "If you don't update your blog, we'll delete it." Even if the corpse of the blog can be reconstructed, for instance through www.archive.org, the problem remains of highly duplicated multimedia content. In his posting "Blogs and Archiving," Alex Halvias suggests that instead of a centralized server the model of a peer-to-peer archive could be a solution.

How can blog culture transcend the true, if banal, accusation that it is only interested in itself? How to deal with this ever-returning accusation—that blogging is merely self-promotion? Having a thriving scene of anonymous personae, as in Iran, is exciting but is not a real alternative for the rest of the world. Anonymous role playing is not going to provide us with an alternative to the self-centered image that blogging haunts, even though it might be interesting to investigate how blogs and MMORPGs (Massively Multiplayer Online Role-Playing Games) relate. At the moment, these are large parallel universes.[96] Instead we could speak, after Stephen Greenblatt, about online self-fashioning. The theatrical pose is made explicit in this term and brings together elements of the self (diary, introspection) with the spectacle of the blogocratic few that fight over the attention of the millions. In the context of blogs, Matthew Berk speaks about "digital self-fashioning." According to Berk, "online people constitute themselves as assemblies of documents and other data designed for people to read and establish some relationship. The more structure in and between this content, the greater is its action potential."[97] The self is defined in a normative way, as the capacity to construct links between content chunks.

Roughtype blogger Nicholas Carr has called the Web 2.0 hype, blogs included, "amoral."[98] "Of course the mainstream media see the blogosphere as a competitor. It *is* a competitor. And, given the economics of the competition, it may well turn out to be a superior competitor. The layoffs we have recently seen at major newspapers may just be the beginning, and those layoffs should be cause not for self-satisfied snickering but for despair. Implicit in the ecstatic visions of Web 2.0 is the hegemony of the amateur." This political empowerment move is captured as a computational "wisdom of crowds." What individual blog owners proudly see as a great post is, seen from the larger picture of the Internet with its one billion users, an ever shifting collection of buzzword clouds consisting of trillions of clicks and micro opinions. The more one knows about this meta level, through sophisticated software tools, the more dispirited one can become about its overall direction. Blogs do not arise from political movements or social concerns. They have an "obsessive focus on the realization of the self, " says Andrew Keen of *The Weekly Standard*. Keen foresees a pessimistic turn: "If you democratize media, then you end up democratizing talent. The unintended consequence of all this democratization, to misquote Web 2.0 apologist Thomas Friedman, is cultural 'flattening.'" Carr adds, "In the end we're left with nothing more than 'the flat noise of opinion'—Socrates's nightmare."[99]

The Carl Schmitt of new media, George Gilder once stated: "As capitalism releases creative energies everywhere, it leads to much greater diversity, including diversity of media. The whole blogosphere is an example of how transcending the top-down hierarchical models of old media technology with new media technology releases diversity and new voices and creations."[100] Against this commonly held view that diversity is a good thing, we can hold onto the loss that comes with the disappearance of familiarity and common references. Blogging alone (in variation of Robert D. Putman's *Bowling Alone*) is a social reality not easily dismissed. Most blogging is what Bernard Siegert calls "ghost communication." "Networking begins and ends with pure self-referentiality," Friedrich Kittler writes, and this autopoiesis is nowhere as clear as in the blogosphere.[101] Social protocols of opinion, deception, and belief cannot be separated from the technical reality of the networks, and in the case of blogs this turns out to be a treadmill.

Once upon a time, back in February 2004, the meme of the Internet being an "ego chamber" showed up. Searls, Weinberg, Ito, and Boyd… they were all there. Danah Boyd wrote: "One of the biggest motivators for a lot of people to get online in the 90s was to find people like them. The goal was not to solidify or to diversity, but to feel validated. Suggesting solidification/diversification implies that the primary motivation behind engaging online is to participate in purposeful dialogue, to be educated and educate. Frankly, I don't believe this to be true."[102] Shelly Parks had noted earlier about blogging: "Do you write to be part of a community? Or do you write to write, and the community part either happens, or doesn't?"[103] In this context, Danah Boyd referred to social networks and the homophilic concept (that birds of a feather flock together). It seems that in the blogging context explicit self-referential group building is still a new concept. Blogs create archipelagos of inward links, but these ties are very weak. On top of that, not only do bloggers usually only refer and answer to members of their online tribe, they have no comprehensive idea of what might happen if they included their adversaries. Blogrolls (link lists) unconsciously presume that if you include a blog you would agree or at least sympathize with its maker. We link to what is interesting and cool.[104] This is a key problem in the Google and Amazon model, in which links are traded as recommendations. This issue has been around since the birth of the browser in 1993–1995, when Netscape built in a category called "What's Cool." The artificial tension that has been designed here is between the blogosphere and the news industry and is used to create an imagined common enemy that does not exist. Once such a crucial, yet artificial, antagonistic relationship is dissolved the ranking hierarchy (and the dynamics behind blogging itself) may well fall apart.

Because of the vastness of the great blog prairie, it is not a contested space. Differences of opinion must first exist—they do not simply fall from the sky. Manufacturing opinion is a fine art of ideology creation. Debating should not be mixed up with a Netwar style of campaigning in which existing (political) fights are played out on the Internet. The pushy tone is what makes blogs so rhetorically poor. What lacks in the software architecture is the very existence of an equal dialogue partner. The result of this is a militarization, expressed in terms such as "blog swarm," defined by Christian right-wing blogger Hugh Hewitt as "an early indicator of an opinion storm brewing, which, when it breaks, will fundamentally alter the general public's understanding of a person, place, product or phenomenon."[105] It is communality of bias, or perhaps conviction, that drives the growth of blogging power and its visibility in other media.

The Land of Kizmiaz

If you agree with the argument, though nonetheless like to avoid cynicism and nihilism because of their heavy moral–historical connotations, simple snarkiness may offer a way out. Snarky language "contains quips or comments containing sarcastic or satirical witticisms intended as blunt irony. Usually delivered in a manner that is somewhat abrupt and out of context and intended to stun and amuse."[106] It cultivates irritable or short-tempered moods into a style. By doing this, it moves the discussion away from attitude and conviction to the level of language. Snark is not just jargon, it jargonizes. The snark is not primarily interested in positive self-promotion. "Because this ass is not going to kiss itself, honey," so says the subtitle of the Snarkiness blog.[107] According to Revenge of the Blog "snarky sounds more like witty sarcasm than cold cynicism, it contributes more to the Young Urban Professional than to the authoritarian character (as described by Adorno) whose cynicism is a way of distancing himself from his own ethical involvement."[108] The author, Pit Schulz, points out that finding one's personal voice is a central aspect of blogging. "Etymologically snarky could be associated with the nasal aspect of snoring or snorting. This sonority refers both to a certain private informality of pajama journalism but also to a state of routine and disconnectedness to a feedback which allows the modulating of expressions." In summary, the opposite of snarky would be emo (emotional); blogging mimics office chats in that it is informal without ever becoming personal. Its brevity stems from the lack of time of the writer, who soon must give his or her attention to work tasks. The short Revenge of the Blog entry noted above ends by stating that procrastination, the habit of putting tasks off to the last possible minute, is there at the opposite side of the time scale. After having drifted off, surfing, mailing, and texting, followed by some routine work, there is the daily panic of unfinished bits, the nagging details, and the unanswered calls. In short, the "new work ethics which follow the subjectification of the knowledge worker in the neo-liberal world society." Robert Scoble, to end this snark, has a cynical-business read of the term.

> The smartest people in my RSS are usually the least snarky. Why? Cause they could give a f**k about all the traffic. Why is all the snark going on? Cause everyone wants traffic. Why did I call this the John Dvorakification? Cause he figured out in the 1980s that if you attack a community everyone will get all up in arms and will start talking about the attack. That translates into traffic. Traffic = advertising dollars. [109]

Can we talk of a fear of media freedom? It is too easy to speak of freedom of speech and that blogs simply materialize this universal human right. The aim of radical freedom, one could argue, is to create autonomy and overcome the dominance of media corporations and state control and no longer be bothered by their channels. Most blogs show an opposite tendency. The obsession with news factoids verges on the extreme. Instead of selective appropriation, there is over-identification and straight out addiction, in particular to the speed of real time reporting. Lists of books that wait to be read, a common feature on blogs, point to this same obsession. After Erich Fromm (the author of *Fear of Freedom*), we could read this subjective stage as a psychological problem because existing information is simply reproduced in a public act of internalization. According to Fromm, freedom has put us in an unbearable isolation. We thus feel anxious and powerless. Either we escape into new dependencies or realize a positive freedom that is based upon "the uniqueness and individuality of man."[110] "The right to express our thoughts means something only if we are able to have thoughts of our own."[111] The freedom from traditional media monopolies leads to new bondages, in this case to the blog paradigm, as there is little emphasis on positive freedom as far as what to do with the overwhelming functionality and the void of the empty, white entry window. We do not hear enough about the tension between the individual self and the community, the swarms, and the mobs, who are also supposed to be part of the online environment. Instead what we see happening on the software side is daily improvements of ever more sophisticated (quantitative) measuring and manipulation tools (such as inbound linking, traffic measurement, or climbing ever higher on the Google ladder). Isn't the document that stands out the one that is not embedded in existing contexts? That the truth lies in the unlinkable?

Blogged Off

This blog is no more. It has ceased to be. It's expired and gone to meet its maker! It's a stiff! Bereft of life, it rests in peace! Its metabolic processes are now 'istory! It's off the twig! It's kicked the bucket, shuffled off its mortal coil, run down the curtain and joined the bleedin' choir invisible!! THIS IS AN EX-BLOG!!

–Geoff Parkes, appropriating Monty Python[112]

What fascinates me about blogs is not so much their hugging and stabbing in the back of news media, but their incredible turnover. The ghost town phenomenon was known early on, around 1997, when scores left their half-finished, gothic HTML homepages and simply signed off, never to be seen again. In early 2006, *The Financial Times* weekend edition dedicated its cover article to disappeared blogs.[113] Of course, we need to be skeptical when a major media outlet announces the death of the blog as just another crock of virtual gold. By early 2006, the Web 2.0 hype had reached such heights that people, for a variety of reasons, started to get nervous. Some, who had experienced the dotcom craze firsthand, feared yet another crash and publicly downplayed the hype, calling for some common sense. Things got serious when first-generation blogger Dave Winer announced his retirement from the blogscene.

For me, writing here is becoming stale. I'm tired, and I don't enjoy being the go-to guy for snarky folk who try to improve their pagerank by leading idiotic tirades about their supposed insights into my character. I want to enjoy the ability to plan and think before my would-be competitors have a chance to position themselves to grab the fruits of my labor. Too much transparency can be a hindrance, so I'm looking for less of that, and more fun, and more options.[114]

Other A-listers, like Joi Ito, also got bored with blogging and turned their attention to games such as Second Life and World of Warcraft. Another sign of mutation (to put it neutrally) has been the baroque multiplication of extra applications that can be attached to a blog, most of them either stimulating or monitoring one's aggregation of content. Stagnation has also been signaled by Clay Shirky, who in 2006 wrote an update of his *2003 powerlaws*. The obsessive focus on a small group of blogs started to backfire, not just on the A-list itself, but also on blogging in general.[115] *Financial Times Weekend* signaled that the imaginary community called the sphere was about to fall apart. "There is no sphere; these people aren't connected; they don't have anything to do with each other" (Choire Sicha, ex-gawker.com).[116] There is fear of fragmentation and segregation, at the moment when bloggers have little else to exchange but technical details. By mid-2006 there was no socially coherent group that had an interest in blogging each other. Blogging itself is a deeply social commitment. If the blog scene disintegrates, so too might blogs as technical platforms. Plenty of rival platforms are waiting to grab the attention that blogs are generating. There are no blogs without a sphere. Bloggers need each other, they need the addictive build-up around rumors and news scoops. What bloggers often lack is an ability to do thorough research and investigative journalism. "The world of blogs is like an entire newspaper composed of op-eds and letters and wire service feeds" (*Financial Times Weekend*). Blogs express and map micro-fluctuations of opinions and moods. In an era of rapid change, crisis, fear, and uncertainty, we can all indulge in such a pool of interlinked human responses. But at some point it is time to shift gears and change scene. It is hard to accept that the course of human-kind is bound for irrelevance. The technology caravan moves on and as do Internet users.

CHAPTER 2

The Cool Obscure
Crisis of New Media Arts

Wer ohne Rücksicht auf den Stand der Kunst philosophiert, betreibt letztlich immer das Geschäft eines Mythos, verdeckt oder offen, und nicht selten mit gefährlichen Konsequenzen.

—Peter Sloterdijk[1]

Explorations beyond the Official Discourse

A scene at Transmediale 2006, a Berlin festival once devoted to video and media art. Armin Medosch interviews festival director Andreas Broeckmann:

> On my repeated insistence, Broeckmann confirmed that media art existed no more. There was no such thing as a distinguished field of practice. It was either art, where it did not matter which technology was employed, or something else (he did not spell out the something else). In this day and age, Broeckmann said, technology cannot be the sole angle from which an art practice can be looked upon. And off he went to another reception. I was left pondering the implications of media art's sudden but not so unexpected death. The signs had been up there already. Peter Weibel had been advertising the age of digital everything for nearly twenty-five years before he abandoned it, all in a rush, this year, by creating a show called "Post-media Condition". What is going on? Are the former captains turning into rats who are the first to leave the sinking ship? And what with all those newly founded faculties and MA media art courses worldwide?[2]

This chapter raises a range of questions.[3] Why is new media art perceived as an obscure and self-referential subculture that is in the process of disappearing?[4] Why is it so hard for artists who experiment with the latest technologies to be part of pop culture or contemporary arts? What makes it so attractive, and yet so difficult, to seek collaborations with scientists? Why did new media art miss out during the exuberant dotcom days and why do geeks and IT millionaires prefer buying cars and other middle class baubles of consumption, and turn their backs on their own art form? Why is there such a subordinate attitude toward the hard sciences? Is the educational sector the only way out when we look at personal biographies? New media art has positioned itself in-between commercial demo design and museum strategies, and instead of being crushed, it has fallen into an abyss of misunderstanding. After years of heroic struggle to create works, install exhibitions, and assemble festivals, conferences, and courses, there is a looming sense of crisis. Is this just a painful moment in a process of growth or do we need to discuss structural problems?

Disclaimer: I am reluctant to list specific examples of artwork for fear of diluting the general argument. Each argument I give can be disproved with references to specific works of art that exemplify the exact opposite of what I am trying to prove. Of course, there are successful new media artists. Only a few of them can be seen at Biennales, where we are mostly treated to single channel video projections. Regional and national differences only make it harder to extract general trends, as in most parts of the world new media art is an unknown entity. Should this failed (commercially speaking) art form be circumvented by emerging artists? I am interested in a general picture of new media art in a time of rapid commercial development and social uptake of new media forms. A call for positive examples and alternatives is not a constructive attitude. In fact, it is part of the problem because it averts making a critical analysis. As Renato Poggioli wrote in his *Theory of the Avant-Garde*, my aim is diagnosis, not therapeutic treatment.[5] I have been involved in new media arts since the late-1980s and have done jury work and organized festivals where these works were shown. Over the years I have met so many artists, seen shows and granted interviews, most of them posted to the nettime list and then collected in *Uncanny Networks*. The connection in my own work to art was always close. Scores of brilliant pieces stand out, and I would not like to stress their importance here. If I speak about a crisis of new media arts, I do not refer to the level of artistic work but to the precarious position of the art form as such and its institutional representations in particular. I wrote this chapter with a pain in my heart, knowing that someone, a relative outsider like me, who is not a curator, artist, or administrator, would be in a position to voice concerns that are, in fact, not all that new and shared by many.

In this chapter I summarize recent debates on mailing lists like the Deep Europe platform Spectre, Empyre, iDC, and Fibreculture from Australia, where in 2005 the Australian federal arts funding agency dismantled its separate New Media Arts Board. Would it be better to integrate new media arts into film, theater, and the visual arts, or do we get works that are more interesting if technology-based art has its own funding structures, media labs, and centers? Besides a critical examination of the premises—and the very existence—of electronic arts, I am making an argument to question the Biennale-centric contemporary arts system—a system that reproduces a retrograde distinction between the fake of the special effect and the authentic struggle of real artists with the raw image.

The world is a big place and there are contradictory movements happening all the time. There are, still, enough asynchronous developments. It is hard and often not very wise to extrapolate a certain tendency, in this case the conceptual stagnation of new media art, and presume it is happening everywhere else. What emerges in A has been stagnant for ages in B. However, there are trends and rumors—memes spread fast. Electronic art, an earlier synonym for new media art, is in crisis. So is virtual art and net.art. These carefully gated communities have proven incapable of communicating their urgency and beauty to their ever-rising (potential) audience. In response to this, there are fewer subsidies and sponsorships available. The crisis is taking place in a culturally conservative era that shies away from experiment in general. Art should hit, slap in the face, go straight through all interference, and not question. It should present itself as an object of desire, a tangible commodity, and not see itself as a prototype. It should be instantly ready for consumption. This leads to questions like, "What are the economic models of new media art with its unstable standards?" and "Are there as yet untapped sources of money and resources?"

Beginnings

I feel compelled to start with a definition. New media art can best be described as a transitional, hybrid art form, and a multi-disciplinary cloud of micro-practices.[6] Historically, new media arose when the boundaries between clearly separated art forms such as film, theater, and photography began to blur, due to the rise of digital technologies.[7] Its beginnings are currently being investigated by scholars such as Dieter Daniels and Inke Arns, Charlie Gere, Stephen Jones, Paul Brown, and Oliver Grau.[8] In October 2005 Refresh!, the first international conference to deal with the multiple new media arts histories from the science perspective, was held in Banff, Canada.[9] The emerging field of media archeology as exercised by Siegfried Zielinski, Erkki Huhtamo, and others will contribute to this effort on another level, as well as studies by sociologists and art historians. Before we can start speculating about its future, it is time to analyze its stagnation, using the tools of institutional criticism.

The birth of new media is closely tied to the democratization of computers with the development of the personal computer (PC). According to some, it is an art form born out of the *Geist* of Fluxus with its video art and performance. Others stress the influence of 1970s electronic music and postindustrial art and activism of the 1980s. Again, others point at the intermedia practices that used a variety of analogue techniques, also called multimedia, such as slides and super-8, projectors, inflammables, and soundscapes. Despite its numerous predecessors and prehistories of telematic art, I see the late 1980s as a starting point when new media art hit the surface, specifically tied to the rise of desktop publishing, hypertext, and the production of CD-ROMs. Internet involvement started relatively late, from 1994–1995 onward, after the World Wide Web had been introduced. New media art is, first of all, part of the larger visual culture picture. While it has strong ties to hypertext discourses, cyberculture, and sound art, as well as abstract and conceptual art and performance, we can nonetheless say that the visual arts element forms the dominant thread. However, the problem with these accounts of the beginnings of new media art is their overemphasis on individual artists and their works. Such accounts usually lack institutional awareness. Institutional understanding in this sector has been as slow as the development of new media technology has been rapid. In this respect, new media art is a misnomer because it reproduced repeatedly the modernist dilemma between aesthetic autonomy and social engagement. Add the word "art" and you instantly create a problem. In the case of new media art, there was—and still is—no significant market, almost no gallery support, precious few curators and critics, and an audience of specialists, bordering on a cult. Most of all, there was no suprematist feeling of acting as an avant-garde. A sense of historical confidence is clearly lacking here. Instead, there is a strong practice of conducting minor interventions in the shadow of established practices such as film, visual arts, television, and graphic design.

"New media art, as defined by the Australia Council, is a process where new technologies are used by artists to create works that explore new modes of artistic expression. These new technologies include computers, information and communications technology, virtual or immersive environments, or sound engineering. They are the brushes and pens of a new generation of artists."[10] The emphasis here is on exploration. New media art is searching for new standards and art forms. Its prime aim is not necessarily to create everlasting universal artwork. Instead, it paves the way for a new generation to make full use of the newly discovered language—outside of the new media arts context. This strength should further be emphasized and explored. However, as this chapter shows, many of the prime energies get lost in the battle to fit in. The emphasis on the creation of a language, an infrastructure, could explain why there is so much hidden, voluntary work done in this scene and why self-exploitation is so common. Only pioneers understand that one first needs to create a language in order to write a poem. However, the laws of new media are simply not there to be uncovered. What some see as an advantage, not having a complex set of rules and references, others judge as an inherently immature situation. How do you drag yourself out of the mud, jump over your own shadow? No one will do it for new media art. There is no sugar daddy. Forget the trophy at the end of the race.

During the early 1990s, a quiet divorce happened. In the midst of the virtual reality, multimedia, and cyberspace excitement, video art slipped off the scene and made a clever move toward contemporary art with its much better infrastructure of biennales, curatorial programs, and exhibition halls. There are a few exceptions, like the New York Postmasters Gallery that in the late-1990s became central for the net.artists it represented. Still, if we speak of new media art we deal with an art form that embodies technological experimentation. Some video art still does this, but most have turned away from frame-within-the-frame and other special effects. Video art can no longer afford to indulge in formal experimentation and has found it needs to transmit ideas which are easily understood in a classic narrative form. Within new media discourse we can see confusion around the exact status of the moving image. What is called "video" these days ranges from the high-end productions of Pipilotti Rist and Stan Douglas to works that look like they have been hacked together in iMovie last weekend by a cousin. In his book *Topology of Art*, Boris Groys includes a chapter called "Media Art in the Museum" in which he reduces new media to video installations and how they relate to cinema. There isn't a single mention of interactivity, immersive issues, the role of sound, networked environments, or performance pieces. Groys should know better as a Karlsruhe-based ZKM art historian. This exclusion is, of course, consciously done and restates that new media, by definition, belongs to the visual arts domain.[11]

We need to remain specific. Political climates in Western countries vary greatly. Whereas "e-culture" funding in the Netherlands has gone up, new media no longer exists as a separate category in the funding of art there. A political coup out of Rotterdam in 2000 tried to centralize the arts, including the V2 centre for "unstable media" into an overarching Centre for Visual Culture, but it failed miserably. The situations in Berlin, Paris, and London are all radically different. Academia remains a safe haven in the United States with little cultural funding available elsewhere, whereas

Europe still struggles with the question of whether art education should be academic. My critique is not meant to disdainfully look down on the "yawning vacancy of the technological sublime."[12] New media art is not a single entity. It is "searching" and does not primarily focus on grand narratives or finished works that can be purchased in a gallery. Electronic art, a somewhat older term that is sometimes used as a synonym for new media art, is a hybrid setup that depends highly on the cultural parameters set by engineers. Many of the key players in the field position their practice in the fragile zone between art and technology, which asks for trouble. Often there are traces back to the practice called intermedia, which deals with transdisciplinary collaboration.[13]

New media artworks are forms in search of a form. They are procedural in the sense of writing material-specific procedures. As test beds they often lack content. Many of the works are neither cool nor ironic, as are so many works of contemporary art. Instead, they often have a playful, naïve feel in that they invite the user to experience alternative interfaces. Many examples of new media art are hot—participatory, dysfunctional, or distributed—frustrating the attempt to detach and frame them in a gallery.[14] New media, to its credit, has been one of the very few art forms that has taken seriously the programmatic wish to blow up the walls of the white cube. This was done in such a systematic manner that it moved itself outside of the art system altogether.

New media artworks have the impossible task of having to impress both computer scientists and art curators. But this undertaking fails tragically. Neither the art world nor ICT professionals are necessarily fans of electronic arts. *Wunderkammer* artworks are not in big demand. From the geek perspective they are made by users, not developers. In their view, such artworks apply new technologies and do not contribute to their further development. There is a lack of interest in engaging with new media artworks as they are often packed with references to philosophy, art history, and its own recent history as a genre.[15] For the art professionals, on the other hand, new media art belongs in educational science museums and amusement parks rather than contemporary art exhibitions. If we read the mainstream critics, they believe art should transmit Beauty, Truth, and Emotion. In today's society of the spectacle there is no place for halfway art, no matter how many policy documents praise new media art for its experimental attitude and will to innovate. The thesis that I develop here is not a critique of experimentation. The question of how to deal with the inevitable self-referentiality that occurs once new media are no longer new and a process of institutionalization sets in that, instead of facilitating its constituency, in the end cuts off more possibilities than not is at stake.

I am by no means the first one to address these issues. In 2002, Cologne-based media theorist Hans Ulrich Reck published a booklet called *Mythos Medienkunst* (*The Myth of Media Art*). I am quoting here from a not (yet) published translation. According to Reck, art is dissolving into various directions. He then proposes to draw a distinction between "art through media" and "media art." "Whereas 'media art' continues the lineage of claiming art as defined by expression, presentation and representation, 'art through media' highlights the 'interventionist' and 'collaborative' claims with a stress on processual methods and findings."[16] Reck argues that there is no compelling reason to attach one and the same—art—to any number of creative processes. Crucial in this context is his thesis that "if something is art, then it is not art because it employs certain media. Painting is not 'oil art'." For Reck, it is absurd to take material characteristics of art to be a defining feature. "What art is does not depend on its media and its materials. Art is a specific statement." At the same time, he warns that no claim can be made to cultural exclusivity in the name of art. Instead of a cold, institutional definition of art, Reck does not question whether something is art or not. What matters is whether something is good, important, relevant, illuminating, or shattering. Reck defines art in a normative sense as an activating force, as something in the realm of the virtual (in the Deleuzian sense), a category that opens a realm of possibilities. Art attempts the impossible—with or without the use of "new" media. "Art is no longer the art of representation, but primarily the art of transformation."

To illustrate the often-felt lack of urgency, I quote from a report of the August 2006 ISEA conference in San Jose, CA, written by the artist kanarinka/Catherine D'Ignazio that focused on one of the festival's main programs called Interactive City.

> The festival's imagination seemed to be characterized by a spirit of play which feels increasingly oriented towards middle-class consumer spectacle and the experience economy. To give you an example of some art experiences that were possible at ISEA:
>
> 1. eating ice cream and singing karaoke
> 2. calling an old person in San Jose to talk about whatever you might have in common with them
> 3. pressing a button on a machine and getting an artsy plane ticket with your photo on it
> 4. drifting through the city as if it were a sports field via applying sports plays in urban space
> 5. visualizing your social network via Bluetooth as you go around the conference and talk to your friends

6. watching/listening to noise music made by people riding skateboards around the conference
7. listening to an erotic sci-fi narrative about San Jose on your cell phone while riding the train
8. flipping light switches to make a one-word message in public space
9. viewing colorful 3D representations of wireless digital data

So, my questions to the artists, the organizers, the attendees and everyone else is—is psycho-geography/locative media work simply R&D for a new generation of entertainment spectacle? Or, what are we actually trying to do with these ideas of "play" in urban space? Who gets to play? And what about the interactive cities in Iraq and Lebanon and elsewhere? Why didn't we address war, security, militarization and terrorism as aspects of the contemporary interactive city? For me, running around making the city into a sandbox, a playground or a playing field feels increasingly irrelevant and irresponsible. A gentleman invited to drift with us summed it up nicely "Sorry, I can't go with you. I have to work here until 8 PM and then I have to go to my other job."[17]

At the 2006 ISEA, Sydney-based theorist Anna Munster witnessed divergence, not convergence. "There is no common thread to new media anymore." "Festivals, like Biennale's, are now events that are pretty much external to the local and the located—they are art imports that come in with lots of talk of global, critiques even of the global and then precisely land like a great big Airbus 380 and do their 'thang' wherever they happen to dock." Anna Munster also observed that, as a visitor to the United States, it was remarkable that none of the artworks or themes in ISEA addressed Iraq, Afghanistan, or the Israel–Lebanon war that raged on during the days of the festival.[18]

Before I will go into specific debates, I would like to present four models to deal with the current stagnation. The first one is what we see happening in most places: a desperate attempt to further carve out a semi-autonomous terrain for technology-based arts practices. This strategy is ambivalent as it attempts to institutionalize itself while simultaneously collaborating with neighboring, and competing, art and research practices such as theater, performance, film and media studies, computer science, humanities, and contemporary arts. The making of a mature discipline is constantly undermined by inter/poly/metadisciplinary approaches. In the field of constant and rapid change, it is hard to go for the long haul. The establishment of a separate field with its own expertise takes decades. Just think how long it takes to set up awards and residencies, organize critical writing and review mechanisms, set up centers and labs where the artists can work, and secure a separate, sustainable funding from federal or local authorities, foundations, or sponsorship.

The second option would be a Hegelian transcendence of new media arts into the existing institutional art practices. One could also call it the strategy of disappearance. It is naïve and real at the same time, as such a synthesis between the traditional and the digital is too good of a deal. It might work for individual artists who escape the ghetto, but will be devastating for the small new media arts infrastructure that has been set up over the past few decades. Where could those with their professional careers so deeply invested—all their dreams, hopes, and ambitions in the new media arts identity—possibly go? The contemporary arts scene can only speak with contempt about the ugly high-tech installations, and this doesn't present much promise for future negotiations. The destiny of new media arts as an autonomous domain looks bleak if it has to merge with established art forms. A possible example here could be to look at video art and how it elegantly disassociated itself from new media in the early 1990s in order to reincarnate itself as a marketable art form.

The third option would be to leave the arts context altogether. Most young new media artists disappear into the commercial sector and find work as Web or games designers, animators, video editors, or, worse, behind the desk of a copy shop. Or they become unemployed and live on social security, if that's an option anyway, and make extra money playing the stock market. Most disappear into the education sector. Another way out would be to seek refuge in science labs, and I will discuss such art and science collaborations in the following.

The fourth option would be renaming new media arts as creativity. The creative industries (CI) concepts thus far have proven to be not much less than a short-term government policy cycle. The CI-hype exists only in the heads of bureaucrats. This is a problem because the CI construct could at least serve as some kind of diversification of money sources (in places where governments give money to start with). The good thing about the CI meme is that, at the very least, it puts the economic question on the table: How do artists survive? It forces artists to think beyond state funding and a gallery market that doesn't exist in the first place. Thus far, new media art has been reluctant to talk about commercial options, at least in Europe. If you work in the business sector, you are no longer an artist. Elsewhere, such as in Japan, most parts of Asia, and the United States, there is little other option than to either work in the private sector or teach in an art school.

Dissolving a New Media Arts Board

In December 2004, the Australia Council announced its intention to disband the New Media Arts Board and the Community Cultural Development Board. These boards gave grants, respectively, to artists working in new media and to artists working with communities such as disadvantaged youth, prison inmates, and the homeless. Some of the responses on the Australian mailing list for new media research and culture, Fibreculture, are summarized here. Paul Brown writes that it has always been his opinion "that setting up special funding bodies essentially marginalizes the practice and allows the conservatives to defer acknowledgment of the inevitable."[19] While Danny Butt appreciates that artists may not want to be pigeonholed, it is his understanding "that you could always apply to the other pots of money and 'compete on your merits' against the landscape painters if you were that concerned about it. This move [by the Australia Council] represents a suppression of the new, the emergent and the political in favor of the known and the commercial (high art is big business)."

Theorist Anna Munster played an important role in the debate and strongly criticized the Council's decision. On Fibreculture she wrote:

> We now live deeply immersed in informationalism as a cultural, social and political set of circumstances. We need fields and infrastructure to support responses to and experiments with this. It doesn't matter whether the New Media Arts Board is stuck in a semantic loop about the term new media. The point is that a huge amount of very interesting and extraordinarily experimental work here in Australia would not have been done without it.

Munster points to the future of the young generation.

> Where will our younger and emerging artists who are feeding and living off information culture go for support now? They will be forced into making tiny amounts of money doing web design, making ring tones, or doing cell clean-up whenever a blockbuster Hollywood production rolls into Fox studios. Or they will tread the grinding road into academia, which is probably going to be the next place new media gets the cut. Of course they/we have to do this anyway in order to live and we attempt to sustain our more experimental practices through these avenues. The previous board supported a range of people that had more sustained periods of time to think through ideas and bring these to fruition. You just don't get that kind of time without funding support.

Munster also points to the current precarious position of artistic practice that exists on the back of unpaid voluntary labor.

The notion that we are now or should be moving from welfare to commercialization is simply adopting the glib election patter of the government. The economic times we live in, as artists, comprise a mix of public and private sector restructuring in the light of global shifts towards a service-based economy. The reality for most artists is that they get a bit of public sector funding, a bit of sponsorship and then the rest of the time they sell their services to sustain their practice. Selling your services is the way in which artists currently self-sustain.

Internet artist, curator, and now director of the Australian Network for Art and Technology, Melinda Rackham saw clear benefits from the situation as it was.

Even if the board was a short term solution, it was a bloody good solution that other countries are following. It helped produce some fantastic work, created dialogue, and promoted our artists globally. And it worked for very little investment.

University of Queensland scholar Lucy Cameron points at another tendency:

There is a suggestion that in the future there will be less 'new talent' funding and more 'virtuous cycles' funding based on the track record of the institution you're attached to—if you got grants/contracts before you're more likely to get grants in the future—a process that is being supported by the current suggestion by the government that in Australia we'll soon be reverting to a two-tier higher education system—of teaching only and more elite teaching and research institutions. The overall effect of this U.S. type free-market, bottom-up, endogenous growth philosophy is that it backs commercial capacity rather than individual talent.[20]

In an open letter to the chair of the Australia Council, media artist Simon Biggs sums up some of the secondary aspects of new media arts, besides the central question of if it is art (or not).

The emergence of new media art can be seen as valuable to society not only for the art that arises from it. Australia is a world leader in the new media industries and in part this is due to the well-documented interchange there has been between the experimental cultural practices that have happened in new media art and the commercial exploitation of these developments. Australia is also a world leader in education and, again, this has been enhanced notably by the emergence of new media arts specialist departments at many of Australia's universities and is also evidenced by the number of

Australian artists employed at similar departments in universities around the world.[21]

Thus far, the New Media Arts Board measured success mainly as individual talent and was hesitant to encourage institutionalization. ANAT (Adelaide), Experimenta (Melbourne), and D'Lux (Sydney) are all tiny and have been stagnant over the last decade (in terms of their budget). The prestigious ACMI centre (Autralian Centre for the Moving Image) on Federation Square, Melbourne will be, as the name already indicates, soon turned into a film center with little emphasis on contemporary arts or technology. The new media arts funding of the Australia Council over the past decade produced a field of dispersed, highly trained and well-informed artists who are now increasingly desperate as the necessary next phase of institutionalization of the field has failed to materialize. The strategy to fund a number of small organizations and dissipate what little money there was to individuals has made the New Media Board, and the sector as a whole, an easy target.

This Brechtian *Lehrstück* (learning play) from down under could lead us to the thesis that the true potential of new media arts is in its ability to dissipate. It is not a goal in itself, even though it obviously has self-referential tendencies, like all activities in society. In the short term, new media art sets out to discover the inner logic, standards, and architectures of new technologies, but apparently, these processes can only last for a short while. The phase of experimentation will necessarily come to an end. Its findings will dissolve into society.

Myth of the Blank Page

If it is all just misery, then why bother about electronic arts in the first place? Is it the road less traveled, the thrill to discover, to write history that attracts artists? For this we need to look into the archetype of the artist as inventor and creator. Whereas those who stress the media aspect will see the role of artists as one that critically comments and questions, for those who focus on technology there are positive and imaginative contributions to be made. There is a widely spread belief that tech-based artworks have the potential to be genius. Supposedly there are not yet traces or fingerprints of society on recently developed technologies and the artist therefore has the full range of all possible forms of expression in front of him or her. Imagine if you were the one to make the first film, or shoot the first photograph. Humans, with their dirty little interests have not yet spoiled the channel. There are no influences of pop culture yet. The apparent absence of digital aesthetics for PDAs, urban screens, RFID tags, smart cloth, mobile phones, and the like is exactly seen as their potential. According to this "myth of the blank page," new media artists are not limited by existing cultural connotations because there are no media-specific references yet. It is the heroic task of the new media artist to define those cultural codes. There is indeed historical evidence that those who work first with a new medium can reach a God-like status (and make fortunes). But in most cases, these artists only start to make real money after they have passed away.

In the myth of the blank page, the situation of new media art is too good to be true. You can do whatever you like and are not bothered by the heavy weight of art history. The problem of this theory of the unspoiled perception is the uncritical belief in art talent that operates outside of its own time-space. Real new media artists are obsessed with deciphering the eternal laws of the new materials. So-called creative, contemporary artists, on the other hand, are focused on the market. They have to subject themselves to the laws of fame and celebrity and cannot waste their time in such uncool environments as computer labs. For them, technology is merely a tool and they will be the last to question the manual, let alone write their own software or build experimental interfaces. The search for the specificities of a new medium requires a long trial-and-error period in which funky images or experiences are not guaranteed. Pop and experiment do not go together very well. The geek as role model had its media moment during the Internet hype of the mid-1990s, but then quickly faded away. And the geek aesthetic remains as bad as it always has been. This is media reality but the new media arts sector finds it hard to deal with. The uncool can only be pop once—after its demise, it is just seen as a failure.

A Motivational Art Intermezzo

"Live to be outstanding." What is new media in the age of the rock 'n roll life coach Anthony Robbins? There is no longer the need to be spectacular. The Situationist critique of the spectacle has won. That would be my assessment of the Anthony Robbins Age in which we now live. Audiences are no longer looking for empty entertainment; they seek help. Art has to motivate—not question, but assist. Art should not primarily reflect, represent, or discover the world but talk to its audience, hit it in the face, so say today's art marketers. Irony can be a medicine as long as it contributes to the healing process of the patient. Be careful not to offend anyone. Today's aesthetic experiences ought to awaken the spiritual side of life. Aesthetics are not there for contemplation only. Art has to become (inter)active and take on the role of coaching. In terms of the self-mastery discourse, the 21st century artist helps to unleash the power from within. No doubt, this is going to be achieved with positive energy. Perverse optimism, as Tibor Kalman called it, is needed. Art has to create, not destroy. A visit to the museum or gallery has to fit into one's personal development program. Art should consult us in transformation techniques and not criticize. In order to be a true experience, the artwork has to be an immediate bodily experience, comparable to the fire walk. It has to be passionate, and should shed its disdain for the viewer, along with its postmodern strategies of irony, reversal, and indifference. In short, artists have to take responsibility and stop their silly plays. The performance artist's perfect day job is the corporate seminar, building trust and distilling the firm's core values from its human resources.

Self-management ideology builds on the 1980s wave of political correctness—liberated from a critical negativism that only questioned existing power structures without giving guidance. As Anthony Robbins says, "Live with passion!" Emotions have to flow. People want to be fired up and move out of their comfort zone. Complex references to intellectual currents within art history are a waste of time. The art experience has to fit in and add to the personal growth agenda. Art has to leverage fears and promise guaranteed success. Part therapist, part consultant, art no longer compensates for a colorless life. Instead, it makes the most of valuable resources and is aware of the attention economy in which it operates. In order to reach such higher planes of awareness, it seems unavoidable to admit and celebrate one's own perverse *Existenz*. Everyone is a pile of shit and has got dirty hands. Or as Tibor Kalman said: "No one gets to work under ethically pure conditions."[22] It is at that Žižekian point that art as a counseling practice comes into being.

Tired Media Art

Let's look into another debate. It is hard to reconstruct the beginnings of the crisis in new media arts debate. The relative isolation of technology-based work probably already existed in the 1950s and 1960s. Here we can only report on the malaise that surfaced around 2004–2006. Transmediale director and moderator of the Spectre list, Andreas Broeckmann kicked off a debate about the "media art centre of the 21st century" with the following overview of festival and center closures.

> Rob van Kranenburg asked on this list: "what's next?", quoting the "restructuring" of IVREA in Italy and the closure of the MIT Media Lab in Dublin; we have also recently seen the termination of the Radiator Festival, Kopenhagen, of CICV, Montbeliard (France), of

the World Wide Video Festival, Amsterdam, as well as the scaling down of Electrohype, Malmö (Sweden), Public Netbase in Vienna, and of HTBA Hull Time Based Arts, Hull (United Kingdom); while each of these cases has its particular local, national or even personal reasons, it is difficult not to think that there is some sort of a pattern which, at least in part, reverses the 1990s institutional expansion of media culture and media art.[23]

Had new media, as a fashion, passed its due date, and if so, what would happen to those who had committed their identity and career to the term? How do you reconcile with the notion of an institutional lifecycle?

Spectre subscriber Tom Holley mentions the dissolvement of the Internet art program of the Walker Art Center (when curator Steve Dietz was fired) and ICA's New Media Centre in London, which was sponsored by Sun Microsystems. Holley was one of a series of curators/producers who tried to direct the ICA lab. New media art struggles with the discrepancy between its own niche status (Joe Kraus: "The twenty-first century is all about millions of markets of dozens of people") and unprecedented ICT growth figures. According to Holley, most media labs close down because of a failure in the funding models.

> With the Sun deal at the ICA the organization accrued a lot of cash, probably saving it from closure, but at the same time the provision of Sun machines that hardly anybody knew how to use alienated the community. Locked doors created a ridiculous sense of exclusion for most, which is at odds with any sense of openness and skill/knowledge. With the millions of pounds value of the sponsorship deal the ICA got its IT infrastructure in place, plus servers and a sys admin guy. When the deal ended a few years on Sun pulled support and it's been dead in the water for years now.[24]

Compare this with triumph of the new media market as described by Andreas Broekmann:

> We see a massive expansion of the field of digital culture, a growing number of mainly young people who inhabit that space, who are "of that tribe", who "live digital culture"—often even without a strong critical reflection, but more as a quasi-natural, techno-social environment in which they grow up—and swim like fish that don't see the water because they don't need to. [25]

In a thread called "Is Modernity our Antiquity?" on the Empyre list, Ben Bogart raised the question of why concept prevails over technology in the art system.

Technology is nothing but the manifestation of concepts. Would a critic deem a painting as poor because the artist spent too much time developing the colors on the canvas? Is "concept" simply a method of sorting those artists that do from those that "create" and leave the implementation to others?

New York artist Millie Nis responded that

a lot of digital art is about technology in an empty, self-referential way that is of little interest to the wider art world. Too much new media is an exercise in demonstrating that a certain technological process is possible rather than an exploration of some area of human interest. Most art makes us think about things that are broader than the specific art techniques employed in the work, such as emotional, cultural, or philosophical issues. It also often reminds us of real life and gives us insight about real life (like when we see a painting that influences our way of seeing the world outside the painting). If a work of digital art does not engage us in this way, then it probably will fail as art, however well-executed the technology is.

GH Hovagimyan agreed. "The problem with digital art is its focus on techne," he writes.

A large amount of digital art doesn't engage art history or the art world at all but rather presents itself as the newest form of creativity that obsoletes all previous forms. Digital art often insists that it be judged by its own rules so that for instance, well-formed code is supposed to be considered on an equal footing with a Jackson Pollack. What digital artists disregard is that Pollack engaged in a rigorous discourse with previous art forms. He painted WPA and regionalist murals, he studied and produced both Surrealist and Cubist paintings and drawings before he got to his drip paintings.

The Desire to Be Science

There is an implicit holistic, New Age element behind the desire to escape and create a synthesis between arts and technology, thereby escaping the confrontation with the art market. With Leonardo da Vinci in mind, the artist–engineer expects the world to embrace the desire to unite humanities and hard science. Much to their surprise, the world is not yet ready for such good ideas. Often the artist is not much more than a willing test user/ early adaptor. In itself this wouldn't be such a problem. Who cares? But most new media art works are neither subversive nor overly conceptual or critical. To make things more complicated, they aren't pop either. The new media art genre cannot work out whether it is underground or urban sub-culture. But new media arts never really became part of the techno, dance, or rave party scene either—let alone a rebel subculture; certainly, it's never had anything to do with rap or other contemporary street cultures. VJ culture, for instance, is not part of the official new media arts canon and hovers at the edge. Like the self-insulated world of the ivory-tower modern academic, new media art situates itself in a media lab rather than a lounge club. The launch bed of works is the new media festival where like-minded colleagues gather.

Instead of being loud and clear about the hybridity-in-flux, the some-what odd and isolated situation of new media arts has turned into a taboo topic. A general discontent has been around for a while, in particularly as a privileged inner-circle has focused on excessively expensive interactive baroque installations that could be found in places like Ars Electronica (Austria), ZKM (Germany), and ICC (Japan). But that excessive period of the late-1990s is over. We could almost become nostalgic about those days. It was a good party for many and a modest goldmine for some. In contrast, this postmillennial period is a time of budget cuts, conceptual stagnation, talk of creative industries, artistic backlashes (with the return of minimal painting), and political uncertainty—while simultaneously new media are penetrating society in an unprecedented fashion.

It is not considered good form to openly raise crisis issues in the new media area for the simple fact that the gloomy mood may endanger future projects, a next job, or your upcoming application. It is often enough said that most new media art is of inferior quality. Negativism sticks to people in this scene, which is silently dominated by New Age positivism, driven by a common cornucopian belief that technology will ultimately save us all. We're on the right side of history, no? There are only rare cases of indi-viduals who speak out openly. The rest shut up and move on to become part of the contemporary arts or to find a job elsewhere. Another reason for the lack of negation could be the influence of techno-libertarianism. Those who protest are quickly condemned as enemies of the future, but this is never done out in the open.

The collective discursive poverty within new media arts explains the virtual absence of lively debates about art works in general. There is little institutional criticism. With mainstream media uninterested, the new media arts scene is fearful of potentially devastating internal debates. Rival academic disciplines and policy makers could be on the lookout to kill budgets. Instead, a fuzzy tribal culture of consensus rules, based on good-will and mutual trust. To develop a genuinely critical perspective on new media arts, one has to either come from elsewhere or move away from the scene to an entirely different field such as the commercial art world, design, pop culture, or dance parties. For all these reasons, the scene remains small and is stagnating, despite the phenomenal growth of new media worldwide. This is not exactly what young, creative tinkerers expect. A growing number of young artists who work with technology carefully avoid the ailing sector and find their own path, via the established art sector, tactical media activism, or small businesses. At the same time, there are painters, sculptors, and fashion designers who use computers as the primary tool of design, yet explicitly leave out new media in their public presentations.

Instead of taking the heroic stand of the avant-garde, many new media practitioners have chosen to simply drift away in clouds of images, texts, and URLs. There is a certain coziness to hanging out in the networks and not being confronted with the exigencies of the world. The importance of vagueness cannot be underestimated. The blurry background aspect of many works needs to be acknowledged and taken seriously. In the present situation of immediate irrelevance, it is genuinely difficult to create a significant work that will have an impact. Digital aesthetics have developed a hyper-modern, formalist approach, and seem to lack the critical rigor of standard contemporary art pieces. The main reason for this is the young age of a field that is constantly on the move, from video, industrial robotics, and CD-ROM to Internet, bio art, and immersive installations to locative media and software art. This makes it hard to develop a critical apparatus.

It is easy to become depressed at this point. Some will deal with this situation, label it as existential, and continue with their work no matter what art critics, the markets, or funding bodies have to say. Such an elegant, self-referential attitude of becoming sovereign media has popped up here and there.[26] The larger issue here is the widely acknowledged impossibility of creating avant-garde movements. Working with computers, the Internet and similar technologies could easily have created specific romantic, agnostic, or nihilistic aesthetics, a set of styles and attached schools that gather around certain ideas and political programs. This did not happen and we all know why there cannot and will not be a repeat of the historical avant-garde. Pop art and then postmodernism have successfully sabotaged every attempt in this direction. Relieved, sad, or angry? The isolated situation of innovative art cannot be discussed without taking into account the mourning phase after the death of avant-garde. So, the question remains: If art is either a perpetual mobile or a fashion spectacle, then why experiment?

Current art and science inquiries, as promoted by Roy Ascott and Jill Scott, could be read in the light of IRCAM's "scientization of art." IRCAM, based in Paris, is the largest institute of its kind that researches electronic music. It was founded in 1977 by the avant-garde composer Pierre Boulez and is funded by the French state. The aim of IRCAM has been to bring together music, science, and technology. The center is best known for its residency program for composers. In her study on IRCAM, Georgina Born describes how the musical avant-garde gradually became legitimized by the academy and gained increasing financial subsidy. It became established, but quite different from the way modernist avant-garde in the visual arts created a commercial market for its artworks. Modernist visual techniques, says Born,

> have become absorbed into wider cultural practices and public consciousness. By contrast, the musical avant-garde has failed to find success with a broad public or to achieve wider cultural currency: it remains an elite form of high culture. Being no longer marginal or critical of the dominant order it has not only undermined its initial raison d'être but it must also continually legitimize its present position of official subsidy in the absence of a larger audience.

This is exactly the position in which electronic art has maneuvered itself, including an "avant-garde view of history, in which the present state is denigrated in promise of greater things to come."[27] The relative isolation in which IRCAM operated does not stem from organizational mismanagement. This is not the case within new media arts organizations either. Born describes IRCAM as an "efficient ship," a "dependable machinery" with a marketing and education department. "IRCAM remains as it has always been: a hierarchical, now increasingly efficient bureaucratic institution."[28] However, what is under debate here is not professionalism but basic categories and presumptions.

If new media art has such an emphasis on experimentation and collaboration with engineers, biological scientists, and innovative interfaces, then why is it not simply giving up this tragic alliance with the arts and ruthlessly seeking to integrate itself in the world of IT business and computer science? It is only outsiders who can accuse the electronic arts of compliance with the capitalist system. The sad reality is that artists are not all that different from ordinary computer users, unless they are part of the celebrity high-end circuit. For the majority of artists, access to technology is limited to consumer hardware and software. Often there is no money for more state-of-the-art machines or resources to acquire strategic knowledge. This strategy is exhausting because today's latest technology is tomorrow's trash technology. The way out here is either to produce works with a lasting aesthetic quality or to use the latest but to override it with powerful material.

A way out could be to accept the demo design status of artist works. But most corporations already have their own networks to do the demo design and don't take art serious—if they take any notice of it in the first place. This is the tragedy of new media arts. Those who turn new media inside out and develop an aesthetic counter-agenda have hardly any place in today's production processes. Despite such institutional, disciplinary, and economic realities, so many artists persist in their pursuit of a formalist Nirvana. Is this symptomatic of a lack of imagination, or perhaps even an oversubscription to the exotica of the artist identity?

If digital formalism, unrecognized by the museum, the market, or the industry, is such a dead-end street, then why aren't artists walking over to the content side and producing narratives? Certainly a lot of the new media artists try this move. But their stories are not connected to the mainstream distribution networks such as film, television, and the publishing industry. This is why numerous CD-ROMs and DVDs do not even reach their own core audiences. It is not seen as a priority to build up distribution networks through, for instance, museum bookshops. Another reason for the reluctance to comply is the wish to alter interfaces, software, and even operating systems. Rightly so (or not?), some new media artists feel uncomfortable using mainstream products such as Windows XP or even Mac OS X. Critique in this context is focused on underlying structures, not the superficial level of mediated representation. It is the architecture of the Internet and open standards of the Web that shape your surf experience, not this or that cool homepage.

New media art operates well beyond the logic of the demo design. Marketing something that has not been conceived of as a product in the first place has proven next to impossible. Putting content online is a last resort, but funnily enough it is not very popular among new media artists. The Internet is looked down upon by some as a primitive device, left to an in-crowd of Internet artists and discourse leaders who prefer to perform formalistic experiments, combined with a subversive political action every now and then, such as those instigated by groups such as www.rtmark. com. New media art is (rightly so) not interested in traditional politics, but has yet to reach its own phase of political correctness. Even though the presence of female curators and administrators is substantial, this does not result in a more open field. Links to contemporary social movements are weak, and the awareness of basic postcolonial issues is often absent. This is not the case if we look at individual works, but certainly if we look at the way festivals and conferences are programmed. The scene, which is largely "white," is, for the most part, a collection of individuals from North–West–Central Europe, United States, Canada, Australia, and Japan; that is, those areas where digital technology is most developed and integrated into the social fabric.

Life for artists in general is an uphill struggle and this particularly counts for those who deliberately position themselves in-between or across disciplines. Instead of curiosity and support, what the pristine new media arts scene finds is stiff competition between scientific disciplines, media, and art forms. There are often fights over decreasing resources within a general climate of jealousy and ignorance. There is no convergence or harmony with the performing arts. Despite all the ideology, multi- and interdisciplinarity are at an all-time low. People simply cannot afford to jump over to a competing form of expression. It seems that all too often people working in theater have to look down on the medium of television, and video people are often snobs when it comes to new media. There is nothing as trashy and third-rate as the Internet.

Online Debates on Art and Science

Until recently, the art and science rhetoric in new media remained obscure and was not debated. People with critical insights could not speak out because they would otherwise lose their funding or would have to quit the Ph.D. program in which they are enrolled. Nonetheless, in early 2006 some exchanges on the Spectre list were devoted to the topic. Australian media theorist Anna Munster argued that the rise of bio art merely reflects the rise of biotech research budgets in Western countries. It is no longer the question of whether or why but how art and science should relate to each other. "Science and art don't actually speak the same language, so then what do we mean by collaboration? What is the mythology created around this idea by using a 'language of collaboration'? Is a 'communication' paradigm useful for describing art-science working strategies or is there a problem here that glides over crucial problems of translation, slippage, praxis?"[29] While it is useless to put forward a grand plan of art–science collaborations, it is also uninformed, says Anna Munster, to dismiss the art–science relationship. "What we need instead are concrete histories and discussions about who is doing what, where and why." The point is, however, that new media arts have made a false start in this respect. On the agenda, says Anna Munster, is the confrontation of art and science collaborations with contemporary forms of visual representation. It is not enough to hide in laboratories and do interesting stuff. Critical Art Ensemble, for instance, is dealing with this challenge by turning laboratory work into performances. Others work on new visualizations of scientific procedures.

Critical interventions that emphasize the DIY approach do exist (Critical Art Ensemble, Natalie Jeremijenko, the Tissue Culture and Art Project, Heath Bunting) but they have not been visible enough to counter the dominant current in which artist works are instrumentalized to promote value-free biosciences. Jose-Carlos Mariadegiu from Peru demands that scientists should reflect on the importance of being critical and open to discussion. But what if they don't? And what exactly has new media art to offer that scientists, beyond their human compassion, would be interested in? They already discuss ethics enough. Paul Brown is curious how "artists and scientists are collaborating on projects for mutual gain. And not, for example, artists appropriating scientific ideas for their own gain—that I see as part of the romantic/postmodern fallacy. When scientists see this latter they quite rightly perceive there's little in it for them apart from at best publicity so they are reluctant to engage."[30] Despite their reluctance, they do still engage in such projects, while devoting little time to actual engagement with the artists, and this is where art and science become so compromising. Anna Munster asks: "What are the epistemological issues raised by media and new media art? Do these challenge or speak to similar issues and questions in some areas of contemporary science?"[31]

New York artist Trebor Scholz gives an insight into why art and science came up in the face of resource scarcity. Due to the lack of art funding, it is hard to imagine how artists who experiment can survive outside of academia.

> In the U.S. the business logic of the university moves the largest part of academic funding to the sciences. Universities see this investment as seed funding to attract corporate involvement aiming for large-scale profits that so far have largely not materialized. In the battle over resources the humanities have no chance of winning and the funding for these areas of inquiry may increasingly be found only at long-established universities who can still afford the luxury. In the context of this funding dynamic a widespread scientification of the arts kicks in. Cultural producers battling over grants adapt to science formats. This is not always their genuine choice. Their work is suddenly framed as "research" and "case studies" are being carried out. A Ph.D. is often necessary to apply for national science grants. The noticeable interest in practice-based doctoral degrees is more often than not related to this funding logic.[32]

Instead of debating with biologists, neuroscientists, or astronomers, it would be good to start closer to home and deal with the relationship between computer science and new media arts. It is well known that even IT engineers show little interest in experimental interfaces and image processing for the sake of art, let alone Internet art. Game designer Chris Crawford deals with the two cultures in his book *Interactive Storytelling*. Why can't programmers and games people communicate with the artists who talk about new media? He confesses:

> Bubble intellectualism arises when a group has become so ingrown that it loses all contact with the rest of the intellectual universe and

drifts off into its own self-reinforcing universe. I must confess that I don't understand any of the artists' discussions on interactive story-telling or, for that matter, games. Despite my substantial credentials as a designer and theoretician, I can't understand what these people are talking about. It's not just one of them that bewilders me—it's the whole kit 'n caboodle. The works of the media theorists impress me with their erudition and cleverness, but they never leave me with anything to grab hold of.

Crawford has to give artists credit for trying to bridge the gap, at least socially, and raves on how the different groups fail to have productive exchanges.

Artists have organized conferences on interactive entertainment and games, to which they always invite some representatives of the techie/games community. (It's revealing that techies have never reciprocated, but merely acquiesced to an artsie initiative.) These conferences always start off with an earnest declaration of the need for academia and industry to work hand in hand. Then a techie gets up and talks about what he wants from academia: students trained in 3D artwork, programming, and animation. An artsie gets up and lectures about the semiotics of Mario Brothers. A techie follows with a lecture on production techniques in the games industry. Another artsie analyses the modalities of mimetics in text adventures. And so it goes, both sides happily talking right past each other, and neither side having the slightest interest in or comprehension of the other side's work.[34]

Writing in 1962, literary scholar Renato Poggioli reminds us that avant-garde movements always had an interest in science and technology. But what these artists explored, says Poggioli, was "the terra incognita of the unconscious, the unexplored of the soul."[35] They play games with technical elements in order to awake unheard and unseen content. What happens is the invasion into realms where technique has no raison d'etre. Poggioli sees that the avant-garde thinker is "particularly susceptible to the scientific myth" and lists numerous titles of works that use scientific metaphors. What makes late-twentieth century electronic artists so different is their lack of superiority. Their scientificism, as Poggioli coins it, grows out of a subordinate feeling that scientists are decades, if not centuries, ahead of ordinary people and that we, artists included, will never be able to fully understand their complex knowledge. It is out of this inferiority complex that the urge grows to collaborate so that the artist at least has a vague notion of what is ahead. Maybe scientists and programmers will start listening if artists regain their sense of superiority in that they possess knowledge that far supersedes ordinary interdisciplinary exchanges. The breakdown of communication between the two cultures of humanities and sciences, as C.P. Snow described in 1959, is still real but rather should be described as asymmetric.[36] Over the past decades progress has been in made, mainly thanks to an increase in scientific journalism that informs the arts and humanities and the public in general about the latest scientific research and its ethical implications. We can no longer state, as Snow did, that artists and humanities scholars are ignorant about science. John Brockmann's third culture of scientists who reach out to the broader public is a real existing media phenomena.[37] What lacks is a critical interest among scientists and technologists for the arts, perhaps not so much on a personal level but in terms of institutional arrangements. In the end, this can only be solved through a reallocation of financial resources. We no longer need accurate information or critical awareness; an overall shift is needed. To suggest that well-intended collaboration will do the job has proven to be a powerless gesture.

Inside Institutional Changes

Much of what I write here has to remain speculative. In a sense, *mafia* is too strong an accusation, as there is little money available in the new media arts scene. Nonetheless, electronic art is an old boys club (including a few old girls). As I have indicated, a lack of a rich and diverse discourse is one of the many problems. Sectarianism is another. The strategy to first build up a self-referential system and then reach out has taken a toll. The new media scene, even on a global scale, is simply too small and is in an increased state of defense as neighboring, competing disciplines such as visual arts, photography, film, and television are eager to kill off the emerging new media scene. Even though the Internet part of the new media arts scene has taken off, its institutional representation is weak and often nonexisting. Administrators and curators find it hard to keep up with the multitude of forums, lists, and blogs, let alone actively participate in them. What is the need of new media as a separate domain if the computer is being integrated in all existing art forms anyway? For instance, theater itself becomes one digital trajectory from concept, production, stage design, light, and music to promotion and ticket sales. It doesn't need the specific new media arts insights. The same could be said of performance, dance, and film.

New media images are not sacred, nor do they have an aura. Instead, we could describe these images as technical in the spirit of Vilém Flusser's definition of "technical images." According to Flusser,

> it is difficult to decipher technical images, because they are apparently in no need of being deciphered. Their meaning seems to impress itself

automatically on their surfaces, as in fingerprints where the meaning (the finger) is the cause and the image (the print) is the effect.
...It seems that what one is seeing while looking at technical images
are not symbols in need of deciphering, but symptoms of the world
they mean, and that we can see this meaning through them however indirectly. This apparent non-symbolic, "objective" character of
technical images has the observer looking at them as if they were not
really images, but a kind of window on the world. He trusts them as
he trusts his own eyes. If he criticizes them at all, he does so not as a
critique of image, but as a critique of vision; his critique is not concerned with their production, but with the world "as seen through"
them. Such a lack of critical attitude towards technical images is dangerous in a situation where these images are about to displace texts.
The uncritical attitude is dangerous because the "objectivity" of the
technical image is a delusion. They are in truth, images, and as such
they are symbolical.

I am quoting Flusser at length because he provides us with a clue
about the fate of new media arts: the technical nature of its images is
in itself not by definition cool. New media arts have a problematic relation with pop culture and the strategy of appropriation. Obviously its
image production is not claimed to be unique. Instead, new media arts
are probes into new laws of perception. The dominant appropriation
point of view in art history can only deal with content, not with the
medium itself. Data from other media are used as resources, as data
trash, fuel that can fire up the exploration. There is no desire to further
deconstruct the already weak modernist project. If there is anything
that needs to be appropriated, it is hardcore scientific knowledge, not
other art works.

The new media arts scene is not in need of further globalization. Its
scope is broad enough, despite the relative lack of work from non-Western
countries. One day it may absorb postcolonial theory but that is not our
concern here. At the moment, the financial resources to operate on a truly
global level are not available. What new media arts cry for is a quantum
leap. The ghetto walls need to be taken down. As a revolt from inside is not
likely to happen, rather we can expect a general implosion. Younger generations that join the education courses in droves will not automatically join
in. Their attention span is even less than the one-minute video. Interactive
installations are often too complex for them, due to the unorthodox interfaces. This surprising lack of interest, if we take into account their absence
at festivals, could cause the field to fade away and to become owned by
specific generations.

What if there are those who do not accept such trends? A first step would be to raise civil courage and get out of closet. Right now people talk with two tongues. They feel compelled to defend the venerable field, and this is completely legitimate. There is policy and good intensions, but that alone will not do the job. Questions are raised in small circles and private conversations but in the end, funding bodies and other officials have to be praised. There is a regime of fear that needs to be broken down. The question of how we cater beyond the small scene has to be seen as a creative challenge. Electronic art is in need of its own whistleblowers. People in positions of power are not questioned and there is not even a basic awareness as to how a controversy could be ignited. We are in a situation much like that of the former socialist countries, with their two cultures and two languages, except that in this case dissidents are even too fearful (or cowardly?) to publicly declare that the real existing culture is one of misguidedness and irrelevance. The only legitimate option that remains is to walk away and change context, or not to enter the scene in the first place—which is what most young artists do.

Electronic Arts and the Dotcoms

Let's focus for a while on the rarely debated topic of the (absent) relation between new media arts and IT business. While many blame new media for being too narrowly focused on technology, the actual influence or presence of IT firms in this field is almost zero. This question of how new media arts related to the dotcom sector might only be of historical interest, but is important as sufficient capital, back then, could have decisively transformed the field. Superficially, the "tech wreck" of 2000–2001 and its following associated scandals did not affect new media arts. It always struck me how slow critical new media practices have been in their response to the rise and the fall of dotcom mania. Whereas Internet use spread quickly in the early to mid-1990s, publicly available knowledge of its economy was hard to find. It seemed as if they were parallel universes with the arts dragging behind events. There was not even a spiritual anticipation of the excess. Everything was business as usual during the mad years of the orgy. The world of IT firms and their volatile valuations on the world's stock market seemed light years away from the new media arts galaxy. One of the explanations of this could have been that the speculative heyday of new media culture was the early 1990s, in fact before the rise of the World Wide Web when video was still in the new media galaxy. Theorists and artists jumped eagerly at not-yet-existing and inaccessible technologies such as virtual reality. Cyberspace generated a rich collection of mythologies. Issues of embodiment and identity were fiercely debated but virtually played no role in the dotcom saga. In fact, new media came too early on the scene but lacked the glamour, or the suspense, to out itself as avant-garde.

Only five years later, with Internet stocks going through the roof, not much was left of the initial excitement in intellectual and artistic circles. The artist-as-virtual-expert had lost its short-lived hype status of the early to mid-1990s when artists could showcase their multimedia capabilities. Once concepts could be turned into money, there was no longer room for people with ideas. At the turn of the millennium, artists and their theorists had lost influence on the public perception of what new media was all about. What could have turned into a pop culture, financed by funny money, degenerated into a shrinking microcosmos. The market, after all, had its own demo designers who spoke the right visual language that could be used in advertisement campaigns. The experimental art resisted too much, insisting on its own autonomy, to become instrumentalized. And maybe dotcom tycoons did not support new media art simply because it did not support *them*.

Dotcom culture has been anti-art in a rather open fashion. It was said that profit should be reinvested in the IT sector, transferred into stocks, and not invested in artworks, as old money was doing. Technology itself was art, and there was no need for artists to substantiate this assumed truth. Real artists were the geeks who worked for firms. Applied art such as design was cool but its role should not be overestimated as it was the abstract and image free code that eventually ruled, not the world of images. Cyberculture of the 1990s was essentially manufactured by Hollywood.

Eventually experimental techno culture missed out on the funny money of venture capitalists. As a result, no commercial arts in this sector have been developed, nor have serious attempts been made to resolve the distribution and revenue/cash crisis. Most new media art is therefore produced with government support that tightly controls and guides production. It is stunning to see how, in detail, pseudo-independent bodies are overseeing the new media arts field, exercising their power over tiny individual applications. This, in turn, explains the relative importance of Northern European countries, Austria, Canada, and Australia. Most work done in the United States originates from universities or is funded by a handful of foundations. Over the past few years there has been a growing stagnation of new media culture, both in terms of its concepts and state funding. With hundreds of millions of new users flocking onto the Internet and over one billion now using mobile phones, new media arts proved unable to keep up with the fast pace of change and had to withdraw into its own world of small festivals and workshops (exceptions here are Ars Electronica in Linz and, lately, Transmediale in Berlin).

Whereas new media arts institutions, begging for goodwill, still portray their artists as working at the forefront of technological developments, collaborating with state of the art scientists, the reality is different. Multidisciplinary goodwill is at an all-time low. At best, the artist's new media products are demo designs, as described by Peter Lunenfeld in his book *Snap to Grid*. Often the work does not even reach that level. New media art, as defined by institutions such as Ars Electronica, ISEA, Transmediale, and the countless educational programs, rarely reaches audiences outside of its own subculture. What, in positive terms, could be described as the heroic fight for the establishment of a self-referential new media arts system through a frantic differentiation of works, concepts, and traditions may as well be thought of as a dead-end street. The acceptance of new media by leading museums and collectors simply will not happen. Why wait a few decades anyway? The majority of the new media artwork on display at ZKM in Karlsruhe, the Linz Ars Electronica Center, and ICC in Tokyo are amazing in their innocence, being neither critical nor radically Utopian, or even vaguely untimely in their approach. It is for this reason that the new media arts sector, despite its steady growth, is becoming increasingly isolated, incapable of addressing the issues of today's globalized world. It is therefore understandable that the contemporary (visual) arts world is continuing the decades-old silent boycott of interactive new media work in galleries, art fairs, biennales, and shows such as Documenta. The relative isolation of new media arts could also explain, in part, the rise of the creative industries discourse, which presents itself explicitly as a way out of the miserable policies that surround the state-funded arts and education businesses. The irony, however, is that the creative industries meme itself does not exist outside of the realm of state policies.

A critical reassessment of the role of arts and culture within today's network society seems necessary. Would artists be happier if they could work within the creative industries and no longer bother with the question of whether they are producing art? Certainly, there is a discursive legitimacy that awaits migrants to the creative industries, but whether it pays their rent is yet to be seen. The information economy is still failing to extract value from content production, and if money is to be made, it profits whoever possesses the IP rights, which typically is not the creative producer, whose role is really one of service provision. So, what is the difference between the artist and the sales clerk in that scenario?

Let's go beyond the tactical intentions of the players involved. The artist-engineer, tinkering away on alternative human–machine interfaces, social software, alternative browsers, or digital aesthetics has effectively been operating in a self-imposed vacuum. Over the last few decades, both science and business have successfully and easily ignored the creative community.

Even worse, artists have actively been sidelined in the name of usability. The backlash movement against Web design, led by usability guru Jakob Nielsen, is a good example of this trend. Other contributing factors may have been fear of corporate dominance. Creative Commons lawyer Lawrence Lessig[38] argues that innovation of the Internet itself is in danger. In the meantime, the younger artists are turning their backs on the specific new media arts related issues and become anticorporate activists, do Web design for a living, teach here and there, struggle in a freelance existence, or turn to other professions altogether. Since the crash of 2001, the Internet has rapidly lost its imaginative attraction. File swapping and cell phones can only temporarily fill the vacuum. It would be foolish to ignore these implosive trends. New media have lost their exclusiveness. Youth culture is engaging with the magic spell on a massive scale and shows little interest in decades-old pioneer work. Unlike previous generations that had to fight for access to high tech, gadgets are now part of everyday life, similar to radio and the vacuum cleaner. The passionate uptake of blogs and social networks does not contradict the normalization trend.

New Media as a War of the Generations

A taboo issue in new media is generationalism. With video and expensive interactive installations being the domain of the baby boomers, the generation of 1989 has embraced the free Internet. But the Internet turned out to be a trap for the young ones. Whereas real assets, positions, and power remain in the hands of the aging baby boomers, the gamble of its successors on the rise of new media did not materialize. After venture capital has melted away, there is still no sustainable revenue system in place for the Internet outside of advertising (viz. Google) and gated content downloads (viz. iTunes). There is no life after demo design. The slow working education bureaucracies have not yet grasped the new media malaise. Universities are still in the process of establishing new media departments. But that will come to a halt at some point. The fifty-something tenured chairs and vice chancellors must feel good about their persistent reluctance. The positive generation (ISP Wanadoo slogan) is unemployed and frustrated and, in a word, precarious.

"What's so new about new media anyway?" many baby boomers ask. Computers are not generating narrative content and what the world needs now is meaning, not empty, ironic net.art. They say technology was hype after all, promoted by the corporate crooks of Enron, Tyco, and WorldCom. It is enough for students to do a bit of e-mail and Web surfing, safeguarded within a filtered and controlled intranet. If there is to be a counter to this cynical reasoning, then we urgently need to analyze the ideology of the excessive 1990s and its associated political consciousness of techno-libertarianism. If we do not disassociate new media quickly from that decade, and if we continue with the same rhetoric, the isolation of the new media sector will eventually result in its demise. Let's transform the new media buzz into something more interesting altogether before others do it for us. The will to subordinate to science is nothing more than a helpless adolescent gesture of powerlessness and victimhood.

One way out of this subordinate position may be to point at the social aspect of the production of science, as Bruno Latour and others do. According to their theory, the work of science consists of the enrollment and juxtaposition of heterogeneous elements—rats, test tubes, colleagues, journal articles, funders, grants, papers at scientific conferences, and so on—which need continual management. They conclude that scientists' work is "the simultaneous reconstruction of social contexts of which they form a part—labs simultaneously rebuild and link the social and natural contexts upon which they act."[39]

U.S. performance artist Coco Fusco wrote a critique of biotech art on the Nettime mailing list (January 26, 2003). "Biotech artists have claimed that they are redefining art practice and therefore the old rules don't apply to them." For Fusco, "bio art's heroic stance and imperviousness to criticism sounds a bit hollow and self-serving after a while, especially when the demand for inclusion in mainstream art institutions, art departments in universities, art curricula, art world money and art press is so strong." From this marginal position, the bio arts posthuman dreams of transcending the body could be better read as desires to transcend its own marginality, being recognized neither as visual arts nor as science. Coco Fusco: "I find the attempts by many biotech art endorsers to celebrate their endeavor, as if it were just about a scientific or aesthetic pursuit, to be disingenuous. Its very rhetoric of transcendence of the human is itself a violent act of erasure, a master discourse that entails the creation of 'slaves' as others that must be dominated." Okay, but what if all this remains but a dream, prototypes of human–machine interfaces that, like demo-design, are going nowhere. The isolated social position of the new media arts in this type of criticism is not taken into consideration. Biotech art has to be almighty in order for the Fusco rhetoric to function.

Fusco rightly points to artists who "attend meetings with 'real' scientists, but in that context they become advisors on how to popularize science, which is hardly what I would call a critical intervention in scientific institutions." Artists are not better scientists and the scientific process is not a better way of making art than any other, Fusco writes. She concludes: "Losing respect for human life is certainly the underbelly of any militaristic adventure, and lies at the root of the racist and classist ideas that have justified the violent use of science for centuries. I don't think there is any reason to believe that suddenly, that kind of science will disappear because some artists find beauty in biotech." It remains an open question where radical criticism of (life) science has gone and why the new media (arts) canon is still in such a primitive, regressive stage. Fusco's remarks were written before the FBI cracked down on Critical Arts Ensemble (mid-2004) because of their alleged biotech terror experiments.[40] This, however, does not affect her overall argument.

Conspiracies of Contemporary Art

Art is what you can get away with.

—**Andy Warhol**

Before we end, I would like to look into some critiques of "contemporary arts" that I find relevant in this context. It was Jean Baudrillard who, in 1996, wrote that contemporary art had no reason to exist. As Baudrillard's editor Sylvère Lothringer remarks, this denunciation came as a slap in the face. Didn't this French simulation thinker side with the new and cool? The contemporary arts markets have been booming, so what is the problem? In *The Conspiracy of Art*, Baudrillard states that visibility and fame, not content, had become the engine of the New Art Order. Art has spread in so many directions that we can no longer distinguish it from society. It is no different from anything else. As the back cover sums up, "spiraling from aesthetic nullity to commercial frenzy, art has entered a 'trans-aesthetic' state." What Baudrillard claims—art that has lost its desire for illusion—could no doubt also count for new media. The suspense of subjectivity seems hard to deny. According to Baudrillard, galleries now primarily deal with the byproducts of art. What happens there is the "management of residues." You can do anything there, which, for Baudrillard leads to virtual reality (VR). VR represents "the end of art and rather resembles a technological activity. It seems to have become the orientation of many artists."[41] At this point, we can closely observe how out of touch Paris intellectuals have become. Not only can we count artists that work with VR on one hand, but also such work is hardly exhibited, let alone seen in New York galleries, as Baudrillard suggests. Even if we would read Baudrillard's use of the VR term in a broader sense as hype and effect, it is still imprecise and untrue as so few galleries deal with technological culture, apart from using video projectors and monitors.

The problem, as I have outlined above, is not the ubiquity of technological art but its marginality. For VR, one has to visit highly specialized hospitals or academic research institutes, not galleries. What is indeed remarkable about this is what I am observing about new media arts; Baudrillard is also witnessing it for contemporary arts, namely its self-referential autonomy, cut off from any real economy of value. For Baudrillard, art has become a "fantastic excrescence." The art market "is formed according to the rules of its own games, and whose disappearance would go unnoticed." Baudrillard blames Duchamp, who set a process in motion of "readymadeness, a trans-aestheticization of everything, which means that there is no illusion to speak of." Whereas the contemporary art system still holds onto the belief that there is a market for its art objects, most new media artists have given up all hope to enter the value chain. Their experimentation has become priceless, to describe it in a more positive way. For Baudrillard contemporary art no longer transcends itself into the past or the future. Its only reality is its operation in real time and its "confusion with this reality." It is questionable if new media art shares a similar obsession with real time. It does when it dreams of interaction as real time manipulation. It does when it focuses on remote presence and live surveillance. But it does not in terms of those works that study the real time reality within networks or even broadcast media. In fact, many new media works create artificial environments that shy away from reality as we know it. What Baudrillard propagates is a tactical indifference. There is too much art. And that may also include new media art if we look at the hundreds, if not thousands, of entries for a growing amount of random, interchangeable categories at festivals such as Ars Electronica and ISEA. Baudrillard argues for form and limits. "More is not better." This may be so, but we cannot turn the clock. Art is no longer a privileged activity and we have to live with its obesity and the impossibility of tracing its circumference.

In a similar publication, published in the same series by Sylvère Lothringer, Paul Virilio contemplates the "accident of art." Like Baudrillard, Virilio questions the term contemporary: "It's contemporary in the sense that it isn't modern, or ancient, or futurist, it's of the moment. But it can only disappear in the shrinking of instantaneity." The due date can be measured in picoseconds. In this context, Virilio surprisingly mentions Stelarc being a "futurist, implying that such body-art is beyond the contemporary." Virilio does not see how the failure of the visual arts can be overcome, as a return to corporeal arts merely results in more spectacle and virtuality. Unlike postmodern strategies of the 1980s that raved on about the sensuality of perception, the body is no longer seen as a counter-strategy to compensate for the unbearable lightness of becoming virtual. For Virilio abstract art is not abstract, it is an art of retreat. Inevitably, Virilio maintains, the figurative will be destroyed as a response to the systems of organized violence of which artists themselves are a part.

According to Virilio, art should stop making camouflage and start recognizing itself as a casualty of war. "Contemporary art has been a war victim through Surrealism, Expressionism, Viennese Actionism and terrorism today." The military origins of new media are common knowledge and part of every curriculum, such as the origin of Internet in the Defense Advanced Research Projects Agency (DARPA). In that sense, Virilio's notion has already been fully incorporated. But is a better understanding of the twentieth century's past really the key to overcoming the impasse and breaking through the current isolation of the arts? If the rehabilitation of the image is not the right answer to decomposition, then what is? How can art be identified if it is stripped of its socioeconomic context and no longer produced and exhibited in the gallery and museum industrial complex? Increasingly, professional critics and curators are no longer capable of legitimizing their moves to bring artwork and practices from one context into another. "We are leaving the image behind—including the conceptual image by Warhol or Duchamp—for optics," Virilio says.[42] But why not drop the presumed primacy of the visual altogether? Why only mention optics? New media not only consists of new arrangements between text, sound, and images, it is also increasingly becoming miniaturized and wireless; in short—invisible to the eye. Spherical, as Peter Sloterdijk would say.

An inside analysis of a different kind comes from San Francisco artist Henry Warwick.[43] He points at Ellen Dissanayake's Homo Aestheticus, in which she writes that art is a way of saying "this is special."[44] Warwick agrees:

> Art is a method of "framing": this isn't just a picture of a chair, it speaks in terms of symbols, it is SPECIAL and requires Special Attention and reverence. When you get something that is, by definition or even intention, inherently meaningless, and then frame it in the "this is special" lens of art, you have an abuse of the aesthetic faculty. Meaning can be brought to a meaningless object—but that doesn't mean that making meaningless objects is a method of making meaning, except in a precise sense of critical awareness. Such a limited stance brings in the range from Duchamp to Warhol to Fluxus to Koons. Their positions are studiously "meaningless" and based in a critique of the cultural signifier as to demonstrate the emptiness of the signifier itself.

Turning to new media art, Warwick submits that

> the influence of Fluxus was not wholly beneficial. It held the new media arts back due to its credentials in academic circles. There is this odd cabal of Fluxus, Post-Modernism, Deconstruction, Conceptualism, and the balkanization of identity politics that has led to the

present impasse. Let's face it: the largest market for professional VJ equipment is in Christian Evangelical Churches. People want and need meaning. For a while, the Modernist impulse became a religion for a secular civilization. But when it turned the corner into the cul de sac of post-modernism, art as a cultural force lost its way. Art can't come back—it lost its credibility when it said that we have to treat meaningless art as "special". As a consequence new media may transform into a new folk art of the techno savvy working class.

After decades of meaningless work, the toll is getting heavy, Warwick concludes,

and I don't think it can be paid much longer. Dissanayake also notes our world is one typified by "unprecedented leisure, comfort, and plenty." This is completely predicated on the petroleum economy, and as we cross into peak production of that resource and watch it contract over the next several decades, we will no longer have the luxury of affording meaningless art—the materials will be too expensive and exotic to permit something that isn't "special."

A surprising message from the American Abendland.

Becomings

What new media art, to my taste, lacks is a sense of superiority, sovereignty, determination, and direction. One can witness such tendency toward digital inferiority at virtually every cyber event. The politically naïve pose of the techno-art tinkerers has not paid off. Neither science nor art is paying much attention to its goodwill projects. Artists, critics, and curators have made themselves subservient to technology and life science in particular, unsuccessfully begging for the attention of the real bioscientists. This ideological stand has grown out of an ignorance that is not easily explained. We are talking here about a mentality that is nearly invisible. The cult practice between dominant science and its servants is taking place in the backrooms of universities and art institutions, all warmly supported by genuinely interested corporate bourgeois elements; the board members, professors, science writers, and journalists that set the techno-cultural agenda. We are not talking about some form of techno celebration.

The corporate world is not interested in electronic art because, in the end, they are too abstract and lack sex appeal. They are not "special" in the Warwick sense, and should in fact raise more interest in science and technology museums. Do not make this mistake. New media art is not merely a servant to corporate interests. There has not been a sellout for the simple reason that there has not been a basic economic interest from the corporate world to start with. If only it were that simple. The accusation of new media arts celebrating technology is a banality, only stated by ill-informed outsiders; the interest in life sciences can easily be sold as a (hidden) longing to take part in science's supra-human triumph of logos, but I won't go there either. Scientists, for their part, are disdainfully looking down at the vaudeville interfaces and well-intentioned weirdness of amateur tech art. Not that they will say anything. But the weak smiles on their faces bespeak a cultural gap of light years. An exquisite non-communication is at hand here. Ever growing markets for Internet-provided content, mobile devices, and digital electronic consumer goods make it hard to sense the true despair. Instead of calling for a more positive attitude toward the future, it could be a more seductive strategy of becoming to disconnect the computer from labels such as new and digital and start building up polyperverse networks across the board with an even more brutal intensity.

In defense of new media art, we have to say that there is a passion for complexity away from the amateur imperfection. If we look at the videos that run in biennales, museums, galleries, and exhibitions, half of the works are video but none of them are experimental or self-reflective about the materiality of the medium. Contemporary videos are nice and provide us with shocking, one-off pictures. It is art that uses a documentary style—long shots, hardly edited, without special effects—in order to present itself as uncompromised. New media art, at its best, is aware of the specifics of the technologies it is utilizing, and explores its underlying architecture. Contemporary arts' video is techno-naive, and sometimes worse; its consciously wobbly camera tries to have a reality claim, sublime superiority over the artificiality of new media art. And in the public's eye, it looks amateurish and pointless compared to the slick entertainment they get from cable, broadcast, or DVD and, therefore, looks like art.

Networked Social Spaces

As a way out of the crisis, on the Spectre list Eric Kluitenberg proposed a new style institution aimed "to bridge between these kinds of cultures deeply immersed in the digital realm, and simultaneously to a broader audience that either tinkers away at home or is not immersed quite as deeply into the digital but finds itself still fascinated." He points at an underlying crisis in presentation formats. "Conventional formats such as the exhibition, stage production and concert all seem a bit incomplete or inadequate to capturing the spirit of the new media cultures. Putting up terminals in a public space is totally inept, better to watch it at home through your DSL or cable modem connection. Workshops, seminars and lectures are all fine but we can do those already now." Eric asks, should the new institution necessarily have to be a place where you can offer experiences audiences cannot possibly have at home? "But wouldn't that make the venue too dependent on expensive high tech? Or conversely, should it be 'just' a meeting place with basic facilities? But what makes it special then?"[45] These are strategic topics as they move beyond the "but is it art?" deliberations. Shu Lea Chang is pondering a "mesh network relay system;" relays, as Andreas Broeckmann suggests, that are managed by medium-size institutions that can work with more fluid segmented structures as well as with the docking stations at molar institutions. Yet, he admits these relays do not have a noteworthy lifespan and cannot offer financial and organizational support to artists. Often they are not rooted enough in the local art infrastructure in order to offer them the possibility of maintaining some sort of stable structure and income.

Large institutions such as ZKM, ICC, and AEC started ambitious programs of both supporting production of new media artwork in their media labs, curating exhibitions, doing festivals and conferences with catalogues, and growing and conserving their collection. This has proven too much. Tim Druckrey in Spectre:

> ZKM has, for example, largely abandoned support for production (and for a decade it was a powerful producer) in favor of bombastic exhibitions. The highly visible exhibition touts itself as encyclopedic rather than exploratory and itself undermines its insulated community in favor of a broader public (no less broader funding). This is the fate—and crisis—of the mega-institution.[46]

New channels for dialogue need to be opened. One of them would be art history. Judith Rodenbeck, writing in her report of the Banff Refresh! conference on new media art history, noticed a disturbed relation between art history that supposedly aligned itself too much with painting and therefore unable to deal with new media. The technical incompetence among general art critics makes it difficult, if not impossible, for them to judge new media works. Rodenbeck rejects this.

> Art history and new media share Walter Benjamin and, for better or worse, Rudolf Arnheim; new media people would do well to read Panofsky and Warburg, just as I and at least some of my colleagues read Wiener and Kittler. Art history may not yet be able to deal with new media, but perhaps it is also the case that new media doesn't know how to deal with art history.[47]

Whether technology-based art should continue to claim a relative autonomy to do research remains open for debate. Artwork should not merely be judged according to its commodity status, or for its capacity to alienate, enlighten, transform, and educate. According to Swiss media theorist Giacco Schiesser, art-as-method emphasizes the process character of creative acts. What artists explore, Schiesser says, is the *Eigensinn*, the willful obstinacy of new media.[48] It is obvious that radical, fundamental research is a risky enterprise with unpredictable outcomes. The artworks that are the outcome of such searches often fail to communicate their initial curiosity. We get to see results without knowing the questions with which they struggled. This is where new media art becomes autistic. Artistic research need not end in self-contained objects. Often it is not the self-referential quality that disturbs, as the tradition of the discipline itself is, in fact, rather weak. Unlike literature and film, new media arts do not suffer from an abundance of insider cross-references. The unfinished deconstruction efforts and the failed attempts to formulate a new media grammar are what disturbs, not some grand Utopian gestures.

From a funding perspective, it might be strategic to negotiate a merger or takeover and strike a deal at the right moment, before all art is being conceived as technological and people can no longer distinguish a difference between digital and non-digital art. Giacco Schiesser discusses an entry point for such negotiations:

> If the *Eigensinn* of a new medium has to some degree been recognized, tried out and developed, the new artistic methods and possibilities have an effect on the old media. Soon after the invention of photography and film, for instance, these media began to exercise a strong influence on literature, and since very recently we can witness a similar influence being exercised by the new media.[49]

This is where the bargaining power of new media art could be located.

Discussing the faith of new media and its relation to the contemporary arts system, Melbourne art theorist Charles Green is using the Concorde analogy. He quotes Francis Spufford, who noted that the

> real flaw in Concorde was not technological but social. The whole project was based on an error in social prediction. Those who commissioned it assumed that air travel would remain, as it was in 1962, something done by the rich... but at the time that Great Britain and France were betting on supersonic speed as the next step in aviation, one of the bosses at Boeing pushed through the development of a subsonic plane that could carry four hundred passengers at a time.[50]

For Green, new media is an "already outmoded disciplinary formulation." Intellectual validation through artistic scientism has been a problematic feature, says Green, who traces this back to Roy Ascott, who is not only influential in ISEA, V2, and Ars Electronica circles, but also played a major role in accrediting practice-based Ph.D.s to a range of new media artists through the U.K. school system. Such links with the scientific method Charles Green judges as arbitrary, "the resulting detachment from artistic genealogies accounts for the shaky relationship—oscillating between awe and amnesia—that the art world has with new media art." The strategic decision of Ascott to move new media away from the gallery and museum world and into academia and research has been detrimental for several generations of artists. Again, Charles Green: "Because new media is only partly concerned with itself as art, its inhabitants tend to have a somewhat touching and definitely naïve belief in either art or its irrelevance."

Following the Concorde analogy, new media art was betting on a close alliance with scientists and engineers. The mistake was to envision the artist-as-developer in a lab situation and suggest that an entire art genre, including its institutions, festivals, exhibitions, and education programs, be wrapped around the lab and science reference. The high speed of computer dissemination in society, including its introduction into and influence on all art forms, was overlooked. It is this democratization of computer use that eventually made new media art as a special category redundant. There is also a reconciliation with consumer electronics necessary here. Many pointed out that access to equipment is becoming less and less of an issue, at least in affluent societies. While prices dropped, performance of machines increased dramatically. This makes it questionable if special new media facilities in art schools and museums should be established and further maintained. Specific software training and tech support in the making of networked pieces, videos, and installations will remain necessary. But that is a point of discussion in the free cooperation context, in that most contemporary artworks are produced in collaborative teams. The ideal of the genius who masters a myriad of programming languages and operating systems is an idea of the past.

Critical Intervention: Warren Neidich

Artist Warren Neidich, inventor of neuroaesthetics,[51] stresses the protest attitude of the first generation of media artists who initially didn't care about the art market. "When Fluxus and early sound and video art started, there was no money in it. These artists were anti-establishment and actually gravitated to those forms of expression to resist what they perceived as the establishment. Art and science and new technology groups are coming from the opposite place. Any wonder that they are now disappointed?" For Neidich, art has to be a form of resistance. Technology is just another tool, not an end in itself. He says:

> Artists throughout modernism have utilized technology for many reasons. First of all because new technologies presented the opportunity to change the morphology and methods of production of the artwork. Norman Bryson writes that it was the invention of numbered pencils with different degrees of hardness of their graphite that allowed Ingres to draw the way he did. New technologies as they fed back into artistic discourse destabilized the dynamic relations with the factographic relationships of the aesthetic form. Nude Descending a Staircase and the work of the Futurists are examples of this process.

For Neidich, new media artists became intoxicated by the power of new technologies. "Maybe artists should not fetishize technology as a reason for making a work." Even when the apparatus was an essential aspect of their work, as in the case of the early experimental films of the 1960s from the likes of Stan Brakhage or Jean Luc Godard, it was in the context of a desire to express the social, political, economic, and psychological relations at the time and in which these technologies were imbedded.

What makes digital culture interesting for Neidich is when that art, instead of stressing the technology, hides the technology and concentrates on the conversation that it is having with culture that surrounds it. For Neidich that could include the culture of science but, he warns, it needs to make science a ready-made and import it into the white cube, the black box where it becomes anew in relation to the history of aesthetic concerns and the history of art. Neidich says:

> If you are going to call yourself an artist then talk in the language of an artist. Too many in new media have forgotten this. There is a conversation out there at all times locally and globally that artists are having between themselves and with the broader culture. Right now, for instance, it is about the handmade. How can new media talk to the handmade object? For new media arts to survive and be interesting to the art world they need to be aware of what that conversation is and figure out how to enter it. I am not talking about the art market which seems to be an obsession with digital artists as they are somehow excluded from it. The reason is not digital or media praxis but rather that it is not addressing the concerns that artists using other media are interested in. Even though painting and figuration is hot now it is finding reverberations in sculpture, installation art, drawing, photography, video and, yes, in digital art. Many digital artists are of course aware of this.

A renewed disdain for digital art is needed. Neidich says:

Until recently artists used to make a distinction between fine art and commercial art. From the very beginning digital art, not media art, was a kind of commercial art. If you look at the creativity industry that is now erupting through art and science and new technology artists, you can see that it is its natural extension. New media artists can't have it both ways. On one hand they cannot act as if the world is an assemblage of global flows and trans-disciplinary practices and on the other insulate themselves in an a-historical moment with themselves as the only rightful authors. As such they are enlisting modernist tropes of medium specificity. So there is a contradiction here.

It would indeed be interesting to reframe new media arts as an arts and crafts movement. The problem with this approach, however, is that new media arts thus far have been a financial failure for most practitioners.

Beyond the Cool Obscure

Everything changes except new media.

—after Paul Valery

Before we launch the next techno art wave (for instance, locative video), we have to figure out how to avoid the cool obscure. At first sight, cool and obscure seem to be opposites. Cool is out there, on the street, whereas the enigmatic hides itself, careful not to overexpose itself. Many artworks seen in galleries today aim to be cool but are completely obscure. Virilio's opt-out is his Museum of Accidents, filled with negative monuments such as Hiroshima and Auschwitz, but also Chernobyl and the World Trade Center. This strategy is radically different from attempts to get new media arts accepted so that it can, finally, enter the temple of high art. However, accidents still operate within the contemporary arts scheme that art has to disrupt. The strength of new media arts is its will to investigate, its curiosity beyond the convention of having to break through conventions. Free software could be a source of inspiration here, as it leaves behind the discontent and antagonists about monopolies such as Microsoft. The tinkering is modest in that it does not claim to be innovation. Neither must it be focused on problem solving, as Judith Donath states.[52] The awareness that new media often causes more problems than it pretends to solve is widely accepted. There are simply too many bugs. Unfinished defines the aesthetic of digital media, as Peter Lunenfeld already noted.[53]

In the period of the historical avant-garde, obscurity has been one of the tools the movement owned to express its antagonism to the public.

More important than the common man and his hostility toward new art is the tactical use of idiom to distinguish itself from previous generations. According to Renato Poggioli, this tendency calls to mind the theory of the young Nietzsche. "Metaphor would originate in the desire of a group of youths to distinguish themselves by a kind of secret language. Their language would be opposed to the prose idiom, since that was the means of communication of the old generation."[54] With a few communication guerilla exceptions, new media arts have lacked such drive. Its obscurity often was default and grew out of its tragic destiny and was not done with intent. The hermeticism of works does not carry secret messages that can only be revealed by next generations or other civilizations. The experiments often want to achieve too much, fighting dozens of battles simultaneously, with painting and TV, popular culture and politics, while also dealing with interface design issues, network architecture, the power of code, and so on. This almost inherent drive to create the multimedia *Gesamtkunstwerk* put the narrative element on the backburner and makes it hard for the artist to reach clarity. The result is a nice looking work whose multitude of intentions, unfortunately, will remain obscure.

"Artists working with new technology often invent by necessity. It's rarely our primary motivation, it just happens," says Michael Naimark in his Rockefeller report on new media arts and sustainability. "We are in an inflection point. We have a clear idea what doesn't work, but not much of a clue what does." He concludes that patents are not a realistic source of income for an art lab and favors a checkbox on U.S. tax forms, which says "I do/don't support weird and difficult art." Thus far, the dotcom millionaires who have entered philanthropy have had little interest in contemporary art, let alone technological arts. Art should nurture a culture that values debate, says Naimark, and the tools we create could radically reshape the world. *But they don't.* Checking out the role of artists in the hundreds of so-called Web 2.0 applications will tell you that their contribution has been minimal. Artists that developed expensive, proprietary VR installations, built for museum purposes only, indeed play no role in "reshaping the world." Perhaps it is time for the virtual artists to step down, give up their obsession with the future, and catch up with contemporary uses of technology.

The pope is no longer a patron of the arts. There is no longer a need for cathedral-sized immersive environments. Society has caught up with techno-Utopia—now it is time for reorientation for the artists. What new media art has yet to deal with is the miniaturization, up to the point of invisibility, of real existing devices. This places the man–machine interface question, played out by so many immersive artists, in a different framework away from the still heavy "machinistic" aspect, with its (post)industrial references, toward a more precise understanding of the "manual" (as in, related to the hand). Software art is another way out. VR as a visual *Gesammtkunstwerk* has proven to be an ideal closed circuit for theorists and art historians. They found all the evidence that was hidden there by the inventors. By now all references, from Lascaux to Richard Wagner, have been retrieved. Information technology developed in another direction, from the exceptional sacred baroque 3D installation toward ordinary, secular mobility—integrating computers into the everyday. We moved from the *Wunderkammer*, owned by aristocrats and later bourgeois classes, toward twenty-first-century Jan Steen scenes: checking your e-mail while doing the dishes, iPodding away on your bike, text-messaging in the subway. What we are witnessing is a radical—and rapid—demystification of technology toward a new form of intimacy in which people from all walks of life have learned to deal with devices that are no longer alien objects. The challenge now is to navigate between empowerment and control, as new media clearly facilitate both.[55]

The culture of unfinished experimentation needs to be overcome. What some see as a celebration of the freedom of expression and the autonomy of the arts, others judge as immaturity and incompetence. Is there a lack of rigorous work in new media arts as an institutional practice? We have to, once again, keep in mind that I am not talking about outstanding experimental qualities of individual works. Often it is the multiplication of different experiments in one work that makes the end result ill conceived. This leads to a growing impatience among viewers who conclude that the "search for a form" cannot last forever. We witness a strange love–hate relationship with the Unfinished. In a rich and dense visual culture, it has become a rarity to see new images and to be surprised about unexpected sounds. Occasionally the technology sector comes up with an unseen feature, but power users are getting used to the unheard of within weeks, if not hours. Therefore, it would be a challenge for new media arts if works would be pushed to their limits. Someone needs to take the art out of its beta stage in which it is stuck and encourage the artist to further develop the work. Often it is a matter of polishing narration and meaning (even if the content is technology itself). Radical clarity concerning the balance between form and content is needed. Such a trend would not necessarily imply commercialization and cooptation. In fact, we do not need less laboratory art but simply better outcomes. Digital works are never finished and whereas some see this as an advantage, others dismiss the culture of preliminary releases. What Fred Camper said about avant-garde film also counts for new media arts. "An avant-garde film addresses each viewer as a unique individual, speaks to him in the isolation of the crowd, invites him to perceive the film according to his own particular and perception."[56] For

Camper, such attitude is the result of the "individuating techniques that make the act of perceiving the film a part of the experience of it." The artist who travels the road that many have traveled before and claims to reinvent his medium has to take into account what happens when experiments continue to convince the audience. Moving on to ever new platforms and gadgets is not the way out and in fact only raises the suspicion of escapist behavior. Camper advises: "It is hopelessly self-destructive, when trying to make a film, to make something great. One can often reach a large goal by thinking in the smallest of terms."

One could argue that new media should align itself with the highest and strongest forms of expression. Instead of looking inward, it needs an older brother or sister. Such points of reference need to be identified and are not similar in any given situation or genre. This much is clear: it is not, by definition, visual arts. In the Dutch context it would be architecture and design. In Australia it would be film and cultural studies. In London it would be music and visual arts, in Berlin the techno club scene. Theater, with its rich tradition and solid infrastructure, would be another context in which new media experiments can flourish. There has been, for instance, a tremendous uptake of digital technologies in fashion, a trend that has thus far been ignored by new media. After an anxious decade, photography has, by and large, dropped the polarized contradiction between the analogue/chemical procedure and digital images. It is also, finally, widely recognized how useful vinyl records and record players are, compared to the flat and crisp sound quality of CDs and the CD's lack of random access to its surface—not to mention the ubiquity of MP3 sound files. Scores of painters have laptops and projectors in their ateliers, precomposing images on the computer. The contradiction between real objects such as canvas, prints, or DVDs and the artificial nature of virtuality has become a farce—the argument is dead. This victory of the digital and the arrival of its own set of postdigital exigencies in all disciplines and parts of life, sadly, will not be credited to new media art, a label that would best be forgotten. If new media has any chance of surviving, it will be as material awareness. New media art, at its best, communicates the underlying premises, and glitches, of the network gadgets we use day and night. Without such critical knowledge, we merely float around in the collective unconscious of the media sphere.

CHAPTER 3

Whereabouts of German Media Theory

Wo Panzer und Raketen den Frieden "sichern"
AKWs und Computer das Leben 'verbessern'
Bewaffnete Roboter überall
Doch Deutschland, wir bringen dich zu Fall
Deutschland muß sterben, damit wir leben können!

—SLIME

In an October 2004 e-mail to Rohrpost, a German-language forum on network culture, I raised the question of whether there was a German media theory. If there ever was an American invention called French philosophy that worked on poststructuralism—something scholars in Paris had never even heard of—then why not start a promotion campaign for German media theory? The world was slowly waking up and many media scholars had already heard about the Humboldt University professor Friedrich Kittler who has written about the intrinsic relationship between media, literature, and the technologies of war. So, are we speaking of a possible future export hit, or rather about a missed opportunity? Should we turn dour and melancholic and denounce a world that no longer recognizes sophistication? Are the often-speculative theories made in Western Germany signs of strength or are they hiding—under an all-too-German avalanche of terminology—in a vast tepid sea of helplessness, cultural pessimism, and a lack of practical knowledge of new media and their functionalities? Who else, apart from me, indulges in grandiose metaphysical statements? And, important in the context of education, why should the many thousands of students of new media the world over solely deal with English-language authors and knowledge? How could a comprehensive overview of German media theory be communicated to the outside world? Does it all have to stop with the male grandmaster voices of Brecht, Krakauer, Benjamin, Adorno, Horkheimer, and Habermas? Is it politically possible, and intellectually productive, to label a cloud of authors as German? As a disclaimer I have to say that in this chapter I will not deal with media theory per se, but discuss its production parameters—its very conditions of possibility.

The day I posted my question to the Rohrpost list, I garnered a great number of responses. Mercedes Bunz answered in the affirmative. "German media theory: there is one. But absurdly, not as an export hit, but as an imported commodity. That means there wasn't one until it was perceived out there, in countries speaking other languages." An acquaintance of Bunz from London formulated it as follows: "Here in the UK there's beginning to be something of a buzz around what's being termed 'German media theory', by which is meant the work mainly of Friedrich Kittler, Bernd Siegert, Vilém Flusser, Niklas Luhmann and Klaus Theweleit, but also Peter Sloterdijk and Hartmut Winkler." Bunz replies: "One thus learns from French theory, which did not exist in France: there will be no German media theory in Germany. But chances look good elsewhere." So, what cannot be discussed in Germany may thrive elsewhere. Around the same time, two media theory anthologies were published in German that, more or less, tried to position German theory production of the past few decades within the Anglo-American context. They provide interesting reads to see how works of Flusser, Kittler and his critical opponent Winkler, and philosophers such as Sandbothe are summarized, popularized, and compared with McLuhan, Baudrillard, De Kerckhove, and Manovich. However, the question cannot be asked if there is something unique or specific about contemporary German-language media theory, apart from, thank God, how it presents itself to the outside world as a theory.[1]

It was foreseeable that the label "German" would be problematic, even though I used it to refer to the language and not to the country. German, many say, stands for mediocrity and missed opportunities. Pit Schultz puts it in a nutshell:

> German would be Transrapid, Space Center Bremen, the toll collect system, the social security website, shifting cargo, Phonoline [a failed music distribution portal], "stocks for the people", the loss making Karstadt department store chain, and reunification, i.e., the logic of failure on a high level. It would have to do with large-scale technological networks and their culture, i.e., more in the direction of Harold Innis and Lewis Mumford or Bruno Latour or H.P. Hughes, or even Avital Ronell's study of stupidity.[2]

As recently as the time prior to the 2006 soccer World Cup, most young intellectuals in Germany were "anti-German"[3] and sympathetic to the idea that Germany, at all cost, should be prevented from expressing national ambitions. Nonetheless, far away from the Heimat, media students bring up the legitimate question of whether there are any successors to the grand thinkers of the Interbellum. Without a corresponding translation policy, the answer is probably not coming soon. Why important contemporary German works are not translated into English could be linked back to the Anglo-Saxon publishing world, but that is not under debate here. It is a fact that German academics have increasingly been focused on their own, deteriorating, situation. To this we should add the fact that the total German readership is around 100 million, a considerable mass compared to other European languages. In response to the globalization of knowledge production, humanities, social sciences, and the arts, German theorists had to endure one defensive issue after another. Poor skills in English are no longer an issue, even though most scholars do not write their papers (let alone their books) in English. They do travel overseas and are very well informed about what is happening outside of the German-speaking world. The issue here is one primarily of time. If an influential work appears, as a rule it should be translated within the next five to ten years after publication in order to contribute to the international discourse. This is not the case with German works. One gets the impression that both Anglo-Saxon publishers and the German scientific foundations do not prioritize contemporary theory and would rather invest in classics and monographs concerning history, anything from the 18th century to the Nazi period. An exception here would be Ulrich Beck, whose work explicitly focuses on globalization and culture. Luckily, two books of media archeologist Siegfried Zielinski have recently been translated. The same can be said for Friedrich Kittler, of whom, of course, more could be translated.

For the sake of those who love the current debates about the canon, let us mention some authors and titles (or, the Internet equivalent: *The Listables*). On top of my personal wish list would be a translation of the collected works of Vilém Flusser. This project should be urgent as it would be of great value. Some of his titles have been published recently, specifically, *The Freedom of the Migrant* and an anthology of his work. A systematic approach of this unique, cosmopolitan Euro-Brazilian thinker would be timely, a project that would best be conducted as an international collaboration, much like the online journal flusserstudies.net, launched in 2005. I recently read a book by a postwar contemporary of Flusser's, Max Bense. His *Aesthetics and Text Theory*, which is Volume 3 of his *Selected Writings,* is excellent. Another must read would be *The Book of Kings* by Klaus Theweleit (two volumes, 1988/1994). I consider these works as important as the translated

Male Fantasies (1977).[4] They provide us with a theory of gender collaboration, media, and creative production, ranging from Claudio Monteverdi to Gottfried Benn and Knut Hamsun, from Bertolt Brecht to Elvis. This rich, narrative, psychoanalytic theory of cultural artifacts, ranging from poetry to films and records, shows that a combination of literary criticism with art history or postcolonial/cultural studies, closely in sync with Kittler's theses, can be applied to a variety of present and future contexts.

Peter Sloterdijk's magnus opus *Sphären* (three volumes, 1998/1999/2004) is another German text I would love to see translated. Its sheer volume (thousands of pages) might scare publishers, but this monumental translation job will need to be done anyway, so why not speed it up? Much like Theweleit, Sloterdijk provides us with a broad and original understanding of media. Sloterdijk explains the basic concept:

> *Spheres* are the spaces where people actually live. The space where human beings exist has always been taken for granted, without ever being made conscious and explicit. And this *lieu* or space I call a *sphere* in order to indicate that we are never in fact naked in totality, in a physical or biological environment of some kind, but that we are ourselves space-creating beings, and that we cannot exist otherwise than in these self-animated spaces.[5]

I predict that spherical media theories will have a great future as so much of the technologies drift that way. Thus far only two of Sloterdijk's books from the 1980s have been translated into English—a rather poor score for Germany's "second biggest philosopher." Besides the sphere trilogy, there are also texts that explicitly deal with (new) media, such as *Medien-Zeit* (Media Time, 1995), while Sloterdijk's 2005 *Innerspace of Capital* contains his take on the globalization discourse.

An introduction to Hartmut Winkler's work also seems desirable. His main work *Docuverse* (1997) on the question of whether the computer is a medium or calculating machine is still worth reading, as is *Discourse Economy* (2004). At least Winkler has a homepage with some texts in English. Where to start? Martin Warnke and the Hypercult festival in Lüneburg; the Cologne-based Hans-Ulrich Reck's studies on media art; Georg Tholen in Basel; Berlin philosophy professor Sybille Krämer; the writings on net.art by Tilman Baumgärtel; and cyberfeminists like Verena Kuni, Claudia Reiche and Yvonne Volkart.[6] I also consider some of Nobert Bolz's texts classics, such as *Theory of New Media* (1989) where he theorizes the Nietzsche–Benjamin–McLuhan troika.[7] Also worthy of note and study are the following: Wolfgang Hagen, who writes about the history of cybernetics; Michael Giesecke and his historical studies on the Gutenberg book culture; Sigrid Schade's studies on art, body, gender, and new media; Wolfgang

Coy, who operates inside computer science; Wolfgang Ernst's work on archives; the highly original media theories of art critic Boris Groys; and Dieter Daniels' histories of media art. It is also valuable to hear the voices of the younger generation, born in the 1960s: Inke Arns, who is an expert in contemporary (Eastern) European new media culture; software theorist Florian Cramer, who is now teaching in Rotterdam; the brilliant storyteller Nils Röller; and the computer historian and game expert Claus Pias.

Mann will nicht viel und kann noch weniger

—Deutschland, 2006

Now, let's return to the Rohrpost online debate. Florian Cramer denies that there is something like a unified, worked-out media theory.

> Since the 1990s, every scholar in the humanities with any pride says the "media" are one of his areas of research. The practical illiteracy in this area, the lack of mastery of elementary "new-media" cultural technologies (starting with e-mail), and the fundamental lack of technical know-how beggars description and continually produces real-life satires of scholars. This is the same as if one is a foreign-language philologist without any knowledge of a foreign language or a musicologist who can neither play an instrument nor read music.

Yes, one ought to expect a media researcher to know at least what TCP/IP, routing, and DNS are. Even though I agree with Cramer here, I have to admit that I do not read German media theory to garner technical knowledge. Instead, what makes this metaphysical writing so enjoyable is the natural way in which media theory is embedded into philosophy, literature, and the humanities in general. It immediately broadens your view and inspires you beyond the latest RSS news feeder, into Greek mythology, the history of warfare, German idealism, and seventeenth-century networks of knowledge. This is, of course, also its weak point. Once you have blown up the media concept to contain the entire human history and all of its cultural artifacts, you run the risk of emptying out a field that has only just begun.

The widespread lack of detailed knowledge among media theorists has to be traced back to an ongoing discontent with media culture among intellectuals. Many of the theorists listed have not made the cultural turn toward Anglo-Saxon cultural studies with its emphasis on discourse analysis and postcolonialism.[8] Despite all the Adorno bashing among media theorists, the distrust of the culture industries in German-speaking countries forms a remarkable consensus across the political spectrum. Cramer, writing on the Rohrpost list:

That "the media" are autonomous, and thus the human being is helplessly at their mercy, and that this means the end of traditional culture, is the thread running through practically all German media theories whose authors were born before approximately 1955. One finds this leitmotif either in a pessimistic-negative coloration or, in dialectical mirror-imaging, as an affirmation of a postmodern "Stop Making Sense."

If there is no school, in the sense of a Frankfurt School, there is certainly a cluster of authors who publish together and invite each other to conferences. For a while, I used to call them the Kassel School of German Media Theory because this network used to meet in the West German town of Kassel during the mid- to late-1980s at the height of its productive years. For Sebastian Lütgert there are at least the students of Friedrich Kittler as an identifiable group also called the Kittler youth. This may sound like a derogative term, but this group of young student–followers actually exists. They can be recognized by their militant techno-determinism, their tendency toward cybernetics matched with war history (Thomas Pynchon) and an unreconstructed anti-Americanism that runs as a not-so-subtle subcurrent through their writings once they start talking about Microsoft or Hollywood. Sebastian Lütgert:

> If there was a britpop in 1995 or young Berlin art in 2002, then of course there is a German media theory—that is, the common interest of the marketing divisions of German universities to position a national trademark in the face of increasing site competition. But it does not refer to a tradition of thought, or even to any thought at all, but merely to the common destiny of German professors.

Stefan Heidenreich, on the other hand, regards the label "German" as weak.

> If one counts every mention of the term "media", it becomes boundless. The word "media" meanwhile stands less for a substantive position than it serves as a trademark to secure monies and positions in the academic battle for a share of the pie.

Verena Kuni, based in Frankfurt, is involved in the small Interfiction conferences in Kassel where every year, in a non-academic setup, media theory mixes up with art-related topics. Kuni believes that theory can be located. But it is more a matter of institutions than of nations. What interests her above all is what relation network cultures have to traditional academic institutions like colleges and universities. No contemporary media theory presently deals critically with contemporary network cultures and also takes account of technologies like wikis in its writing processes. Cramer says:

The dot-com crash has strengthened conservative attitudes of defensiveness and resentment and has made many people certain that the Internet is a dead hype. On the other hand, those network cultures that, like nettime almost ten years ago, came with the ambition of "collaboratively filtering" a "network critique" have not come up with any alternatives.

Till von Heiseler sums up the current situation:

Media theory today does not manage to understand itself as theory and to draw the corresponding consequences. It is attached to academia and, without reflection, mostly uses the traditional formats of research that result from the history of science and the many contingent individual decisions for reputation. In this context, everyone battles for the book as the sole worthy laurels.

During the Rohrpost debate, Kuni warned against an over-generalizing essentialism because every practice and every discipline produces its respective blind spots.

What one ought to be able to demand from theoreticians is that the objects to which what is said/written refer to something and the limits, including one's own, should be precisely named. Unfortunately, the latter is not one of the promising strategies when one wants to establish his or her theory.

Nevertheless, there are also alternatives like the text archive initiated by Sebastian Lütgert, www.textz.com. Cramer remarks on this:

The role of subversive importer, eclectic filter, thought-provocateur, unofficial institution of discourse, and counter-Suhrkamp publisher that the German Semiotext(e) called Merve Verlag once had, is now assumed by textz.com, the latter even in a legal sense and more radically than Merve ever dared. But textz.com's selection of texts, for example "Heidegger for Illiterates", stands athwart any subsumation as "German." Equally, only very few of the texts on the server qualify as "theory". Instead, textz.com gathers and indexes tangential discourses that, for long stretches, are also a discourse on media. In a certain way, textz.com thus fulfills medially and epistemologically what is described, precisely in Merve books, as discourse theory, but which Merve hardly implemented.

My original question did not aim at lists of favorite authors, but at how European languages can position themselves globally. At least 100 million people speak German as their first language, and yet it is often regarded as irrelevant and provincial. The translating machines in the Unired King-dom and the United States are still in the hands of necrophilian publishing houses. Only dead thinkers can be marketed. More and more authors will have to pay for their works to be translated into English. But in German-speaking countries, theorists are often not aware of these new economic circumstances. They just sit there and patiently wait until they are discovered. This is lethal for current theory. We live in a real-time era, and readers should not have to wait thirty to fifty years for translation of important foreign-language texts. Additionally, Gutenberg-centrism is beginning to totter. Under these conditions, how can new forms of dialogue within Europe be shaped? Is it possible to debate German media theory or should we just forget about it and focus on what everyone else is talking about? Let's look into a concrete case. I posed the question on Rohrpost; if I organized a conference on German media theory, to be held in Amsterdam, should it be in English? There was a mixed response. At home, among my University of Amsterdam students, only a few read German, let alone have an active interest in Germany or have any interest in actively participating in a conference on this topic. It is simply out of the question to require Dutch students to read texts in German today. International students will not either, as most of them have a hard enough time struggling with English. In times of globalization, the isolation of cultures inside Europe has risen dramatically. Here Cramer is, as always, very direct:

> German-language academic media and cultural sciences encapsu-late themselves off from the rest of the world because in their home countries they are communicated and taught only in German, their academic conferences are held only in German, and they publish only on paper and in German.

In a posting to Rohrpost, Janus von Abaton already knows what course a possible Amsterdam conference on German media theory might take.

> It's easy to chat just under the level of actual developments of thought. Who honors whom? No one insults anyone. Of course one is intel-ligent and speaks English hardly any worse than German. And then one regards this as internationalism. One also thinks a little bit, as far as one's career permits and as long as it doesn't hurt. At the end, one goes to a good Amsterdam restaurant, allows oneself to be served, and feels good. One is in one's element. One thinks about a hooker one saw while strolling. She must come from South America. And then—whaddaya know!—a talk actually comes about.

By the way, Janus forgot to mention the mandatory visit to an Amster-dam coffee shop. For a variety of reasons, the conference never took place.

Maybe it was a bad idea in the first place to discuss German media theory with Germans. According to Pit Schultz, the original question should be reformulated: *Is there a European media theory?* So, should we forget German altogether? Outside of Germany, curiosity about contemporary theory from Old Europe is growing. Berlin is cool, mainly because it is so cheap. An exotic niche might be there for everyone, ready to be discovered. But we do not find much (new) media or technology business or research in the real existing Berlin, where the talk is more about music, clubs, fashion, cultural theory, visual arts, and architecture. Let's face it. Despite its still large theory production, even in Germany book culture is going south. Since export-oriented translation politics are probably stuck in the reform jam, individual authors have little choice but to compose their texts directly in English—a decision I myself made in the middle of the 1990s, uncomfortably. But this, too, demands no less than a revolution in the education system and will only fuel the shift of knowledge toward a network-based learning, away from the Gutenberg galaxy and the safety of surrounding oneself with Great Dead Authors.

Apart from the translation and language issue, I would like to discuss the proposal of a new subdiscipline: media philosophy. Whereas media theory is a general term that points to a broad public domain in which intellectuals from all disciplines and backgrounds (not just academic) contribute to the discourse, media philosophy is a specific term that intervenes within an institutionalized discipline. I had an online dialogue about this latest academic current with the Viennese media theorist and philosopher Frank Hartmann. To further discuss the media philosophy meme I asked Sybille Krämer, Marie-Luise Angerer, Mike Sandbothe, and Wolfgang Ernst to respond to Frank Hartmann's theses.[9] Mike Sandbothe, professor for media philosophy in Aalborg (Denmark) claims that media philosophy is an expression that media people like to use and specialized researchers prefer to avoid. Yet, something is happening. In November 2003, a conference was held on the subject in Stuttgart.

In 2003, Fischer publishing house released the volume *Medienphilosophie. Beiträge zur Klärung eines Begriffs* (Media Philosophy: Papers toward Clarifying a Term). In twelve programmatic essays, it delves into the question of what media philosophy could be. Let's take a brief look into this anthology. There are contributions from the neo-rationalist Matthias Vogel; the aesthetics of Lorenz Engell, a media philosopher in Weimar; the critical approach of Elena Esposito of Italy; the online identity researcher Barbara Becker; philosopher Martin Seel from Giessen; and the systems theoretician Stefan Weber of Salzburg. While some define scholarly media philosophy strictly as a program of instruction and research, others advocate a pragmatic approach oriented toward art and design. Skeptics see the project media philosophy as a renovation enterprise with a limited mission (Seel), while others seem quite prepared to get their hands dirty dealing with media practice. For example, Lorenz Engell writes, "Media philosophy is a happening, possibly a practice, and one of the media. It does not wait for the philosophers before being written. It always has already happened: in and through the media."[10] Stefan Weber, by contrast, sees an "intellectual counter-movement, as a renaissance of the luxury of reflecting thought in the context of a media science that is increasingly submitting to the tyranny of practice."[11]

A few years earlier, in 2000, the Vienna-based media theorist Frank Hartmann published a book with the title *Medienphilosophie*. If you start fearing you missed something because you do not know which side you're on in the media philosophy debate, don't worry, there is not much at stake. At least the antagonists have thus far failed to make clear what the controversy over this concept is all about—presuming there is one. From the outside, it looks like a failed cockfight over nonexisting institutional arrangements, in a time of rising student numbers and shrinking education budgets. Maybe there was no controversy after all, but no strong collective will either. Like all academic disciplines, philosophy is also confronted with the rise of the computer. This has been the case for half a century, but it is only now that the knowledge itself is being produced and stored in networks and databases. Technology is no longer an obscure object of study for some (like the history of science scholars), but alters production of knowledge in general.

The advance of computer networking has reached philosophers' rooms for good. Technology is no longer the research field of individuals, but is transforming the production of knowledge as a whole, including that of philosophy, whether we are talking about ethics or logic. And that is where the current discussion begins. While some think that the core of philosophy (thinking in itself) remains untouched by the fashionable machines, others believe the survival of the whole discipline depends on dealing with the issue of media. The debates center on the goals of this new subdiscipline called "media philosophy." The choice of this label was not coincidental, for the choice of name clearly aims to position it within this millennia-old field. Parallel projects like media theory, mediology, media studies, and even media science are popping up all over the place, inside both Germany and elsewhere.

In 2000, I interviewed Frank Hartmann. He talked about media philosophy and how this emerging discipline relates to Kittler's media theory and the dirty little practice of "net criticism."[12] In 2003, Hartmann published *Mediologie*. Like his previous book *Medienphilosophie*, it is written as a general introduction to current topics. Unlike most of his continental colleagues, Hartmann's style is free of high-flying hermeneutic exercises. Hartmann's new media analysis is free of fear and disdain. Without becoming affirmative, he is keen to avoid "totalizing" concepts that try to explain everything and exclude most anything that does not fit into the newly carved-out discursive cave. One neither has to be subjected to the Empire of Images, nor does one have to flee it. In early 2004, I had a second e-mail exchange with Hartmann. This time we wrote about his interpretation of the mediology concept and tension between concept-centered theory and digital image culture. To summarize the debate: For some, new media and the Internet are fads that will fade away, not affecting the eternal philosophical questions, whereas others believe that the philosophical practice will indeed be fundamentally transformed once the introduction of new media is complete.

In the Anglo-Saxon world, the term *media philosophy* was compromised from the start—*Imagologies*, the cyber-hype book from Mark C. Taylor and Esa Saarinen published in 1994 contributed substantially to the derogation of the term. The tragic superficiality of *Imagologies* proved finally that it is not enough to merely link up students and scholars via e-mail and satellite and then expect them to have interesting conversations. As the Canadian communications theorist and political economist Harold Innis realized, one's techniques of practice—or appraisal of technology—is peculiar to the medium of communication and will change according to the type of medium adopted. Human action is after all an extension of media forms; for a critical, reflexive practice to emerge, it is essential to go beyond the excitement and hubris of being early adapters. Praise of technology is not enough; readers expect philosophers to negate, to circumvent society and its PR propaganda, and not just celebrate the latest slogans. Only radical futurism is worth debating. Speculative philosophies need to transcend the present, explore unlikely futures, and reject the temptation to extrapolate the cool present. Nor is it sufficient to retreat to the safe Gutenberg galaxy of critical theory. Media philosophy has to take risks and cut across disciplinary borders. The "iconic turn" debate[13] as summarized by Hartmann can only be one of many beginnings and proves just how difficult, and immature, pictorial thinking really is.

Deep incursions of real-time global media into everyday life continue. There seems to be no end to the technology boom, despite the latest bust. Media enters the realms of imagination and reality from all sides, as *Big Brother* and similar reality television programs demonstrate. Infotainment has elements of both war and game, contributing to what Paul Virilio termed the "militarization of civil society." In this fluid, transient world, people long for ethics and values, and dream of a fantasy future of a society in which the individual knows his or her place. Philosophy can be one of those pseudo religions. In *Infinite Thought*, Alain Badiou calls for a return to philosophy. He no longer wants philosophy to be subordinated to a "multiplicity of language games" and claims that language is not the absolute horizon of thought. He calls for the return of an unconditional principle. How could we translate this into media philosophy terms? Or rather should we dismiss Badiou's call because he looks down on the mediasphere—as one would expect from a French philosopher of 1968. According to Badiou, "the world is submitted to the profoundly illogical regime of communication" that "transmits a universe made up of disconnected images, remarks, statements." This is the dilemma media philosophy faces. Should it return to something stable or jump into the unknown and risk losing all ties with the institutionalized knowledge? Nietzsche would certainly have opted for the latter, but then Nietzsche himself has become captured, framed, and institutionalized (no pun intended) like no other philosopher.

A surprising amount of the media philosophy is about institutional arrangements. Should an ancient discipline open itself up to contemporary topics, not just as an object of study, but incorporate it as a fully integrated branch of knowledge within the wider field? It is only when media philosophy has been properly defined, and its existence authorized and, hence, legitimized that people will enter this field. Prior to that, the central concept needs to be loaded with hermeneutic speculations, while at the same time sheltered against attacks from neighboring tribes that envy philosophy's long history. Philosophers can only start thinking when there is a properly defined discipline that fits neatly into the academic structures, including all its institutional arrangements. There is not much "thinking on the fence" going on. To start thinking that something like media philosophy could be a feasible proposition almost sounds like a subversive act. Frank Hartmann: "What are the incentives for someone in a tenured position to go for new topics? Why bother when by the time you have reached your job as professor you're so inculcated into a largely corrupt feudalistic system of patronage? What else can you be but exhausted and demoralized?"

A form of philosophy that is open for dialogue needs to be introduced. Hartmann:

> European philosophers are trained to produce texts relating to texts. The classical attitude is to "defend" the thesis you have formulated in your text, and to "destroy" any opposing argument. There is no dialogue, no lively thought—even at workshops people do nothing else but read their prefabricated texts to each other. The inbred discourse produced in this manner is only of interest for the philosophers themselves.

Hartmann considers Marshall McLuhan, the first media philosopher. "McLuhan pointed out that writing texts is but one form of processing ideas, and that new media culture points beyond this singular form, and even beyond the medium of language itself. This certainly is something a German philosopher does not want to hear." Following the approach of mediology, Hartmann favors a materialistic model over the metaphysical cloud. "Mediology means to come up with concrete research questions that could indeed be the needle to pop this bubble called 'media philosophy'. Rather than having a precise definition of the term 'medium', I imagine a raw mix of sociological, philosophical and semiotic questions that deal with the problems of our technologically advanced culture."

In the twentieth century, technology, including media technology, was mostly viewed as being external, alien. When someone says the word "philosophy," one involuntarily thinks of dusty cultural pessimism and the laments of those who foresee the apocalypse. Again and again, one encounters reservations, conservative generalizing judgments without any relation to practice. Philosophy seems to be imprisoned in a concept jail and easily does without the actual object of its considerations. We find little curiosity and few questions. For Berlin professor Sybille Krämer, however, the linguistic turn has long since run into a dead end. She writes, "Philosophically radically thinking the idea of mediality inevitably leads to questioning the a priori quality, the 'unavoidability', and the ultimately foundational power of language." The eternal flirtation with a ban on images should come to an end if philosophy does not want to sink completely to the level of esoteric life problem counseling. But academians see the media drifting past after the natural order of script, including its classics, is restored.

But there are also positive things to report. As I pointed out earlier, in the German-speaking world, unique and vibrant media theory production has developed since the 1980s. These studies are often archaeological and conceptual and attempt to find the historical place of the computer and image technologies beyond the ordinary chronology. But this valuable endeavor remains a double-edged sword. Meanwhile, many clearly recognize that new media has been around longer than the day before yesterday, and that it makes political and cultural sense to understand it purely on the basis of its prehistory. However, this rage to order things can also be understood as a rage to fence them in, as a kind of retroactive mastery, since media practice has long eluded the control of the intellectual class. This domestication of computer culture then only serves the higher purpose of maintaining old, hierarchical academic structures. Nevertheless, many of these theories can be remodeled easily into conceptual fuel rods to power imaginative digital force. Mike Sandbothe says, "New concepts, like mediology, media ecology, and media philosophy, develop intellectual tools with whose help the current processes of digitalization and globalization cannot only be passively analyzed, but also actively co-shaped."

The motor of this debate is the constantly increasing demand to open up and establish new courses of study that are explicitly concerned with new media. New textbooks are published and teaching positions offered. Frank Hartmann:

> It is no longer a question of whether there should be new disciplines, but how to shape them in reality. There is lots of valuable material in the philosophical tradition, but we do not necessarily receive answers to the questions of our situation, which have to be posed in an entirely new and different way. But the problem of media theory is not just a theoretical or methodological one; institutional reputations and academic careers are also at stake.

What do media philosophers actually study? Hartmann:

> There are problems with our understanding of knowledge, with semantics and information, with "intelligent" information-processing machines. When treating these new questions, we are more in an area of involvement and intervention than in one of interpretation and hermeneutics. One has to work together with other disciplines, for example with sociological prognoses of the consequences of technology, or look around in a computer laboratory, listen to the programmers, or take part in a discussion about the effects of open source in our culture—all contemporary issues that should be central to what is being called media philosophy. The Italian philosopher Luciano Floridi, who teaches at Oxford and suggests precisely that, says we should stop merely cloning academics and should instead, as Plato called for long ago, begin to train the citizens of our society in all the competencies demanded by a reflecting media culture.

Surprisingly, according to Hartmann, plenty of media theoreticians have not even managed to create their own Web presence, much less new forms of publication such as blogs and wikis. We do not see a specific Internet competence that goes beyond the basic reception of Web content. This is joined and reinforced by a slave mentality toward publishers concerning copyright.

Wolfgang Ernst is the new Humboldt University Professor for media science. He pleads for a convergence with entirely different practices beyond philosophy, from engineering and art to quantum physics. The reality of media requires an independent disciplinary matrix, says Ernst. "While philosophers analyze the media decidedly from the phenomenological side, media scientists go to the trouble of, for example, carrying out the mathematical operations of programming or of analyzing the electro-technical details of chip architecture (for this is the first level upon which media exist as epistemic things)." In the combination of academic reflection and technological competence, Ernst sees "the critical chance of media theory to position itself in high definition against a wildly inflationary use of the term media. Here, the concrete archaeology of the media is the litmus test for all media theory—while in this regard media philosophy is occasionally negligent, even fuzzy."

Learning something about technology is one thing we all must ultimately do. Using computers is something like driving a car. Useful and unavoidable, you have to learn by doing. On top of this, in the networked area of science there is also a different approach to text—an approach that has difficulty for some media philosophers. What new media put into question is the hegemony of text-based scholarship. The composing of texts is only one form among many for the processing of thought. Hartmann: "New media culture points beyond the singular form, indeed, beyond the medium of language itself. No German philosopher wants to hear anything like this." Wolfgang Ernst writes: "I agree with Frank Hartmann, who underscores that visual design, DJ-ing, and programming are also to be regarded as forms of philosophical reflection. Digital media themselves are potentially theorizable—including in the sense that, without theory (purely as machines), they would never have come to be."

Marie-Luise Angerer, professor at the Academy of Media Arts Cologne, remarks that the German-language discussion of media focuses on the master-definition of *medium*. Angerer:

> It is less about what the medium does or how it stages itself than it is, again and again, about: who is your master? This strikes me as a very male attitude, to talk about the end of the master narratives but always to come with a new one. The university's media discourse in Germany and Austria does not cover Europe either. What is happening in Italy and France, in England or in Slovenia, are other things that do not appear in Hartmann's field of vision. In addition, it would be worth looking not only at the university's media discussion, but also to include media labs, art colleges, and others.

In this sense, the entire field of German media theory can be termed prefeminist, pre-1989, still having its postcolonial period ahead of it. But the question is also whether more practice-oriented discourses would be fundamentally in a position to change power constellations like gender and geography.

Imagine Internet-competent philosophers heading the A-list of European bloggers. Why does this sound so unlikely, even ridiculous? Many underscore that media is not the solution to all problems. Sybille Krämer: "Media should not occupy the 'void' left behind by the erosion of the modern concept of the subject. The challenge of media philosophy thus consists in showing the fundamental role of mediality, without thereby establishing a media apriorism and media fundamentalism." According to Wolfgang Ernst, synergism should definitely not be striven for: "If media are considered in the discipline of philosophy, this is useful, as long as the terms media and philosophy do not converge in hybridization, but remain productive in their mutual difference in observers." Media philosophy should provide neither encouraging promises for the future nor prognoses of dark consequences, but untimely blueprints. Media needs no monopolistic standards, but endless variations: techno-difference. An impassioned media philosophy opens up spaces of possibilities, but only after the reevaluation of all course catalogs. This leads to the conclusion that the study of media and networks should not threaten existing disciplines. But they do, and this is causing a great deal of anxiety in German-speaking countries. The strategy of the mainstream institutions is one of containment and denial: if we hide, the storm might pass. Why should philosophy, art history, and *Germanistik* deal with contemporary topics anyway? Just leave us alone in our comfortable eighteenth century or, even better, our cozy dead antiquity. Surprisingly enough, research funds are all ears for this retreat into history. In such a conservative climate, proposals such as media philosophy have a refreshing touch and feel. The question should be how to distinguish the value between the provincial nostalgia of the historical approach and the conceptual richness of untimely thinking.

CHAPTER **4**

Blogging and Building
The Netherlands after Digitization

Dedicated to *Bob the Builder* and the game *Design a House with Mr. Bentley*[1] (with thanks to Kazimir).

The architectural firm, Citythoughts, in Amsterdam commissioned this chapter. An earlier version appeared in the publication *Suburban Scenarios* and on February 24, 2006 was presented at an event that took place at Club 11, inside the former post office next to Amsterdam's Central Station. Bastiaan Gribling invited a number of non-architects (writers, artists, critics) to discuss the notion that in the next ten years the Dutch "randstad," the metropolitan area between Amsterdam, Utrecht, Rotterdam, and The Hague, will coagulate to become one big, built-up congested urban area.[2] What characterizes the densely populated Netherlands is not that it is the model of a mega-city, but instead it is a collection of small and medium sized cities located within close proximity of one another. This urban archipelago is bound by a vast network of waterways, train connections, highways, the Rotterdam harbor, Schiphol airport, and, lest we forget, a telecommunications infrastructure. The leftover, mostly manmade, empty space is often called the *Groene Hart* (the Green Heart) and, as a "cultural landscape," dates from the early Middle Ages. Until now, a great deal of the urban architectural efforts have focused on creating a clear line between the encroaching suburban housing, office, and industrial park development, and the patchwork of deeply green and boggy meadows. But it seems that this encroaching urbanization can no longer be restrained. A fatal blow will likely be dealt this rural countryside when the European Union (EU) ultimately reduces its agricultural subsidies. If, in the near future, all the small farms should disappear, who will remain behind to manage the agrarian landscape?[3]

Bastiaan Gribling asked us to address the question of what the "actual process of the formation of metropolises means in relation to contemporary cultural developments. What is the role of art and culture in the genesis of Dutch metropolitan areas?" It became quite obvious that I could contribute something from an Internet perspective. I was more concerned with how architecture is networked and less how the network obtains architecture. The assignment came, coincidentally enough, during a period when the Netherlands became the country with the highest rate of ADSL-broadband usage worldwide. What I propose is that the Internet is already being seriously considered and used in the planning of the nation's general housing character but, at the same time, is not being adequately recognized—and utilized—by Dutch architects and urban developers who continue to view computer networks as little more than technical and promotional tools and not as a full-fledged medium and interactive environment—a place where we have already been residing for some time now. It is not enough to see the role of the Internet as merely an input device in the planning machinery. The Internet has changed the very logic of the machine itself.

My starting point here is the radical democratization of architectural tools that were facilitated by a combination of the computer, software, and fiber-optic networks. I pose this thesis as a conscious dilettante, well aware that such an intervention in the architecture discipline is rather unwelcome. The increased role of the Internet in Dutch everyday life seems to have largely passed by the urban planners and architectural theoreticians. In this futuristic scenario, we assume an accelerated discarding of planological devices with all of their associated rituals by a group of professionals that no longer has a need for "involvement." AutoCAD4all or Sketchup will eventually replace the e-governance meme, especially now that Google has made Sketchup free. Meanwhile, "blog building"[4] is not based on the notion of artificial scarcity that the Dutch elite have for centuries imposed on their subjects. In the Internet period, do-it-yourself builders have assumed the right to a minimum of 1000 square meters. The fairy tale that there would no longer be enough land left on which to build or that it would be unaffordable is no longer accepted.[5]

The generic suburbs of the twenty-first century will be the final projects involving the individualization of society as expressed in interior rooms, dominated by mass manufactured subjectivity.[6] Finally we will be able to leave behind that nineteenth century notion of row houses and closed city blocks. If this is not going to be permitted in the Netherlands, then we will just look elsewhere. If we recognize the relationship between urban development and computer networks, we begin to notice the emergence of all sorts of challenges and possibilities. However, the Internet and mobile phones remain largely overlooked in the environmental planning debates. The major parties continue to view the computer as nothing more than a simulation game, a combination of drawing and calculating machine, and computer work is still often delegated to assistants. The mentality of this "transitional generation" (with one foot in the old media and the other in the new) is at the heart of this chapter.

The global architecture and urban development market is, for the time being, still dominated by the Baby Boom Generation. Chronologically speaking, they were there at the birth of the computer age, and yet they have managed to maintain their critical and skeptical distance. Intellectually speaking, the computer and its related networks remained in the background and continue to be viewed as tools that lack their own voices. Marxism, as well as the poststructuralist and deconstructionist movements did not welcome the digitalization of society—including its own disciplines—with open arms. All we need to do is look to the examples set by Heidegger and Virilio. Modernism à la Bauhaus had the potential to leave its mark but ultimately lost its credibility some time ago. The arrival of Koolhaas, in any case, came too late, and the influence of people like Spuybroek, Oosterhuis, and Lynn, among others, has remained relatively limited, although there are recent signs that this may be changing. Rightly so or not, virtual architecture is all too often cast aside as nothing more than some inconsequential trick of the trade or marketing tool. Viewed from another angle, we could also say that architecture, as a discourse, has not had a substantial influence on the development of new media theory. The reason is quite simple: the computer, in architectural circles, is still considered just a black box and not what McLuhan proposed—an environment with its own characteristics. While plenty of attention is paid to aesthetics and design in the Netherlands, the pragmatic aspects remain limited by the form. The age-old traditional belief is that the computer, however powerful a tool it may be, remains a development that summons up few critical reflections.

The notion of the Internet as little more than a tool is countered by the vision of the Internet as an "intensifying machine." The Internet increases the velocity of social processes we observe around us. This process accelerator makes no distinction between the formation of urban areas and the preservation of the Dutch landscape. The Internet encourages both a hectic city life and the more sluggish lifestyle of the telecommunications employee who lives in the more visually correct and bucolic countryside. Research by sociologist Saskia Sassen reveals that the crowded information networks have not led to the demise of the inner city. They have actually facilitated quite the opposite.[7] On the other hand, everyone knows that telecommunications work, from the suburb to a foreign country, continues to increase and continues to have a bright future. Once teleconferencing becomes more democratic and emerges as a real alternative to going to conferences and meetings, it will only serve to increase the necessity of telecommunications work.[8] Thus, the choice presented here—between urban metropolis and protected landscape—is perhaps a false dichotomy.

Rem Koolhaas has for years operated at the center of this debate. In 2002, a former architecture student, Lorne Haycock, created an Internet site dedicated to "digital architecture and urbanism." In a related essay, Hayock chastises Koolhaas for coming up with a diagnosis but offering no answers. "The current position of society is described by Koolhaas as frantic, fast moving and, as a, generally, more accelerated way of life. Koolhaas embraces this freneticism and seeks to glorify it in his architecture." According to Haycock, Koolhaas is "guilty of almost creating a technological metaphor for the time rather than prescribing a solution. Where he offers a symbolic gesture of the time rather than an appreciation of the potential within this new technology."[9] In this analysis, new media is presented as nothing more than an instrument in an uncritical strategy that seeks to further glorify capitalism. This is an old criticism of the computer that radical activists had already cast aside in the early 1990s.

Haycock describes the arrival of the computer in professional practice as follows: "Computer modelling techniques allow architects to email special details direct to manufacturers for production. The introduction of computer technology into nearly every aspect of the construction industry has led to the demise of the drawing board and given designers a uniform tool, in that of the computer." What we have today is a "tangible architectural testing zone, where, we as architects can conduct architectural experiments indefinitely, until we formulate an appropriate, well-tested solution. As architecture tries to synthesize contemporary culture to understand it, we can now decode our new social, economic, and technological advancements, as we are obliged to, in the relative safety of 'virtual space'." While in contemporary Internet theory, the exchange between network and society is considered its most significant feature, Haycock sees the isolated "sandbox" aspect of virtual space as its most important characteristic.[10]

Space, the Final Frontier

One of the reasons that Internet theory and architecture have had such a difficult relationship centers on the various interpretations of the term "virtual space." Architects who use AutoCAD, ArchiCAD, 3D Studio Max, and others believe that cyberspace actually exists; they see it every day, all day long on their computer screens. The point here is that from an Internet perspective, this glitzy 3D perspective is nothing more than dead space used only for PR purposes. This eye candy may lead an offline existence but it is not interactive and is not linked to other documents. The show-stealing drawings are conceptual dream palaces without users or, in other words, nice pictures to impress potential clients and nothing more.[11] The two worlds I sketch here "shift" like plateaus past one another. In the mid-1990s, when everything to do with the Internet was still new, there were numerous conferences where the Internet and architecture had the opportunity to communicate with one another (i.e., the *Stadt am Netz* Conference in Munich and Luxembourg in 1996).[12] But after that, communication between the two camps grew silent.

Jennifer W. Leung is a New York-based architect, formerly with Diller Scofidio + Renfro. She speaks about 3D software and diversity of architecture practices. "The perspective may be architecture's most theorized and historicized trick of simulation, however simulation is more than the previewing of static form, visual affect, and the city from the point of view of architecture and vice-versa." For Leung, simulation implies a performance model that is about plasticity, iconicity, and environment, not simply a remake of Cartesian space. She says:

> For architecture, as opposed to video gaming and CGI, simulation is less reality by proxy, less Baudrillardian hyper-real, than a disciplinary experiment which plays with current epistemological tropes to varying levels of literalness. As network logics have caused the re-description of infrastructure, urbanism, consumerism, energy, the stock market, economy, and ecology, so too novel terms challenge architecture's description of itself.

Leung hopes that such experiments

> refrain from recasting architecture as a fetishized object vis-à-vis the mediation of computing, but the profession bears almost any number of forms of practice. On one extreme you may have architects *modeling* dynamic models of swarms and flocks or producing form through such an algorithm. On the other, you have architects working *live* within network effects, positioning themselves vis-à-vis media, branding, investing, advocacy, energy policy, and social welfare.[13]

Melbourne theorist Scott McQuire, who has been working on the relation between city and (new) media for many years, adds a historical explanation of the preoccupation with 3D images, in an interesting parallel to the film industry to do with how computers were channeled into high-tech special effects rather than new distribution systems.

There was more concern for the computer as a networking tool for control and communication in the 1960s than there was in the 1980s and 1990s, when digital imaging became more sophisticated and shifted architecture to visual experiments. From Yona Friedman to Constant to Archigram, even to people like MIT Medialab's Nicholas Negroponte, the author of *Soft Architecture Machines* (1975), for which Friedman wrote an intro to one section, there was a displacement of the architect as God in favor of user-configuration. Already in 1967 Peter Cook wrote: "Does consumer choice of pre-fabricated living units and the like imply that every man might become his own architect?"[14]

McQuire asks, "How did these ideas disappear and did we witness such an unprecedented celebrity system, in constant need of slick demo design?" and he tries to come up with an answer. "The lack of a critical analysis of technology in Constant meant that his utopia got overtaken by alternative uses of automation, while the lack of analysis of power in Archigram and Negroponte meant that their stance on computing was co-opted easily into a consumer version of 'choice'."

Lars Spuybroek writes in the introduction to his book *NOX: Machining Architecture* (2004) that he sees the computer as a "steering device" that is concerned with direction and flexibility. "The architecture of continuous variation is not one of 'free form' but of articulation and structure."[15] Even a huge computer fan like Spuybroek defends the profession of architecture against the freedom that the computer has buried inside itself. He believes that architecture should not be caught off guard by technology. Should free forms endlessly generated by the computer be restricted? Spuybroek rejects such a question and emphasizes that free forms themselves do not exist. For Spuybroek, such a notion is a contradiction in terms, as form is always in-formed and thus organized and never free, and whether it is a cloud or a building is irrelevant. Spuybroek notes,

> …the architectural form is organized in its own specific way and is not free either. Not every form that can be calculated bottom-up using algorithms is an architectural form. The "free" form is something therapeutic, for hobbyists on a lost Saturday afternoon, not for architecture. It is a form without information, or, if you like, a form with a low IQ[16]

Spuybroek believes that the computer period of daydreaming has luckily ended. "Disembodied dreams of an architecture floating in cyberspace—those years are over." The *NOX* agenda is based on a new level of discipline. "An architecture of complex, topological geometry can be pursued only through rigorous means, and though its main theory is of vagueness, its practice is of obsessive precision." Here, Spuybroek opens a polemic debate with, among others, Marcos Novak, whose strategy consists of declaring certain mathematical forms in architecture. "This is the same as providing apes with paint and declaring the result a painting." For Spuybroek, this is unrelated to the question of amateurism. How does he judge the "long line of brilliant amateurs"[17] who, with their wild clicking in virtual space, create boundary-blurring works that do not fit neatly inside the architectural discourse? To Spruybroek, their work has no relevance for architecture. "In the past we occasionally discussed how 'architecture without architects' could look like. But providing amateurs with software usually results in painstakingly bad designs." For Spuybroek, architecture is a discipline with a long history of professionals who are judged by people who have worked within this field for a lifetime. "There is no place here for amateurs. Web designers for instance consult Christopher Alexander (author of *The Nature of Order* and *A Pattern Language*) about the meaning of 'windows' but within architecture Alexander is considered a junk theorist."

In this context, it is impossible not to mention DDS, De Digitale Stad (the Digital City) in Amsterdam. For those who missed it, The Digital City was an early Internet initiative by Marleen Stikker from the Balie, with the assistance of numerous xs4all hackers. Users could get a free e-mail address and Web site. The system was launched in January 1994 in a trial run and proved an enormous success. At its peak, some fifty thousand people participated. The Waag Society, located in the Waag on Amsterdam's Nieuwmarkt Square is one of many DDS offshoots. I was also involved in the original early phases of this initiative and through thick and thin published many articles about DDS right up until its passing.[18] The choice of a city metaphor was a conscious one, and expressed the wish back then that the very technical and boyish Western Internet could mirror the compact diversity of the global intersection that is Amsterdam.

The Digital City ran relatively well for five years, despite financial problems. Finally, a long overdue attack of dotcom fever put an end to this colorful gathering of virtual communities and individual online projects. One of the surprising aspects of DDS was the way local information and debates and international usage all crossed paths. With the disappearance of DDS, the discussion concerning urbanism and the Internet effectively ended. The local Internet initiatives of today are preoccupied with establishing wireless networks in neighborhoods. A site like www.amsterdam.nl is run only by local people. This has been, for the most part, the international trend as well (for example, www.berlin.de). Most of the local Internet systems that evolved in the 1990s have collapsed or fallen by the wayside. Various policies, such as "digital empty lots" have come and gone, but could easily happen again with the whole new creative industries hype. These kinds of myopic policies may support a few projects but in the end, they do not result in any long-term initiatives. However, a trend that has become a reality is that of writing in one's own language. The fear that the Dutch language would disappear and that everyone would end up communicating in English has not panned out at all. The breakthrough of blogs somewhere around 2004 has led to an enormous broadening of native-language usage resulting in a rise of a Dutch (or rather Dutch-language) Internet.[19]

More Songs about Buildings and Blobs

Architecture and urban development continue to find themselves in a twentieth-century discursive space characterized by a closed celebrity system with strict peer assessment verification at the front door. The internal media system where the real masters (mostly men) present themselves consists of discussions that largely devolve around questions of cost, presentations at schools and institutions, exhibitions that include catalogues, and to a lesser degree, journals where critics can comment on a specific architect's work. It is remarkable that since the establishment of the public Internet some ten to fifteen years ago, no authoritative list, newsgroup, Web site, portal, or blog has developed where contemporary global architecture and urban development is regularly discussed,[20] despite the fact that there has been plenty to talk about and plenty of debate as well. This scene has failed to develop not because of some paralyzing consensus, but quite the contrary. It is still astonishing that this rich tradition, certainly in the Netherlands, has isolated itself to such an extent from the available innovative communications media and continues to assume an aloof and conservative position. ArchiNed, the Dutch Internet portal, represents a prime example of this posture. This informational portal has little more than journalistic pretensions. A long-term (online) intellectual debate would necessarily have to assume an international character and appear in English. Even the former (bilingual) journal *Archis* (now called *Volume*), whose editor-in-chief Ole Bouwman tried to keep up with the latest Internet developments, failed to establish a long-term discussion forum. The strength of Dutch architectural discourse is its self-reflection, which is also its weakness. The stronger the discipline, the harder it is to look outside and work on a trans-disciplinary level. While architecture is the most important intellectual discipline with an international character in the Netherlands, it has failed to find an Internet equivalent. This is actually a general problem that is not specific to the Netherlands, but this argument cannot be used as an excuse. As is so often the case, Google represents the search order trend. When we type in "Internet" and then "architecture," we repeatedly end up at "network architecture." This is also an interesting, albeit technical, subject but not the one for which we were searching.

According to Dutch architecture theorist Wim Nijenhuis, for Holland everything changed in the 1990s when neo-liberalism took over and the construction sector started to flourish.[21] The few architects who reached world fame with their ideas started to earn large amounts of money through the realization of their projects. The positions that architects articulate, says Nijenhuis, are media-focused and no longer derive from intellectual debates. Today's key concepts seem to be operationality, realization, acquisition, and public relations. From now on, Dutch architecture has to operate within the "economy of attention" paradigm. Whether it concerns theoretical projects or actual designs, without media coverage the architect's position may be endangered. Theory has to support their superior position. Consequently, related questions such as the Internet and broader social changes in society have been marginalized. A critical culture, such as existed in the 1970s and 1980s, is no longer supported. How architecture should relate to media theory is perceived as too complex a question because it is seen as irrelevant to the clients and the commissions that make decisions regarding design.

One would think that in a country where the architecture discipline not only has such a long tradition but also gained hegemonic status inside its own culture as the dominant global practice of the Netherlands, critical theory would be seen as a crucial component of the current success. This is not the case. Architecture theorists in the Netherlands are becoming an endangered species. If a publication goes beyond the anecdotal stage of the anthology, there is no longer a market for it. A case in point here is the Ph.D. thesis of Wim Nijenhui. It deals with the theory and history of urban planning and extensively elaborates the theses of Paul Virilio about urbanism, war, and communication technology. To date, it has been completely neglected in the Netherlands.

Granted, things are not that great on the Internet side either. This no-longer-so-minty-fresh medium has gone into a kind of postspeculative phase since its first slump in 2001–2002. This means that, among other things, terms like *cyberspace* and *virtual space* have ended up tossed into the dustbin forever. While architecture seemed to find itself more and more in virtuality, the Internet culture was becoming more and more real. That Deleuze turned the virtuality–reality notion into hype did nothing to help resolve some of the problems surrounding this bipolarity. Cultural curiosity shifted from the speculative 1990s, when everything still seemed possible (the virtual), to the cold and cynical reality of the post-9/11 period, which has become dominated by phenomena like reality television.[22] We know by now that nearly anything can be simulated on a computer. But what is even more spectacular than the virtually impossible is the clash with reality, which is established and interpreted by numerous media producers. The virtual 3D worlds of computer games have been opened up to its many fans and users. In the meantime, the Internet train roars further down the tracks, and under the code name of Web 2.0 has taken on a new shape with the development of blogs, RSS-feeds, wikis, podcasting, and the attention economy.

"Computers make the impossible aspects of architecture possible," Ken Sakamura proposes. What Sakamura's quote nicely illustrates is the aspect that the computer works in the service of architecture and not the other way around. The computer facilitates a metamorphosis of the profession and construction. However, this process does not lead to any essential adaptations. The development process becomes more pleasurable, producing plans becomes an automated process, but it does not go much beyond that. The influence computers could have as a network remains undiscussed and that goes for virtual theoreticians such as Greg Lynn, Brian Massumi, and Markos Novak as well.

According to Wim Nijenhuis, "blobarchitecture" is in danger of becoming a style, an architectural sculpture that is hooked on the ever-expanding possibilities offered by computer software. The blobs are an art form that would love to be avant-garde, knowing well that in this posthistoric era such a status can no longer be claimed. Occupying a position between many others, this architecture style has to defend itself and self-promote, says Nijenhuis. The "primacy of the visual" (the title of a book by Dutch critic Camiel van Winkel) is something that architects have to take into account. If you have no visibility, you do not exist. Nijenhuis agrees that we know very little of the relation between urban planning and networks but points to the work of Professor Luuk Boelens who works inside the city planning department of Utrecht University. Boelens researches the relationship between the communication networks and the city on the level of finance and planning regimes. He promotes new approaches in urbanism that deal with the hypermobility of money and power, approaches that question traditional institutions, including the political. He states that we have to move from government to governance, from the institutions to the actors in the field. In the great play of influencing the urban and regional development, the role of design is to influence the networks that actually decide.

In a recent Dutch newspaper article, architecture critic Bernard Huisman described the blobarchitecture movement as "neo expressionistic."[23] The main characteristic would be "the sculptural." This is odd, says Nijenhuis, "as with one stroke major differences are being erased and such a variety of architects as Frank Gehry, Kas Oosterhuis, Lars Spuybroek, Liesbeth van der Pol, Onix, Neutelings/Riedijk and others find themselves suddenly categorized under this one rubric, having Mendelsohn, Wijdeveld and the Amsterdamse School as their secret sources of inspiration." This, according to Nijenhuis, should be read as a test of art history whether it is still able to draw these architects, no matter how diverse they are, inside its categories. One has to understand that architects are not particularly happy with such a move because other, more authentic, motivations are neglected.

And the Fourth Little Piggie Made His House Out of Electrons

The way to move out of the grip of art history is to move into urban planning. Concerning this move into urbanism, iconoclastic idea lab and architecture firm MVRDV recently seems to have taken up an equal position as Constant and Archigram did in the past. Although a lot of thinking about the relation between the networks and the city has been focusing on the work of these two, in *Km3: Excursions on Capacity* MVRDV makes the argument for a return to radical utopianism, even referring to the works developed by Soviet engineers under Stalin. What we see here is an attempt to play with the logic of the media in speeding up the circle of fashion in image and theory. This results in an acceleration (and trashing) of ideas and concepts not yet seen in the architecture discipline. It is likely that, together with the message, their own brand is brought to the attention of potential clients by shooting off some controversial viewpoint with a theme that is somewhat against the current.[24]

Utopian thought has a considerable power of fascination. Students pick up radical utopianism as a trend and start dreaming of being radical themselves in order to realize large projects. It is not hard to see this mechanism at work. But we are twenty years into postmodernism and all ethics today are anti-utopian. Designers cannot be fuelled by utopian ideas of 30 or 40 years ago. We see then that these ideas remain circulating inside large heavily insulated and slow-moving institutions that remain unaffected. The underlying paradigm, if there is any, is the typical postmodern search for energy that can (re)fuel independent and critical architectural practices. Certainly in the case of MVRDV, one could say that such architecture is in a frantic search for new impulses, conflicts, and forms.

Let's go back to the Internet as the Netherlands enters the age of gigabyte access for all. When it comes to bandwidth, we are approaching the eve of a spectacular third round. After the simple modems of the 1990s, and the ADSL and cable modems currently in use, many Dutch households will soon be hooked up directly to fiber optic networks that will provide full screen high definition television with movie image quality. Telecommunications researcher James Encks recently predicted that there would be a great revolution that would ultimately benefit the users. The big losers will be those who hold on to the past.

The impact that computer networks and telecommunications have on environmental planning does not necessarily need to be interpreted literally. Quite the contrary, the infrastructural aspect often has little to say about the nature and extent of utilization. The importance of user cultures over the past few decades has become clear. Merely having a link, however, does not reveal much. Connection speed is also not an accurate indication of an online culture. What really matters is the density of social links.[25] The time someone spends online, or the number of gigabytes one downloads does not reveal much about the quality of the interaction. They could just be downloading Hollywood films; you cannot object to it, but this in itself does not herald an alternative media culture. If the Internet was nothing more than an extrapolation of the daily newspaper, film, radio, and television, then there would be nothing new under the sun, and we would not need to discuss this any further. The recycling of old content that is reheated online is a good indication of the integration of the Internet into our society, but is not particularly innovative.

The point that I am making has little to do with actual computer use by architects but does emphasize their sometimes rudimentary understanding of Internet, reducing this rich and layered environment to a mere tool. Again, we turn to Jennifer W. Leung, who informs us about actual cultures of use:

> Architects email, upload to wikis and ftp sites; we have websites for branding, linking, advertising, polemicizing, false flattery, and representing our work. The omissions regarding our commissions speak to intellectual property protection on the client's or our own behalf, the perceived limitation of the effectiveness of the Internet as an infrastructure of formal and informal communication, and the incongruity of scales and metrics which manifest as large file size and poor resolution.

Believe it or not, even architects Google! Leung says:

> Because we are not searchable by specialty, ideology, relationship to technology and form-making, or even fees, the website is rarely the site of first contact; though it is almost always the second. Often, we are "looked up" when we have exchanged business cards, have been referred or linked to, have appeared at a lecture, party, in a magazine or online discussion, or have work on other websites. In this sense, perhaps the web exacerbates the need for name recognition. On the other hand, it is not true of architects that we don't exist if we cannot

be found on Google. In addition to what we choose to upload or make public, architects engage, often laboriously, in data mining.

Considering the undeveloped potential of the network society, it is better to see the current disciplines for what they are. From an Internet politics perspective, it does not make sense to keep begging the big disinterested architects and stressed out politicians for attention. This is also true for mass media—radio, television, and newspapers—they all see the Internet as a competitor, and rightly so. Now that the strategies of belittling and ignoring have failed, and the Internet as mass medium has earned its right to exist, it no longer makes any difference whether the Dutch cultural elite ignores or embraces it. This makes it possible to ask questions about how the Internet and urban development can ultimately be linked. Of course, there could be online participation. There have been campaigns to stop the (further) expansion of Schiphol Airport and, meanwhile, other local citizen groups can better prepare themselves for the next IJburg urban development project.[26] But there are also other possibilities. I believe that there is, for instance, plenty of potential for someone to develop his or her own plans for a home or apartment (autoCAD for all), develop new building materials, and manage the costs of construction.

Complex building components can be produced elsewhere in the world and shipped by container to some Dutch polder destination, where it would be unfolded and pieced together. Without going to the extreme where everyone is his or her own contractor, we can also foresee residents[27] eliminating the architect as an important go-between and, in the future, approaching local governments directly to submit their designs for tests based on structural regulations and fire safety. Naturally, houses can also be built elsewhere in this manner. The idea that the Dutch will want to build their homes with the "4-wheel drive next to their own scaffolding"[28] in this expensive, densely populated, cold, and swampy land seems to be a bit of an old-fashioned notion to me. It is already possible to build your own house with a DIY kit at a comfortable distance from your neighbors, without actually having to be there yourself. Banality knows no borders. If they are prohibited by the Van Toorns from building what they want, the highly networked Dutch simply click on a new location. Let it be in Turkey or somewhere in Africa then. What I am describing here is not a futuristic scenario but a development that has already been going on for some time. Now it is not just about that second home in France. That *passé* region is left to the postwar generation. There is plenty of room in the world. Petroleum prices are the limit then. The democratization that occurred in the 1960s is now emerging as a reality because of technical methods. This goes way beyond "involvement" and "participation" for so-called "residents." Unabated individualization, combined with privatized public housing, will only continue to threaten further the visual uniformity of the row house. Those who thought that the final battle of the 20th century would be one between Spuybroek and the modernist housing corporations were very wrong. Before you know it, NOX software will be applied to the lifestyle of the masses.

The Dutch "architect without a title," Job Goedhart, a squatter from the Weijers generation, sees himself first and foremost as a builder–contemplator. After years of working as a carpenter and furniture builder, specializing in kitchens and flower stalls, in the 1990s he became a digital developer of constructions that are made of standard construction elements,[29] "Going from the physical to the meditative qualities of manual labour, moving mentally towards a conceptual, virtual plan," as he likes to describe it. Goedhart's process involves viewing the structure as it exists in the computer from every possible physical angle. It can be sent in a number of formats, such as a list of all its constituent parts, a blueprint, a visualization (a line drawing or a color/data rendering), or a walk-through animation. The results are then saved as a PDF and sent to the client and customer, and are used to determine prices. This is commonly followed by a presentation in the form of a printed blueprint with samples of the materials before the job is contracted out. Goedhart observes, "I wouldn't call what I do assembling because it really does involve producing a design. No matter how much use I make of standard elements the largest portion of a model is made up of new materials."

Goedhart: "Not unlike in the realm of sexuality, construction has moved from the physical and material plane to a virtual plan." He observes that there is currently a great deal being built on computers.

> If you have the time and/or money there are an almost unlimited number of possibilities. A building like the ING House (the so-called "Petty Thief") in Amsterdam's Zuidas (southern axis) district can no longer simply be interpreted as just a building because it is actually an industrial design. It could also be seen as a waste of design efforts if this ends up being just some one-off project. It would seem more logical to produce and sell this kind of high-tech accommodation on an industrial scale. Then you'd have to deal with having to spot a couple of Petty Thieves in Shanghai as part of the bargain. Whether one considers that a good thing is a matter of taste, and maybe a question of morality if you were to apply a set of environmental standards to this industrial product.

Goedhart also treats software as a tool.

> From an evolutionary standpoint, it is what has contributed to mankind's current status. The development of tools (machinery, industry)

has brought mankind to where it currently stands. The question is now what kind of data or material is being reworked by software. They are basically only placeholders, representatives of materials that are being manipulated by our software to then later—via a blueprint or a list of necessary components—materialise en place at the construction site. The software puts us in a position that enables us to sell the draft commercially using polished (multimedia) presentations. A new 3-D printer will be introduced shortly. It is a sort of upside-down laser scanner that allows a data cloud to materialise in the very shapes and colours the designer has elicited from the computer. This will mark the moment when the revolution becomes a fact.

However, the printer Goedhart is describing has been used by the auto industry for years. For Goedhart, the revolution will finally have arrived only when every telecommunications worker like himself has one of these on his or her desk.

The democratization of computer-generated design begs the moral question of whether everything that *can* be designed, should be *allowed* to be built. Goedhart observes:

> You will have to decide per project whether a design should or shouldn't be built. Hasn't that actually always been the practice anyway? Whether it be the Aesthetic Commission, the Building Commission, environmental effects reports, the involvement procedures or the zoning plans, there are brakes applied at every juncture of the image-producing capacity of the Dutch design world.

He wonders whether there is not some kind of demand for stronger regulations hidden behind that question. "Are today's regulations too vague? Do they cover the entire spectrum? Have we forgotten something? Or is it all just a veiled complaint about excessive regulations in the built-up world of the Netherlands?"

Goedhart believes that the question highlights the difference between "designer" and "engineer," the two poles in architecture. "The designer focuses on form, colour, and expression, while the engineer is concerned with the technical and procedural aspects. The easy-going, communicative, creative 'designer' with his paint box stands face-to-face with the typical techno-nerd 'engineer' with her AutoCAD programme. If they work well together they can both learn a lot from each other." It remains unclear, however, whether this synthesis process is as easy as 1, 2, 3. Much could be gained if the education system were to make use of an integrated, interdisciplinary approach. The curriculum would have to be adapted in close consultation with those in the profession. But does that mean that the insulated profession of architect will be under review? In any case, the coming design revolution will stir up plenty of dust and cause for complaint by the culture pessimists who can then rail against the bad taste of the intercultural online masses.

For some concluding ideas, let's switch to New York where architect Marisa Yiu has been working on an experiment called Chinatown Work. Together with Eric Schuldenfrei, Yiu realized an interactive installation on Canal Street to raise public participation and awareness around post-9/11 labor and work politics in Lower Manhattan. According to Yiu, one should not only focus on the form makers and celebrity architects. The use of Internet might have more potential when we look into social engagement. How can architecture, design, technology, and the public intersect with civic issues and raise questions that could help with planning or revitalization of areas in need? Yiu says:

> It is true the architecture scene is dominated by certain figures; however there are many other types of architects and non-profit organizations that operate differently in the service to the public or humanity. Just look at organizations that have put together competitions right after the tsunami in Thailand and Indonesia, or how some magazines put a call out to the public to submit designs for new types of houses relating to the hurricane Katrina devastation.

The examples of 9/11 and Katrina prompted Yiu to say, "perhaps architecture and the Internet can only be powerfully integrated when catastrophes or disasters occur."[30]

The change, as is so often the case, will have to come from education. Steffen Lehmann, architecture professor at the University of Newcastle, Australia, writes about the current discussions regarding how best to teach digital design:

> I believe, in a post-digital era, we simply use whatever tool is most appropriate for the job. However, we need to rethink how we engage with digital design in a more meaningful way and not limit ourselves by the capacity of some software applications. The use of the computer needs to be grounded in direct experiences, in a human-centered way, beyond the production of rendered images. Our explorations need to reflect on the dramatic transformations in the nature of work, that is, the speed in which we handle information. Work has shifted from paper processing to knowledge brokering, which affects the shape of our cities, and this is where the Internet comes into play. A worry for me in this respect is the emerging Spectacle City. I am thinking here of my recent visits to Dubai and Abu Dhabi, but also Darling

Harbour in Sydney. There, the authentic working harbor completely vanished and was turned into a dull Landscape of Consumption.[31]

Lehmann is confident that the computer will be crucial in achieving sustainable urban design, and this will probably be the most important influence on architecture and planning since the Industrial Revolution.

New York architect Jennifer W. Leung is seeing the first signs of change.

Architects are only beginning to experiment with script writing in the framework of proprietary software—AUTOLisp, RHINOLisp, Turtle Graphics, etc., or writing their own software programs—as in the maturation of datascaping into coding as MVRDV software: Climatizer™, Regionmaker™, Function Mixer.™ Scripting, as other programming, involves the extensive design of systematic limits, whether this involves formal iterations driven by algorithms, or various efficiency models of cost and performance.

Leung asks, is this packaging of strategy, method, and controlled randomization the first in a series of what will become an infinity of architectural plug-in software or a new form of consultancy? She writes, "The absence of an end user group or refusal to go open source would likely forestall this. But it suggests that the ideality of universal form will shift to claims about best methods, adjudicated by number of downloads or hits."[32]

Home Again, Home Again, Jiggety Jig

The conclusion of this story is not that everyone will become an artist and that with the online dissemination of building know-how, the world will become a more livable—or for that matter, a more beautiful—place. Not everyone has the ambition to build or own his or her own home. But architecture, as a distinguished old profession, has lost its claim that it knows what is best for the people. That people have taken the mouse or graphics tablet in their own hands to make their own drawings comes as no surprise. The urban development ruins left behind or abandoned and detonated by the twentieth century say plenty about the moral bankruptcy of architecture. It will be left to future historians to give an accurate portrayal of this drama. Nevertheless, an impressive array of interesting design practices and styles exists today. We are in the middle of a revolution involving new building materials. Nor is the profession sitting still, either.

And yet, architecture is too often nothing more than a strange spacecraft that has landed on a devastated landscape à la Bilbao and Berlin. "Architecture" appears, just like all other social phenomena, under the constellation of the media spectacle. The phenomenon of DIY building on the Internet has happened in the shadow of the stagnating mass media. "Middlemen" are being scrapped from the budget, as is the case everywhere. Chances are that the architect's guild may well react in a heavily reactionary and conservative way to this development.

Against the neglect within Dutch architecture of media and network issues, one could pose the question of how can innovative, subversive, and obstinate architectonic principles be poured into new software? How can the unpredictable form become the most likely option? It can clearly end up being that the "variations within a standard" are nonetheless disappointingly small. Technology does not automatically lead to "wild living."[33] For that we need advanced and differentiated user cultures. The tastes of the average Internet user are quite distorted. The villa with a swimming pool, a garage plus a dock for the boat is the basic starting point for many designs. Still, that is a dramatic advance over the cardboard box-like chicken shacks where people are still being forced to live. It is especially galling that the all-too-Dutch conglomerate of banks, pension funds, building contractors, corporations, and real estate types dare to ask 300,000 euros or more for these houses. By destroying this alliance of power brokers, architecture's position could be that it chooses the side of the Internet users. For example, they could engage the copyright topics that Creative Commons so clearly addresses. On the other hand, will they remain, as they have in the past, on the side of the established order of capital and clients? This choice concerns the establishment of a contagious variety of "best practice" models. The menu of styles could be nearly infinite in variety. Long live architectural freedom. This might lead to a bandwagon effect, so that the *rapaille* or lumpen proletariat begins to copy innovative designs. If this does not end up being the case, then there will once again be a call by the elite for more regulations so that they can remain on top of the heap.

CHAPTER 5

Indifference of the Networked Presence[1]
On Internet Time

We don't just want airtime, we want all the time all of the time.

—Refused, Liberation Frequency

Time, time, what is time? Swiss manufacture it. French hoard it. Italians squander it. Americans say it is money. Hindus say it does not exist. Do you know what I say? I say time is a crook!

—Peter Lorre in *Beat the Devil*, directed by John Huston, written by Truman Capote

The Theory

From an Internet perspective, it is banal to complain about the danger of a "global time regime." The Internet is here to stay; understanding its architecture is necessary if we are to make it serve us, rather than enslave us—there is no negation without knowledge. Paul Virilio was right when he said that we no longer live in local time as we did in the past, when we were prisoners of history. We now live in the age of global time. We are experiencing an epoch, which for Virilio is equivalent to a global accident. As Virilio points out,

> …this is the way I interpret simultaneity and its imposition upon us, as well as the immediacy and the ubiquity, that is, the omnipresence of the

information bomb, which, at the moment, thanks to the information (super)highways and all the technological breakthroughs and developments in the field of telecommunication, is just about to explode.[2]

Stefan Heidenreich observed that thus far the Internet is seen as a timeless environment. A good example of this would be Google's search results—they fail to mention the time when documents have appeared on the Web. Heidenreich predicts a paradigmatic change toward a time-embedded Internet.[3]

Doug Kellner provides a concise summary of Virilio's theses on time and the Internet:

> Cyberspace, Virilio claims, supplies another space without the usual space-time coordinates that generates a disorienting and disembodying form of experience in which communication and interaction takes place instantaneously in a new global time, overcoming boundaries of time and space. It is a disembodied space with no fixed coordinates in which one loses anchorage in one's body, nature, and social community. It is thus for Virilio a dematerialized and abstract realm in which cybernauts can become lost in space and divorced from their bodies and social world.[4]

Note that Paul Virilio rarely speaks of computer networks or the Internet in particular, let alone of browsers, instant messaging, games, search engines, VoIP, or blogging. Critics from Virilio to Žižek have locked themselves up in a general jargon of 1990s metaphors such as cyberspace, information highway, and disembodiment, terms that are first related to the offline virtual reality discourse and it is exactly these mythological terms that have helped bring us to such an apocalyptic mood while reading contemporary theory. Instead of countering skeptical thought with similarly uninformed techno-optimism, it is my proposal to look into the time regimes under which today's Internet users are actually operating.

Italian theorist Franco Berardi (Bifo), in one of his more pessimistic moods, sees the problem

> that the rhythms of the technological mutation are a lot faster than those of the mental mutation. Hence the expansion of cyberspace is incommensurably faster than the human brain's capacity to expand and adapt (to cybertime). We can increase the length of time an organism is exposed to information, but experience can't be intensified beyond a certain limit. Acceleration provokes an impoverishment of experience, given that we are exposed to a growing mass of stimuli that we can't digest in the intensive modes of enjoyment and knowledge.[5]

For Bifo, the very slowness of emotion is transformed little by little into a commodity, "an artificial condition that can be exchanged for money. Time is scarce; time can be exchanged for money. Time, an indispensable dimension of pleasure, is cut into fragments that can no longer be enjoyed." Instead of indulging in such undisputable downward trends, I propose practice of the art of going nowhere. We have all had experiences of getting lost amid all the open windows and applications on our computer screens, search queries that lead nowhere, e-mails from friends that got stuck in spam filters, the dead links to closed-down Web sites and disappeared blogs. Instead of conservative complaints about the downfall of civilization due to new media, psychogeography teaches us how to morph lost time into an endless source of imagination and subversion.

The Praxis

Let's look into the case of Timi, a self-proclaimed Internet junkie who wrote me about her recent online experiences.

> I enjoy spending time on the Net. From emailing to researching to playing or just plain googling. I like hanging around in this virtual world. I often miss it, and in the past few years, I couldn't pry myself away from it. First thing I do in the morning is go online. The last thing I do before going to bed is go offline. I've never really devoted too much analysis about my own Internet time, though.[6]

This is what German media theorist Wolfgang Hagen describes as *Gegenwartsvergessenheit*, forgetting the presence, or *topical amnesty* as he also calls it.[7] Repeatedly media make themselves invisible. Despite free and open source software, the computer as experience provokes blind tactics. We get lost in a technical environment, characterized by highly precise transmissions of choices.

But let's go back to Timi:

> I'm basically always online. At home, the TV might be on, or I might be cooking, but I remain online. Whether I'm studying or on vacation, time on the Internet is vital for me. I find it difficult not to be online. My Internet time is now so intertwined in my daily life that when my husband and I moved to a new house and were disconnected from the Net, I personally felt "lost" and disconnected from the world. Distress and panic come close to the feeling. Impatience, too and a great curiosity about who had tried to contact me.

What is lacking here, as Hagen would say, is *living presence* (*lebendige Gegenwart*).

What most critics cannot comprehend is the media's indifference to today's users. They classify individuals into two categories: users are either complicit or victims and even those who work for the system are also victims. Against this image of the Machine that overwhelms its subjects, I propose the "calculating citizen"[8] who builds a harness around his or her daily life in order to cope with the ever-growing demands of society to perform, participate, and communicate. The resource in this context is not money but time (and, as we all know, time is money). What is calculated here is the time spent with certain media devices. Getting lost in the media sphere does not stand in opposition to strict time management. It is sometimes a luxury to get lost and the data dandies that can freely stroll around the Internet are the ideal netizen-prosumers.

No matter how sexy or horrible we judge time management, there is no simple synthesis of the local with the global. Nowhere do we get a better picture of how workers struggle with different time zones than in the IT outsourcing industry. Once a week, in California, a friend explains how his wife, Beth, a project manager, holds a 7 a.m. telephone meeting.

> The people in Germany are zoning out because it's 4 o'clock, and those in Singapore are exhausted because it's 10 at night. For Beth it's the crack of dawn, she is half asleep and sitting there in her pajamas trying to wake up over a cup of tea... everyone is tired, but it's the only time where everyone can talk at once. It's one of those odd irreducible facts that technology can't really remove for the sake of efficiency—the diurnal cycle of the human animal.

Rachel Konrad reports about a Silicon Valley company that collaborates with partners in India. At the end of the working day in California,

> managers move into a conference room to dial India, where engineers twelve and a half time zones ahead are just arriving in Hyderabad. As colleagues on opposite sides of the globe discuss circuit board configurations and debugging strategies for a project code-named "Doppelganger," it's just the start of another endless day for the company. Within twelve hours, Indian workers will end their day with calls and e-mails to California, where managers in the Santa Clara headquarters will just be waking up. "We keep passing the baton between California and India, and that way we can cram a lot more work into a 24-hour period," said Jeff Hawkey, vice president of hardware engineering, who conducts evening meetings from the office or on his laptop at home. "A lot of nights, I go home, tuck the kids into bed and then get on the conference call."

Take Bombay-based consulting powerhouse Tata Consultancy Services which employs 42,000 workers worldwide, including 14,000 people in India who handle projects from the United States. Their shifts are from 7 a.m. to 3 p.m. or 2 p.m. to 10 p.m. local time, not including frequent early or late meetings with overseas clients. The human cost of the fifty-plus hour workweeks are becoming apparent. "It's one thing to do it for a couple weeks, but it's another to put up with this pain in the neck permanently," Konrad is told. "When executives talk about the efficiencies of offshoring, they're often not factoring in the long-term human toll on management."[9]

In *Fast Boat to China, Lessons from Shanghai, Corporate Flight and the Consequences of Free Trade* (2006), Andrew Ross visits the Shanghai Pudong Software Park cafeteria where Chinese programmers, project managers, and engineers meet for lunch. There he met Emiy Zhang. She spoke of how the young generation finds working hard important. Bodies get run down and have to be toned and recharged at the gym. She said that visiting the park in the late evening is the way of seeing what the park is all about. She is often at work until 10 p.m. and the company pays for a car to take her home. Workweeks of seventy or eighty hours are normal in this industry. But the nightshift, says Ross,

> was something quite specific. The employees in many of these offices were doing business process outsourcing (BPO) for clients in other time zones. The timing of their work shifts was a significant factor in the development of a project or delivery of a service that required global input on a daily basis. ...It is in this environment, where clients who called the shots could be in Sydney, Singapore, Yokohama, London or Chicago, the standard nine-to-five workday was a rapidly vanishing luxury. If they were very lucky, employees might still only put in a forty-hour week—they just may not know which forty hours they would be working.[10]

Several years back I published an online polemic against Swiss watch company Swatch's intention to launch their own Internet time standard.[11] Ignoring the developers' community, and Internet users in general, this corporation tried to push through a proprietary time standard! It failed miserably. Swatch Time is still around,[12] and has even been installed by a number of Web sites but it was never endorsed by hackers or early adaptors. Most would not even know it exists. Whereas blogs have bizarre collections of banners and additional functionalities on the left and the right columns, the Swatch Time applet is curiously missing, and rightly so. What is needed is not Global Standard Time, a "One Time," but rather enhanced global time awareness. Are you aware of people in Brazil right now? Are they still asleep, having breakfast, or are they out on the town because it is evening in Sao Paolo? It is this time knowledge—combined with sensitivity for cultural differences—that counts if you are participating in online collaborations. A growing number of sites are now announcing their local time, which is extremely useful if you collaborate with a large variety of people, dispersed over the planet.[13]

Complaints about global time often come from theorists who fail to distinguish between radio and television on the one hand and the Internet on the other. The real-time regime to which they refer is actually live global television events that use satellite uplinks.[14] Strictly speaking we have already left the real-time era when BBC News announced that it installed delay technology to monitor incoming live news feeds. From now on "live" television can be controlled without viewers being aware of it. This move happened in response to the uncensored broadcasting of the bloody Beslan school siege in Russia conducted by Chechen fighters in 2004.

Media philosophy professor Sybille Krämer, who recently ran a marathon, told me: "If you're not jogging, you lack time; if you exercise, you do have time." Obviously our experience of time is subjective and the objective time measuring a mere convention. Mastering techniques that allow one to experience the sense of having more time is linked to quality of life considerations. However, what I have witnessed over the course of 10 to 15 years of online experience is not time shortage but time indifference. This is a quality of life one learns to appreciate. Most users complain about the computer eating up time instead of empowering them to arrange their lives freely. Colleagues I know typically spend up to five hours responding to their e-mail, and then wonder what they have accomplished. But there are solutions for this most modern feeling of discomfort.

The answer to time panic is not, as personal development gurus like Anthony Robbins and David Allen suggest, to make lists and prioritize. A similar New Age guru, Steve Pavlina, suggests: "The real gains in time management are realized at the top, not the bottom. If your high-level strategic decisions are based on an inaccurate understanding of reality, then your mission, goals, projects, and actions will be virtually meaningless in the grand scheme of things. All of your accomplishments will be little more than busywork."[15] Agreed, Steve. What then is the reality of the Internet? What if distraction is the ruling principle and not efficiency? The "temps perdu" is not noticed immediately and the indifference is not there from the start. One starts to take notice only after a while when sessions can be identified. The online session is perhaps the best time unit to express what time on the Internet could look like. Think of more sessions happening simultaneously, such as chatting, talking on Skype, surfing MySpace, watching videos, following blog links, reading and answering incoming e-mails, and conducting a search. When you are online all the time (with a DSL broadband Internet connection), it is the bundle of these never-ending sessions that defines the Internet experience.

The better we understand the architecture of certain media, its interfaces, and programs, the less time we have to spend with it and can then drift off in conversational spaces, either technically mediated or with people around us in "real life." The problems, however, are numerous—security threats, companies that force us to upgrade their software, hardware that breaks down. On average, every three years users purchase a new computer. If this high circulation did not occur, chances are much more likely that we would drift farther, and in an unconscious manner. Now we are constantly barraged by e-mails that warn us to download the latest anti-virus definition and software patch.

The time spent interacting with media needs to be understood in terms of three distinctly different activities. The first involves the time needed to configure the machine, install, learn, and operate the software, and to become familiar with the tools for navigation. The second is the time spent with certain application-related content such as blogs, e-mail, SMS, and iPods. Only after we have downloaded all the e-mail, checked intranets, and blogs do we then enter the third activity, the flat, eternal time of pure communication—be it with humans or machines. Techno-illiterate intellectuals have little knowledge about the difference between the meta-instruction of the machine and the flows of interaction once the connection or application is up and running. The calculating citizen[16] has an efficient handle on the first activity and, subsequently, a great abundance of the second and third activities. Indeed, it is a pleasure when we leave the world of stark necessity behind and drift off to enter the buzzing sphere of floating data.

In the attention economy,[17] value is measured in the amount of time you happen to spend with any given media object or person. This can be a Web site, watching your favorite show on television, text messaging a friend, talking on the phone, or blogging about the concert you attended last night. For a long time the attention economy remained a hyped-up concept, launched during the speculative 1990s to point to the shift from the production of tangible goods to immaterial services. The point that makes attention such an interesting commodity is the fact that it is so scarce. As Michael Goldhaber writes in his 1996 Principles of the New Economy: "Attention is scarce because each of us has only so much of it to give, and it can come only from us—not machines, computers or anywhere else."[18] Attention is another way of saying "time," as in "where I choose to spend my time."[19]

However, that was ten years ago. Attempts are now under way to lay the foundation for an actual Web-based attention economy. This is happening as one of numerous initiatives in the Web 2.0/blogosphere realm. The attention technology builds on recent experiences and developments with XML, RSS-feeds, del.iou.us, furl archives (link collections that people share publicly), and so on. The next development is that users would make the information about the time they visited a site available to others. Because of serious and systematic abuses of privacy by governments and corporations, users have been reluctant to share data related to their surfing behavior. The attention economy heats up once users start trading this type of information and sell the meta-data of their surf behavior to interested parties. Social Internet entrepreneurs recently set up a nonprofit foundation, Attention Trust, which will set standards and limits regarding what companies can and cannot do with the collected attention data.[20] Without trust and transparency, the attention economy, no matter how cool and geeky it might look, will not take off. The foundation has also developed its own attention recorder built in a browser to capture the click stream of the user.

Whereas the Internet as an information environment provokes observations of timelessness and is perceived as a vast space of never-ending databases and linked sites, most of its users remain locked up in the small triumphs and tragedies of their everyday lives. Trading data on how many seconds visitors might visit a particular Web page only shows how low we have sunk in terms of the exploration of micro time-related activities. Attention data, as the new currency of the time economy, may be interesting to gather from a select group of young, high-end users and professional knowledge workers. But for the most part, it would likely show how little time average users spend on the Internet. The discrepancy between colossal libraries and the limits of the short-lived individual must have existed throughout time. What makes the current data excess so pertinent is the intimacy and everlasting accessibility of such pico knowledge.

Japanese-American venture capitalist and Internet guru Joi Ito wisely keeps sensitive information about his financial deals outside of his blog. Nonetheless, it is relatively easy to trace how he integrates real world travel (in his case, Japan–United States–Europe) with his online presence. It is interesting to note how Ito became bored with his hugely successful blog. In the latter half of 2005, Ito became involved in World of Warcraft (WoW), a massive multiplayer online role-playing game. In the following blog entry, Ito describes how he juggles with different media such as a PC and cell phone.

> I'm sitting in a car on the way home from the airport after arriving in Japan from New York. I had a fourteen-hour plane trip where I

caught up on email and wrote some reports. As it has been noted, the frequency of my posts (as well as the number of blogs I read) has decreased significantly since I started playing World of Warcraft. Originally I was attributing this entirely to the addictive nature of WoW, but I wonder if I'm also slightly bored.

Ito admits to being an early adopter type.

Reflecting back on my personal early days of blogging, there was something nifty and cool coming out every week. Blogrolls, facerolls, Technorati, etc. My traffic was growing, blogs were becoming global, and it was all new… at least to me.

Ito describes in detail how applications and platforms are being consumed through the investment of time. But no matter how powerful these "killer apps" are, the nervous innovator has to move on, leaving behind one data ruin after another. After having abolished e-mail and homepages, it is now time to turn away from blogs.

Ito says:

New things continue to be developed, but more and more of the work seems to involve growing pains like scalability, oversized communities and integration of "normal people" as we cross the chasm. Also, the new consumer Internet bubble is attracting attention from non-participant investors. This is an important part of making blogs a truly ubiquitous phenomenon, but it definitely feels more and more like real work.

And work means dedicating more and more "idle time" to a technology of the past. Prime time is used for private passions, to hack the new. Ito continues:

When I was in Helsinki visiting Nokia a few days ago, I playing with my phone waiting in line and in cabs. It dawned on me that what I really want is better moblogging. Now, when I am in front of a computer connected to the Internet, I'm mostly immersed in IM (instant messaging) for business or Warcraft for fun. When I am mobile, I have idle time that I could spend reading blogs and writing to my blog. I guess this is a sign that, at least for me, blogging has moved from my primary online activity to my idle time filler.

Constantly switching between texting, blogging, gaming, and talking, Ito is in search of further optimizing his machine time. Ito: "Considering how much idle time I have with my phone, I think I could still blog at a relatively consistent rate. Also, I wish there were better ways to read and write when I am with my computer without a connection."[21]

Other Time

To me, the issue is not being online from anywhere, twenty-four hours a day, but to develop an awareness of other times. This is easier said than done. Even senior Internet scholars and high profile techies have difficulties remembering if a person on another continent is ahead or behind compared to one's own time zone. This confusion only gets worse if you start traveling overseas yourself. It still comes as a surprise to many that the maximum time difference is not twenty-four hours, but in fact only twelve hours. It is important to drop the GMT reference, which suggests that you can have up to twenty-four hours' time difference. For instance, if at Robert Hassan's little desktop World Clock it says Wed 3:43 p.m. in Melbourne and Tue 6:43 p.m. in Honolulu, this does not mean a twenty-one hour time difference but merely three. Teams in Australia and Hawaii have little trouble working together, except three days a week around Sunday, provided one takes off from work during the weekend (as once defined by the Christian church fathers).

Developing a sense for local time elsewhere starts with the abstract idea that you have to go either forward or backward in time. So, it is not global time but a shortage of time itself that is perceived as the bigger problem. You have not even started aimless surfing when you are already aborting the session because your attention has drifted off elsewhere or another technology interferes. It feels as if time reserves are drying up. Bosses in high-tech work environments are very aware of time management and can closely monitor what individual workers are doing online. New media is renowned for eating up time, the "temps perdu" caused by computer games, instant messaging, social networks, blogging, and e-mail is astonishing. The crackdown on lost time has to begin at some point. Sophisticated surveillance software already exists, not only to monitor employees, but also to sanction them. The time you use for private e-mail during work hours is automatically deducted from your monthly work time and salary.

In his *Small Pieces Loosely Joined, A Unified Theory of the Web*, David Weinberger remarks that Internet time supposedly is seven times faster than real-world time. And more important than the speed of time, on the Web you are in control of your time. Weinberger notes that Web time is threaded. He defines a thread as a set of messages on a topic. This means that conversations have two dimensions: chronological, flowing in time, and systematic, meaning not time-based. Threads bind the flux of the Web into meaningful currents and make it possible to leave a context and come back. Whereas in a real-world conversation, topics come one upon another in a hyperthreaded medium like the Web, free of the drag of space and our permission-based social structure, Weinberger says we can "unstick our interests." Weinberger, praising Heidegger, concludes that the "fundamental unit of time isn't a moment, it's a story, and the string that holds time together isn't the mere proximity of moments but our interest in the story." We should follow our hearts, not the time beat of the Machine. "The Web, unlike a communications medium, accretes value. It is the persistent sum of the stories we are telling to each other."

"Vita brevis, ars longa." Francis Bacon translated this Hippocrates aphorism as "Life is Short; Art is Long." Transferred to a contemporary context, your art outlives your life. Transposed onto the online world we could translate like this: "Art is long and Internet postings are the insects of a day." The amount of Internet sites disappearing is alarming. No medium is as unstable as the Internet. That today's chatter is stored as digital information does not mean that we can compare it to historical records. Only techno-determinists, with little experience in computer culture, state that because everything is being recorded no data will ever get lost. That is why they now suffer from information overload ("Das Leiden des jungen Bloggers" [The Sorrows of Young Bloggers]).

The Internet is not a time machine that teleports us from here to nowhere and back. Despite its public image as a "virtualizer" and an "accelerator," the Internet is still not particularly futuristic. No matter how much progress has been made, its interface and speed remain clumsy and slightly disappointing. Compared with virtual reality systems and computer games, the Internet is nearly as rudimentary as it was 10 or 15 years ago. Browsers still crash and connections still fail, no matter how much the speed has increased over the years.[22] Similar to the usability debate in the late 1990s, we can now start wondering if the measured attention was really spent on that particular content and whether we are not constantly daydreaming. This leads to the next level of reification and commodification where our unconscious looking-away and micro sleeps would be measured, ranked, and readied for sale. The construct of users as conscious persons—as people who know what they are looking for and want to get it in the shortest amount of time—remains questionable.

In *The Intelligence of Evil or the Lucidity Pact*, Jean Baudrillard writes: "Time itself, lived time, no longer has time to take place." In this pathology of postmodernity, the Internet is no doubt the epiphany of the real-time power. With regime change no longer possible, we are completely stuck. In this darkest of hours it feels like being locked-up in the Soviet Union during the 1970s. "The possible itself is no longer possible. What happens happens, and that's all there is to it." Even the event and its radical discontinuity have come to an end. "All that remains is the blatant self-evidence of actuality."[23] The problem of this outsiders' view on matters digital is its lack of irony and humor. New media are judged as perfect machines, holistic enterprises. The "notworking" is taken out of the daily experience and replaced with disgust for the perfect simulacrum.

In his essay *Time to Revolt—Reflections on Empire*, John Holloway proposes breaking "the homogeneity of time."[24] He calls for creation of a world in which "duration is shattered, in which time is not a long railway track or a slice of pizza, but tends towards the intensity of the Jetztzeit (now-time) of Benjamin or the nunc stans of Bloch, towards the timeless-time." "Bourgeois thought, of course, will have none of this. Built upon identity, upon extending what is into what will be, bourgeois thought is obsessed with labeling, with classifying, with fitting things together, with creating neat boxes, with paradigms." We need to revolt against Time itself. "Time becomes stodgy, almost solid, something that can be cut into wedges, into periods, into paradigms, a million miles removed from the timeless-time of intense love or engagement."

Instead of repeating the classic opposition of subversive living versus machine time, we can observe, experience, and shape timeless net cultures that undercut and undermine capitalistic time logic, even in the midst of nearly Orwellian surveillance systems and data tracking. In this context Robert Hassan asks,

> What kind of time do we experience online, when we get lost amid dead links, get blocked at restricted access sites, search queries that lead to who knows where? It's not clock time, and it's not Swatch time, it's a time of lags and latencies, of waiting and clicking through, of fast and slow. It is the experience of differing speeds and asynchronicity. [25]

But it is not only disruption that characterizes Internet time. We have to find a way to transpose the figure of the *flaneur* into today's world and remove it from its identity-centered context. Being online is not a lifestyle. This was a fundamental mistake of the California-based Boing-Boing/Mondo 2000 faction that dominated cyberculture for a while during the early 1990s, before *Wired* magazine massaged the aggressive business agenda into a haze of techno-libertarianism. In the Internet, to get lost is not an exception, *but the rule*. It will be hard to portray the vague user as an outsider or even a rebel. No more relocations. As Bruce Sterling states, "We have past the line of no return."[26] The "gizmofication" of the world makes it impossible to marginalize the Internet as a sandbox of micro-identities. There is no avant-garde or bohemia anymore that leads us into some radical Wonderland—only "neocrats" hold sway, the punditocracy that claims to possess knowledge of the latest and coolest functionalities.

Instead of administrating ever smaller (and larger[27]) amounts of time, it is interesting to investigate how, given the current constraints, we can step out of time, given the digital constraints of "mental capitalism" (Georg Franck). It may not be sufficient to merely criticize linear timetables or introduce the cyclical time model as a way out of time exploitation. Instead of development and progress, we would simply go around in circles—a feeling we all have anyway. It seems unavoidable to track through the "desert of the real," camp here and there for the night, without a promise of ever escaping the current time-space capsule. To provide a critical diagnostics of the chronopolitics of our times is one thing, but to inscribe alternative models into the network architectures is another matter. It is not sufficient to delegate quasi-spiritual time experiences into the private realm, a tactic that New Age leaders preach and so-called "change managers" practice. Radical time experiences should not be promoted as compensation for stressful work. Quality time does not save us from quantity misery. In addition, we should be careful not to easily adopt the language that talks of change and transformation of, in this case, time regimes. There is nothing inherently good or bad about what is coming up. What we can do is research, remember, and repeat forgotten concepts that help us overcome the unbearable lightness of real-time living. What we need are autonomous strategies: Time Management of the Self. How can we surf in style, without manifesting or glorifying the digital drift? "Self knowledge is power."[28]

CHAPTER **6**

Revisiting Sarai

Five Years of New Media Culture in India

Early in 2001, the Sarai new media center opened in Delhi, India. Soon, Sarai became famous for its high quality work and critical engagements. I have been involved with Sarai since its inception in 1998. Around the opening of Sarai in early 2001, I wrote a chapter in my previous book *Dark Fiber* about its founding and first programs. As of 2006, Sarai has gone through a phase of spectacular growth, expanding to 120 people who are part of the network of employees and fellows. Most of them are not working in the Sarai building or even in Delhi. This chapter is by no means a comprehensive overview of Sarai's activities as there is simply too much going on. I am emphasizing new media related research, knowing that Sarai's agenda is much broader than that. I will discuss my own limited selection of projects as well as the international dimension of Sarai's work.

This chapter is divided into three sections. First, I describe my visit to Sarai in late 2002. In the second part, I discuss the new projects and developments I witnessed in late 2004. In the last part, written around mid-2006, I focus on the international aspect of Sarai's work. To date, many artists from overseas have done residencies at Sarai. What was their experience and how do Sarai members deal with this growing number of travelers? I will also discuss the Dutch–Indian exchange program between Sarai and the new media center, Waag Society in Amsterdam, which secured the initial funding for Sarai and is partnering with Sarai in this program.[1] In 2004, the Dutch–Indian exchange program opened and became a platform with initiatives in Bangalore, Brazil, and Beirut. As is so often the case with new media projects, internationalization happened at an incredible pace. Sarai has developed partnerships in the cities of Hamburg, Liverpool, Vienna, and others. Sarai is not only receiving many guests from overseas, but also has an impressive international presence.

Sarai's buzz began with its eight core members—Ravi Sundaram, Ravi Vasuderan, and the three members of the Raqs Media Collective: Monica Narula, Jeebesh Bagchi, and Shuddha Sengupta.[2] Dipu (Awadhendra Sharan), who works on environmental discourse in the city, joined in 2004, around the same time as Ravikant Sharma. Ashish Mahajan joined in 2005.

Sarai is a subsidiary program of the Center for the Study of Developing Societies (CSDS). CSDS was founded in 1964, and is one of India's best-known independent research institutes with a commitment to critical social thought and democratic political values. Bringing together some of South Asia's most famous social theorists, writers, and critics such as Ashis Nandy and Rajni Kothari, the CSDS has played an important part in shaping the intellectual and creative map of South Asia. Raqs, an autonomous unit within Sarai, was originally a documentary film collective. Founded in 1991, Raqs has moved from its original focus on film into contemporary arts, exhibiting in major shows such as Documenta XI in Kassel, Germany and the 2005 Venice Biennale. The Raqs members travel a lot, but return to Delhi over the winter months when the annual Sarai journal, *Reader*, is being produced, and when conferences take place at Sarai. Ravi Sundaram and Ravi Vasuderan both worked as fellows at CSDS before Sarai started. In the front building of the compound, CSDS operates as the center, and Sarai is still a subsidiary program of CSDS. All Sarai staff touch base in August when the 40, mostly younger, people from all over India gather in Delhi to present the results of their research.

Sundaram explains the original drive behind the global aspect of Sarai's work:

Sarai has always been comfortably international, in contrast to nationalist intellectual traditions in India. This is because we recognized the logic of the new network-critique, which buried nationalist state-centered analysis for good. This comfort with international intellectual traditions has set us apart from so many others, and may account for some of our successes in collaborations and intellectual debate.

Sundaram admits that it has another side.

Success has meant too many demands internationally from a mix including well-meaning liberals, narrow counter culture Western characters, and in some cases first rate and wonderful collaborations. Demands are great. The international cultural (arts, new media, academic) economy globally loves "success." since Sarai has been represented as that it increases traffic, some of it not always easy to handle.[3]

At the same time that Sarai's profile has increased internationally, so has that of the Raqs collective, which existed well before Sarai's founding. The work of Raqs has become increasingly global while at the same time its content, strictly speaking, remains Indian. The potential tension between a sophisticated global audience and an even more sophisticated local context is hitting the surface. For instance, freelance journalists Johny ML and Mrinal asked, back in 2000,

> We do not insist that the art to be pedagogic. But when you leave the gallery you need to carry something in your mind to brood over. What does Raqs Collective give us to ruminate? Where is the critique? What does the Raqs Collective think about the malnutrition in India? What does it think about the Indian beauty industry? On what level does it wants the participants to play the game of participation? What is the computer density in India? And what percentage of the Indian populace is connected to WWW?[4]

They ask a lot. Beyond moralism and political correctness, really, what does it mean to work in a Delhi settlement one day and a European art exhibit the next? What are the challenges here? And what is my position in this, as an engaged insider and observer? Rather than leap to an immediate judgment here, instead let us get a glimpse of what it means in India today to run a politically engaged new media center with a global outreach.

In October 2002, nearly two years after Sarai started its operations, I visited the center for a second time, curious to meet the new staff and see how projects had evolved.[5] The center was a buzzing hub, full of energy. During the six days of my stay, I only got a glimpse of what was going on. Delhi, as hot and polluted as ever, was undergoing a major transformation. The construction of the subway was still under way. Due to the tense situation in Gujarat and Kashmir, Delhi felt under siege. Surveillance and control were stepped up; there were police roadblocks here and there. Politically, the week was marked by the elections in Jammu and Kashmir, which resulted in a defeat for the ruling National Conference, a partner in the Hindu nationalist BJP-led National Democratic Alliance coalition. By positioning itself off the radar, Sarai had not yet had to deal with state interference. The impression one got of Sarai was that of a dynamic cultural center where new media are center stage but not the sole denominator. Instead, what was driving Sarai was a passion for cosmopolitan intellectual debate on contemporary urban culture. The central concern of Sarai was the connection between urban culture, media, and daily life. The annually published Sarai *Reader* is proof of the strong ties to book culture. At the same time the Sarai server was, and is, host to a range of electronic mailing lists, from its own reader-list, commons-law, picturepost ("a forum to share and discuss images") to cr-india, a discussion forum on community radio in India.

At Sarai there was a weekly public screening program, using easy to obtain VHS and DVD copies of feature films and documentaries. On the program that week was an Iranian film, *Kandahar*, by Mohsen Makhmalbaf. The day I arrived, Michael Saup of ZKM, the German center for art and technology, gave a workshop that was supported by the Goethe Institute—a technological event the Institute itself could not host. In addition, there were two Australians there in residency. In the midst of it all, there were countless staff meetings. And, yes, there was the occasional electricity outage. Because of road construction, the ISDN connection to the Internet had been down for a while, but this improved later on that week.[6] One of the Sarai founders, Ravi Sundaram, said bandwidth could have been better, but that the government was holding up connectivity because of the post-9/11 security clearance of cable landings.

In the following paragraphs, we will examine some of the projects.

The Hindi Language and Computing

Ravikant Sharma, a former historian, is responsible for the language and popular culture program. Hindi is perhaps one of the largest languages in the world.[7] However, it is a pity to see that the best books on the Hindi public domain are all written in English. Experts on Hindi film only publish in English. Sharma's research looks at the implications—and possibilities—of new media for Hindi popular culture. He is the editor of the *Hindi Media Reader*, arguably the first new media publication in Hindi with commissioned articles on free software, satellite channels, and tactical media. The *Reader* also contains specific essays about the Indian context for new media. The first book in this series deals with new media theory seen from a broad context. Ravikant: "The Hindi world has been obsessed with print culture, which rose in the late nineteenth century. Related is the love for literature. But in our age there are more ways of looking at the world. Film and television now constitute language." In the Hindi context, it is important to discuss the anxiety between "high" literature and popular media. The *Hindi Media Reader* discusses the relationship between the book and the computer. Sarai wants to play a mediator role, lift the knowledge of one sphere, and transfer it into another. Ravikant knows only of a few

Indian media theorists, post-Marxist scholars, and writers who have been struggling against the dominant trend of treating audio-visual media as suspect. New media are usually seen as part of the package called "globalization."

By 2002, considerable progress had been made concerning the introduction of Hindi as a computer user language, both on the level of software interfaces and on the Internet. Still a lot of work needed to be done. Like Japanese, Hindi has its own set of characters. Programs and the keyboard required adjustment. Sharma:

> At the moment there are three levels at which work is being done. There is the font solution, in which you have to install fonts within the application you use. Then there are the dynamic fonts. Thirdly, there is the Hindi Unicode (the extended standard of ASCII), which will be the long-term solution. However, you can't use it yet for the Linux-based Star Office. Compared to open source programs, Windows has a much better support for Hindi Unicode. The BBC Hindi site has started using Unicode. You can download fonts from there, which are for free. But keyboards have not yet been adapted.

For those interested, there is a Yahoo! group that deals with Hindi and computing.[8] Lately, Linux groups in India have woken up and started to deal with the language issue. Sharma:

> I just came back from a conference in Bangalore that dealt with all the issues of standardization—mainly visited by Linux users.[9] Whatever input devices we use, we should give people choices. In India old school typists—turned DTP operators—do most of the work. Their needs should also be taken into account. Many are bi-lingual workers. But there are also those who only speak Hindi. For them we should also offer the phonetic choice at the QWERTY keyboard level.

Despite rampant nationalism, the Hindi part of the Internet is much more tolerant than one might expect. Sharma:

> We learned to live with the tension of hate sites. There are limits to what you can do against Hindi nationalists. There is such an obsession in India with the protection of the "purity" of culture. We therefore have to find ways to talk about other topics. There is always the danger that the Hindi language agenda gets hi-jacked by the guardians of cultural purity but that should not stop us from getting involved. I am hopeful. The Hindu right wing forces are losing one election after another. The ruling class is in fact not following the nationalist economic agenda.

Cybermohalla

Cybermohalla (CM) is perhaps one of Sarai's most impressive projects.[10] In May 2001 a media lab was established in a squatters' settlement called LNJP, a *basti*, next to a hospital in central Delhi. The settlement lives under the permanent threat of eviction. Bulldozers could come at any time and force the inhabitants to resettle on the outskirts of the 9 million people metropolis. The project is based in a small room nicknamed Compughar, has three computers (two of them Linux), mainly used by a group of young people, most of whom are young Muslim women. Shveta Sarda, who trained as a social worker before coming to Sarai to work on the CM project, has taken me to Compughar and translates from Hindi to English the many stories the youngsters have to tell. The co-coordinator Azra Tabassum, a lively 20-year-old, shows us around. Compughar is a self-regulated space. Tabassum looks into the everyday functioning of the lab. Monday to Saturday everyone meets from 10 to 4. There is lots of laughter—and expertise. The CM project is now well under way. The frequent visitors, most of them school dropouts, have quickly learned to master word processing (in Hindi), drawing and animation programs (Gimp), games, the digital camera, and a scanner. There is even a phone and e-mail access via a modem but the connection is not always stable. At length we discuss the use of Hindi fonts, compare chemical processed pictures with digital ones, and go through the countless animations the children and young people have made of their computer drawings.

CM is not like many digital divide projects in that its emphasis is not focused primarily on access and IT education. Unlike most telecenters, the emphasis is not on access but on raising cultural competence within the locality. Sarai, together with the non-governmental organization (NGO), Ankur (the Society for Alternatives in Education) have developed their own methodology. Ankur's philosophy is to give young people what they are deprived of in schools. Prabhat Jha, who works for Ankur, writes: "What is needed is that we be excited by innovation, but not get swept away by blind faith in it. That there be creativity, along with a critical attitude." Unlike most projects in this area, the focus is not primarily on (micro) software training. It takes courage to step outside of the development logic that IT is solely about bringing prosperity. CM is first about digital story telling. The participants go out into the narrow streets and bring back what they have heard and seen. Technical training is only one aspect. The ability to tell a story is just as important. Jha: "Within a month, the children understood that they were not doing a normal computer course." A community media memory was in the making. Sarda explains that Ankur has an extensive local, national, and international network and many visitors from that network visit CM labs on a regular basis.

This is a substantial volume. The content from Ankur circulates within this network, and critically, many invitations to CM to host workshops, make presentations, develop projects come from here. Ankur has made Cybermohalla a critical vantage point to begin rethinking the idea of critical pedagogy within the development/NGO sector.[11]

Sarda told me more about the CM methodology.

We use a variety of media forms, from wall magazines to html pages, animation, stickers and diaries (texts, audio recordings, photographs). The participants write about the basti, about the neighbourhood, they make excursions into Delhi (short walks, for instance), as well as to other cities. Excursions are often in small groups. The texts—narratives, reflections, descriptions—written individually, are shared within the group. It is through this loop of writing, readings and sharing, and very significantly, the conversations these engender, through the words and ideas that they move through, that members like Azra, Nilofer, Shamsher, Suraj, Babli, Shahana, Mehrunisa, Yashoda, and others discover and evolve the various concepts we engage with.

The conversations, Sarda explained, are critical to the process of concept making at CM. Ruchika Negi, another researcher at CM, brought into the labs through readings and discussions her own narratives about the city— narratives she was currently working on through her interactions with scavengers, people who live on the streets, who subsist on the invisible margins in the city.

Besides Sarda, there is Joy Chatterjee, a Web designer in the Sarai media lab, who provides support and shares skills in text editing and image manipulation. Also part of the team is Ashish Mahajan, who oversees the technical skill sharing for the use of low-end consumer technology (camera, Dictaphone, sound equipment, and microphones). Ravikant Sharma, involved in CM because of the Hindi language aspect, agreed that the project has a posteducational emphasis.

The mainstream understanding is that there is a direct link between technology and development. And between education and employment. We could say that at Cybermohalla these kids gain critical skills. But we should not pretend that we provide existential comfort to the people associated with us.

Sarda says:

It's not just the mainstream understanding of a link between technology and development, or between education and employment, but also the notion, a class-based bias of looking at certain peoples as culture deficits, waiting for a delivery system of ideas, words, concepts and skills, that invariably gets articulated under the garb of the language of "lack" and "empowerment." Sadly, this masks the significance of "cultural creativity," or that of users and producers contributing to and guiding (technical) innovation.

In July 2002, material was brought together in a beautifully designed, bilingual book called *By Lanes*.[12] All the children, parents, and others came to Sarai. The place had never been so packed. The Compughar group read their stories. The response of the basti community was mixed. Sharma: "There was some opposition, but now there is openness about what the women are doing. For the first time there are reports coming in from the basti citizens themselves. Before reports were usually written by outsiders." The Compughar group made an animation about the fierce debate within the basti community. "Why would the outside world be interested about the everyday life of a settlement?" some asked. The style of diary-type entries in *By Lanes* about daily life in the settlement is reflexive, poetic, and at times nostalgic, whereas, for instance, the online stories in CM's 'Ibarat' newsletter about a train journey to Mumbai are more fragmented and narrative.[13]

In the afternoon, we visited the second CM media lab in the Dakshin-puri resettlement colony in South Delhi. The lab had opened only two months ago, with Pinki as the co-coordinator. The growing group of participants was still in the process of finding out about the possibilities of the software. Both exhausted from the encounters and the long journey through town by car, Shveta and I returned to Sarai.

In an e-mail exchange a few weeks later, Shveta wrote:

> What Cybermohalla creates is a context for researchers, media practitioners, web designers, programmers—from different contexts, with our specificities, pursuits, subjectivities—to interact, to collaboratively, dialogically create and transform our own, and one another's practices through an awareness of and a critical engagement with one another, to participate in the process—as Jeebesh puts it—not as unequals. It is a dialogic reflection among peers. The processes are not determined by their ultimate purposes. Skills, forms and materials are not introduced into the labs with a fixed, predetermined purpose or instrumentality. We're not working with or within a curriculum, or "evolving" one. Otherwise where would the room exist for experimentation, or a playfulness with forms, an interrogation of these?

Sarai and the Arts

Sarai is by no means a national center only. From the beginning, it has been embedded in regional South Asian and international networks. The Raqs

Media Collective, Jeebesh, Monica, and Shuddha, are founding members of Sarai who have worked together for many years and have shown their work abroad for a long time. In 2002, Raqs had an installation at the Documenta 11 art exhibition in Kassel, Germany.[14] A year before the opening of the show, one of the platforms (D11 curator Okwui Enwezor's term for public debate) had taken place in Delhi.[15] Raqs's Documenta installation, "Coordinates of Everyday Life," consists of two parts. The video section, using a few projectors in a dark room, engaged with Delhi urban culture. Shuddha writes:

> Many hours of shooting were done over a period of one and a half years. It is 90 minutes of video material if you want to see everything. We engaged with the city in a systematic way, each week identifying an element of city life. We would then go to that particular spot and shoot. There are for instance parts taken from one shot of us in the fog, standing on a bridge at one camera angle for one and a half hours. We learned a lot from that discipline. In filmmaking you are always under the pressure to move your camera and yourself. This shift is related to our move into the arts. It is a move away from the "universal clock" of television. At the same time it is a sign of our ongoing engagement with documentary filmmaking. Before, the "clock" of television was still running in our heads. Now, there is no search for any spectacular, decisive moment. We did not look for the significant shot. In that sense creating a work for an arts context allowed us to re-engage with the documentary sensibility.

The work also looks at the law and the legal regime governing space. This forms the textual component of the work. Shuddha adds:

> Certainly the presence of rules and regulations in urban space has increased dramatically. The first piece that you see in the installation is the law on land rights, dating back to the 19th century. It defines what is property in land. What matters here is not so much the codification as such but its precise articulation in today's context through regimes of surveillance and urban relocation.

The paranoia about security is significant in Delhi. For the installation, RAQS also produced stickers. They contained simple messages such as "look under your seat," "do not touch abandoned objects," and "missing persons report immediately."

The second part of "Coordinates of Everyday Life" at Documenta 11 was a piece of open source software presented on PC monitors. Opus (Open Platform for Unlimited Signification) is a Web-based database structure for shared content.[16] Opus is an attempt to create a digital commons in culture, based on the principle of a sharing of work, while at the same time retaining the possibility (if and when desired) of maintaining traces of individual authorship and identity. I asked Shuddha to what extent the conceptual nature of the Opus database was related to the precise nature of everyday life imagery in Delhi. Shuddha replied:

> Both are about inhabiting space in a different way. One is about being restrained by legal regimes in offline space, the other reflects on the possibility of sharing space in a much more free-floating, dispersed fashion. We started to be interested in work that enables work. Opus means work. It's a work about work. It's not an object that can be contemplated. Rather, Opus is a playground. I look at Opus as a building or an architecture, as a blueprint. It is like a building waiting to be inhabited. It takes some talking to communicate to an art audience what the implications of Opus are.

Those familiar with free software immediately understand the basic ideas behind Opus. But they would ask: Why label it art? Shuddha:

> Certainly. Software questions the boundaries of art. The most interesting response came from a group in Brazil called Recombo who were doing something similar with music. They take the idea of the remix culture literally and built an online architecture for people to make collaborative music. In this way peer-to-peer distribution is extended with peer-to-peer creation. Others are interested in the source code. Now we are translating the Opus ideas into physical space. It is a work commissioned by the Walker Art Center, in collaboration with Atelier Bow Wow, a group of Japanese architects. The show opens in February 2003. We are trying to figure out what kind of analogue manifestations Opus can have in a gallery space.

In August 2002, a delegation from Sarai flew to Sao Paolo, Brazil to install a work of Raqs Media Collective at the new media arts exhibition Emoção Art.ficial.[17] The installation called location (n) has eight clocks and eight monitors. Shuddha explains:

> The crucial idea is one of time zone. The clocks represent different cities such as Sao Paolo, New York, Lisbon and Delhi. Instead of hours the face of the clock has emotions such as epiphany at 12 o'clock, or anxiety... nostalgia. The fun of the work is that visitors can compare the different states of being in each city. The whole room is filled with the sound of a heartbeat, layered on to which are the sounds of global electronic transactions, modems, fax machines, and phones. On the monitors you see a face slowly moving from left to right. It's a

mysterious image because it looks like as if the face disappears from one and then reappears on another monitor. The face seems to be travelling between the time zones. We are playing with the Kulishov effect in early cinema where expressions and objects each produce different emotional effects. In our case it was about the expression of the same emotions in different time zones. Globally speaking we always had the same emotions. It's just that there is no singularity. Everyone feels the same but at different point of time.

My journey around the Sarai projects ended with an interesting exchange on free software and open source in the Indian context. Tripta Chandola is responsible for the free software public outreach project of Sarai.[18] Before stumbling into the Linux scene Chandola studied ancient Indian history. In retrospect, Chandola explains, she had already encountered open source issues during her study when she could not access artifacts and primary sources. Six months ago, she became a member of the Delhi Linux User Group.[19] At the first meeting she was appointed general secretary. In the beginning, her curiosity was born out of activism. The group produced its own distribution CD and went to schools to give presentations. Chandola: "After a while I realized that the group did not manage to penetrate into the schools and break through the barriers of preconceived ideas. Microsoft is the software that authorities use." In response to this impasse, the Delhi group decided to put up a Web site and post the research results of each of its members. The main issue is how can Microsoft's hegemony be broken in more than technical ways? The aim of Chandola's research is to get more people interested in the cultural aspects of free software related issues. She believes that without research such work cannot happen.

Chandola: "For me open source and free software is not an isolated body of knowledge. It should be placed in a specific context. In my research I am not only looking at the rival factions between the free software purists and the open source pragmatists. I am mainly looking at the Indian context. I am also interested in the media representation." I asked Chandola what the specific situation of Linux in India is. She replied:

Programmers here are not into the development of Linux itself. They are more involved in the service industry. Linux is new here and only few people have expertise in this field. So Indian programmers do not change the source code (despite the philosophy). They even develop code and then release it as proprietary software, parallel to their free software activities. Not only does this lead to a personality split between daytime and evening, but also the overall development of open source stagnates. There is certainly the image that Indian programmers are not designers. They are not good at conceptualizing software. Instead you tell them to do a certain thing and they will program it. This might be a caricature but there is some truth in it. There is a sense that Indian techies cannot penetrate other disciplines. In order for this to change a different sensibility towards technology needs to be developed. For most of us, technology is still this overwhelming thing. The distance between us and technology needs to be broken down.

Then there has to be a viable business model. This is a universal problem but here it has significant local consequences. Chandola:

> Free software cannot be isolated from the social reality in India. I don't want to see our efforts as a hobby as that wouldn't bring us very far. Maybe within programmers' circles it might be a heroic thing to do—to sit through the night and hack the code—but in the larger picture it reduces its own importance.

Another global and troublesome topic is the total absence of women. Chandola:

> Recently I visited one of the colleges. There were lots of women around in the computer science department. Later I realized that all these women, after their graduation in computer science will either study psychology, do an MBA or history or whatever. But none of them will pursue programming. They said that men were better at it. There is the widespread idea that women cannot think logically. The issue is not that women are not using computers. What we should do is break down the barrier between users and programmers.

A cultural turn seems inevitable.

The cultural change we speak about here will not come overnight and might need to be accelerated through conflict and dialogue. Hacker versus artist is a conflict that also exists within Sarai, as in so many new media arts organizations. There are tensions with the first generation of young programmers and the artists/intellectuals. Chandola, trapped between the two, explains:

> In both "camps" there is this arrogance: what I know you won't be able to understand. Then the conversations cease to happen. Techies should be involved on all levels. Programming should not be seen as a commissioned job. Techies have to be fully aware of what the ideas behind a certain project are. The problem is: techies at Sarai do not see why technology should be used within arts and culture. They do not see the point of net art and prefer to do "more substantial"' stuff. It is important that these issues are addressed in this space, because

if they are not discussed in Sarai, then where would they be? Businessmen wouldn't even bother to look into such issues.

For Chandola the conflict is all about sensitivities and people's backgrounds. She stresses the importance of going into schools.

We are building a web portal for students to put their open content on. That could be a beginning. The continuing use of Microsoft products has led to a closed sensibility towards software. In that sense, the use of open source software in daily life would indeed make a difference. But that's only a long-term solution. For artists and critics it doesn't really matter what software they use. What counts is the openness towards the ideas and the willingness to start the dialogue with programmers.

When I left Sarai, the staff was examining the 100+ applications that had arrived for the second round of the seed grants program for students and young researchers. Sarai is committed to generating public knowledge and creativity through research. The Independent Research Fellowship Program is one of Sarai's most successful initiatives and, in particular, Bangalore initiatives have benefited. It does not just support Delhi-based projects. Themes are as diverse as habitation, sexuality, labor, social/digital interfaces, urban violence, street life, technologies of urban control, health and the city, migration, and transportation. Around twenty to thirty microgrants are awarded. Every year in August, fellows meet in Delhi to discuss their results and it is the highlight in the Sarai annual calendar because of the eloquent presentations and lively debates. Project topics range from the use of celluloid and compact disks in Punjab to exploring the space of psychiatric hospitals in Srinagar, from the culture of telephone booths to identities and aspirations of Tibetan Youth in New Delhi, from the impact of Urdu women's magazines on Muslim women to student politics in Allahabad.[20]

In response to the pogrom in Gujarat (early 2002) and the worsening global situation following September 11, 2001, Shuddha Dasgupta and I produced a conference on crisis media.[21] When he and I were at the No Border camp in Strassbourg, Germany in July 2002, we sat apart and devised the program in the midst of the Euro-autonomous crowds who were indulging themselves in endless plenary sessions. In March 2003, a few weeks before the U.S.-led invasion in Iraq, I traveled to Delhi to discuss how media interventions are possible in times of war and crisis. We invited journalists, media practitioners, writers, theorists, and activists to talk about the crisis of representation and reportage in situations as diverse as ethnic conflicts in ex-Yugoslavia and Central Africa, the economic collapse in Argentina, the conflicts in Israel and the Palestinian territories, the impending war against Iraq, violence in Gujarat and Kashmir, and the displacement of people by big dam building projects in the Narmada Valley. During the meeting, the sense of urgency was palpable. "Crisis Media: The Uncertain States of Reportage" was less playful and undefined compared to many new media and hacker events. The workshop opened with a provocation that stated, "The crises in the media are the crises of the media." The main speaker was novelist Arundhati Roy, who compared the mainstream media to a buffalo surrounded by a swarm of bees that were all the alternative and independent voices emerging from within a politicized new media culture.

When I visited Sarai in December 2004, it looked as if the place had doubled in size. Here, I will give a report of my meetings and experiences.

A group of students from Pakistan was visiting the center. Shevta Sarda gave me an update of the CM project. It had expanded, there were now three labs, and a fourth, solely for R&D purposes, had been established at the partner organization, Ankur. Labs were now regularly distributing broadsheets throughout their settlements. What had been developed over the years, Sarda tells me, is the methodology of digital storytelling that, besides e-mail, the Web, video, and performances, was using paper as a medium, for example, the scratch book[22] and the broadsheet.[23] As the Web site presently explains, the youngsters who meet regularly in the Compughars acquire considerable technical skills in handling computers, digital cameras, audio recorders, and scanners in order to create interviews, stories, write-ups, photographs, audio recordings, wall magazines, pamphlets, stickers, and short animations. "They play with words, ideas, concepts and images to narrate the every day and make an evolving networked collection of diary entries. Diaries are a specific mode of writing: intensely subjective, personal."[24] The diaries talk about the lanes, elections, perceptions, celebrations, accidents, dislocation, migration, evictions, work situations, technology, life stories, and deaths. CM experiences have been taken to Gujurat, where communal riots took place in 2002. A successful residency happened with a community group in Bootle, a suburb of Liverpool, England, in collaboration with the FACT new media center.[25] The locality labs have developed dynamics of their own, independent of one another and Ankur/ Sarai. According to Sarda, the number of localities could increase to five but there are no ambitious plans to expand. The CM project is wary of branches and does not intend to be marketed as a global concept and developed into a brand. Over the years the use of mobile phones and VCD players have increased, but magazines still have their importance.

With Raqs and Sarai founding member and CM coordinator Jeebesh Bagchi, we discussed the latest lab project. He says that Delhi is changing rapidly due to the Commonwealth Games in 2010. The metro, the construction of huge new complexes, all of the development is escalating real estate prices, and the periphery is quickly expanding. This is the current condition of the city and the context in which Sarai looks at possible encounters in a newly established lab. The lab is located in Nangla Maanchi, a squatter settlement along the west bank of the river Yamuna, on the fly ash deposits of the thermal power station, its neighbor. The settlement started 25 years ago and now numbers around 100,000 people. It is a mixed population, resource-rich in terms of language, ethnicity, and religion. However, the land on which they live is now a part of urban redevelopment plans, which will become more aggressive with the approaching Commonwealth Games. The authorities have conducted preliminary surveys, and the Supreme Court has been pushing for faster and more effective action from the municipality in matters of cleaning up. This resulted in the eviction of Nangla in the Spring of 2006. A blog was installed to report on this traumatic event and a broadsheet was produced.[26] Sarda writes:

> Nangla has been a difficult experience for Cybermohalla. The violence of the law and the plan has been enacted in a very brutal way in the daily lives of Cybermohalla practitioners and their worlds. For instance, we're talking about slums. It is a category developed by the Law and the Plan, and acts as a self-explanatory form of describing social life. Throughout its five years, one of the challenges of the Cybermohalla project has been to articulate a different way of talking about these spaces, and see them as self-organized settlements with no legal claims to the land on which they emerge. Nangla narratives have been an attempt to narrate this within the sharply conflict-ridden urban re-designing. Interestingly, even the Old City of Delhi was named "slum" by the new elite in the 1950s. Slum is not a neutral word of description.[27]

The Nangla lab, which no longer exists, had a core group of six. Five two-member teams from the other two labs joined to build it up. It was an experiment to try to make a new lab by drawing from the collective experiences of other labs. This was not only a question of setting up newer labs, but of entering this process each time with a recognition of the change in location, through the density accreting around each existing node. The idea to set up a separate R&D lab for CM grew from the desire to create a reflective space for the practitioners from the various locality labs. To understand the necessity of a discreet R&D lab, one must first understand the rhythms of the locality lab. Jeebesh says that there are, at any given moment, fifteen to twenty young people in each of the locality labs. There is a daily practice of sharing materials with each other, of making things together. This also means there is increasing confidence in creating contexts for sharing outside the lab itself, with the other localities. He sees this as an outward impetus of the labs—what he calls "breathing out."

Second, he says that new young people join the labs at different points in time. At the same time, there are older practitioners, with a longer history of practice at each lab. This is a differentiation within the space, one that demands innovation in expansion. That is, the question is not one of making new labs alone, but responding to the inner demands of a lab's social contexts. Third, the labs periodically host other researcher-practitioners—for instance, techies and designers—and work on projects with them. Depending on the procedural demands of these interactions, sometimes these projects are absorbed into the daily practice of the labs, while at other times they require a shift in the rhythm. Jeebesh:

> The question before was how to think all of these aspects. And so, to think of a space which responds to each of these concerns. The R&D lab was then thought of as a nodal space, a space which connects the locality labs, where older practitioners can spend some quiet time for deepening their own practices while still being at the locality labs, where lab practitioners from all three labs can spend time to make things in a sustained way for circulation (along with doing this at their own locality lab), and where researcher-practitioners who come from outside can enter into a context for dialogue without disrupting the daily rhythms of the locality labs.

By 2006, fifteen to twenty people were engaged in CM across all the projects on a full-time basis, so a lot could come out of it. The practice itself is open to dialogue. The participants share their excitement, not only with their peers at the labs, but also in creative contexts outside the labs. The confidence is there. For example, following a one-hour storytelling performance in a theater in Hamburg in March 2004, they started making radio programs. In this way, each encounter is seen as replete with possibilities of newer questions and practices for the locality labs.

Daily writing is now a basic practice at the labs. One associated practice is doing (non-fiction) streetlogs. The idea of the streetlog is, for instance, to sit for hours in a tea or a barbershop, where people move in and out. Practitioners describe the space and lock in a few characters in their descriptions. From here they can tell one story about a face they like. What they learn from this is the art of listening. The dignity of listening becomes part of the creative practice—and that is even more important than writing.

Jeebesh also noted an interesting shift in the approach to images with the arrival of digital cameras. They would take a large number of shots, change the colors, resize the images, and make them into short animated films. Photography enables a different kind of interaction. One of the localities invited old people of the colony to come to the lab and have a conversation. They took photographs of each person, blew them up, put them in frames, and gifted them. On another occasion, they revisited the schoolteachers from whom they had once run away. They invited them into the lab and made recordings of conversations of the teachers' school days. The teachers emerged as human beings, not just social functionaries. Computer skills are not an issue. Participants teach each other the software. Some of them fight their way into English. They see people working as programming and designing. Those who excel at animation do not call themselves "animators." One would say, "I talk, I think, and can do fun things with computers." Jeebesh is convinced that technology should not translate into a self-definition of identity.

Tripta Chandola, whom I met in 2002, and was involved in the free software activities then, has since left Sarai to become a (new) media ethnographer. She is doing participatory observations in the computer market Nehru Place, in the Govindpuri settlement and a rural area out of Delhi, together with Jo Tacchi, a U.K. community media researcher who works out of the Queensland University of Technology in Brisbane. In 2004, Chandola took me to Nehru Place, a business hub in South Delhi and one of the oldest hardware and software markets in Delhi, now undergoing rapid transition.[28] Large, grey 1970s concrete structures and squares are encircled by the shiny mirror high-rises mushrooming all over Asia. The pavement is being renewed. Because of the drastic fall of consumer electronics prices, the old market for second-hand reassembled hardware is still there but cheap high-tech products that compete with recycled old models are rapidly overtaking it. Whereas a brand-new computer printer can be sold for a discount price, the refilling of old ink cartridges is still a lucrative business. Chandola knows most of the vendors and we talk with some of them. Early in her fieldwork, Chandola had tried to mold some of her experiences into semi-fictional narratives, but then she started to keep a diary in notebooks—writing down her observations in an anthropological manner, revisiting her encounters. In such instances, the technology steps back.

A few months after having worked in the settlement in 2004, she wrote to me: "Working with issues like poverty, with communications on the forefront and its aura of 'development' looming behind, we realized that things are not as straightforward as they are put out to be."[29] You have to give up stereotypes. Using electronics is part of the everyday everywhere.

This should not surprise us, as it is easier to obtain a television than get clean tap water. Chandola is trying to understand poverty as a lived experience rather than a page of statistics and mere access to resources. In government reports, the poor are constantly referred to as "others." What struck Chandola , for instance, was the difference between those who were mobile (not only in the sense of transportation but also related to the use of telecommunications) and those who were trapped in the slum. Being the first settler in a slum makes a big difference in status, income, and access to media. Poverty in this context, so Chandola thinks, is "displaced" poverty and can best be measured, in relative terms, within the settlement itself. Those deprived and in crisis work inside the settlement and do not buy or rent the places in which they live. They are illiterate and their children do not go to school.

Tripta Chandola is fascinated by her city. She loves the crowds and writes,

> the calls, missed calls, dirt and grime, romantic indulgences, despairing temptations, casual conversations, borrowed breaths, scattered lives, makeovers, turnovers, lost landmarks, missing milestones, carved corners, shared fears, scared dreams, dirty desires, the sparse places, the wide imaginations, incessant honking, deafening silence, orderly commotions, confusing conversations, comic interludes, defeating collusions and amidst this, the convoluted connections.

Whereas in the West cities are taken for granted and fiercely compete with each other, in India we find a genuine fascination for "the city" as such. In China, we see a similar hype around the phenomenal growth of cities. Whereas in the decade of The Club of Rome urbanization was portrayed as the prime cause of the planet's problems (together with population growth), since the 1990s there has been a shift away from the apocalyptic toward the view of the city as a complex arrangement of difference. The collective imaginary that Sarai embodies is one of critical engagement or even passion for the daily contradictions they must endure. Think of Walter Ruttmann's *Symphony of a City* (Berlin, 1927) and then put that frantic energy into the Indian context. Sarai artists and scholars are obsessed with capturing the spirit of this fast-changing place.

Sarai's Involvement with the Internet

Sarai's *Reader* list provides an interesting read. Unlike most e-mail–based mailing lists, it is not overly dominated by announcements or short responses. It regularly comes up with unique content that cannot be found elsewhere. The usually lengthy postings are, for the most part, essays written by the 40 to 50 Sarai independent fellows. They use the list to disseminate their research results—a sign that, in India, e-mail is still the predominant channel to exchange texts and ideas. The topics over the past several years, just to mention a few, include excavating Indian experimental film; the position of research into the lives of Kashmiris in Delhi; Dastangoi, the culture of storytelling in Urdu; the cultural aspects of the finance business in Vijayawada; spooked vision, cyclists on Delhi roads; the contribution of the Christian missionaries in the construction of Assamese identity; golf in South Asia; entrepreneurship in Mumbai; and railway notes from the Imperial Survey of 1881.

In the Sarai media lab, the room where most of the design work is done, I met Anand Vivek Taneja, a writer and filmmaker who is part of the Publics and Practices in the History of the Present project, in short, PPHP. He gives me a photocopied reader full of articles on copy culture, media markets, and illegality. Since its inception, this cluster of topics has been a central focus of research at Sarai. In December 2002 there was a workshop called The Daily Life of Intellectual Property Law,[30] followed by City One, a South Asian Conference on the Urban Experience in January 2003 and in January 2005 Contested Commons/Trespassing Publics, a conference on inequalities, conflicts, and intellectual property. The background to all this is the emergence in Indian cities of new informal distribution networks. Small shops selling MP3 CDs and films on CD (VCDs) have sprung up everywhere, even in settlements. Material is also distributed through neighborhood cable networks. At the center of this research stands a dynamic "culture of the copy" that started with copying music cassettes, then VHS and VCDs, MP3s and DVDs, and now moves toward downloadable digital films through peer-to-peer networks on the Internet. Each of these technologies has produced its own pirate culture. With Anand I talked about the countless small factories that assemble consumer electronics from parts they order in China or Southeast Asia. Competition between these factories is fierce as they often depend on orders where individuals might require a customized Sony or Samsung. People prefer to purchase such goods during the festival seasons and outside of these periods they can be out of work. When urban markets are exhausted, sellers carry the players on their scooters deep into the small towns and rural areas.

Information society does not always mean what you expect. Taha Mehmood is a young researcher who joined Sarai in 2004. He looks into security service agencies, databases, identification practices, and the Multiple-purpose National Identification Card (MNIC), which is poised at a critical juncture. He started to map the information flows from security firms in the city. Mehmood tells me that surveillance in India is not that technical because there is no shortage of labor. They use people the old-fashioned way. Not all of them even have a mobile phone. Surveillance here is an informal activity. The security guards map the area of the establishment under surveillance and gate it accordingly. They keep registers of every car going in and out, what persons, at what time. That is information society in India. Mehmood thinks his definition is more literal, basic.

> In every instance that you move through town, you are registered. We don't know what the state or private companies are doing with this massive form of data collection. What's the need to be so specific about every entry point? It looks as if we're guilty of something, until proven innocent. With all these forms you create vicious circles. To apply for a passport, you need a driver's license, identity cards and vice versa. The form is forming us.[31]

Physical mapping is being done in preparation for the introduction in India of a smart card for every individual. Mehmood:

> There is a drive in each of us to hide away from this fixation of identity into one static data body. Everyone likes anonymity. Remember, it's not an easy task to keep track of a billion people. Tens of thousands of them have the same surname plus first name. A huge chunk of the population is mobile. So how do you fix them? It is still possible to have fake papers that can claim land property.

As part of his MA in mass communication, Mehmood made a film about the topic. All of the security executives were too frightened to speak on camera, so Mehmood talked with them off camera. One of them is a retired colonel who has been in the security business for the last thirteen years and employs 1000 guards. That is his private army. The entire army model is replicated in his organization. Six or seven guards report to a head guard who reports to a supervisor. They wear the name of the firm on their uniform, belt, and cap. They look very smart in their uniforms. Mehmood explained these men come from Bihar and Rajistan, the most impoverished states in India. They have little clue about much of anything and they receive no training. Nobody knows how many security personnel there are in this city. Even Sarai has one. Security guards are guarding entire areas like public parks and streets, grabbing municipal property. This happens throughout Delhi. For Mehmood, security starts to look like a façade to hide the divisions in society. The irony is that these are the most insecure people in the world providing security to the richest in the city. This situation mirrors the working of the state, in terms of the fencing of the border between India and Pakistan. However, in the newly developed shopping malls, condominiums, and conceptual cities near Delhi, there is a greater reliance on surveillance equipment and not the usual assemblage of guards, something that did not seem to be the case when Mehmood started his research. Consequently, there is an increasingly complex interplay of both technical and manual forms of control.

An important part of Sarai's activity is to host international residencies. Sometimes artists come to do their own work, in other instances they are attached to specific Sarai programs. There have been many, so here I will feature a few of the residencies as illustration of the program.

Sara Kolster

Sara is a Dutch visual artist with a background in design who shifted toward film and video. She was at Sarai in late 2005 for two months to work on a project called LivingSpaces. It was her aim to photograph home interiors. She imagined visiting different houses of people with various socioeconomic backgrounds. Sara:

> During my city-journeys, a completely different view of the city arose. Soon it became clear to me that a visual of the variety of living spaces would be impossible. I however continued my collection of photographs of interiors. I focused on specific neighborhoods and localities which had caught my interest during the walks.

With the assistance of the Sarai broadsheet group, she worked in Kilokri—a district with a chaotic stacking of houses.

> Narrow paths, which sometimes make you wonder whether you are in- or outside, take you past schools, mosques, public buildings, parks and labor workshops. In residential buildings the basement is used for sewing a special kind of Indian dress, to be sold in the United States. Since the houses are so narrowly built, you can almost touch your neighbors when hanging out the window.

What struck Sara about Sarai was the broad definition of research. The final shape often varies from a documentary film, sound pieces, an exhibition, and a lot of research text. Sara observes that,

> the Sarai researcher (artist, writer or filmmaker) mostly enjoys the "new" style of expression. The exchange between research and art, seen as "theory" and "practice", seems to be interwoven at Sarai, although the "thinking" part sometimes takes over and gets stuck in discussions.

Sarai and ALF

The Waag–Sarai exchange program that was the financial backbone during the founding of the center had finished by 2004.[32] Sarai then received money from a host of sources such as the Rockefeller Foundation, Dutch development aid from HIVOS, IDPAD, and the Ministry of Foreign Affairs, and the Canadian Langois Foundation. Securing a multitude of donors had been crucial from early on. After four years, the model of the one-to-one exchange between Waag and Sarai was replaced by the concept of the "platform" in which the two original partners would, for another four years, support emerging, even not-yet-existing new media centers. The idea was to transfer knowledge on how to set up an institution. There are plenty of virtual networks, collaborations, and temporary structures such as festivals and talks, but new media culture seems to shy away from the question of how sustainable organizations can be set up and support research from cultural, political, and artistic perspectives.

As a first partner, the Bangalore Alternative Law Forum (ALF) was invited to submit a proposal.[33] ALF started in March 2000 as a group of lawyers mainly involved in litigation work. Not entirely by coincidence, Bangalore being one of India's main IT centers, ALF was involved in a number of new media related topics such as software piracy, intellectual property disputes, and free software/open source initiatives. I visited ALF in December 2002 on my first trip to Bangalore. ALF is centrally located, on the top floor of a private home. At that time, the organization consisted mostly of law students doing litigation work. We had a meeting on their rooftop and discussed how ALF could grow into a sustainable organization using the possibilities of the new media buzz while continuing to support people marginalized on the grounds of gender, sexuality, class, and caste. ALF has taken on cases of contract laborers, women who are victims of domestic violence, divorce, guardianship and custody of children, the right to residence, property rights, child labor, bonded labor, and sex workers who have been abused by the police.[34]

By 2006, ALF had become a close collaboration partner of Sarai. Over time, ALF developed an interest in the impact the technology industry was having on the city, in the way businesses grabbed land, the environmental impact of such development, and the working conditions in industry. According to its Web site, ALF "integrates alternative lawyering with critical research, alternative dispute resolution, pedagogic interventions and more generally maintain sustained legal interventions in various social issues." Much like Sarai, the focal point of ALF's activities is not labeled "technology," "art," or "culture." Over the years, the center has grown. In 2005, ten to twelve ALF members were on payroll, being able to commit themselves fully to the projects at hand. In November 2005, the Austrian new media organization Netbase showed its traveling world-information.org exhibition in Bangalore, co-produced with ALF and other local partners.[35]

Sarai and Tactical Media

After an open fellowship application process in 2004, the Waag–Sarai platform chose two partners in Brazil and three of its own members to attend a meeting in Bangalore. The tactical media scene had been very much alive there over the past few years. Until 2002, most Brazilian new media art had been formalistic, elitist, and New Age, carefully kept outside of society by a small group of artists, theorists, and curators who worked with a mainly international focus inside art institutions, festivals, and universities. The rise of an independent scene of activists who were into music, street art, video, performance, and free software was imminent. Here, I will mention a few projects that are more relevant to this discussion of Sarai and tactical media.

The first Midia Tática event in Sao Paolo, Brazil in March 2003 worked as a catalyst to bring together dispersed groups and individuals. Out of it emerged the Midia Tática group, which spawned Auto Labs—three temporary autonomous media labs in the city's *favelas*.[36] Its concept was a mix between the classic telecenter work (training) facility, free software, promoting AIDS awareness, and an ABC primer of digital cultural production. Despite, or because of, its ambiguous success, the project was discontinued after five months. A second event the group put together soon after was the art and activist new media festival Digitofagia (October 2004). Parallel, and in close collaboration, ran Metarecyclagem, a successful computer-recycling project that opened various workshops throughout the country. Their hallmark is twofold: not only do they refurbish the hardware and install free software, but they also paint the gray PC covers in flashy, tropical Brazilian colors.

The size and dynamics were such that a center would have been a logical next step, so as to consolidate and support further initiatives. Both the Midia Tática group and Metarecyclagem applied for the Waag–Sarai Platform grant that was launched in mid-2004. By the time proposals had been worked out for a center, Midia Tática had fallen apart with core members moving away from Sao Paolo to Rio de Janeiro and Belém. Simultaneously, the "third way" Lula government's plan to set up a network of so-called cultural hotspots was under way, coordinated by the minister of culture— the popular singer Gilberto Gill—and thusly taking a considerable part of the ideas, energy, and people away from Auto Labs and the emerging tactical media field. A unique opportunity to work with "at most" six hundred cultural centers that had to be equipped with free software computers to edit audio and video was then taken up. These so-called cultural hotspots that had been identified were going to get funding through the Cultura Viva program of the Ministry of Culture. By early 2006, at least 250 were mapped and 100 of them equipped with free software media labs.[37] Similar to the case of Auto Labs—which could not really sustain itself compared to official telecenter NGO structures—things started to become really big, fluid, and messy. The shadow side of such a large undertaking was Big Politics. Corruption scandals haunted the Lula administration during 2005, which meant constant delays and uncertainties. The Cultura Digital project had reached such momentum by 2006 that any contribution of Waag Society and Sarai seemed futile.

The enormous geographic distance to Brazil and lack of local knowledge and language on the side of Amsterdam and Delhi started to kick in. What to do? The program was clearly intended to support emerging physical spaces, not networks, as there were enough of those anyway. For much of that year the confusion only grew. In October 2005, a small conference called Submidialogia took place in Campinas, near Sao Paolo, where a decentralized research network proposal was discussed. At first, a serious publication in Portuguese on Brazilian indie electronic pop culture appeared, but the momentum to found a center seemed to have passed. The euphoric tactical media phase was over.

Meanwhile, the caravan Sarai moved on to another corner of world— Beirut. It seemed ironic to try your luck in the Middle East, but that's exactly what the plucky protagonists set out to do. Initial contacts in Iran sounded promising, but proved unrealistic. Contacts were established in Beirut; however, no group (then or now) came forward with the intention to set up a center. How about Bandung? With Waag and Sarai members roaming around the world, giving talks and exhibiting work, doing screenings and hosting events, the initiative had reached its zenith, and showcased what new media was doing at a global level, with so much more to come. Was all of this only a start, a mere beginning, of international collaboration between cultural workers with radically different backgrounds, or was this the end of an era?

One of the things in which I have always been interested is organizational forms and whether intensive use of new media might produce alternative work forms and different power structures within projects. A member of the Sarai team wrote to me that Sarai in the popular imagination is a space that is spread out horizontally rather than vertically. It is normal that outsiders' expectations differ from the reality inside an organization, and Sarai is not an exception here.

> In this horizontal space, the nodes are fluid and the networks constantly evolving. As it is presented, hierarchies based on backgrounds, expertise, affiliations do not form a part of this loosely yet intricately knit network. In this network, nodes exchange freely, conversations flow smoothly, one can without any inhibitions present or

critique any works/ideas. This network is welcoming and constantly warming up to new nodes, evoking a romanticized *flaneur* set on a stroll to explore the spaces and the various landscapes. The reality is far from this representation. Sarai as a space is highly bureaucratic and sustains well-consolidated vertical networks. In essence, I prefer horizontal, spread out networks but I must admit I do not have a problem with vertical-hierarchy based networks.

Then what, you may ask, is the problem with Sarai?

It is the silence it maintains in this regard. The fact that it does not accept that the network is sustained through vertical nodes. It becomes difficult for others who can critically see the power politics as well as take the projected "freedom of speech and ideas" a bit too seriously, to address this. The discrepancy of the projected and practiced remains high.

Another sensitive topic is the question of how open or closed the media labs in the settlements would have to be. CM labs are kept relatively insulated, even from insider entries and open only for specific viewership.

"I completely understand the need to not let the space become a site spectacle," the Sarai team member continues, "but my commonsensical understanding tells me that a site becomes a spectacle when conscious attempts are made to filter/control the gaze. Cybermohallas are treated as precariously delicate spaces sustained through very delicate and sensitive networks and aspirations and the only ones allowed in this space are 'viewers'. One needn't step out of Sarai to see instances of this insulation. Of the entire Sarai populace, only 5% or less would have visited Cybermohalla labs. People from the Development/NGO sector who wanted to visit were supposedly denied because it was stated they will not understand the 'creative' 'intellectual' energy of the space, and would rather disrupt it."

Again the Sarai member: "What needs one to have read to enter this space? Where needs one have to have visited to qualify as a visitor into the space? Why is it treated with kid gloves? A magical object becomes a magical one only when it is kept away. Isn't dialogue, sustained and meaningful, needed to make a space more definite? What are they afraid of? By guarding them (the young researchers from the settlements) so fiercely, are they not in sense implying that they need to be guarded thus reinforcing the very insecurities of/about these spaces and people which they intend to address through their practices?"

Shveta Sarda counters this critique with a long list of encounters between Sarai staff and CM practitioners. CM is regularly discussed in the Sarai Monday meetings, and the internal mailing list is the first site for circulation of CM content, says Sarda. Productions like the broadsheets, radio, and video (for circulation on local cable networks) often happen at Sarai itself. Members of Sarai's network often visit the CM labs: Lawrence Liang did a great workshop on law and juridical reason; Hansa Thapliyal, a filmmaker from Bombay, has spent time at the labs discussing her films and stories; Samina Mishra, author of *Henna in the City*, came and discussed her book. On one occasion, by request from CSDS, an Australian anthropologist of Indian origin was given total access to the CM labs in Dakshinpuri and Nangla Maanchi. After a brief encounter, he coldly dumped the lab. Clearly, this was not a good experience. Jaanu blogged about this occasion, describing the researcher as an absent-minded, indifferent observer.[38] Student interns from universities and design schools have also been coming. A very successful internship, Sarda writes, was a graduation project by Lekhoni Gupto with the Dakshinpuri lab who was encouraged to blog about her research.[39]

The pressure to receive international guests is a real concern, Sarda admits. The labs spend most of their time interacting with their neighborhoods. "They meet visitors, they go out and seek conversations, set up spaces in weekly markets and use local infrastructure for content circulation such as the suburbs' cable networks." Sarda:

> I have refused some international visitors simply because they show an entitlement to be taken to the labs. They either think that we in Sarai have no work other than pandering to their requests, and when they have done no reading, no thinking with the CM content and want to see the site for immediate gratification. This is a great imposition as a visit to a lab takes away 5-6 hours of critical lab time. The labs themselves are extremely critical of these visitors and have articulated the feeling of being "zoo creatures."

Sarda also denies that CM participants have been overly protected against the outside world.

> Personally, over the last two months since the Nangla demolition, seeing CM practitioners interact with a wide spectrum of people—journalists, lawyers' assistants, local politicians, school administrators, police, municipal workers and administrators, film makers, NGO workers—I realise how prepared and confident they are for these conversations. Surely a protective model would not have enabled this. CM now is a network of about 75 people engaging full time with a

very complex weave of practices, public forms and events. They travel extensively in the city and, on invitation, to other spaces.[40]

Ravi Sundaram further elaborates on the politics of Western traffic:

When visitors come, they are not all like you, talking to everyone in Sarai. They sometimes assume that they will be taken to places, typically make a demand to be "seen" the cybermohalla labs. This is part of circuit of travel culture, this rush for representation. If you do not see the Taj, then see the cool alternative circuit—Sarai. But who do we bear responsibility to—our public, or the "traffic cultures" as the anthropologist James Clifford once said?[41]

In an update of the Fellowship Program, Sarda reports that Vivek Narayanan, who joined Sarai to engage with Independent Fellows on a day-to-day basis in 2004, is building up a team with ex-fellows in Sarai and in other cities. To support eighty people's intensive interactions over eight months is a complex process. The aim is to build a researcher and practitioner community around Independent Fellowship. Sarda:

Sarai members are encouraged to engage with the fellows and everyone has few fellows they dialogue with through the period of the fellowship. This is both through personal correspondence and mails on the reader and urban study list, as well as sharing of books, articles and other resources. Sarai-txt, a collective of three women who bring out the Sarai broadsheet every three months, regularly go through all the postings and make collations for public renditions.[42]

Needless to say, postings and discussions are discussed during Sarai's Monday meetings. Since 2005, Fellows in different cities have organized meetings in their own cities during the period of the fellowship for face-to-face interactions, and Sarai members have been invited to these. Recently, Fellows have also become part of this process. In 2006, Fellows in different cities will play hosts to their counterparts, and be guests to others in return. Networking, Sarai style.

How new media centers should be run is not much debated, no matter where you go. There are little traces left of an active search for alternative organizational models such as cooperatives, associations, or collectives. The organizations presented in this chapter are too small for trade unions and somehow already too big to be run in an informal way. These new media organizations are similar to NGOs and for-profit businesses and are light years removed from the consensus-focused autonomous movements of old and tired Western Europe. Their virtual network component is strong. Despite all cultural differences, Waag and Sarai have a similar way of running their organizations, in that there is not much collective decision making. In the end, the founders are the ones in charge and have grouped a management structure around them; in the Waag case, a formal one, at Sarai a perhaps more informal one. It is not possible to remove or vote out the founders and a system of rotation of leadership is unknown. Therefore, whereas the substance of the work has the aura of innovation, the internal structure has, in fact, regressed to levels well before the cultural upheavals of the 1960s. In certain places, if you start a cultural organization or NGO, it is considered private property. This leaves newcomers and next generations with little other choice to either start a similar organization themselves, work as freelancers and workers underneath the existing organization, or not enter the field in the first place.

Oliver Leistert, a West German visitor on a three-month residency in Sarai, wrote down his observations in an e-mail that was discussed among all Sarai staff. Oliver:

> I found it unbelievable that the founding team of Sarai plus two CSDS members are selecting the stipends, even though they are doing a great job. I would love to witness an open discussion process involving anyone interested in this from Sarai. Maybe my expectations are too much shaped by my own collective experiences, which—summarized—say: the more people are part of the decision, the better is the collaborative effort. I see a paradox when peer-to-peer and collaborative software is being highlighted, without much fallout of this on the social scheme.
>
> "The hierarchical model made me feel sad," Oliver continues. "As always in such cases, it was the less people from the coordination team were present, which happened quite a few times, when the power vacuum could be felt most intensively. There was an inability to decide. Instead of sorting out the problem, most preferred to accept this as a condition sine qua non, without expressing the need to reorganize Sarai. The organizational model looks like it hasn't changed for years, ignoring the fact of substantial changes in quantity and quality."

His letter concludes:

> The most interesting future question for a project like Sarai is how to transform, mutate, wander into a new form. Though Sarai has much interest about what happens outside of India and a lot of their people are much better informed than those from European initiatives usually are, the interest in translating this knowledge and experience into a new region has its limits. I didn't find traces of a

fascination for difference. The Western view on "the other" (in this case Indian people) must have had such an impact that "the other" for an Indian person is coded as "do not touch, don't be curious." Another possible reason might be the endless research field that Delhi and India offer itself.

There are disappointments here, but also a realization of how difficult it is to aspire to truly egalitarian global collaboration, having to take into consideration colonial history and unequal power relations in terms of money and resources. How is one to debate issues if there is no clear common political agenda and all that exists are good intentions? What is mutual aid in an equal relationship? It is questionable if such values from autonomous movements in "Old Europe" can—and should—be transferred into radically different cultural contexts. But that is what is under debate here.

Sarai members rejected Oliver's criticism. Sarda: "His comments on hierarchy and decision making in Sarai are ill-informed, and at their best evoke a shrug." For Sarda, the frequent traveling around the world of Sarai members has not caused alarm.

My peers and I watch them critically as they move between worlds— from the Venice Biennale to the self-organized settlements with no legal claims to the land on which they emerge. I enjoy their complicated dance in multiple sites, which makes the world less abstract for me. I enjoy watching my peers take on an understanding of the world and appreciate the complexity of demands that come with having open conversations in many directions. They create a demand on each of us to take global publicness seriously and engage with it.

According to Ravi Sundaram, Sarai's problem lies elsewhere.

We are awful with organization and bureaucracy to our great loss at times. We do not have the heart to fire people, nor do we exert the faintest measure of hierarchy. That has been our problem. How do we come to terms with this? Part of what draws people to Sarai is precisely our reasonably open environment, but we face the aporia of unending openness. To be sure there is hierarchy of age and experience in Sarai but that is not "bureaucracy". In fact if there is any self criticism it would be that we should quickly design a new organisational form that is network-based and less demanding.

Sarai is well connected; there are thousands of contacts. The center is well known to many initiatives that work in the fields of visual arts and new media culture. This exposure gradually might have turned into a problem. Does it suffice to open up even more CMs, have more international residencies, programs, and exchanges? Growth is the main challenge for Sarai. It is not simply a question of sustainability, a buzzword that often tries to discredit the temporality of project-based initiatives and tactical interventions. Nor has Sarai fallen into the new media arts trap, so that is one less problem to worry about. Being an institution with a steering body should be accepted first. Studies about the history and structures of institutions could be undertaken. Where is the new media equivalent of revolutionary Third World educator Paolo Freire?

Expansion of the intercultural dialogue to differences in organizational modes is needed. Agenda setting, as used in international policy contexts, as tried with the "Delhi Declaration,"[43] might be a promising possibility—but that, too easily, positions politics outside of Sarai and international collaborations such as the Waag–Sarai exchange. The questions I raise here are partly local but are also relevant elsewhere as the search for new institutional forms is well under way. Ashis Nandy, eminent grise at CSDS, recommends a reorientation of Sarai's primary concerns once the new media hype has died down. In a private conversation, Nandy summed up the Sarai agenda: the city, media, and access. Urban culture is a relatively new field of study for India's intellectuals, he explains, as still seventy-five percent of its population is living in rural areas and previous generations of intellectuals were mainly preoccupied with rural issues. The abstract machinery of high-rises, freeways, and subways has not yet been the subject of serious engagement. Sarai has to be seen as an attempt to create a rich cultural-political vocabulary to interpret the everyday of urban life, says Nandy, asking what constitutes democracy and public life in the age of the Internet and free software. According to Jeebesh Bagchi,

> one should not be too obsessed with the difficulties of entry and exit, which anybody will face in encountering any other spaces, institutions and networks. It is critical to understand how interesting and innovative work and collaborations happen in spite of these difficulties.

The most interesting thing about Sarai as an institution, says Jeebesh, "is the production of new critical bodies of knowledge, energies that sustain collaborations and improvisations on architectures of sharing and participation."

CHAPTER 7

ICT after Development

The Incommunicado Agenda

This chapter is a personal account of how I navigated the rapidly expanding Information and Communication Technologies (ICT) for Development field.[1] In December 2003 and November 2005 I attended the World Summit on the Information Society (WSIS) in Geneva and Tunis, two UN gatherings where each time 15,000 to 20,000 government officials, NGOs, and businesses met to discuss telecom and Internet issues within the development context. The former Third World has been relabeled a developing market. Tens of thousands saw these summits as an opportunity to meet, discuss, and do business. Through my engagement with the Sarai new media center in Delhi, I had the privilege of first-hand experience in this field. I was so inspired by the work going on at Sarai to begin formulating a critique of ICT4D, as this sector became known.

XS4US and XS4ALL

My first encounter with this field was in the late 1980s, when I met Michael Polman of the NGO Antenna—the Dutch affiliate of the International Association for Progressive Communication (APC). Until the Internet took off in 1993 and the World Wide Web became the default standard, there were some interesting debates among hackers and activists about the usefulness of the direction of (alternative) computer-aided communications. This was the time of bulletin board systems (BBS), with store-forward networks like Fido, and patchy access to a text-only Internet that solely operated through UNIX commands. A schism developed over the "access for all" versus "access for us" issue. Antenna mainly worked with NGOs in non-Western countries, training them to set up BBS and early Internet systems. In their view, it was of little value to provide individual users with computer access. Remember, this was a time of scarce bandwidth, even in Western countries. It was the organization, not the individual, that needed to get Internet access first. Against this institutional approach stood the anarcho-libertarian view of groups like Hacktic/xs4all that stressed the rights of the individual user. The debate over this choice—in situations of limited bandwidth and hardware—can be seen as fundamental, but it has a tactical angle as well. Over the years, I saw this debate being repeated numerous times. Ever since the first computer hackers' event I participated in, the Galactic Hacker Party held in the Amsterdam Paradiso building in August 1989, I have repeatedly come across this dilemma and argument. For instance, in 2006, critics of the MIT Lab initiative, One Laptop per Child, voiced concerns that school kids could very well share computer facilities and that it was a Western idea that children would need individual laptops. In some pedagogical approaches we find groups identified as the user, a concept that leaves behind the individual as user. The cost of devices, even a cheap radio, is still a factor, not to mention the cost of access. In a telecenter or cybercafe, one still has to pay for bandwidth. It would be unwise to deny these realities in the name of some higher goal, in this case, (Western) subjectivity.

While preparing for the Sarai funding round in 1999, we noticed that the Dutch development ministry and related funding bodies were still new to the idea that a diverse and sophisticated new media culture should be encouraged. Focusing on health care, women, and the environment were all worthy NGO goals, but ICTs should not be reduced to mere tools. There is also an autonomous, creative element to all these cultures that should be recognized and nurtured. ICT was (and often still is) a terribly poor monoculture, worldwide, that cried to be opened up. Nonetheless, things were on the move. Not long before in 1997 the International Institute for Communication and Development (IICD) had been established in The Hague.[2] Apart from the APC praxis equipping Western and Southern NGOs with computers and modems, connected through often-expensive long distance calls, the concept of developing a cultural politics around new media was a contested topic. In the early 1990s, the "water pump policy" was still in place. This meant that Western development had the (moral) priority to reach the poorest of the poor, mostly situated in rural areas, who were in need of basic infrastructure, health, and education. Computers and Internet access were considered Western luxuries that would only benefit the local urban elite and emerging middle class populations. Since the late 1990s, there has been a rapid shift away from this policy in spite of some surveys showing that those without Internet access placed higher priority on other forms of assistance and technology.

The "Digital Divide" became a buzzword of the late 1990s. At the official level, the report of the Maitland Commission for the International Telecommunications Union (1984) was seen as the founding document of the ICT for Development discourse.[3] The first summit of this emerging field on a global institutional scale might have been the Global Knowledge event in Toronto (June 1997), out of which the multi-stakeholder network Global Knowledge Partnership (GKP) emerged, a network of ICT4D organizations managed from Kuala Lumpur.

That many of the ICT4D organizations are from Canada is no coincidence. There are only a handful of ministries and affiliated organizations that play an innovative role in this field. Among them are the Canadians and their IDRC in Ottawa (Ontario), the Swiss Agency for Development and Cooperation (SDC), DFID and Panos in the U.K., and IICD and Hivos in the Netherlands. Oddly, the U.S. government's presence is minimal in this context. Instead, we see more involvement of foundations, including the Soros Foundation (OSI), Project Harmony, and Intermedia foundations. This does not mean that USAID has no priority for ICT for Development projects. Their Leland project, for instance, has connected twenty African countries since 1994. However, there is a lot of competition and non-cooperation on the international level. The outcome has been a clear loss of global hegemony for U.S. government agencies—a situation completely different from the dominant positions of U.S. companies like Google, Microsoft, eBay, and Yahoo. A former Peace Corps volunteer wrote to me,

> The main U.S. presence in many countries is military. U.S. Embassies are not only fortified (with good reason) but all groups like DEA and USAID now have to reside inside the embassy. The Peace Corps always wanted to be seen as separate and much closer to "the people" and it still does, but security issues associated with anti-Americanism have really had an impact on how they work. USAID having to fit its strategic planning in with State and Defense is the biggest change.

We should not make the mistake of presuming that U.S. firms are in the same situation (yet) and blindly follow the orders and dictates of the White House. The engagement of Microsoft, Sun, Dell, and HP in the ICT4D circus is substantial. United Nations or not, there is money to be made. For instance, Microsoft became the main sponsor of the global telecenter support effort, telecenter.org, a Canadian IDRC initiative.

Another WSIS predecessor worth mentioning was the DOT Force (or Digital Opportunity Taskforce) following the G8 Summit in Okinawa (2000), a global policy meeting where bureaucrats, global NGOs, academics, and corporations gathered to set an agenda on how to tackle the digital divide. A comparable, related forum was the UN ICT Task Force, established in 2001. Large sums were spent on meetings in Cape Town and Sienna, with little outcome. Within these circles rumors began to spread that a UN summit was going to deal with the Internet and global telecommunications. For those who have been around for a number of decades, it looked like a follow-up of the efforts in the 1970s and 1980s to create a "New International Information Order." This movement grew out of the postcolonial phase where countries that had recently gained independence resisted cultural synchronization with the West. The press agency Inter Press Service in Rome, an "independent voice from the South," is a concrete materialization of this demand to stem the one-sided news stream flowing from the North to the South, in order to make way for "stories from underneath."[4] However, the global political landscape had changed.

Worldwide, there were hardly any leftist movements or parties in charge. Most socialist projects on a national level had vanished. UNESCO, as the UN's cultural organization, was no longer in charge of media matters. The organization of the WSIS summits was given to ITU (International Telecommunications Union), an ancient technical body that dealt with standards of national telecoms (PTTs). This was a most unfortunate start, as it was the ITU that, throughout the 1990s, had unsuccessfully tried to take over, limit, and regulate the Internet. There are hilarious stories how national PTTs tried to crackdown on modems and charge a fortune for ISDN lines. The disgraceful witchhunt against hackers made it impossible to create a broad coalition against the privatization of the telecom industry as prices fell sharply. Unlike other sectors such as water, health care, and electricity, the main population ironically benefited from what can be considered a strategic loss in public infrastructure. Even in 2005, the telcos versus Internet controversy echoed through the WSIS conference halls. The ITU, still dominated by "Bell heads," was not supportive of the packed-switched TCP/IP religion espoused by Internet advocates. This lack of support and understanding was witnessed in the poorly covered part of WSIS that dealt with the future of the Internet telephony (VoIP). What had also changed since the 1970s was that the debate was no longer limited to government officials. As telcos were privatized all over the world, companies were sitting at the table with the ITU. There was a multi-stakeholder approach with participants from governments, corporations, and civil society. From the civil society side there was progressive anti-corporate rhetoric voiced by a number of people including media critic and sociologist Herbert I. Schiller. By the 1990s, the stringent vision had been replaced with the adoption of a much milder human rights discourse, which was seen as a "set of universally accepted moral claims." Instead of rebel talk, activists claimed legitimacy in the belief that they could appeal to an "international political consensus."[5]

I did not attend the Geneva and Tunis summits in the capacity of a delegate nor did I run around like a journalist covering the event. Instead, I took up observer status, indulging in the variety of presentations from two hundred or so countries. I spent most of the time in conferences and talked to representatives of organizations that were taking part in the ICT4ALL trade show. WSIS was the first truly global conference I attended, a dream come true, with thousands of participants in a truly futuristic event. Since then, I have spent much time conceptualizing festivals and events with a similar diversity of participants and ideas. For decades we have heard the politically correct criticism about the under-representation of women, minorities, and people from the South in new media events—and such criticism was well justified. Most Internet conferences are still U.S.-centered, with a few Europeans here and there. Web 2.0, Internet2, grid technology, and WiFi are the latest examples of such white, male monoculture. Most Internet governance and cyber rights lobbyists are Anglo-Saxon. Meanwhile, the vast majority of media users are post-Western. It is somewhat ironic in this context that even the international organization Internet Society (ISOC) is battling with these same issues and struggles to keep up with the globalization caused by its very own medium. Instead of taking the lead, the cyber elite are now paying the price for their triumphalism and related cultural indifference.

A related question then becomes how does one enforce change and embody "globalness" in Linux forums, new media arts festivals, and tactical media events, contexts in which financial resources are, by definition, limited? The point is not to reach for a world parliament model. It is no longer desirable to organize Olympic conferences in which all nations, minorities, and social groups are represented, let alone vote. Contemporary politics is postrepresentational. The multi-stakeholder approach, so dominant in WSIS, embodies this change. The stakeholders have an active interest, are engaged in the process, and are not merely representing some absent entity. The discontent in multi-stakeholderism is widespread, but that is a discussion of such enormous scope and consequence that I cannot reasonably cover it here.[6]

WSIS was one of the first global conventions that dealt with the multiplication of possibilities. Unlike summits that deal with immense problems such as HIV/AIDS, urbanization, global warming, gender inequality, and the environment, WSIS had the luxury to focus on possibilities. Leaving aside the obvious danger of techno-centrism, there was a genuine excitement in the air that access to technology and communication would be improved for hundreds of millions of people. That scale was not to be found in any projects with which I had dealt thus far. During the WSIS negotiations, little was achieved mainly because the stakes and legitimacy of WSIS were not clearly defined. I don't believe in resolutions and that was not what made the buzz. At some point after the first summit in Geneva, Internet governance emerged as the only intractable topic because the WSIS, ITU, or the UN did not have authority over the Internet domain name realm. For the global consultancy class that made the effort to come, WSIS and its preparatory meetings (the so-called prepconfs) were just another stop in a series of meetings. I rejected the cynical references to expensive hotels and large ministry delegations from African countries enjoying the shopping opportunity. For me it was enough to envision what a post-Western techno-culture could look like. The WSIS summits gave me a glimpse of things to come.

The carton box full of WSIS material I gathered contains reports like Mainstreaming ICTs: Africa Lives the Information Society, The Global Status of ICT Indicators, From Digital Divide to Digital Opportunities, Status of the Internet in Iran, Digital Review of Asia Pacific, and African Media and ICT4D: Documentary Evidence. Many of these are surveys, statistics, and policy reports but there were many exceptions. In one of the brochures, Global Process, Local Reality; Nigerian Youth Lead Action in Information Society, I found a story that summed up for me what WSIS was all about, far away from the conference rooms. It is a story about Mashi, a village near Duara, the origin of the Hausa/Fulani tribe, where ten young volunteers set up computers in the open square of the market. Groups of villagers trouped out to attend the event.

> Many of them were shown how to use the computer while the older teenagers were given questionnaires and were interviewed (audio and video) to find out their perspectives on the inclusion of ICTs in their everyday life in the village. A total of about 103 villagers participated in the campaign.[7]

What is clear from this is the role of WSIS as a contextualizer, providing actors-to-be a framework within which to work, legitimacy to contact authorities, and to create new platforms and contacts. Without such an insight it becomes too easy to critique such summits as wasteful gatherings that lack tangible outcomes. Even though such remarks are justified, and many of the postings on the Incommunicado email list deal with the (in)efficient use of resources, cynicism should not overshadow genuine enthusiasm and, again, silence the voices from "everybody else."

An invaluable account comes from Sylvestre Ouédraogo from Ouagadougou in Burkina Faso, a country in Sub-Saharan Africa. In The Computer and the Djembe, an illustrated, bilingual English-French collection of short stories and observations, economist Ouédraogo recalls his first encounter with computers and his engagement in ICT for Development. Ouédraogo sees the introduction of ICT in Africa as a profound rupture. "Traditional ways are still manifest, not only in village life but also in urban centers, in family life and interpersonal relationships."[8] There is a shortage of commentaries on the changes by Africans themselves, says Ouédraogo. As a founder of the Yam Pukri (Intelligence Awakening) association, Ouédraogo deals with a wide range of issues. In this capacity, he became part of the ICT4D spectacle of going to conferences, writing applications, and dealing with Western donors. "We have been told that if we want financial support, we should create associations because people abroad generally think that the African is a collective individual and that it is easier to support a group than individuals having different interests." Soon after founding, Yam Pukri's efforts to become autonomous were hampered. There was no other way than to provide services free of charge, creating the danger of donor dependency, so familiar in similar development projects.

Ouédraogo makes detailed observations about early Internet culture in Africa. At first the computer is seen as a black box. "Several times I tried to fill the toner cartridge with Chinese ink but it didn't work. I even tried in vain to use the traditional dye that my wife applied on cotton clothes. How can I manage to use this tool which may never be helpful to my brothers?" Ouédraogo continues the textile metaphor, as Sadie Plant once did in *Zeros + Ones*, comparing the computer with a traditional weaving work.

> You just introduce a pattern of loincloth you would like to obtain and you actually get it. Don't ask it to make a dress or a coat. It has been created to reproduce loincloths. Now, do you know the computer scientist? In fact, he is the weaver. He tightens the ropes and adjusts the threads. He makes a pattern of the loincloth you wish to have.

Then there is the usual confusion of the man who asks to get back the e-mail he just sent. Or the man who showed up happily with a big box and said: "I just bought a brand new computer. I opened the box and found that the machine was over twenty years old!" The discrepancy between real-time communication, expecting an immediate answer, and the reality of other users can be big. "You ask your African correspondent to answer your urgent message but he can't do it because he has just used up his Internet credit at the cyber cafe. He has just a little money left for his breakfast." Or this one: "You send an e-mail to an African friend living in the heart of the Savannah. He hasn't answered it for two months. What you don't know is that he has to cover a hundred kilometers to access the first Internet site and he goes there every three months!"

Concerning the Internet and development, there are two positions that are not, by definition, contrary. In the holistic approach, there is no special position given to technology, media, and telecommunications. Not even gross domestic product (GDP) is considered a reliable indicator. What counts are the overall living conditions—health, education, working conditions, childcare—and for some even immaterial values such as social well-being or happiness. In this regard, technology is often seen as part of a larger modernization package that increases pollution, stress, working hours, travel distances to work, and exploitation in general, in exchange for an increase of Western goods. Even though individual activists can make effective use of ICTs, the overall impact is, at best, neutral. Within ICT for Development, one hardly hears such concerns. For that, one probably has to attend the World Social Forum, whose leaders are, by and large, skeptical about the positive effect of almost all technologies.

The second approach argues from within the techno discourse and measures the impact of different programs. In this context, it is easy to point to the failures of a technocratic approach that only focuses on access. Repeatedly it has been said that access is vital—and meaningless. This also counts for general IT training that often ends up enlarging the Microsoft workforce, which can search the Web for known content, including porn. Thus far, ICT for Development projects have mainly been small scale so this type of critique is often unjustified. It is only recently that we see new initiatives to connect, for instance, all schools in Macedonia. Or MIT's One Laptop per Child initiative that aims to produce extremely low-cost laptops, which are sold only by the million, for children in developing countries.

The problem of ICT4D is its temporary conceptual nature, not its large scale. Thus far most ICT4D projects have been pilots focusing on training, setting up telecenters and other community facilities, policy assistance, and NGO capacity building. Recently we have seen a tendency among innovators to move away from training and access and to move toward a more political approach that emphasizes the "openness and freedom of the virtual domain" since donors have also become reluctant to continue investing in hardware and connectivity. You got your PCs in 2000, why do you need more? In part, we should read this as a response to the avalanche of anti-terror legislation after 9/11. Unlike the impression that outsiders sometimes have, within most ICT4D projects new and old media feed off each other.

Unlike other issues, ICT4D has not yet attracted much autonomous activism. Apart from the official human rights agenda of NGOs and global civil society, surprisingly little has come from radical groups. Unlike the case of biotech and gene manipulation, Internet and telecom issues have attracted little or no fundamental criticism. Real existing activism is focused on free software, wireless networks, and the connection between old and new media (for instance, radio). A few months prior to the 2003 summit, *WSIS We Seize* was created by a number of tactical media groups at a side event of the European Social Forum in Paris. This effort was meant to counterbalance the Geneva WSIS summit from the outside. Instrumental in this effort was Alan Toner, who published a text in *Mute* magazine in the lead-up to the event. After the obligatory intellectual property rights critique, he wrote:

> The draft declaration indicates the questionable content of the "information society" concept itself, comprising seventy-one different points and resuscitating a ruse reminiscent of the heights of the "dot com" folly: addition of prefix "E"- to any given area of human activity to cast it as an "ICT issue" (E-administration, E-Learning and so on). Meanwhile substantial media-themes have been marginalized.

Toner talked about the problems NGOs had getting access to WSIS procedures, but fell short in developing a critique of the human rights discourse or global civil society. In the months leading up to WSIS, interesting strategic debates emerged between the organizing autonomous groups over the "open source, open borders" slogan. If one favors open source, open knowledge, open access, and so on, then why not extend these demands to open borders, as the Was Tun group of immigration activists proposed. This issue split the *We Seize* campaign into two and caused some arguments during preparatory meetings and in chat rooms. The history of this controversy has yet to be written.

For some, the relation between freedom of speech and freedom of movement was obvious, while others failed to see the connection and criticized the unrealistic "open borders" demand. The term *freedom* had been discredited to such an extent by neo-liberal governments and conservatives alike that it could no longer be used. In the meantime, there was no autonomous position concerning, for instance, Internet governance and other WSIS issues.[9] The relation between activists outside and NGOs inside remained unclear from the start, and during WSIS II in Tunis there was no autonomous space whatsoever due to heavy police surveillance and repression by the authoritarian Tunisian regime.

Postdevelopmental?

Summits are mere culmination points. The long-term shift we see here is a move away from a power analysis (who has access and control to communication) to one that stresses the enabling factor of ICTs in fields such as environmental concerns, the fight against HIV/AIDS, gender inequality, and poverty reduction through various economic practices, for instance, micro finance. What I call for is a renewed analysis of power, as technology never operates as a neutral tool. We need to go beyond the good intention and its critique. My aim here is to create common ground for strategic debate. Too often, such discussions have moralistic underpinnings. Without having to go back to a technophobic position, it is important to deconstruct the agendas that come with an uncritical acceptance of ICTs as if they were an innocent medicine. Aid, development, and well-meant NGO structures all come with agendas that go beyond good intentions. This classic insight of development critique is in urgent need to be voiced again. My attempt is to update and rewrite the critique of development by Arturo Escobar and others for the ICT4D context. The point is not that technology in general is harmful, as much as there always looms the danger of hype—the presumption that social problems can be solved by the use of technology. Unless proven otherwise, activists, researchers, and policy officials should instead be humble about the effects of their projects and, at the very least, study the new power arrangements their ICTs introduce. It is also still very much of an open question whether the global poor actually benefit from ICTs. In particular, because this field is crowded by people engaged in new media, including myself, it is sometimes hard to distinguish between our personal beliefs and hopes, and the facts and figures on the ground. Many of us do not have the experience or talent to assist in other ways, just as agriculture, nutrition, and health advisors may not see how ICT can support their goals.

In his classic 1995 study, *Encountering Development,* Arturo Escobar writes:

> The empty defense of development must be left to the bureaucrats of the development apparatus and those who support it, such as the military and (not all of) the corporations. It is up to us, however, to make sure that the life span of the bureaucrats and the experts as producers and enforcers of costly gestures is limited. Development unmade means the inauguration of a discontinuity with the discursive practice of the last forty years of incredibly irresponsible policies and programs.[10]

Escobar argues for a hybrid modernity that supports a heterogeneity of hypermodern and premodern, amodern and even antimodern forms. It is the task of the critic, says Escobar, "to learn to look at and recognize hybrid cultural differences of political relevance."[11] Cultural differences, for Escobar, "embody possibilities for transforming the politics of representation, that is, for transforming social life itself. Out of hybrid or minority cultural situations might emerge other ways of building economies, of dealing with basic needs, of coming together into social groups." The aim is "to resist and subvert the axioms of capitalism and modernity in their hegemonic form."[12] No matter how appealing this position may be, we have to ask how this radical position relates to current debates around campaigns such as Make Poverty History. Is more development money, this time spent on ICTs, really the best approach? We might argue for this from a given sector's perspective, but it should be possible to transcend such a limited point of view, even though I have not seen people doing this.

Around 2002 I was able to observe the workings of the info development industry from the inside when I was invited, together with Ravi Sundaram, to be on the advisory board of the ICT section of the Indo-Dutch Programme on Alternatives in Development (IDPAD). In its fifth phase (2002–2006), emphasis was given to ICTs. The committee had to go through a high number of research applications and then select a few to be further developed into full-fledged proposals. A number of topics were covered—telemedicine in Karnataka, gender issues in the Kerala software industry, use of ICTs and local radio in social movements, and a study, conducted out of Hyderabad, on how women in both urban and rural areas in Andra Pradesh engage with ICT. There were also comparative studies between the Netherlands and India—for example, a study concerning working conditions in IT-enabled services. What it showed me was how far advanced reality is compared to the social and economic sciences that claim to study it. At the end of the selection process, project proposals were presented at a conference in Bangalore. Most of the studies were going to look into the impact of technologies on certain sectors, and more specifically their "network readiness." These are all relevant issues but what is often left out is the strategic question of how the direction of technology itself can be steered. India's large group of programmers potentially can direct the software industry as outsourcing of Western work that is being sent back will decrease in importance. The "techno-coolies" exist, but one may as well read this image as an easy copy-paste from colonial studies into the messy reality of transnational networks. Comparisons with China are interesting; for instance, to what extent the division of labor thesis (India software, China hardware) is valid and for how long.

The Solaris Dialogues

Inspired by Sarai's critique of information development as voiced by Ashis Nandy, Ravi Sundaram, and others, I started a mailing list together with the Canadian scholar Michael Gurstein in late 2001 called Solaris.[13] The discontent with the conventional discourse around IT and Development had been growing steadily for some time. Since most, if not all, NGOs in this sector were dependent on government funding, there were hardly any independent researchers. There was little independent theory in the making. Freelance consultants in this field were doing the main work but it was hard to say how openly they could discuss their findings.[14] Most of their work was commissioned by large NGOs and government agencies and their reports often reflect the language and formats of funding bodies. Before Solaris, there had not been an online institutionally independent forum. What the development community needed was free speech (there was certainly enough free beer). Within mailing list culture, there had been little interest debating digital divide discourses and the new power relations of digitally enabled economies. Solaris called for a "critical discourse (that) comes from "within" and is not meant to spread a new form of techno-cultural pessimism. The last thing we need is a moralistic analysis of the Internet as a 'US-American imperialist tool'."[15]

Our Internet era was blinded by the light. As network technology was still an expanding universe, it was hard to see its limits or to recognize its damages without falling back into technophobia and cultural pessimism. An engaged form of research was necessary to overcome dry economism and its spiritual counterpart, technodeterminism—the all too often heard notion that technology will automatically bring salvation and result in prosperity for all, worldwide. In the early 2000s, a need was felt to analyze the agendas of all agents involved, including G8 DOT Force, U.S.-American foundations (Markle, Soros, Rockefeller, Ford), the charity/marketing input from IT companies, government ICT4D programs, NGOs, and media activists. Topics on Solaris were, to name but a few, the dumping of used computers, the role of local radio in relation to Internet, intellectual property in the NGO world, the Indian handheld device called Simputer, and similar cheap solutions.

In this context, it was important to state that information technology had not solved world poverty. The fight against poverty has proven to be an uphill battle. We cannot blame the Internet for this, but to ignore the bare facts would be negligent. What we should look for instead is a revolutionary modesty that is willing to take the faults in the Development Industries seriously. Unfortunately, we cannot answer the question of whether the money spent on computers and networks could be put to better use elsewhere. A shantytown community may not say, "Give us the money, not the computers, and we will decide how to use it." ITC arguably has contributed even further to the growing income inequality on both global and national levels. The rhetoric of UN initiatives, such as DOT Force and other digital divide programs such as WSIS, appears to recycle outdated neo-liberal dotcom models. PowerPoint optimism of successful projects is often used against those who ask questions. Before 2001, there was an "end of history" culture in the making driven by the almost religious belief that technology times market-driven business models would automatically result in democracy and prosperity for all. Debates around the World Summit on the Information Society have not changed these basic parameters. There is a broad consensus, from activists to government officials and business leaders, that ICTs have an overall positive effect. In such a climate, it becomes all too easy to ignore criticism and accuse those who call for more research and reflection of spoiling the party.

For example, the worldwide bandwidth gap is widening at an accelerating pace. While Africa struggles with modems, Western scientists fool around with grid technology. Linux is still stagnating as an alternative to Microsoft, thereby limiting its role as a competitive operating system, and is too often merely used as a platform for server software. The Solaris initiative intended to ask in which areas could strategic software be developed. Information technology does not always come with turnkey "out of the box" solutions. The overall picture is a complex and often paradoxical one. There is no longer a need for technology transfer from North to South. "Everyone is an expert" is not just a phrase—it is a daily reality. IT specialists are everywhere. However, there are numerous economic roadblocks preventing software production from below. The time has come to stress and examine the structural obstacles—and Western NGOs could be one of them. Another one could be unreconstructed (post)colonialism. It is becoming increasingly questionable whether we can continue to think in terms of technology deficits.

The use of information technology worldwide is causing paradoxical, sometimes contradictory, confusing effects, with occasional miracles and widely spread new forms of exclusion. Still, the overall sense is one of empowerment and surprise. The primal drive to discover, adapt, mutate, and further develop technology is a truly global phenomenon, one that cannot be overrun by a culture of complaint or the desire of corporate interests to create and capture markets. The Solaris initiators felt the need to emphasize the complexity of the picture and as the call said,

> involve all those who feel attracted to a rich multidisciplinary form of digital story telling beyond dull politics, sterile academicism, paper tiger task forces and self-reflexive policy conglomerates. It is time to get rid of the almost dead phrase "IT is about people, stupid" and move it beyond the massing ranks of the Digital Divide industry.

Information Technology for Everybody Else

In early 2004, the rather small conversations on Solaris were integrated into another initiative coined Incommunicado, a list and Web site that I founded with German scholar Soenke Zehle. The term *incommunicado* refers to a state of being without the means or rights to communicate, especially in the case of incommunicado detention and the threat of massive human rights violations. The latter also implies an extra-judicial space of exception, where torture, executions, and disappearances occur all-too-frequently in the lives of journalists and media activists, online or offline, around the world. Compared to Solaris, Incommunicado had a broader agenda, and focused on global civil society, environmental issues, and academic papers, which were distributed through its blog, www.incommunicado.info. Central to Incommunicado was the "info rights" discourse that had become prominent within the WSIS discourse. After the end of the Cold War and the collapse of the bilateral order, the discourse on human rights had become an important placeholder for agendas of social change and transformation, a discourse no longer articulated in Third-Worldist or tri-continentalist terms. The info rights agenda is a copy-paste strategy that follows a simple logic. If human rights are such a successful context for activists and NGOs, then why not use the same arguments, rhetoric, and organizational structures when it comes to emerging issues such as telecommunications? Search: human. Replace: info. Why not rewrite the Universal Declaration of Human Rights? This then became the strategy of a small group of activists, mostly from APC and related organizations to set up a so-called campaign that would work itself into the ITU and UN structures in the preparation phase of WSIS I and II.

The term *incommunicado* was chosen as the name for this research network of activists, academics, and geeks to acknowledge that while questions related to info-development and info-politics are often explored in a broader human rights context, this does not imply embracing a politics of rights as such. Instead, one of the aims of the Incommunicado project was to explore tactical mobilizations of rights-based claims to access, communication, or information, as well as the limits of any politics of rights, its concepts, and its absolutism as a political perspective. The program of the first Incommunicado conference, held in Amsterdam on June 15–17, 2005, had an explicitly broad and investigative character. Besides WSIS topics such as Internet governance and open source, the event put a few critical topics on the agenda, such as the role of NGOs, the critique of development in the Internet age, and the question of how useful it is to talk about info-rights. Some debates were also new and had to be explored, such as the role of ICT corporations as partners in development within the UN or the role of culture and corporate sponsorship in the ICT4D context.

While participants at Incommunicado 05 agreed that the standard scope of ICT4D debates and research needed to expand, there was no agreement on how this might best be done. What was certain was that the kind of critique the Incommunicado network was set up to explore and facilitate was unlikely to proceed through the consensus-building model of civil society caucuses and inter-institutional networks. Given the commitment to different, even mutually exclusive, logics and models of institutionalization in different camps from media activists to development NGOs and academic ICT analysts, the mutual engagement in a spirit of self-critique had its limits. But this was not necessarily a weakness. Part of the Incommunicado agenda was the assumption of a general comprehensibility and commensurability of efforts grouped under "civil society." As noted earlier, the aim was not to come to a real form of representation but to exemplify power relations between the real existing actors.

Digital Bandung

Also discussed at the Incommunicado 05 event was the shift in the techno-cultural development of the Web—a shift from an essentially Euro-American postindustrialist project toward a more complexly mapped post-Third-World network. These new South–South alliances are already upsetting our common definitions of info-development as an exclusively North-South affair. Let's call it the China–India–Brazil axis or Bandung II, named after the Bandung conference in 1955 where the Non-Aligned Movement was formed, aimed at promoting Asian-Afro cooperation. Before the recent "flattening of the world" as described by Thomas Friedman, most computer networks and ICT expertise were located in the North. The emergence of South-South relationships calls into question the old school relationships within ICT4D, which mainly focuses on North America/Europe and its involvement in Africa and, to a lesser extent, Asia and Latin America. However tempting, the new developments and particularly the emerging alliances should not be romanticized in terms of a new tri-continentalism. The cohesion of the new South-South alliances originates in part from the shared resistance to an emergent Euro-American front on intellectual property rights (IPR) and related matters, and is profiting from a U.S. American preoccupation with the Middle East.

In ICT there is no given recipe for success. Ambitious info-development projects struggle to find a role for themselves either as basic infrastructure and support for other development activity, or as a complement to older forms of infrastructure and service-oriented development. Often they are expected to meet a host of contradictory aims: alleviating poverty, catapulting peasants into the information age, producing localized content, promoting knowledge-based industries, or facilitating democratization through increased participation and local empowerment. Meanwhile, of course, info-development also facilitates transnational corporate efforts to offshore IT-related jobs and services in ever-shorter cycles of transposition. This often leaves local stakeholders at a loss to decide whether scarce public subsidies should even be used to attract and retain industries that are likely to move on anyway.

Info-development creates new conflicts, putting communities in competition with each other. But it also creates new alliances, bringing NGOs and civil society groups to the negotiating table. Below the traditional thresholds of sovereignty, grassroots efforts are calling into question the entire IPR regime of access restriction on which commercial info-development is based. Common- or open-source-oriented organizations are challenging northern countries on their self-serving commitment to IPR and their dominance of key info-political organizations. Meanwhile, lesser-known members of the UN family, such as the World Intellectual Property Organization (WIPO), are beginning to feel the heat brought on by activist campaigns that are targeting the entire international range of public actors to bring an agenda of accountability to the institutions of multilateral governance. As a response to the increasingly contradictory info-political activities of the major agencies like the ITU, UNDP, UNESCO, and WIPO, even the UN has begun to lose its aura. Its defense of profit-driven property rights is no longer sustainable and is making way for a new understanding of the digital public domain. As public perception of a positive UN role in governance, humanitarianism, and peacekeeping shifts toward corruption and inter-agency rivalry (carefully guided by neo-conservative think tanks), the ensemble of supra-state apparatuses that are supposed to sustain the vision of a postimperial order suddenly seem mired in a frightening family dispute. In the case of the dispute between ITU technocrats and the so-called progressive UNESCO cultural bureaucrats, it threatens to spin out of control.

The critique of development and its institutional arrangements—of its conceptual apparatus as well as the economic and social policies implemented in its name—have traditionally been a theoretical project and the agenda of a multitude of "subaltern" social movements. However, in the case of ICT4D we have heard surprisingly little thus far.[16] The reason for this could be the long shadow of the technophobia of NGOs in the past. Much work in ICT4D shows little awareness of or interest in the history of development critique. In fact, the ICT4D debate, whose terms are frequently reproduced in the members-only loop of a few influential NGO networks (APC, OneWorld, or PANOS, and other states and organizations), remains surprisingly inward looking, unable or unwilling to actively challenge the hegemony of an ahistorical techno-determinism. These global NGOs and Western government info-development agencies are new to the fact that there are now a multitude of actors operating in "their" field. The Incommunicado project is just one of many efforts to broaden the ICT4D scope, for instance those who work on free software, wireless network groups, and blog portals such as Global Voices.[17] A part of this process is a critical investigation into the role of info-developmental NGOs and how the office culture of such institutions could be transformed into open networks that initiate and facilitate campaigns. In this process, there would be a necessary shift away from (global) policy making toward decentralized citizen-to-citizen networks where collaboration, not aid, is the central driver.

Many believe that ICT leads to economic progress and eventually contributes to poverty reduction and that those who are being critical are doing it just for the sake of it. However, we should nonetheless ask: have development skepticism and the multiplicity of alternative visions it created simply been forgotten? We should not accept that postcolonialism has been hidden away in literature departments. Instead, we should inject these insights in current practices—to aim for a collateral thinking that includes antagonisms, and counter the trend of forced optimism where every public statement has to be some kind of sales pitch. Do we need to add ever more legitimacy to the strategies of "preemptive" development that are based on an intimate alliance between the politics of aid, development, and security? Are analyses based on the assumption of the inherent goodness of the Internet and its promise of connectivity already transcending existing power analyses of global media and communication structures? How can we reflect on the booming ICT4D industry beyond best practice suggestions, as listed in the many reports that have been produced over the years?

Civil Society versus Grassroots

We have become accustomed to thinking of civil society organizations and NGOs as natural development actors. However, their presence is indicative of a fundamental transformation from an originally state-centered development regime to their self-perception as representatives of civic and grassroots interests. Their growing influence raises difficult issues regarding their relationship to state and corporate actors. In spite of the neat sociological grammar of declarations and manifestos, increasingly these hybrid actors no longer follow the simple schema of state, market, or civil society, but engage in cross-sector alliances. Responding to the crisis of older top-down approaches to development, corporations and aid donors are increasingly bypassing states and international agencies to work directly with smaller NGOs. While national and international development agencies now have to defend their activity against both pro- and anti-neo-liberal critics, info-NGOs participating in public-private partnerships and info-capitalist ventures suddenly find themselves in the midst of another heated controversy over their new role as junior partners of both states and corporations. Responding by stepping up their own brand-protection and professional reputation management, major NGOs even conclude that it is no longer their organizational culture but *their agenda alone* that differentiates them from corporate actors.

The two world summits on the information society united many cyber-libertarians afraid of UN interventions into key questions of Internet governance. While many info-activists were assessing (and re-assessing) the hidden cost of invitations to sit at multi-stakeholder tables with mega-NGOs and corporate associations, others are already refusing to allow grassroots or subaltern agendas into the managed consensus being built around the dynamic of an international civil society. Others, such as Bernardo Sorj in Brazil, play down the importance of the global level altogether and show how important initiatives and legislation at the national level remain. Summits such as WSIS, at best, facilitate international exchange of information and ideas but have little or no impact at the political level or on everyday life. Mirroring the withdrawal from traditional mechanisms of political participation, there has been a growing disaffection with the high art of diplomatic multilateralism as the necessary default perspective for any counter-imperial politics. Unwilling to accept the idioms of sovereignty, some abandoned the very logic of summits and counter-summits to articulate postsovereign perspectives. If summits are good for anything, they at least provoke the question of what postrepresentational politics might look like. Is it possible to run a campaign in such closed surroundings like hotels and conference centers? How can activists intervene inside meetings that solely focus on the wording of declarations when they are actively taking part in the negotiations themselves?

Often the space of critique is defined in terms of an almost mythological grassroots and popular democracy. So combined, they are perceived as authentic sources of legitimacy and the last instance of accountability. In this way all you need for a critique of civil society and NGOs is to show their gradual (and almost inevitable, it seems) estrangement from a social movement grassroots. This critique is facilitated by the NGOs' adoption of corporate models of professionalization and emphasis on organizing efforts that are compatible with a professional intergovernmental summit. Meanwhile, the summit machine continues to hum right along, largely unimpressed by action plans, civil society declarations, and manifestos. In this failure of uncritical and unreflected action, it seems to produce its own critique.

ICTs and the NGO Question

When it comes to the innovative use of ICTs, NGOs have lost ground in the past decade and are largely indistinguishable from other users. The advantage NGOs had in the 1980s and early 1990s (mainly in the use of e-mail) was lost. It is well known that, perhaps with the exception of the APC, most NGOs have thus far resisted innovative use of the World Wide Web and continue their reluctance to use blogs, wikis, and social networks. In part, this is a question of generational demographics. Civil society has been anything but innovative when it comes to the adoption of ICTs. In many instances they were last and remain last. There is hardly any interest in new software, other platforms, or even public discussion as such. The skepticism toward open source and free software is widespread. The Web is often used in a static top-down mode. Blogs are nowhere to be seen. There is hardly any in-house software or interface development. It is, therefore, questionable to presume that NGOs are playing a key role in the development of ICT in non-Western countries. What they do best, and have always done, is to give access and training to their own staff and surrounding communities. NGO officials are not known for sharing their resources. In fact, more and more of their IT systems have been copied from the corporate world. The reason for this is the shift in consultancy culture. Because of a push to professionalize and to be accountable, large consultancy firms such as KPMG, PwC, Ernst & Young, and Deloitte are getting a tight grip on the NGO sector. It is known that NGOs are getting locked up in closed offices and compounds. Their ICT culture is merely a mirror of such enclosures and cannot be discussed outside of these developments.

The story I tell here is connected to a wider reservation on my side about the role that NGOs are playing and their stubborn responses when called upon for reflection. In my view, NGOs are memories in stone and papers about actual struggles and movements. They are institutional residue, condensed memories of events, and themselves not the real motors of social change. We cannot blame the NGO for its remnant status. These points are important for the ICT context. Today's movements are dramatically fluid and consist of a variety of temporary elements that we find in new media, but do not find in the NGO sector. Please note, however, that NGOs come into play toward the end of social processes. There is nothing wrong with this, but it is important to note as it indicates that NGOs are not necessarily the bodies that drive social or technological innovation, despite their good intentions. In the mainstream media and press and conservative think tanks, NGOs are charged with being undemocratic and unaccountable. From a movement perspective this is more or less irrelevant. What is more interesting is how the NGO model can be dissolved into virtual networks. In the last chapter of this book, I discuss how network organizations could relate to organized networks.

No tears have been shed. NGOs have become part of the establishment. Instead of bemoaning this decline and indulging in the defeat, we may as well move on and look for new forms of organization. We can leave the NGO criticism to conservatives like www.ngowatch.org, which writes: "NGO officials and their activities are widely cited in the media and relied upon in congressional testimony; corporations regularly consult with NGOs prior to major investments. Many groups have strayed beyond their original mandates and assumed quasi-governmental roles." There is a lot of truth in this. Just think of the tragic role NGOs played in the Kyoto treaty negotiations and how NGO negotiators remained silent when police arrested protesters during summits in The Hague (2000) and Bonn (2001). During a 2002 global warming conference in Marrakesh, Morocco, local authorities, in close collaboration with organizers, made it virtually impossible to protest.[18]

It is remarkable that there are no global NGOs like Greenpeace, Amnesty, or Oxfam that critically investigate the Internet and the new media/telecom sector. The Electronic Frontier Foundation has attempted to globalize, but it must have become clear that their libertarian worldview does not fit well into other cultural contexts. Sites like icannwatch.org that do such important work merely focus on the United States. For most NGOs, ICT is a tool, not a separate field of contestation that needs scrutiny. This lack was badly felt during the dotcom years and the following years of scandal, in which civil society played hardly any role at all. Often NGOs were the last to adapt, not the first.[19] Worldwide, there are few independent investigative journalists who specialize in ICT issues. This lack has grave consequences for the general understanding of the field. It is time to go beyond the understanding of ICT as a tool to develop a broadly distributed understanding of this crucial sector beyond the next thing.

There is the general discontent about the ICT and Development discourse, mainly in non-Western countries. This criticism is widely felt but not that advanced in terms of writing and key texts. There is something fundamentally fraudulent about this discourse and it is not the usual critique that people need clean water, food, and health care instead of computers. At WSIS, one saw many bureaucrats and their "researchers," a.k.a. consultants, but not many initiatives. Such summits are incentives to create an apparatus, not to link networks with networks. It is an interesting anomaly to see how governments like India on the one hand endorse ICT for development schemes and rhetoric, while simultaneously announcing that they will no longer accept Western ICT development assistance.

Academic research and critical theory have thus far been remarkably absent in this field. The whole idea of research such as the Social Science Research Council in New York was too slow for the rapidly changing IT environment, as it is stuck in decades-old academic procedures.[20] The way most academics conduct research these days makes their work often irrelevant once it is published—caused by slow peer-reviewed journals and publishing houses. We all complain about it, but there are actually quite effective ways to do something about this. For instance, it could be a requirement that research data be published online immediately and comply with open access rules. Instead of following, it is time for social science to take the lead. It is not that difficult. One way out would be to change social science from a discipline that only gathers data about the long-term impact of ICT, toward a laboratory model that invents, initiates, and connects. There should be a much bigger commitment to free software, open source, Wikipedia, and wireless networks, just to name a few examples of a diverse digital public domain in the making. These areas are so unique that we can drop the *development* label and enter a much more interesting area of collaboration.

WSIS made evident that there are only a few forces willing and able to analyze and criticize the information society concept. The air in Geneva was filled with the spirit of network naiveté—no matter on what side one stood. Both the hegemonic and the alternative view of the information society is characterized by a persistent transcendentalism, as if the spread of ICT would increase development, as if access to the Internet would improve living conditions, as if free software would override capitalism, as if file sharing equals altruism, as if open publishing would promote democracy. As if. Leaving Amand Mattelart's *The Information Society: An Introduction* (2003) aside, one could say that a post-Luddite critique of information society, written from the radical inside, does not yet exist. There is the NGO-type civil society story about human rights and unequal access, but that's about it. The weak spot with this approach is its charity mentality: please donate some computers and share your bandwidth with the poor. What is lacking is a sovereign autonomist perspective. Let's say, a Hardt and Negri of the Internet generation. Hardt and Negri have processed political experiences of the Baby Boom/Cold War generation; now it is time to move beyond 1989. Such programmatic works should have been written during the raving 1990s, but instead we are stuck with remnant bits of anti-imperialist thinking and other reworkings of a past that was not ours. Much of the anti-globalization discourse sets us back in time. All we got in return was this peculiar blend of utopia, violence, and retreat. In the past decade, collective work on ideas has been replaced by informal networking, a move away from old school macho politics toward culture and the arts, shifting the focus toward software, interface design, and just playing around. Instead of blaming Generation X for their disinterest in theory, one could also stress that theory can only grow out of reflected experience. In that sense, we might be too impatient. The question should rather be: how can theory exist in an age of real-time events?

Quixotic projects and idealism pervade the rhetoric of the vast majority of those who did not ignore the summit. That was the disappointment of the WSIS process but it did not come as a much of a surprise. What could it mean to put the information society under a radical critique? One has to track down the material basis of information and communication in order to turn the whole discourse upside down. For instance, one could research the impact of precarious and migrant labor in hardware and software industries, such as the service sector call centers, and their armies of temporary workers. This would mean tearing down the exclusive notion of information as something ephemeral, spiritual, and immaterial and revealing the dirty side of the technology with its grease and steel.

It would be a mistake to look at this other or, more accurately, real information society with an attitude of charity, and to commiserate with these poor people who work so damned hard so we can play and entertain ourselves with ever-cheaper computers. Often this perspective comes along with a romantic, anti-technological attitude—full of ignorance and resentment against informatization, deregularization, and globalization. These processes that constitute the current situation are direct and indirect results of struggles (against the working day, for a better living, or for any job at all) that are disconnected and abstracted from a common, daily experience.

A radical critique always implies practical consequences. There is no other way out of the intellectual stagnation than to stage unlikely encounters and unexpected alliances—between coders, activists, and researchers, artists, and unionists. We have to bring on irrelevant moments and leave the programmed density of the event-time for what it is. Shouldn't a radical critique of the information society in the first instance confront the common notion of sovereignty and its media saturation with something that reaches out beyond the increasing banality of networking? What happens after the excitement of the encounter has faded? Should the motor of creativity and subversion continue to be supplied with an ever-changing focus on yet-to-be discovered (and soon-to-be exploited) cultural differences?

Incommunicado Research

Thus far, the Incommunicado agenda has been a broad one, bringing together different threads of critique into one platform. The topics that Incommunicado covered in 2006 varied from public-private partnerships, e-waste, which PC is best for the poor, Internet governance (again), emergency technologies, first mile solutions, design that matters, ICTs and remittances to Africa, and open source. Such a wide approach is a high-risk strategy as the mix of different concerns can be perceived as bohemian, if not to say radical chic. We have to take into account the enormous scale of global poverty with the next billion or two people that will get a mobile phone and be introduced to the Internet over the next decade. Within ICT4D both critical and visionary research has not been much of a priority. What we found most often are best practice stories that are supposed to feed into policy documents. While there must be critical assessment reports, these are usually written for internal use only. To discuss openly the question "Why did my project fail" is so twenty-second century. Ministries, funding bodies, foundations, and NGOs are not eager to share their inside knowledge with outsiders for fear that any negative information will compromise their position in the scramble for funds, and could eventually lead to budget cuts. This makes it hard, if not impossible, to have an open debate about the terms that are floating around, and to come up with new concepts.

Beyond organizing meetings and setting up lists and collaborative Weblogs, research is also a means of opening up a space, both in terms of activism and knowledge production. This also requires calling into question the assemblage of "mots d'ordre" that make up the info-development discourse. Such "mots d'ordre"—including, but not limited to, access, capacity building, poverty alleviation, and stakeholderism—are not made to encourage debate, but more to foster agreement on a consensual perception of what info-development is. We have witnessed this in the context of WSIS, and Incommunicado was started in the context of WSIS. However, even if it maintains a critical distance from this perception—as do, by now, virtually all groups that have been involved—it is still marked by this focus on the critique of a policy-driven process organized around a fairly standard set of actors. At the same time, what is actually happening below the threshold of civil society is a rich and dynamic source of new forms of info-political engagement and new conceptual approaches. Hence, future research on the development discourse must engage such micro-level studies as well as the donor discourse that serves to filter such efforts from the outside of the established research system. Such engagement is especially important, as the donor discourse has reproduced into a transnational regime that includes state and non-state agencies, philanthropic and profit-oriented efforts. Groups such as IT for Change (Bangalore), Third World Institute (Montevideo), and Sarai (Delhi) are all doing interesting work in this direction. It is now time for the critical academic development studies to catch up and start up long-term ICT research that will go beyond WSIS monitoring.

Finally, ICT4D research needs to be considered in the context of shifts in the mode of production of science. Some sociologists argue, for example, that we are witnessing a transition from an academically centered mode that values scientific autonomy and peer evaluation, to a flexible mode that is participatory and transdisciplinary. Such a flexible mode would address a host of economic and social questions through research that is accountable, open, and transparent. Flexible scientific production is the ultimate wet dream of donors more committed to the vague notion of a knowledge society than to the controversial questions of what such a new scientific ethic might actually mean in practice. This would include a controversy over the criteria of relevance and reliability that determine whether efforts that do not uncritically accept the hegemonic assemblage of "mots d'ordre" would still receive support.

NGOs, new media activists, and artists are still at the very beginning of formulating demands. The official talk rarely goes beyond universal access. For example, at-large membership participation within the technical coordination body ICANN—a private non-profit corporation controlled by the U.S. government, that is directed to govern the global Internet domain name structure—has had recent traumatic experiences that have hardly been digested. The idea that another Internet is possible, one that is no longer exclusively ruled by the worthy white male engineering class who protect their closed consensus culture while claiming to work for the common good, is still a long way off. On the other hand, no one wants to return to a model in which intergovernmental relations make all decisions. A radical critique of the multi-stakeholder approach cannot easily circumvent this dilemma. Proposals for alternative global governance of the new media sphere have yet to be made. It is even unclear who the stakeholders are and how national governments, telcos, and civil society (whoever that is) might relate to each other. On the formal, political level WSIS may not have any outcome. As one among many summits, WSIS will be crushed by the much larger multilateral crisis that affects all UN bodies. But that will not stop thousands from fiercely debating the issues and defining the next new world network disorder.

CHAPTER 8

Updating Tactical Media
Strategies for Media Activism

Running updates is an integral part of our technological culture. It is considered a necessary evil. To not download the necessary patches is seen as suicidal. In contemporary theory production, this practice has not yet been introduced. Within the humanities and the arts, wikis remain underutilized. Theory is still considered a terrain of the sole author who contemplates the world, preferably offline, surrounded by a pile of books, a fountain pen, and a notebook. This is of course a caricature, but where exactly is the obstacle located? Apart from a text having different versions before it is published, most writers do not take out bugs or flaws after publishing the text even though word processing and online text editing have become so easy. Instead of updating old texts, the consensus is that it is better to come up with something new altogether. This not only satisfies producers and users; newness is what the market demands. Radio maker and programmer Alexander Klosch from Weimar led me to the difference between updating and upgrading. Wikipedia continuously upgrades and downgrades its articles. Whereas updating has a time element, upgrading usually refers to quality and status. A change does not by definition result in an improvement or a disqualification. According to Klosch, the update is best placed in collaborative work. A single maintainer is often overstretched, keeping a complex structure up-to-date. This is where a community or smaller group of maintainers comes into play. Thus far, online platforms are rarely used to create—and change—theoretical concepts. Theory books rarely make it to a next print run, much less are ever rewritten for a second edition. The common belief holds that outdated theories are hard to use, have bugs and limitations, and can only be read under the rubric of history. In the Change Society in which we are stuck, yesterday's concepts are not just worn out; they are by definition wrong as they are deconstructed at the time of their release.

In this chapter, I propose critical updates for the concept of tactical media. I provide a subjective overview of current debates about new media and the role they play in global social movements.[1] In the first part, I look into the status of the tactical media meme since it embarked on its remarkable journey. Then I discuss strategies of the biggest emerging political force in decades—the so-called antiglobalization movement—and discuss some books about this topic. It has often been remarked that this movement is not one, it has many faces and names. In some instances, I speak of the global justice movement, in others of multitudes. Some call this multi-headed dragon the "movement of movements." Another name, the "other-globalization movement," expresses the desire to go beyond the anti-position of street protests in order to emphasize the common search for alternatives. Here I specifically look into strategies of critical new media culture in the postspeculative phase after dotcommania, 9/11, the big mobilizations from Seattle to Gleneagles and, in particular, inquire about the relationship between the real and the virtual. Instead of burying the tactical media concept, which could have been done years ago, we may as well celebrate its robustness. Missed the autumn of tactical media? Then join the renaissance of tactics!

Revisiting Tactical Media

Let's briefly look back. The term *tactical media* arose in the aftermath of the fall of the Berlin Wall as a renaissance of media activism, blending old school political work and artists' engagement with new technologies. The early 1990s saw a growing awareness of gender issues, an exponential growth of media industries, and the increasing availability of cheap DIY equipment—creating a new sense of self-awareness among activists, programmers, theorists, curators, and artists. Media were no longer seen as merely tools for the struggle, but experienced as virtual environments whose parameters were permanently under construction. This was the golden age of tactical media, open to issues of aesthetics and experimentation with alternative forms of storytelling. However, these liberating techno-practices did not immediately translate into visible social movements. Rather, they symbolized the celebration of media freedom, in itself a great political goal. The DIY media that was used varied widely—from video, DVDs, cassettes, 'zines and flyers to music styles such as rap and techno—and the content was equally diverse. A commonly shared feeling was that politically motivated activities, be they art or research or advocacy work, were no longer part of a closed and suspicious identity circuit. They could intervene in pop culture without necessarily having to compromise with the system. With everything up for negotiation, new coalitions could be formed.

The origins of tactical media go back to the Next Five Minutes (N5M) festival in Amsterdam, a new media event with a clear political angle that grew out of a coalition of cultural institutions, individuals, and groups. Around mid-1992 a name had to be chosen for an art, activism, and media festival and it became "N5M: Tactical Television." The first N5M took place in January 1993 and focused on the camcorder revolution and the events in Eastern Europe after the fall of the Berlin Wall. In March 1996, during the Internet boom, the second edition took place, and the name was changed to Tactical Media. The first systematic text on the topic, written by David Garcia and me, appeared in 1997.[2] The third festival was held in March 1999, days before the outbreak of the Kosovo war. The post-9/11 fourth edition took place in September 2003. N5M never culminated into an organization. It did not become an annual or biannual event and never obtained a legal structure or a stable Web site. From the beginning, N5M had been a temporary coalition of individuals and institutions that came together to organize the festival—and then separate. Also remarkable is the fact that the event thus far has not resulted in a (sustainable) network. To some extent, Indymedia took over this role from 2000 onward, but Indymedia misses an imaginative and artistic agenda, mainly due to its narrow focus on news.

The current movements worldwide cannot be understood outside of the diverse and often very personal desire for digital freedom of expression. Tactical media is a short-term concept, born out of disgust for ideology. It surfs on the waves of events, enjoying the opening up of scenes and borders, on the lookout for new alliances. Curious, not afraid of difference, it is not bound to certain formats or platforms. It comes with a positive attitude toward contemporary digital technology. It is more exploratory than confrontational. It wants to make a new start for activism and reach new audiences. But, as Paul Garrin warns, "Tactical Media is not only something that Media Activists engage in. It's advertising, corporate psychological warfare of Perception Management."[3] My critique of tactical media is not its short-lived character. By definition, tactical media is nonsustainable, always on the verge of disappearance. Its unstable nature creates situations while setting clear limits for further growth.

Let's not repeat the definitions that are floating around. Since early 2006, there has been a Wikipedia entry for tactical media. What is worth mentioning is the way in which this term has been adopted by numerous groups and individuals worldwide. Besides the tactical media scene in Brazil, one could think of Tactical Tech, an Amsterdam-based network of free software open source developers in non-Western countries, or of the Slovenian artist Marko Peljhan, whose Makrolab has been given the tactical media adjective. In his book *Protocol*, Alex Galloway mentions a few more projects, from computer viruses to cyberfeminism and games.[4] What brings these tactical initiatives together is their carefully designed workings, their aesthetics beyond the question of taste. Being neither cute nor ugly, neither good nor bad, tactical media appears, strikes, and disappears again. Instead of the old school rituals of negation and refusal, tactical media engages makers and users, producers and viewers, into a game of appearances and disappearances. Key to tactical media is its mix of art and activism, and a shared critical awareness of style, design, and aesthetics. This is also its most vulnerable part, as most activists, journalists, and intellectuals do not necessarily subscribe to its agenda, or are even informed about its existence.

Tactical media celebrates disorganization. There is not even an electronic mailing list that brings together tactical media practitioners. Nettime, Spectre, Fibreculture, and IDC might do this, in part, but none of these lists is focused on media activists. Agreed, tactical media makers meet up every now and then, but rarely create networks among themselves, yet they are often grouped around an event or incident. Tactical media workers seem to have other identities. It is a remarkable historical detail that if you type "tactical media network" into a search engine, you end up on a empty red page, produced in mid-1997 for Documenta X in Kassel by the Amsterdam N5M, a page that leads nowhere. What we find there are definitions, not a network. Its provisional character is stressed. The tactical generation is wary of institutionalization and loves to operate undercover. Weak ties between artists and activists are carefully being conserved.

Within the tactical media context, what does it mean to create a global platform? Isn't that pure ideology? Are we merely nostalgic revolutionaries who dream of revitalizing the good old international solidarity that communist functionaries once preached? On a Waag–Sarai collaboration Web site, we can read the following, long quotation:

> Finances have to be organized, technology installed, content curated. A well functioning interconnected system may be the proud result of the intense exchanges of ideas, software and other resources. Yet, the network itself remains fragile and unseen. It is the metaphysical entity of our days ("Ceci n'est pas une reseau"). The techno-civic maze always remains under construction. Networks are never merely tools. They are sensitive environments, mutating organisms where people

and institutions constantly negotiate, question, argue, contribute, feeding each other with an ever-growing stream of information. Networks are never finished channels of Babel. They are an intercultural grid that's always in flux and grown out of a never-ending passion for coding and streaming, designing, and writing. We have passed the stage of the one-way "technology transfer" and arrived in the age of global collaboration. This is not to say that worldwide economic inequality has all but disappeared overnight due to the arrival of the computer. However, the image of the "digital divide" is a much too passive description for the titanic turmoil caused by proliferation of new technologies on a planetary scale.[5]

What is exchanged between new media centers and practitioners on a truly global scale? Isn't it a megalomaniacal project to aim for universal representation? Tactical media can easily operate on micro-levels, but why should it mimic a United Nations? Just because we now have the tools, do we know how to utilize them and stumble into the most amazing compatriots? What is this promiscuous "contact between continents" all about? What is so attractive about this essentially Christian imagery? How can a meme maintain its power while operating in wildly diverse cultures? It is not hard to see that the challenge for tactical media is no longer technical but resides in knowing how to negotiate differences within a loose and temporal network structure.

All too easily, the energy of tactical media practitioners is getting lost inside the locality called Internet, a place we all love to hate. It is tempting to get lost there and believe in the Internet as the "medium to end all media." What tactical media makers do is discourage high expectations around the liberating potential of all technologies, both old and new, while not falling into the trap of cultural pessimism. Instead, we look for ways to connect the banal with the exclusive, the popular with high art, common trash with expensive branded commodities. On a technical level this means finding ways to connect, relay, disconnect—and again reconnect—a veritable stampede of pirate radio waves, video art, animations, hoaxes, wi-fi networks, music jam sessions, Xerox cultures, performances, grassroots robotics, cinema screenings, street graffiti, and (don't forget!) computer code. There is a lot of mutual aid in building up centers and networks, up to the point when it is time to leave them to others, to history, and move on. The strength of tactical media is that it can bring people together. Its weakness is its lack of borders and programmatic statements. Tactical media has a tendency to fall apart in numerous micro swarms. There is nothing against that—that is the nature of coalitions. What actually happens goes global. There are realities that cut across borders and across the old

North-South divide, says Saskia Sassen.[6] Activists in Sao Paolo and Manila share an emergent geography of centrality that connects them, through rather unstable connections, with groups in New York or Paris. Small organizations that have little financial resources meet up with like-minded initiatives from dozens of countries, spread across the planet, from Latin America to South Asia. We see similar connections established in visual arts, music, and free software. How do we gain cultural sensitivity? How do we master the labor-intensive task of arranging visas for African partici- pants? Think twice if you think you want to use the term *global*.

The Time of the Movement

Different phases of the global movement are becoming visible, all of which have distinct political, artistic, and aesthetic qualities. By the end of the 1990s, the postmodern "time without movements" had come to pass. Orga- nized discontent began to rise against neo-liberalism, global warming, labor exploitation, and numerous other issues. Equipped with networks and arguments, backed up by decades of research, a hybrid movement— wrongly labeled as "antiglobalization" —gained momentum. One of the particular features of this movement was its apparent inability and unwill- ingness to answer the question that is typical of any kind of movement on the rise or any generation on the move: What is to be done? There was and is no answer, no alternative—either strategic or tactical—to the existing world order, to the dominant mode of globalization.

Moreover, maybe this is the most important and liberating conclu- sion: There is no way back to the twentieth century, the protective nation state, and the gruesome tragedies of the "left." It has been good to remem- ber—but equally good to throw off—the past. The question "What is to be done?" should not be read as an attempt to reintroduce some form of Leninist principle. The issues of strategy, organization, and democracy belong to all times. We neither want to bring old policies back through the backdoor, nor do we think that this urgent question can be dismissed by invoking crimes committed under the banner of Lenin, however justified such arguments are. When Slavoj Žižek looks in the mirror he may see Father Lenin, but that's not the case for everyone. It is possible to wake up from the nightmare of the history of communism and ask: What is to be done? Can a multitude of interests and backgrounds still ask that question, or is the only agenda the one defined by the summit calendar of world leaders and the business elite?

Nevertheless, the movement of movements has spread like wildfire. At first sight, it appeared to use a traditional medium: the mass-mobilization of tens of thousands in the streets of Seattle, hundreds of thousands in the streets of Genoa. Tactical media networks played an important role in this coming into being. From now on, pluriformity of issues and identities was a given reality. Difference is here to stay and no longer needs to legitimize itself against higher authorities such as the Party, the Union, or the Media. Compared to previous decades, this is its biggest gain. There are no longer any central meaning structures. The Church has been replaced by a never-ending parade of celebrities that provide us with comfort and hope. The multitudes are not a dream or some theoretical construct, but a reality. This world is decentralized and fragmented. That is where the trouble starts: How do multitudes communicate over distances, and in what language? How do they create common ground without using traditional intermediaries? How do they operate in the market of micro-identities? And most of all, once they gather, how do they discuss and come to make decisions?

If there is a strategy, it is not contradiction but complementary existence. Despite theoretical deliberations, there is no contradiction between the street and cyberspace—one fuels the other. Protests against the WTO, neo-liberal EU policies, and party conventions have all been staged in front of the gathered world press. Indymedia centers crop up as parasites of mainstream media. Instead of having to beg for attention, protests take place under the eyes of the world media during summits of politicians and business leaders, seeking direct confrontation. Alternatively, symbolic sites are chosen. These include border regions such as in East-West Europe, South Europe–Africa, United States–Mexico, or refugee detention centers at the Amsterdam and Frankfurt airports, the centralized Eurocop database in Strasbourg, or the Woomera detention center in the South Australian desert. Rather than merely objecting to it, the global entitlement of the movement adds to the ruling mode of globalization a new layer of globalization from below.

Confusion and Resignation after 9/11

At first glance, the future of the movement is a confusing and irritating one. Old-leftist grand vistas, explaining the imperialism of the willing and its aggressive unilateralist policies, provided by Chomsky, Pilger, Fisk, and Roy are consumed with enthusiasm but no longer given religious certainty. In a polycentric world, conspiracy theories that highlight only one aspect (in this case oil and U.S. foreign policy) can only provide temporary comfort for the confused. No moralist condemnation of capitalism is necessary as facts and events speak for themselves. People are driven to the street by the situation, not by theories. The few remaining leftists can no longer provide the movement with an ideology, as it works perfectly without one. Even the fermented social movements that emerged in the

1970s and 1980s, and now locked up in their NGO structures, are having a hard time keeping up. New social formations are taking possession of the streets and media spaces without feeling the need for representation by some higher authority—not even the heterogeneous committees gathering in Porto Alegre.

Thus far, this movement has been bound in clearly defined time/space coordinates. It still takes months to mobilize multitudes and organize the logistics, from buses and planes, camping grounds and youth hostels, to independent media centers. Thus far, the global movement has been anything but spontaneous (and does not even claim to be so). The people who travel hundreds or thousands of miles to attend protest rallies are driven by real concerns, not by some romantic notion of socialism. The worn-out question: "Reform or revolution?" sounds more like blackmail to provoke the politically correct answer. On both the local and national level, however, we see a different picture—that crowds grow rapidly, even within days. Euromayday, on the other hand, gathers once a year, and has spread over the continent in a slow but steady pace.

The contradiction between selfishness and altruism has proven to be a false one. State-sponsored corporate globalization affects everyone. International bodies such as the WTO, IMF, the Kyoto Agreement on global warming, or the privatization of the energy sector are no longer abstract items, once dealt with by a handfull of experts, bureaucrats, and NGO lobbyists. This political insight has been the major quantum leap of recent times. Is this the last Internationale? There is no way back to the old nation state, to traditional concepts of liberation, to the logic of transgression and transcendence, exclusion and inclusion. Struggles are no longer projected onto a distant Other that begs for moral support and money. We have finally arrived in the postsolidarity age. It is seen as a colonial insult to speak on behalf of the world's poor. Consequently, national liberation movements have been replaced by a new analysis of power, which is simultaneously incredibly abstract, symbolic, and virtual, while terribly concrete, detailed, and intimate. This shortcut marks the quality and vitality of the new movements.

The challenge lately has been to liquidate the regressive period of marginal moral protest that followed the slow demise of mass mobilizations. Fortunately, 9/11 has had no immediate impact on the movement. The choice between Bush and bin Laden was irrelevant. Both agendas were rejected as devastating fundamentalisms. The all too obvious question "Whose terror is worse?" was carefully avoided as it led away from the pressing exigencies of everyday life: the struggle for a living wage, decent public transportation, health care, water, and education. As both social democracy and existing socialism depend heavily on the nation state, a return to the twentieth century sounds as disastrous as all the catastrophes it produced.

The concept of a digital multitude is fundamentally different from previous ideas about the multitude, and is based entirely on openness. Over the last few years, the creative struggles of the multitudes have produced outputs on many different layers: the dialectics of open sources, open borders, and open knowledge. Yet the deep penetration of the concepts of openness and freedom into the principle of struggle is by no means a quick compromise to the cynical and greedy neoliberal class. Progressive movements have always dealt with a radical democratization of the rules of access, decision-making, and the sharing of gained capacities. Usually this began with an illegal or illegitimate common ground. Within the bounds of the analog world, it led to all sorts of cooperatives and self-organized enterprises. Their specific notions of justice were based on efforts to circumvent the brutal regime of the market, and on different ways of dealing with the scarcity of material resources.

Mainstreaming the Debate: George Monbiot

No doubt the times they are a-changin' when internal strategic debates of the other-globalization movement make it into mainstream publishing. According to Amazon.com, "Naomi Klein's *No Logo* told us what was wrong. Now George Monbiot's *The Age of Consent* shows us how to put it right." Publisher Rupert Murdoch's HarperCollins sells Monbiot's manifesto as "authoritative and persuasive de facto figurehead for the contrarian movements in the UK." Environmental activist Monbiot is a columnist for *The Guardian* and author of a bestseller about the United Kingdom's privatization disasters. Thanks to Murdoch's distribution network, *The Age of Consent* made it onto a newsstand at the Sydney airport, where I purchased a copy.[7]

The change Monbiot has in mind falls nothing short of a "metaphysical mutation," a concept he took from French novelist Michel Houellebecq. Or rather an epistemological mutation, a revolutionary process somewhat similar to Thomas Kuhn's concept of the paradigm shift.[8] Monbiot sees a "global civil society" emerging out of protest movements against the WTO, WEF, and the G8 and counter summits such as the World Social Forum. He calls for these movements to seize the moment "and become the catalyst for the new mutation." It has been often said that global problems need global solutions, beyond the interaction between nations. Unlike critics of global corporations such as David Korten, Monbiot is not a "localizer" who believes that self-sufficient small enterprises are the solution. Empire with its global corporations can only be matched with global democracy.

For many of these activists, there is no way back to the nation state. Facing challenges such as the AIDS crisis and global warming, activists see an urgency to collectively dream up new global entities and construct them from the bottom up. "Small is beautiful" may be a worthy sentiment, but it ultimately disadvantages the poor. It is a waste of time to demand global governance and wait until the current political class voluntarily implements such models. I will go into detail with Monbiot's arguments because tactical media have thus far not yet been dealt with in such a global context.

Monbiot makes a case for democracy as the least worst system. As there is nothing better, we may as well work within its premises. What activists often push aside is the question of who guards the guards. Inside movements, and within Internet culture, democracy is being preached but not practiced. This was a problem of the left in the past. Accountability is again an issue in relation to NGOs that get invited to participate in global summits. Whom do they represent and for whom are they accounting? Conservative "astroturf" (opposite of grassroots) campaigns such as ngowatch. org raise this issue, but until recently there was no answer beyond conspiracy theory as to who was behind this NGO watch.[9] Despite its own weak democratic tradition, Monbiot calls for a "global democratic revolution" that will push aside "hopeless realism." Monbiot believes in the power of momentary happenings or even slightly more abstract, "the event," as it is called in philosophical circles. He writes, "What is realistic is what happens. The moment we make it happen. It becomes realistic. A global democratic revolution is the only option we have. It is the only strategy which could deliver us from the global dictatorship of vested interests." After the Age of Dissent, "it is time to invoke the Age of Consent."

Most of the manifesto is dedicated to three proposed global institutions: a world parliament, an International Clearing Union, and a Fair Trade Organization. The idea of a world parliament stems from the complaint that NGOs lack transparency and accountability. Monbiot believes that the ultimate solution for this would be a global forum that is a directly representative one. His world parliament would not be a legislative body, at least not from the start, but would hold global players to account. At the same time we would get rid of the Security Council, where only five countries hold veto right. In addition, we would have to rethink the "one nation one vote" system of the UN General Assembly, as the Pacific island of Vanuatu now holds the same voting power as India and China.

Despite my initial reservation about his Murdoch affiliation, I came to admire Monbiot's spirit. This manifesto is an example of brave, strategic thinking, free of the usual New Age mumbo jumbo that often accompanies "positive" literature. Organized positivism has apparently moved on from dotcom business circles to the translocal messengers of hope. Monbiot's rhetorical fire is yet another example of how wrong the Blairist spin-doctor Charles Leadbeater was in his *Up the Down Escalator: Why the Global Pessimists are Wrong*. Movements such as ATTAC[10] operate like distributed think tanks that have taken up the task to design alternatives in global finance and trade. One may not agree with some elements of the ATTAC story but the direction is clear. Today's movements sense an urgency to materialize their own slogan of "Another World is Possible." Many have taken up this task, moved on and away from the presumably apocalyptic protest mode in order to transform the energy of the growing movements onto other levels. We could mention, for instance, World Changing, Global Voices, Planetwork, and Open Democracy as the most mainstream U.S. examples. To simply map the many global postpolitical workshops of change is a large project in itself.

We no longer live in the dark 1980s, Mr. Leadbeater. There may be mass outbreaks of depression, but these psycho-pandemics are quickly treated with Prozac and Viagra. If we were to live in the Age of Pessimism, who then would be today's Arthur Schopenhauer? Which contemporary thinker can match "Man, the insomniac animal" Emile Cioran? How can we approach the dark mind who wrote "negation is the mind's first freedom"? There is in fact too much artificial optimism. We are forced to mention alternatives that do not exist. Leadbeater's compulsory upbeat sales talk, which presents itself as a quasi-moderate, balanced view on matters, in fact is the present authoritarian voice of the State. His hypocrisy is lying in the denial of force, violence, and the very existence of power. It is an easy job to dump on last century's utopias and accuse your opponents of totalitarianism. What Leadbeater in fact celebrates is the Death of Ideas. Let the experts such as Leadbeater do the thinking for you! Leadbeater favors "innovation" over radical transformation and promotes the comfortable normalcy of his pajama consultancy life as the solution to the world's problems. Leadbeater does not understand it all. Aren't we having a nice life? What are all these critics such as Monbiot whining about?

The Age of Consent is neither utopian nor idealistic, even though many dismissed Monbiot's proposals in such a way. His blueprint for a new world may as well be dismissed as too detailed, too pragmatic. Monbiot writes from an insider's perspective of the global justice movement. It is this explicit position that makes his proposals so appealing and potentially powerful. Finally, it is comforting to know there is someone who has overcome the quasi-neutrality that has made current affairs journalism so cold, cynical, and deliberately out of the touch with the realm of ideas.

Monbiot's manifesto should be read as an example of an emerging genre. *The Age of Consent* reminds one of nonacademic socialist and anarchist pamphlets from before World War I, when the question "What is to be done?" had an urgency—and the answers to that question had an impact on the course of world events. In his writing, you can sense there is something at stake. What Monbiot shares with Negri and Hardt's *Empire* is the belief in power of the multitudes to constitute the world. Everything may have been commodified and integrated into the Spectacle—except the collective imagination. We can find traces of people's sovereignty everywhere. The same can be said of inspirational tactical media groups that develop experimental software, interfaces, and networks. Germination may take a long time.[11] Seeds may sit on the soil for ages. Not that I agree with much of what Monbiot is proposing, but that is exactly the point. Certain texts open up spaces and imaginative possibilities—and that is what is dangerous about ideas. It is what makes those in power so suspicious about those ideas that break the innovation barrier and aim at an overall metamorphosis of society.

After decades of rampant anti-intellectualism, we find ourselves in a Golden Age of Ideas and Monbiot is part of this trend. Festivals of Ideas are popular as never before.[12] Within this wave, ideas are traded as the "currency of our information age." The economic recession, 9/11, climate change, and the violent, unilateral policies of the Bush administration only accelerate this process. "Sticky" ideas have gone beyond the j'accuse! level and can mobilize media users into a growing multiplicity of what Internet critic Howard Rheingold has called "smart mobs." "Our opinions count for nothing until we act upon them," Monbiot writes. But this is becoming less and less of a problem. People are increasingly willing to act and the global antiwar protests in early 2003 have illustrated this in unmistakable terms. Movements increasingly operate outside of the ritualized political realm. There is no way old broadcast media can cover their influence. In the network age, ideas are carefully designed memes that travel far and wide without losing their core meaning. No matter how hard ignorant and obsequious newsroom editors try, ideas cannot be turned into lies. Until recently, they could just be ignored and condemned as marginal, academic, or irrelevant, but the present demand can no longer be denied. Ideas easily withstand misinterpretations caused by sloppy journalists or Menoporsche commentators. The main reason for this is that we live in the postdeconstruction age. It is no longer entertaining or even necessary to take apart every single sentence or concept in order to place each notion within the history of ideas. Every new idea can be disassembled easily into a range of old ideas. Media literacy has risen to such an extent that attractive ideas will reach their audience anyway. This mechanism is also having an impact on the work of spin-doctors.

The 2003 invasion of Iraq can be read in two ways: as a successful campaign to manipulate world opinion or as the end of spin spread by global news media. Already months before the war, millions refused to buy into the media hype that was fanning the flames of war, and public anger only grew after the events. This is the problem of the "Chomsky-style media equals propaganda legacy" that the other globalization movement still embraces. The issue is not the truth that Web sites such as PR-Watch, GNN, Media Channel, or Adbusters are revealing. The problem is that only a few still believe in the media. As I indicated before, blogs are an essential vehicle in this process of demystification of mass media. The enlightenment work has already been done, and it is only cynicism and fear that fuels populism, not the fabricated truth. Media spin itself now has a due date.

It is not freedom of speech that matters so much. If you can say anything you like, outside of a lively social context, there is no threat, no matter what you have to say. It is the freedom of ideas that is truly subversive. Reading the reviews it is interesting to see how both old-school Marxists and free marketers dismiss Monbiot's arguments without seriously engaging with his proposals. To portray capitalists as from Mars and the Movement from Venus, as *The Economist* did, is an easy rhetorical trick that runs away from the very real global crisis in economic, ecological, and political affairs. The breakdown of free trade talks in the Doha-round show that the WTO is at the brink of collapse—and that NGOs are playing a key role in this process. On the other hand, to accuse Monbiot of being a Keynesian whose only wish is to save capitalism is another move that no longer makes sense and is obviously contrary to the message of his book. As Monbiot clearly writes, "The existing institutions cannot reform themselves. Their power relies upon the injustice of the arrangements which gave rise to them, and to tackle that injustice would be to accept their own dissolution."

Monbiot dares to think big and that is what both old-school Marxists and ruling neo-liberals do not like about *The Age of Consent*. "Our task," Monbiot writes, "is not to overthrow globalization, but to capture it, and to use it as a vehicle for humanity's first global democratic revolution." What is on the agenda is nothing less than democracy at a global level. Both the traditional left and the neo-conservatives do not like to talk about "global governance," as it is called in international relations. Whereas the left has over-identified itself with the nation state, neo-liberals believe that it is the global business class's sole right to define the terms of operation on a transnational level. Monbiot rightly points at the strategic opportunity for the movement of movements to draw up models for global democracy. No one will do that for us—unless you believe in the paranoid conspiracy theory that a world government is already in full control.

What if there are global parliamentary elections and no one goes out to vote? Monbiot goes out of the way to ask such questions. Voter turnout has been a problem, for instance for the European parliament that, much like Monbiot's parliament, lacks legitimacy and power. Democracy may be "the least worst system," compared to the nightmares of twentieth century Marxism or the anti-power model of Western anarchists. Nevertheless, that should not withhold a critic from looking into the very real problems facing representative democracy. It would be useful if Monbiot would engage himself with the current democracy debate, as for instance the ideas voiced by the conservative Fareed Zakaria in his *The Future of Freedom*. According to Zakaria, what we need in politics today is not more democracy but less.[13] Unlike what Monbiot suggests, Zakaria is not stating this to defend global business elites. At least, that is not the argument. There are plenty of examples where elections have brought dictators and fundamentalists into power. This problem cannot be overlooked.

Global democracy should not be equated with progress and justice. A world parliament could easily vote for a war on homosexuality or call for a closure of the Internet, for example. In fact, this is quite likely to happen. Libertarian pagans have the most to fear from world opinion. Instead of pushing for more empty institutions, Zakaria argues that a worldwide increase in liberty could strengthen an emerging global democratic culture. An extension and deepening of liberties, such as the freedom of press and the freedom of movement, could counter policymaking dominated by short-term political and electoral considerations. This argument, in my view, is unrelated to the issue of whether some people are "incapable of democracy." In one way or another, Western democracies also have to redefine their relationship toward the media spectacle. It is not enough to argue for frequent online elections because that may only further increase the dangers of populism. Nowhere does Monbiot mention such issues, and one can only guess why. The crisis of democracy is often linked to the media question. Another interesting confrontation would be between Monbiot's global institutional designs and Chantal Mouffe's agonistic model of democracy.

Like many other-globalists, Monbiot's understanding of media and technology issues is virtually nonexistent. One might think that as a journalist Monbiot might have something to say about media, but there is not a single trace of this to be found in *The Age of Content*. One can only ask why. His personal Web site looks fine. It is remarkable that his blueprint does not contain a single reference to new media or network-related topics, let alone tactical media. Fair trade plus global democracy will do the job, so it seems. It is curiously reminiscent of old Marxism to think that today's problems can be solved solely on the level of classic political economy, as if cultural differences, issues of race and gender, and ethnic and religious wars can simply be ignored. Decades of Gramsci, Althusser, Foucault, postmodernism, cultural studies, and new media studies have thus far failed to find their way into the globalization debate. The ideology level, which includes the media realm, remains a secondary instance. Monbiot, and with him scores of other contemporary analysts, has either not yet made the cultural turn or has mysteriously managed to surpass it. One could also blame those who have been seeking shelter in the postmodern (institutional) ghettos. It is time to understand that media is more than representation or spectacle. Societies are deeply networked. There are no democracies, only media democracies. The network society is a fact, not a proposal. The flows Saskia Sassen and Manuel Castells talk about are all too real. Monbiot's viewpoint may be fine if you are not a theory fan, but really becomes a problem if the entire trend toward immaterial labor, creative industries, and the growing importance of knowledge as production factors is left out of consideration. In many respects, it is still 1968 for many of today's leading thinkers. We have never been postmodern.

Mythologies, Logos, Slogans

In search for mythology, social movements have historically needed to create events to which later activities can refer. For the global justice movement, this could be January 1, 1994—the beginning of the Zapatista uprising (symbolized in the Ya Basta! slogan). It is apparently not enough to believe in polysequential events that suddenly find the right alchemy and kick start history. The multitudes are still in need of a plot when it comes to storytelling. It is not satisfying enough that "we are from everywhere." Contrary to its own philosophy, the Movement that hit the media surface in Seattle, in late 1999, has been, and still is, secretly searching for a plausible source that could give the global uprising meaning and direction. However, simultaneously, there are indications that this movement can very well thrive without roots and leadership. This is a contradiction, and one that needs to be examined. The ups and downs of global protest thus far have not followed the usual plots; otherwise, the movement would have died already due to repression, weapons and drugs, infiltration, sectarian infighting, or simple exhaustion. The need for a linear story about the rise and fall, with a beginning, middle, and necessary end, can be pushed aside as an all-too-human weakness.

British environmental journalist Paul Kingsnorth has not necessarily cracked mythology-in-the-making. His *One No, Many Yeses* reads like an honest and representative overview of the movement of movements, without much critical distance or reflection. During 2002 Kingsnorth, a former editor of *The Ecologist* in his early thirties, traveled the globe from Chiapas in Mexico to the riots in Genoa, Italy, visiting Reverend Billy in New York and anti-corporate groups in California. Among the travelogues, a few stories stood out for me. The first is a visit to groups in Soweto that opposed the ANC privatization policies of electricity. Second is his visit to West Papua where he witnessed the emergence of the independence movement. His description of the Landless Rural Workers' Movement (MST) while visiting Brazil for the World Social Forum also stands out.

The absence of a theoretical apparatus is obvious, but does not seem to matter. No Deleuze or Foucault quotes this time, let alone Negri or Agamben. The same can be said of Kingsnorth's media understanding, which does not surpass "Chomsky's media equals propaganda." Big corporations control media and our news agency Indymedia is the answer. This primitive understanding of (new) media is widespread. The absence of new media related topics can be found in the agendas of the social forums, from Porto Alegro to Florence. The surprisingly low awareness of free software issues and open network architectures may as well be blamed on the social disability of geeks, hackers, and Internet artists who thus far have failed to directly address their Baby Boom leaders. Despite countless efforts of grassroots groups, free software principles and Internet issues, in general, have not made it to the higher echelons of the World Social Forum and its regional and national versions.

Repeatedly we see that local events, not general ideas, make up the movements. In that sense the movement is "post-1989" in its refusal of ideologies, and this is an element the theorists, in particular those from Italy and France, still have yet to come to grips with. The "protestivals" have a carnivalesque militancy that has not yet been properly described—Spinoza and Heidegger may not be the adequate sources for it. Even though we read a strong sense of urgency in Kingsnorth's stories, there is no "state of exception" or even a permanent crisis. Kingsnorth rightly analyses the State of the Globe in its full potentiality. One might also read this as the naïve optimism of youth, but that easy judgment overlooks the wild social variety of participants in the protests worldwide. This is not a wave. Rather, it is a set of eruptions that have started to resonate and are transforming into something else.

During the late 1990s, the Seattle movement against corporate globalization gained momentum, both on the street and online. But, can we really speak of a synergy between street protests and online "hacktivism"? What the street and the Internet had in common was their conceptual stage. The sheer potentiality was enormous. Both real and virtual protests risk being stuck at the level of demo design, no longer grounded in actual topics and local situations. This means the movement never gets out of its beta stage. Only at an abstract level can we link struggles and events, but often this type of analysis is more of a religious nature in order to provide people with hope. There is a networked solidarity, yes, but no synergy effect. At first glance, reconciling the virtual and the real seems to be a rhetorical act. Radical pragmatists have often emphasized the embodiment of online networks in real-life society, dispensing with the real/virtual contradiction. Internet activism, like the Internet itself, is always a hybrid, a blend of old and new input and output devices, haunted by geography, gender, race, and other political factors. There is no pure disembodied zone of global communication, as the 1990s cyber-mythology claimed. Nevertheless, can we make a jump over these all too obvious statements? Instead of promoting correctness, it may be more interesting to instigate education initiatives aimed at bringing social movements into the Web 2.0 age. Instead of promoting the use of obscure free software that is still in a beta version, it may be better to install easy-to-use blogs and wikis.

Limits of Tactical Networks

The call of many artists and activists to return to real life does not provide us with a solution as to how alternative new media models can be raised to the level of mass (pop) culture. Yes, street demonstrations raise solidarity levels and lift us up from the daily solitude of one-way media interfaces. However, we should ask the question "What comes after the demo (design)?" of both new media and the movements. In his text *Demoradical vs. Demoliberal Regulation*, Alex Foti proposes labeling the postmovement activity The Pink Conspiracy.[14]

> Women's emancipation and the end of the patriarchal family with its unequal gender roles, feminist movements, gay mobilizations, queer politics, full civil rights for lesbian-gay-bisexual-transgender people, the assertion of reproductive rights against papist reaction and equality of access to political representation for women represent an epochal earthquake for Western politics. In a movement context, the pink carnival of rebellion was the major innovative form of political expression emerging from the Prague-Göteborg-Genoa cauldron, next to, but separate from, the white overalls and black blocs, the two other distinctive youth expressions of the anti-globalization movement. Pink collars are the present of social work and pink movements are the future of social progress.

The pink coalition, says Foti,

> would already manifest itself in the precarity movement that is at the brink of becoming a global movement. On Mayday 2006 one single, huge yell was heard from Berlin to Los Angeles: "No borders! Stop persecution! Halt discrimination! Fuck precarity! Beat inequality!" It is to me self-evident that Mondo Mayday cannot wait any longer.

Foti also admits this isn't the heady 1960s. The 1960s movements resulted in environmentalism, so where will today's movement go after its adolescence? The negative, pure, and modernist level of the conceptual has hit the hard wall of demo design as Peter Lunenfeld described it in his book *Snap to Grid*. The question thus becomes how to jump beyond the one-off event and start prototyping? What comes after the siege of yet another summit of CEOs and their politicians? How long can a movement grow and stay virtual? Or in IT terms, what comes after demo design, after the countless PowerPoint presentations, broadband trials, and Flash animations? Will Linux ever break out of the geek ghetto? The feel-good factor of the open, ever growing crowd, as conceived by novelist and theorist of crowds and power Elias Canetti, will wear out; demo fatigue will set in. We could ask, does your Utopia version have a use-by date? We cannot merely answer such questions in terms of the inevitable cycles of excitement-experience-confrontation-frustration. Kenneth Wirbin discusses another aspect of Internet activism, namely the danger of mistaking forwarding of information with activism.

> People hide behind references and theories, they are also increasingly inclined, in our ever expanding open social order, to hide behind forwarding information; not taking a position one way or the other, just forwarding. In a world that favors forwarding information over personal positions, critical engagement will continue to wane and ultimately vanish, not just on listservs and blogs, but everywhere. These are the contradictions and ambiguities of living in a social order in which life is controlled through its very openness.[15]

Rather than making up yet another concept, it is time to ask the question of how software, interfaces, and alternative standards can be installed in society. Ideas may take the shape of a virus, but society can hit back with even more successful immunization programs: appropriation, repression, and general neglect. We face a scalability crisis. Most movements and initiatives find themselves in a trap. The strategy of becoming "minor" (as in Deleuze and Guattari's concept of a "minor literature") is no longer a positive choice but the default option. Small groups are presently being catered to—what has yet to be facilitated is how to scale up and build temporary coalitions that can claim hegemony. At the moment, designing a successful cultural virus and getting thousands of visitors to your Weblog will not bring you beyond the level of a short-lived spectacle. The challenge is to use media while going beyond them. Culture jammers are no longer outlaws but should be seen as established rebel experts in guerrilla communication.[16]

Today's movements are in danger of being stuck in self-satisfying protest mode. With access to the political process effectively blocked, further mediation seems the only available option. However, gaining more and more brand value in terms of global awareness may turn out to be like overvalued stocks: they might pay off; they might turn out to be worthless. The pride of "We have always told you so" is boosting the morale of minority multitudes, while delegating legitimate fights to the level of Truth and Reconciliation Commissions (often parliamentary or Congressional), long after the damage is done.

Instead of arguing for reconciliation between the real and the virtual, I would call for a rigorous synthesis of social movements' technology. Instead of taking the "the future is now" position derived from cyber-punk, a lot could be gained from a radical reassessment of the techno-revolutions of the last ten to fifteen years. Dotcoms invested their entire venture capital in (old media) advertisements. Their belief that media-generated attention would automatically draw users in and turn them into customers proved unfounded. This is still the case. Social networks such as Flickr, Orkut, and MySpace did not grow because of a giant television advertisement budget. To remix old and new media sounds good but is not necessarily the way to go if you want to create movements. Information forms us. However, new consciousness results less and less in measurable action. Activists are only starting to understand the impact of this paradigm. What if information merely circles around in its own parallel world? What is to be done if carnival-like demonstrations cannot transcend the level of the Spectacle and the transnational protester gets tired of summit hopping?

The hype of networks reveals a conceptual crisis of collaboration and cooperation. The confusing aspect of networking is the fact that large formations of power apparently defy networks. There is growing confusion if blogs and social networks are mainstream or remain a hobby in the fringes, placed outside of the economy where real money circulates. The same can be said of Internet-based activism, in which case it becomes unclear whether the Internet is marginal or vital in today's struggles. Habermas' Internet description as an informal public sphere that has to submit to the higher authority of formal media such as publishing houses, newspapers, and magazines is, in the end, a moral judgment as to how the world should function. Both positions are perfectly valid. The Internet can be secondary while becoming powerful at the same time. There is nothing spectacular about networking. This is exactly why leading intellectuals and theorists are not aware of the current power transformations. They still sit in front of the television, watch the news, and perhaps recently bought a DVD player. Corporations and institutions are still in the process of opening up. The introduction of computer networks within organizations over the past decade has changed workflows but has not reached the level of decision-making. In this period of transition and consolidation, we get confusing answers to the question of whether new media is part of mainstream pop culture and this puts tactical media in a difficult position of stagnation, much like new media arts (see chapter 8). Whereas it is easy to see that networks have become the dominant mode of power, this is still not the case for power in the narrow sense. This is why the call for openness, transparency, and democracy, on both micro- and macro-levels, can still contain progressive elements and should be seen as a counterpart to popular conspiracy theories that complain about closed elites, knowing that openness is the new frontier of power formation.

The classical dichotomies of public/private and global/local have become useless and even obsolete. These binaries are replaced by the flexible attitudes of managing singularities and fluid differences. Rather than challenging power, networking environments act as carriers for virtual self-management and self-control, right up to the point of crashing. Networked environments are inherently unstable and their temporality is key, much like events. Networks are dense social structures on the brink of collapse and it is questionable that there are sustainable models that can "freeze" them. Maybe it is better to understand networking as syncope of power, a temporary loss of consciousness and posture, rather than a panacea against corruption, commodification, resentment, and the general dumbness of traditional hierarchies. The result of networking often is a rampant will to powerlessness that escapes the idea of collective progress under the pretext of participation, fluidity, escapism, and over-commitment.

Many activists easily get lost in the overload of e-mail messages, Weblogs, and chat exchanges. The subjective feeling, having to swim against a tsunami of noise and random tension, can no longer be explained by a lack of media literacy. Activists no longer care about the next wave of technologies, or simply use them without bothering too much about the politics and potentials that are attached to the features. Software and interface solutions can be helpful, but often only temporarily assist users to get a handle on complex information flows. This often results in the abandoning of collective communication somewhere halfway—leaving the online participants with the unsatisfactory feeling that the online conversation got stuck or is broken and unable to reach a conclusion. After an exciting first phase of introductions and debates, networks are put to the test: either they transform into a body that is capable of acting or they remain stable on a flat line of information exchange, with the occasional reply of an individual who dares to disagree. In the meantime, street events occur—the anti-Iraq war demonstrations, the riots in the outskirts of Paris in November 2005, and the student protests in Paris in early 2006—proving that network technologies can support protests, but not necessarily ignite them.

At the same time, we are facing a backlash toward romantic and out-dated forms of representation, hierarchies, and command on many terrains. Due to the conceptual wall that an online community often finds hard to cross, and unable to deal with its own democracy (let alone the one that rules society), classic, informal forms of representation fill the gap. This is part of a larger process of normalization, in which networks are integrated in existing management styles and institutional rituals. However, the progress of networking technologies are not linear nor are they irreversible, as it appears in the techno-naivety of some NGOs. It is often hard to admit that the realm of power (agenda setting, decision making) exists relatively autonomous of the techno-sphere as F2F (face-to-face) meetings. Instead, we all hang onto the idea that decentralized networks somehow dissolve power over time. Meanwhile, networking environments also create specific dispositives that are coordinating new forms of power, consisting of a variety of elements. To research these new elements—the statements, norms, standardizations, practices, and institutions as an ensemble organizing the transactions from power to knowledge and knowledge to power—goes far beyond the current talk about the information society. It also exceeds the attempts to find and replace information with knowledge, as well as any attempt to locate and identify an object of networking, let alone a purpose.

CHAPTER **9**

Axioms of Free Cooperation

Contesting Online Collaboration

A key issue for critical Internet culture is the art of collaboration.[1] The Internet is not merely used for interdevice file transfer (the technical reading) or rampant self-promotion (the economic version). There is life beyond the exhibitionist Weblog. Often people interact and work together on tasks and exchange opinions and materials. They also assist each other in technical matters. What defines the Internet and its protocols is not just its publicity potential, but also the deep underlying social architecture of this emerging medium. It is more than a tool—it is a social environment. Even though this element has been stressed since the 1980s, it is only recently that a critical understanding of the social aspect has reached the top of the agenda of the movers and shakers. Social software, social networks, and social media are all buzzwords that point to a realization that we are in this together. The social is not the latest marketing concept but goes to the core of the medium and its inherent architecture.[2]

To tackle these issues, New York artist Trebor Scholz and I organized a conference on free cooperation that took place on the Buffalo campus of the State University of New York, April 23–24, 2004.[3] I have had extensive exchanges with Scholz on this topic and I consider him the coauthor of this chapter. Early in 2003, while working on the collaborative blog *Discordia*, Scholz and I decided to investigate further the art of (online) collaboration from the media activist/artist perspective. Our starting point, however, was technological change. From cell phones to e-mail, multiplayer online games, free software and open source production, social networks, Weblogs, and wikis—our everyday lives are increasingly enmeshed with technology in which collaboration is constitutional and not merely a free option for the bored. The event, which more resembled a wild collection of workshops than a sober series of staid theory presentations, discussed topics such as leveling the ivory tower, collective writing, open content, expression of women through pixels, social network architectures, art and science collaborations, radio topographies, "who says artists can't organize?", and self-organized universities. Brian Holmes gave a precise account of the creative chaos:

> Free Cooperation was not a conference but an experimental event— by which I mean funny, improvisational, intriguing, full of people with good ideas, always offering a chance to change your ordinary formats and styles of expression. I did a radio broadcast (ultra-short range, but it makes you play the role of "being on the air"), a video interview and a fake TV talk show with a simultaneous performance. I watched monster footage and had a great time talking with everybody in the endless corridors of the State University in Buffalo. There was a kind of B-movie aesthetic to the whole thing, allowing everybody the self-parody they need to say what really matters. It was such a pleasure to do the opposite of the typical academic shtick, in a literally desktop environment![4]

The Buffalo event brought together an odd group of around 100 artists and activists who preferred to enter vague territories. How can we find independence and enhance freedom in the context of networked collaboration? How do you collectively manage and own a shared resource, such as a network? We have to distinguish between the necessity of working in groups—for instance, to produce large and complex art works, conferences, festivals, protests, or publications—and the desire to overcome isolation when you work alone. In both instances, one has to relate the abstract effect with the pleasure and pain of working with, and for, others. The film industry has a long history around the birth and battles of the credits. When I hear the word *collaboration*, I often think about anonymous early renaissance painters and how individuals emerged out of that studio system. These days one would say it is a mix of knowledge of group dynamics and the legal arrangements around collective ownership.

Group exhibitions are on the rise. People are curious about the internal social dynamics within collectives. Collaboration provokes that kind of voyeurism because people presuppose trouble—which always surprises me. For over 15 years, a few of my friends and I published material under the name of Adilkno (or Bilwet in Dutch/German). An important notion in this context was the Third Mind, a reference to the collaborations between Brion Gysin and William S. Burroughs,[5] which implies that if two minds create something, the outcome is not the sum of the two but something different altogether. In the case of Adilkno, it was an easy job to call into being a singular Third Mind. Melbourne art theorist Charles Green called his book on collaborations in contemporary arts *The Third Hand* and it also uses the term Third Artist. Allen Ginsberg saw working together as a "ripening of good karma." What I like about the Third Mind approach is the transformative aspect of these "third" terms, creating something of another order altogether, and something very different from (shared) drug experiences.⁶ One can only guess the problematic part of such vague and dreamy terms, but at least they open up spaces for imagination and show in detail what happens if you passionately create something together. Out of my Adilkno experience grew a close collaboration with Pit Schultz. In the mid-1990s, during the heyday of net criticism, we built up the Nettime project. Many collaborations followed and this book is, in part, a result of several of those collaborations. Nowadays, my plural authorships are mostly virtual. In my view, a lot of the offline issues, in real life (IRL) and online, are the same. I find working IRL to be a luxury and great fun. It is unique if you can collaborate with a group in your own town and continue that collaborative effort on a long-term basis.

In the months leading up to the 2004 gathering, an interesting online debate took place around the event on a specially created e-mail list. The content it generated was edited into a thirty-two-page free newspaper, which was then printed with a circulation of ten thousand. In his introduction for the newspaper Trebor Scholz lists a range of artist collaborations, including Bureau d'Etudes, Dorkbot, Luther Blissett, RTMark, and Group Material.⁷ We could add Mongrel, SubReal, Guerilla Girls, General Idea and, of course, Art & Language. Group work is not only fun and brings into question individual authorship, it is also increasingly facilitated and promoted by technology providers. There is almost an element of inevitability toward social media in which production, reception, and remixing become one flow of collective experiences. This makes it interesting to see how the anarchist tradition of mutual aid—from Proudhon and Kropotkin to today's collectives—will respond to this development in the capitalist mode of cultural production.

Before Buffalo, on October 25, 2003, somewhat similar conferences took place in Banff and London. "The Diffusion: Collaborative Practice in Contemporary Art" conference took place at the Tate Modern in London. Speakers included Bureau d'Etudes, Eve Chiapello, Cornford & Cross, François Deck, Jochen Gerz, Charles Green, John Roberts, and Stephen Wright. In his London talk, Brian Holmes remarked that the strategy of creating a collective in order to get into the museum system is absurd.

> The values of transnational state capitalism have permeated the art world, not only through the commodity form, but also and even primarily, through the artists' adoption of management techniques and branded subjectivities. It is in this sense that contemporary capitalism has absorbed the artistic critique of the 1960s, transforming it into the networked discipline of "neomanagement," as Eve Chiapello says in her work, or into the opportunism of what I call "the flexible personality."[8]

To celebrate the social as such can easily turn into moralism. Communities, groups, networks, and other forms of association have no intrinsic subversive qualities, nor would the celebration of the lonesome power user.

Among others, Scholz and I invited the Bremen-based media critic Christoph Spehr who coined the term "free cooperation" in his extra-extra-large essay *Gleicher als andere* (*More Equal Than the Other*).[9] In 2003, I did an online interview with Spehr and discovered his critical work on collaboration.[10] At that time, most of Spehr's writings were not translated into English and Buffalo was an opportunity to introduce his ideas into Anglophone discourses.[11] Spehr uses references to the 1960s sci-fi movies to think about contemporary cooperation insisting on the option of refusal, independence, negotiation, and renegotiation with alien corporate or state monsters. Spehr's writing is a keen mixture of subversive utopian science fiction and a radical social analysis of contemporary global capitalism. Spehr writes theory fiction for the postdeconstruction age where the question "What is to be done?" opens up new spaces for the collective imagination and action.

What makes Spehr, a historian and political scientist, unique is his free, non-academic style of writing. As a theorist, Spehr brings together contemporary social science, practicalities of everyday life, with strategies for autonomous movements. Spehr has the ability to load up concepts with new meaning. In his theory novel *The Aliens are Amongst Us!* (1999) Spehr makes a distinction between three social categories: aliens, maquis, and civilians. Much like in a science fiction novel, all three have their own civilizations. It would be too easy to describe aliens as evil capitalists. Aliens, in Spehr's view, are first and foremost friendly parasites, post-1945 creatures who are interested in any type of surplus value they can extract from humans. Aliens do not do this in the old manner of attacking or suppressing people, but by assisting them. Power is no longer personal but abstract and can no longer be reduced to characteristics of individuals. Alien power is free, open, and most of all, on a constant search for creative, new ideas. Typical aliens would be intermediaries such as cultural entrepreneurs, social democratic welfare state officials, NGOs, or Green Party members, and they all live off the movements, events, ideas, and expressions of others. What the aliens all have in common is their good intentions. Alien hegemony is politically correct, multicultural, feminist, ecological, and almost impossible to defeat on a discursive level. In Spehr's science friction, the antagonists of the aliens are the maquis, the French word for bush, a term used by the French resistance in World War II to describe zones not occupied by the Nazis. Maquis can be read as a synonym for multitudes. The maquis experiment with posteconomic models of free cooperation—a topic that Spehr further explored after finishing his political novel. The free cooperation model, which discusses ways of establishing a "GPL-society," based on the "Gnu Public License," the principles under which free software is often and currently produced[12] brought him in contact with the free software movement in Germany.

Spehr's key idea is that everyone should have the freedom to dissolve a collaboration at any given time. It is important to define a language in which we can openly talk about difference and power within groups, or even in online networks for that matter. Spehr:

> Free cooperation is based on the acknowledgement that given rules and given distributions of control and possession are a changeable fact and do not deserve any higher objectifiable right. In a free cooperation, all members of the cooperation are free to quit, to give limits or conditions for its cooperative activity in order to influence the rules according to their interests; they can do this at a price that is similar and bearable for all members; and the members really practice it, individually and collectively. Free cooperation needs a policy that materializes it again and again anew, challenging in practice the limits of freedom and the reality of equality, getting through the external and internal preconditions of a similar and bearable price.[13]

For Spehr, it is important to theorize individual and collective experiences, to recognize that there must be a freedom to refuse to collaborate. There must be an exit strategy. At first instance this may seem a mysterious and somewhat paradoxical statement. Why should the idea of refusal be promoted as an *a priori*, as the very foundation of all collaboration, as Spehr has suggested? It almost sounds like a new dogma, a new rule, yet another human right. The question of free cooperation is, in essence, one of organization and comes up after the crisis of the (Fordist) factory model and its political mirror, the political party. This may be obvious. The Italian focus on (post)Fordism is too narrowly engaged with the experience of the twentieth-century. It is up to us in the 21st century to update these concepts and come up with compelling stories about the hidden power structures in social networks, NGO office culture, dotcom leisure work, call center boredom, project management of events, and the working conditions of the freelance labor force.

Spehr's free cooperation is not an alternative concept that fell from the sky, as if free subjects congregate to work together. Cooperation is the very foundation of all work in society. It is just a matter of how we make it visible. Spehr:

> Individualistic ways of living are possible because society has developed in such a way that life is no longer precarious. We need basic security to be established and have access to public wealth. Direct social control weakens because markets allow us to change co-operations, to move city, to leave a company. On the Internet you can do enormous things because someone has already built and maintains it. It's this stage of 'abstract cooperation' that makes individualization possible—and not only for a few individuals but also as a mass phenomenon, not only in the cultural sphere but also as a productive force itself. From this point on, cooperation looks as if it is something special, voluntarily engaged, as if we were monads that come together to collaborate. While the truth is that we can only act in this monad-like way because we are embedded in an elaborated abstract cooperation and so many resources and structures ready at hand. [14]

At first sight, postmodern forms of cooperation have the look and feel of being anti-institutional. Spehr: "We're anti-institution in our attitude, but there is some distinct flavour of neoliberalism in this. We tend to think that the institution is black and autonomy white. But it's not that easy." Spehr calls "to study the complicity between neoliberalism and institutions, to destroy its aura of "freedom for everybody" by re-telling the real story and its facts. Second, we have to think about new ways to imagine institutions and markets." We have to be clear that a new attitude, that of living in a society that is ours, cannot be obtained without institutions. "Social power lies not only in the fact that we are allowed to do this or that, or that we can do it no matter what. Much more important is that social power lies in the fact that we can prevent others from doing this or that, and that we can make others do this or that. That's real power."

Spehr is not trying to formulate a new political utopia. But he is not a pragmatist either. He believes that ideas, shaped through experience, can help us negotiate so the outcome will be beneficial for both the individual and the surrounding others. Spehr, summarizing his key concept:

> All rules in the cooperation can be questioned by everybody, there are no holy rules that people cannot question or reject or bargain and negotiate about—which is not the case in most of the cooperations and organizational forms that we know. Then, people can question and change these rules by using this primary material force of

refusing to cooperate, by restricting their cooperation, by holding back what they do for these cooperations, making conditions under which they are willing to cooperate, or leaving cooperations. They must be guaranteed the right to use these measures to influence the rules and that everybody in the cooperation can do this. The price of not cooperating, the price that it costs if you restrict your cooperation or if the cooperation splits up, should be not exactly equal but similar for all participants in this cooperation, and should be affordable.[15]

What is so deeply Old European about Spehr's approach is his passion for negative thinking. What he proposes is the study of group dynamics of failed collaborations. Let us remember them and reconstruct them in our memories. Let us reconstruct the social workings, instead of repeatedly pushing the harmony ideology and only focusing on the exciting beginnings. The more networked technology we use, the more important it will become to put the psychoanalysis of collaboration high on the curriculum of each school. The feel good factor of success appeals to everyone and this is why it is so unpopular to study mistakes. Why repress real, existing, unresolved conflicts? We know that they will inappropriately explode at any time if we don't address them properly. This is a call for more research into cooperation studies. The more social online tools become available and are used, on a massive worldwide scale, the more material we can study and the more urgent the outcomes will be. This work should be done on a critical-conceptual level, with additional case studies. We can integrate these insights into a collaboration with studies about situations of (online) conflict. This may sound rather mundane, but consider this: how many artists collaborate in the making of a work? Almost all. How visible is this togetherness in the artwork? Hardly at all. How much do we know about the process of working together? Next to nothing.

From Canada came a report by Tobias van Veen, posted on the Empyre list, where in February 2004 a month-long debate took place centered on free cooperation.[16] According to van Veen, you cannot simply walk away. The key is to negotiate.

For cooperation to work, it seems to me that one's relation is only "free" insofar as one makes the choice to "cooperate" in a fashion that may be less than free. At a certain point one realizes one *should* leave, but if you want something to happen, you just grin and bear it. How does one go about dealing with issues of free-riding when walking away would simply jettison the entire project? I like the idea of safe haven to step into, to negotiate such territory; it sounds like a psychic-geography where the balance can be tipped in favor of a subtle reminder to freeloaders to chip in their part.

Speaking from his DJ experience, he asks how collectively organized rave culture fits into the idea of the "third entity." The event itself is the third entity, says van Veen. He admits that the most effective groups "were the ones that have embraced a totalitarian, short-term leader—these have led to the most spectacular projects, but the most serious consequences in terms of the bonds of friendship being subjected to severe strain."

How do the totalitarian myths of art relate to networked, collaborative practices? van Veen asks just that, and gives the example of the DJ versus collaborative laptop music.

> The DJ is totalitarian; although a feedback loop is affected between dancer and DJ the limits of this loop lie in the DJ's desire and ability to read and utilize the feedback on a level which mixes with the unconscious and affective. There is a process of negotiation but often it is in terms of "feeding the floor" what it wants vs. attempts to "educate" the crowd on new styles. On the other channel, shared, jazz-like jamming situations, such as laptop plug-in jam sessions, operate on different levels of feedback. They are fun and neat yet often their only listeners are the musicians themselves. The audience has forsaken them, as the result is often a rather chaotic and unorchestrated mess. With enough structure, the results can be pleasing—but often the feedback is between the musicians, and the audience is left out. For example, the massive Narod Niki jam at MUTEK 2003 in Montréal, featuring eight technoheads on their laptops jamming away, was exciting and wonderful, but lacked the responsive qualities and precision of a class turntablist. The question is: do we need to retune our ears to hear the chaos or is it just that not everybody is a musician and not everybody should be playing at once?

The more people work online, the more important it is to understand that the technical architecture of the tools we use is shaping our social experiences. There would be a lot gained if there was more awareness of the limitations of new media. But we should not separate the technical and put it outside of social interactions. For instance, it is crucial to include aspects of gender and the productive power relationships of male-male, male-female, and female-female collaborations. The German theorist Klaus Theweleit has shaped some of my thinking on collaboration in this respect. In the early 1980s, he worked in the same department as Friedrich Kittler in Freiburg. Their work on gender, media, and collaboration has striking similarities, and I am sure they must have discussed this topic a lot back then. Both Theweleit and Kittler stress the importance of the (Deleuzian) productive element of the male-female-machine triangle. The quintessential image here would be the male writer dictating his Orpheus poems to his female lover who happens to be a fast and remarkably accurate typist. This can also be a male-medium-male connection or a female-medium-female one, but obviously, in male-dominated heterosexual societies, the male-female-machine scenario is the dominant one. Theweleit looks into the oppressive aspect, in which males "sacrifice" female bodies as their medium. The man who uses a woman to start off his production, and then sacrifices her to enter a new productive cycle is a well-known pattern. By himself, he cannot produce songs. The question here would be how to use the other in a creative and non-oppressive way that re-energizes and is cautious not to abuse or exploit, let alone kill (in a real or symbolic way) the other—something that happened in many of Theweleit's case studies. The artist, if he or she is to continue to make real art, must constantly renew him or herself.[17] I wonder if such (cruel) stories are still out there. I can imagine that the gender aspect is still there but is not being played out through computer technology. If I think about the PC and the Internet, I think of the bachelor's machine, not the male genius author who dictates his poems to his secretary/lover. However, I may be wrong. Why was the shift from the typewriter to PC-based word processor so crucial in this respect?

During the Empyre debate, Anna Munster warned us not to narrow down the polymorphous field of collaboration to the everyday psychodrama between partners. Much artistic (and intellectual) collaboration is reintegrated socially and discursively into the model of the couple. "In the couple, one term usually becomes privileged over the other (Deleuze over Guattari) or else it is only in the endless reflectiveness of the couple and their acts that the outcome takes place (Ulay and Abramovic). Often, part of the couple has to break free in order to work again. It's necessary to constantly work against this recuperation, perhaps with multiplying collaborations with different people, by continuing to work outside them in one's own space, and by hanging onto the passion generated in them rather than losing oneself in the safety of their identity."[18] Lloyd Sharp adds: "It is often the case in art/technology based collaborative works that collaborators who appear to have more technical experience, and who often consequently contribute in a more 'practical' way, find it leads to their relegation later in the relationship as simply being a technician who facilitates production for the other 'thinking' collaborators."

Another entry point could be the Italian debates on multitude, precarity, and collaboration. In *A Grammar of the Multitude*, Paulo Virno describes the nature of contemporary production. The questions discussed are subjective and come up after the very act of "refusal." What is collaboration once we conclude that life is being reduced to work? I would argue that it is important to leave behind the initial, decisive stage of refusal because one otherwise ends up in individual anarchism or a Max Stirner type of egoism in which there is nothing left on which to collaborate. There must be a basic consensus on what is on the agenda and what is to be done. The collaboration question follows from there and cannot be discussed in a political vacuum either, otherwise it transforms into a managerial issue. It is a secondary issue with nonetheless grave consequences. Still, we have to keep in mind that collaboration itself is not generating issues that are easily translated into campaigns.

For Virno, the crisis of the society of labor is reflected in the multitude itself. We could extend this and say that multitudes are a problematic category, not only for capital or for the control society. The multitudes themselves as organizational forms for this social grouping are fluid and not yet existing. The multitude is "becoming," to put it in terms that are more diplomatic. It will take a while to get used to the fact that there is no consciousness in and for itself, that revolutionaries can be wary—and bored—of their own potential revolutions. There is talk of a collective ecstasy without a grand resolution. For the multitudes, fragmentation is not a romantic agony but the primary condition of political life.

According to Virno, "social wealth is produced from science, from the general intellect, rather than from the work delivered by individuals. The work demanded seems reducible to a virtually negligible portion of a life. Science, information, knowledge in general, cooperation, these present themselves as the key support system of production—these, rather than labor time." This puts cooperation in a state of exception. It is not the rule, not the everyday life condition, it is rare, uncertain, and always on the verge of dissolution. For Virno, the difference between labor time and non-labor time falls short. This is exactly why there is so much uncertainty (and curiosity) about collaboration. In what act, work, gesture, or idea are the traces of collaboration not included? The distinction between collaboration and non-collaboration becomes increasingly difficult to make. The oppositional linkage of the lonely genius and the multidisciplinary team sounds more like an odd lifestyle choice and is not relevant.[19]

I asked Italian theorist Matteo Pasquinelli how the multitude, precarity, and free cooperation relate as concepts.

> Multitude is the brainchild of Italian post-Operaism and French post-Structuralism (Deleuze, Negri and Virno, all reading Spinoza). It rose out of the quest for a new social subject—multiple and not identitary—after the collapse of the working class in western countries and the rise of post-Fordism. It is more a theoretical than an

historical category. Let's say, it is a new mask for an old movement still alive. Precarity, on the contrary, is in front of our eyes, the daily work condition of the youngest generation, and an effect of the wild turbo-capitalism. However, the political acknowledgement around precarity and the rise of a movement of precarious workers took place in the same cultural context that produced the term "multitude"—not in the Anglo-American world but in Old Europe and Italy. The idea of free cooperation on the other hand is pushed by the Internet revolution, in particular by Free Software developers.

Do they connect? Matteo:

> I do not see the multitude around me. I see a lot of precarious workers and migrants in my daily experience here in Barcelona. I do not see a real—effective—economy based on free collaboration. I see large cultural movements growing around the values of cooperation, sharing, networking, and commons. Moreover, I see coders developing immaterial machines that can manage and exploit tomorrow's temporary workers. So sorry, my honeymoon with collective subjectivity is over. Now I am keen to investigate where conflict is produced, looking for the points of friction of post-Fordist production, on a molecular and not collective scale. In my humble opinion, autonomy without conflict sounds like Playstation. In the realm of digital and "free" cooperation I am looking forward an "immaterial" civil war.[20]

What is at stake is the way in which negotiations take place inside each particular "credit" economy. Which traces remain visible of a collaboration? Can terms of ownership be (re)negotiated further down the line or are the forms of ownership and division of labor fixed at Day One? How many "defeated collaborations" one can bear? Humans may once have been social animals, but that does not mean we always act like ants. There is enough herd mentality, and this makes it hard, even impossible, to promote collaboration as a virtue. Yet, both wisdom and knowledge have blocked the road back to the land of Zarathustra. It is not society that keeps us away from individuation—the main concern is the method of evaluation. Do we look back in anger when groups fall apart?

Collaboration and in particular free cooperation sounds somewhat idealistic. It is perceived as therapy for those who are handicapped with lesser capacities. Humans remain social animals, after all, and it is up to the next generation to leave behind that primitive mingling with others. But amusingly enough, our technologies promote increased sophistication in social interaction. The individualized subject is forced into the tribe, now rebranded as virtual community, the wise crowd, the smart mob, social networking, and the like. Look at how businesses force employees to work in teams. Professionalization (higher salaries and social security) cannot be separated from the inevitable division of labor. The focus on new social movements or autonomous groups (renamed as maquis, multitude, or precariat) in Spehr and Virno's texts may be too narrow and should be enriched with more contemporary ruptures. What is the political after its decentralization? Perhaps it is no longer useful to talk about movements (as in "movement of the movements"). Movement might suggest too much unity and continuity. While the term is accurate if we want to express political and cultural diversity, it still has that promise of continuity in it— and with it comes the suggestion that decline and disappearance can be upheld. The movement should never stop. The energy of the event that gave the movement its character and direction ought not to die. This is where the gestalt of the true believer enters the story. Rituals will be invented to bring back the masses to the street, at any price. But does that necessarily translate to the Internet?

This becomes particularly interesting when informal networks and peer-to-peer collaborations reach critical mass and transform into something entirely different. It is a marvelous, mysterious moment when small and dispersed groups converge into a larger social movement and cause an Event (as Alain Badiou calls it). However, that is the exception. Individual collaborations are geared toward creating historical events. I see that as a rather classic twentieth-century approach, in which creative work is always seen as part of a larger, metaphysical process of history making. On the Internet, no one knows you are a multitude. Common efforts have to be made visible. In the previous chapter, I discussed with the state of media activism. One thing is clear: social movements do not emerge out of the Web. Their beginnings lay somewhere else, not in the act of online communication. Technology aids our dispatches. We build social devices and they, in turn, construct us. Our language is filtered and changed by the technology that facilitates its transmission. The way we learn changes, and what we learn changes in the way it is distributed. However, events, visualized collectivity, such as the February 15, 2003 anti-Iraq War demonstrations, run more on the grammar of the streets than the protocols of the World Wide Web.

It is hard to distinguish between the necessity of working in groups, for instance to produce large and complex art works, conferences, festivals, protests, or publications, and the desire to overcome isolation when you perform individual work. For many new media artworks, collaboration is an absolute requirement because the individual artist simply does not have all the requisite skills to do visuals, 3D, sound, editing, and performance, much less manage the whole process in terms of human resources and finance. The question therefore is one of an "economy of acknowledge-ment"—whether works are produced under the name of a single artist (for example, video artist Bill Viola) or confirm the reality by using a group name. In our times, it is seen as something unique if individuals can work together in the first place. An artist with social skills is praised. The ordi-nary creative genius has to be protected by an army of assistants, produc-ers, interns, lovers, and friends because (a) on their own they could not survive and (b) constant energy has to be invested in social management and networking because of the ongoing irreparable damage the bad-tem-pered artist is causing.

We cannot merely praise collaboration as if it were a product—or deconstruct it as just another ideology (which it is). What we are looking for is nothing less ambitious than laws, underlying mechanisms, common experiences that can be boiled down to strong, everlasting memes; rec-ommendations and sayings that will stay with us for times to come. The problem is that we seem to learn little when it comes to sophisticated social interaction, particularly because, at least in the West, it has become hard to transmit from one generation to the next. The knowledge of collaboration is not a passive one that you acquire and then apply. The question is not: how do I fit in? We are only human once and are destined to fail. Rather, we should ask ourselves what social interaction might be found in larger groups. There is a place for social sophistication. Nonetheless, with a taste for self-reflection we can evolve. With the rise of individualization, col-laboration becomes increasingly something that we perceive as voluntary, almost like a commodity one can purchase. One can witness a growing curiosity, as if it were some old, forgotten ritual, or exotic experience. "Col-laboration? Sounds interesting. Can I try it? Please do—we offer a thirty-day free trial."

The challenge for Internet-based cooperation is how to interface with the real world. It is hard to collaborate online without having meetings in real life. Online work can be very ineffective and slow. To succeed at that level requires some patience. Some people believe in the dotcom phrases about "communicating with the speed of light," but that is not at all the case if you work on more complicated projects with a group of active con-tributing people dispersed all over the globe.

There is a growing desire for open forms of participation. As an incen-tive for online contribution, cooperative projects are increasingly com-mon. The issue here is to distinguish between top-down teamwork in the labor mill and the management rhetoric that surrounds it. "Please empty your tray in the trash—thank you for your cooperation" is not a free coop-eration. It is "friendly fascism" (Bertram Gross). Between free and forced, there is a growing gray zone of projects, applications, and practices that are not aimed at productivity gains, nor are they are entirely autonomous and renegade. There is no complete snow-white innocence. There is no absolute autonomy of collaborative projects that claim to work outside the system. Of course, people will remain fascinated by social mechanisms. The more we understand networked technologies, the more we might find out how to mobilize people and create masses. But even more importantly, the more we understand networked technologies, the more we can liberate ourselves from the pressures of these technologies and their intimidating and seducing character. A process of normalization is important in order to remove the magic spell of gadgets and applications, and the scores of people who live inside today's machines.

Romantics praise cooperation. They think it must be like a love affair. Ferocious pragmatists on the other hand just chant their to-do lists. They think that they can force a genuine smile onto the faces of team players. Such mechanical application of rules simply does not work! A cooperation can indeed be similar to a flirt or a new friendship. It can be an overwhelming encounter. But there is no recipe for such matchmaking. It is an event. You cannot schedule such circumstances for 11 a.m. followed by a business lunch. The event of true collaboration takes you to a place where you have not been before. It makes you forget about time. At other times, collaboration kicks fully into gear when trust is built, and building trust takes time. Professional and personal interests need to be appeased. Those involved need to be willing and able to put in the hours. This can be a tough call. It is grim if you work on many projects at the same time. Collaboration asks for concentration. Online collaboration can have a bitter aftertaste for some; they might think it a pure waste of time. Endless e-mail exchanges, noisy chats, fatiguing time differences, defunct or incompatible software, and unstable bandwidth are all part of this uninviting picture. And it doesn't stop there. The exploitative, precarious character of immaterial, networked labor adds to this busy scenario.

There is, no doubt, such a thing as the high art of collaboration. It is possible to exchange experiences and reflections and to theorize them. However, often these propositions are prescriptive. They end up in a procedure that you are supposed to follow. Collaboration is the science of lists. The do's and don'ts can be read as normative statements. But we can also interpret them as loose guidelines, a bit like walking through rugged terrain with a compass. You approximate the direction. Collaboration is frequently a thorny subject. It is not the highway to heaven. It is muddled by human desires for recognition. It screams for attention at a time when you are just too busy with other affairs. It is like considering having a child—it never seems to be the right time. The issue of shadow labor matters a great deal in collaboration. All too often credit is given to the most visible individual in a collaboration, which brings a project to the breaking point. Group dynamics are also part and parcel in this context. Leadership in collaboration is yet another hot-button topic. There are always hierarchies and rules in collaborations. They need to be acknowledged and the captains of directorship should be compelled to rotate.

The term *spontaneous* frequently comes up when talking about online togetherness. But Web-enhanced collaboration is hardly ever spontaneous. It is slow. However, it can be accelerated by meetings in person. Embodied, it is often only a handful of people who get together. Online, mortals come together in the thousands. Internet collaborations become most intensive if collaborators live in proximity and use the Web-based communication to add to their regular in-person meetings. Research by University of Toronto communication scholar Barry Wellman showed that Internet access increased frequency of communication between people who live in close physical proximity.[21] Clay Shirky noticed that today's media artists often create software tools that are geographically specific. He calls such tools *situated software*.[22] The anywhere and nowhere of the Internet is challenged by site-specific software art that addresses a particular community or location.

For business analyst Chris Shipley, online collaboration stands for social networking through advanced e-mail systems with shared address books or common access to a database. In her essay "2006, The Year of Collaboration" she reminds us of relatively recent collaborative settings such as friends of friends networks like Friendster.[23] Shipley argues that these ways of working together do not really qualify as collaboration. Does the collective throwing in and taking out of data from a box constitute collaboration? Collaboration is a risky, interconnected thing. It is an intensive affair in which individuals who are part of a group share a common goal. They split benefits or losses. Cooperation is a much less involved affair in which sole, independent participants advance separately. Finally, consultation is the loosest model of working together.

Soon we will see collaborations that are more genuine. Men and women create massive amounts of content online. We don't just customize, use, and purchase commodities online. We pitch in our resources and thoughts and feelings. The culture of free sharing blossoms. But still mentalities toward sharing vary widely. Some realize that they benefit from giving everything away. Yet others feel threatened by such openness. They prefer to hold things close to their chest, as they fear to lose out in the rumble of exchanges. Creativity is geographically distributed. We are producers. We are authors. We are columnists and instigators. We support others and are aided in turn. People are getting used to social software tools. They make unexpected uses of them. Bumplist by the researcher and artist Jonah

Brucker Cohen is a good example. On Bumplist, only a limited number of participants can be subscribed to a mailing list at any moment. Once new contributors join, the previous members exceeding the limit for the list are bumped off.

Participatory, creative online tools rule in media art. This holds true at least when it comes to collaboration and cooperation. Artists set up cultural contexts to which others contribute. There is a long history of participation in art that is traced in an essay by Inke Arns.[24] She points to a trajectory from the early 1960s until today that includes Duchamp, Kaprow, Cage, and Lyotard (*Les Immateriaux*). We see many such participatory design projects emerge online. The static, closed online art project has fallen out of favor. Collaboration in the art world happens often at an early stage in the artist's life, after graduation from college when coalitions are built that make entry into the art world easier.

Some artists dropped out of the art world to seek alternative platforms for exposure and dialogue. Low-level collaborations in the form of consultation are the day-to-day bread and butter of technologists. Artists working with technologies need to work with programmers as no one person can know all that is needed to finish a project. While the number of nonbelievers in the model of the lone star is on the decline, the idea of the individual artist genius is vividly alive. Collaboration is not for everyone! And it can be abused! Collaborative tricksters frequently inflate their own social capital by not crediting their cohorts.

Collaborations between artists and scientists are also not a new occurrence. In these working scenarios, artists are more often than not in the role of the illustrator. They visualize the results of scientists and thus help to communicate their findings to the public. But different professional languages and maybe even political leanings may run counter to each other. Do artists and scientists need to have the same goal when working together? It takes a long time to establish a true connection between artists and scientists that might lead to consequential results.

What makes collaboration online so attractive? Essentially, collaborators can find geographically dispersed team members who have the skill sets to fit the demands of their project. On the other hand, critics are quick to condemn sharply the network serfdom of immaterial labor that turns dispersed workers into laptop-lapdogs who are ready to work at any hour anywhere. The network society allows capital to sneak into every minute of our every day. There is no place that could not become a collaborative workplace. Downtime becomes download time. Health insurance and pensions do not need to be paid for what Howard Rheingold calls part-of-the-solution workers. Work and leisure fade into one another. Computers pervade every corner of our existence. The wolf of networked exploitation needs to be recognized when it comes along in the sheepskin of shiny locative gadgets.

Generation after generation, there are experiences made inside collectives, groups, firms, and movements. How do you write an account of collective actions? How do you capture the complexity of collective production? This is rarely captured and theorized, let alone ready to be transferred into other social contexts. Bruno Latour's Actor-Network Theory only gets us so far. Let's put our ear to the ground of collaboration. A surprising majority of collaboration theory is written in support of the Amazon.coms of the world. Theorists think through group coordination and consensus building—all aimed at getting things done. The key term is *effective*. We ask if these business conglomerates really need our help. Is social software the contemporary equivalent to Ford's assembly line? Will we need self-help manuals and psychopharmacology to heal us from the world created by these tools? How do new tools like SMS, IM, VoIP, Skype, Writely, Opinity, Facebook, and MySpace affect the way we act? Corporate sirens lure the online millions into the net of their interactive enterprises. But what can we learn from this? How can we escape the cynical truth that all that is left to do is either appropriate yesterday's knowledge of the consultant class or be appropriated ourselves? What is there beyond Web 2.0 that cannot be appropriated?

Prepare for collaboration. That is all we can do. We cannot predict if it will happen. At best, energizing inspiration grows amid a group. We do not get up, have coffee, and then collaborate. We have to acquire a set of tools and learn the art of collaboration that we can then apply whenever needed. Rheingold defines the ability to take part in technology-enhanced social networks a key skill for the next decade. We try it over and over again, convinced that the sum of all parts is bigger than the number of its pieces. Collaboration flourishes when team members are experienced in such situations. Collaboration needs trust. It needs time. Scale also matters. How does a small team branch out successfully? Charles Green reminds us that we should not mix up cooperation with friendship.

> Friendship is always fragile since its contract is so unenforceable. Demands in and on friendship are always ultimately unsustainable, unless friendship is governed by an economy of civility. Collaboration involves much, much more, namely the articulation of contractual relations.[25]

CHAPTER 10

Theses on Distributed Aesthetics

This chapter examines a concept that emerged within the Australian Fibreculture group.[1] During the preparation of the *Fibreculture Journal* issue on distributed aesthetics, editor Anna Munster and I wrote a number of theses on this matter. These formed the basis of a workshop that was organized by Anna Munster and me on May 11–12, 2006 at the Wissenschaftskolleg/Institute of Advanced Study in Berlin.[2] The theses presented here were initially written together with Anna Munster, around mid-2005, and then rewritten after the Berlin workshop. This text may be considered a classic example of multiple authorship.

There was a wish to open up a new field of inquiry after the demise of net.art and the rise of Web 2.0, locative media, and various mapping efforts. During the roaring 1990s net.art opened up spaces, brought people together, and provoked interesting work and collaborations. This creative and subversive energy dissipated later on when the (failed) attempt was made to seek recognition of the museum and gallery world. Floating dotcom money went to MBAs, not to net.artists. In the end, it was "art" that divided people. However, many of the issues and desires remained. How can aesthetics in a network society be defined beyond the question of if this or that site, blog, or application is, or is not, art? These days, there are still a lot of interesting individual artists and groups that produce sublime and provocative work. But that is not the point. The crucial point is how, and where, the works connect. This collection of ideas proposes a new consolidated thinking through of the (sensual) experience—the "aesthesia"—of networked events. How do we experience the current wave of blogs, podcasts, and mobile phone games? What network theory is used and is it adequate to the task of engaging networks on their own terms?

Obviously, we are not concerned about "eternal beauty." Neither would it be useful to define "aesthesis" as perception of the eyes. There is no need to privilege the visual. Communication is something people do with their hands as much as with their eyes and ears. The manual aspect of, for instance, texting needs to be stressed. Writing an SMS is as much a manual exercise as it is textual, and it all occurs on a screen. Sensing presence through GPS does not have to culminate in an image. There is no necessity to, again, reproduce or question visual domination. We should reject attempts to reduce media and the arts to *Bildwissenschaften*. We are not talking about screen culture as a way to talk only about painting, film, and television. It is the abstract, the conceptual, the unseen, and the immanent that the distributed brings into play. Let's face it, we have passed the aesthetic turn, and there is no way back. There is a link to be made to Nicolas Bourriaud's relational aesthetics, of judging artworks because of the inter-human relations they represent, produce, or prompt. However, we must time and again spoil such a humanistic, subject-centered approach with machinic logic. Seminar participant Warren Sack argues for a nonvisual, conceptual, art-based understanding of artistic work in information visualization. He relies on what Benjamin Buchloh, writing about conceptual art practices, called an "aesthetic of administration."[3] What we need are new entry points, radical and imaginative concepts that enable us to describe what is happening around us. Distributed aesthetics is one such attempt. What is "sensual recognition" in the age of networks and what critical terms need to develop in order to describe properly our mediated experiences?

Another entry point for distributed aesthetics could be the longstanding discontent in interface design as if it were a static image. How can blogs, wikis, and social network sites become more interesting in terms of design, while not giving away the critical mass that many such sites have managed to create? In other words, how can usability be granted in a time when users no longer want to be fooled by quasi-interesting tricks? How can we lose track, wander around, get lost, while still being able to find that telephone number, e-mail, or postal address? Do useful information and the "link to Lorelei" sirens that lure us away from functional tasks have to be contradictory? The codeword, distributed aesthetics, expresses the wish to move on from the virtual and the visual toward an integrated approach—an approach that no longer highlights technology as something revolutionary or disruptive, but focuses on the overall architecture of flows and disruptions; be it immaterial, mechanical, aerodynamic, or static. It is in the art of distribution that we can trace new possibilities of use that go beyond techno-determinist readings that only stress the limitations that we, the trash users, have.

The distributed element not only refers to decentralized and parallel computing, in the sense of "using two or more computers communicating over a network to accomplish a common objective or task" (Wikipedia). It also points to social formations that mobile technologies provoke, such as groups, mobs, crowds, multitudes, and swarms. The distribution over a network of objects, power, work, and people not only caters to diversity and freedom, but also leads to anonymity and isolation. The difficulty of how to transform distant collaboration, solidarity, and friendship into actual situations and social change has increased to such an extent that the social has become fetishized into an exotic entity. No one would even remotely associate it with The Social Question, much less matters of class struggle or socialism. During the Berlin seminar, Brian Holmes commented that institutions have the function to discipline crowds into citizenry with predictable norms. He argued that there is something prepolitical and unruly about the crowd, the mob, and the multitude. The idea of the masses has been associated with citizen formation. In any crowd there are individuals who write its algorithm. The power is with those who are able to set the terms of the debate.[4] This is why the manufacture of concepts is such a strategic undertaking. Instead of borrowing terms from the dead discipline of mass psychology, it would be better to come up with descriptions for what we actually witness, like Warren Sack, who called the networked dialogs on lists, newsgroups, chat rooms, and blogs "very large-scale conversations," as they are often a form of conversation that involves many more people in far more complicated social and semantic dynamics compared to previous eras.[5]

Form, Forming, Format

The premise here is that we are moving from living, analyzing, and imaging contemporary culture as an information society technically underwritten by the computer, to inhabiting and imagining relays of entwined and fragmented techno-social networks. New media is increasingly distributed media and it requires a rethinking of aesthetics beyond the twinned concepts of form and medium that continue to shape analysis of the social and the aesthetic.[6] It requires *distributed aesthetics*. Distributed aesthetics must deal simultaneously with the dispersed and the situated, with asynchronous production and multi-user access to artifacts (both material and immaterial) on the one hand, and the highly individuated and dispensed allotment of information/media on the other. The aesthetics of distributed media, practices, and experience cannot be located in the formal principles of their dispersal. This only provides us with the conditions for serving information via a network to end-users and reduces it to a simplistic schema, one that echoes all the problems of a communications systems transmission model: server-network-users. Nor can we simply derive distributed aesthetics from the viewpoint of use. There is no singular or end use of information but rather the endless relaying of media, practices, and experience as successive dispersals. Distributed aesthetics might be better characterized as an emergent project, situated between the drift away from coherent form on the one hand, and the drift of aesthetics into relations with the social and networked formations on the other.

Networks cannot be fully studied if seen only as mere tools with schematizations and diagrams. They need to be apprehended as complex environments, within the complex networked ecologies in which they are forming. This can easily become an empty statement. By complex, we mean unpredictable, often poor, harsh, and not exactly rich expressions of the social. To project positive predictions, hopes, and desires onto networks is deceptive as it often distracts by focusing solely on the first, founding, and euphoric phase of networks. Consequently, this positivism is ill equipped to deal with the conflict, boredom, confusion, stagnation, and other expressions of our playfully nihilistic culture, which turn up in unmoderated channels such as lists, blogs, and chat rooms. If we call for distributed aesthetics, it needs to account for those experiences of stagnation within network formations. It also needs to couple these networked experiences with a network's potential to transform and mutate into something not yet fully codified. It is not enough to celebrate networks as social realities. What we call for is a systematic reflection on the formats of distribution we use. What counts are cultures of use that understand enough to alter the given software, interfaces, and content into something unprecedented. Can the user really become a network architect and not just a subject that merely leaves traces? How do users turn into developers? And, importantly, how do they develop the critical skills to resist responding at crucial moments? Besides this capacity, we also have to study the consumption of technical distribution (as Sebastian Lütgert suggested at the Berlin seminar), sitting quietly watching the P2P files being downloaded. There is not much left of the autonomy of the user, and Western subjectivity in general. It is important to reassess the status of user, as Pit Schultz has done in his essay "The Producer as Power User."[7]

The Map Is Not the Network

A concrete instance of distributed aesthetics can be found in the widespread eagerness to produce maps. What is so fascinating about mapping?[8]

If we began first with a question and now follow with a gesture of negation, this is precisely because the network—so opaque, so ubiquitous and non-formal—is recruited to serve various strategies of representation. Maps of networks abound. Software for visualizing criminal networks such as PatternTracer are easily available online; an entire discursive field—social network analysis—has arisen around the mapping of networks from corporate to terrorist; and the noncartographic specialist can now log on to an entire map of the Internet, drop in, and link his or her own computer address as a 3D-visualization in the network of all other addresses.[9] Richard Rogers suggests that mapping networks, especially as an intelligence task, carries with it more than just an aesthetic outcome; we are in the midst of a techno-epistemological impulse in which the form(at) of the map has a structuring effect on how we understand the organization (structure) and dynamics (movement) of networks.[10]

Theorizing networks (as opposed to direct network visualization) must struggle with the abstraction of dispersed elements—elements that cannot be captured into one image. The very notion of a network is in conflict with the desire to gain an overview. Mapping software, the technological answer to this problem, by its own nature reduces complexity in order to produce a limited amount of general categories, which then can be applied to the map and linked. The art of network visualization deals with several limitations, those of the screen, algorithms, and the boundaries of human perception. We can read—and understand—only so many linked elements. In order to understand and appreciate network maps, we have to familiarize ourselves with "cloud thinking" in which we zoom out from relational levels in order to obtain a bigger picture. Having moved away from a chaotic cluster, we can then move into the cloud again and look for specific links between items.

Maps make visible what we have already sensed. Maps provoke a sense of recognition. Network maps may also organize our perception of a social object in formation without being forthright about the premises upon which this organizing impulse rests. Network mapping exposes a desire to be in the know, "a way of coming to know and making particular claims only with a technological apparatus that desires to grow to satisfy its cravings for 'really knowing' and, especially 'really knowing what our' intelligence also knows or should know," as Richard Rogers sees it.[11] Mapping information—the aesthetics of contemporary visualization—provides a sense of relief that the twisted and unstructured info-bits that roam around in our cognitive unconscious are finally laid out and put to rest. A beast is tamed. Against today's presumed transparency of the maps, Nils Röller, speaking at the Berlin seminar, emphasized its traditional secrecy. Often the ownership of maps gave the explorer unprecedented access to resources and power. Why would one need a map if one knows where to go, Röller asked. Instead, he proposed the use of the term *compass*. The factors that determine computational environments are too often perceived as being merely oriented on the interface level. Is it the exclusion mechanism that further fuels the open access movement? Is it still relevant to ask what information is revealed and what is hidden? Obviously today's capture devices, from satellites to handy cameras, contain other limits. What to make of Archive.org's wild claim that it provides "universal access to human knowledge?" What if the interfaces are becoming too complex and the databases overgrown with nonsense data? The drive to have a complete overview at that point collapses into madness or resentment.

Network mapping underwent a significant shift in geometry and visualization in the late 1990s.[12] As we moved from the superimposition of flows onto geo-political space, toward the abstraction of topology, similarly our understandings of what comprised networks shifted. We became interested in relations, dynamics, and sociability as opposed to traffic, connections, and community. This change in network mapping visualization has had advantages and disadvantages—we are now aware that networks are different kinds of formations that cannot be understood according to the old distinctions between society (*Gesellschaft*) and community (*Gemeinschaft*). But the increasingly abstract topological visualization of networks removes us from an analysis of the ways in which networks engage and are engaged by current political, economic, and social relations.

At any rate, maps reveal the ways in which we perceive things to be at a given historical time. The Mercator Map (circa 1569), now analyzed from a moment "post" its particular partitioning of perception along a colonial set of axes, reveals what was at stake politically and economically in making the world run according to a north–south cartography. Perhaps network mapping will similarly reveal the logic of its own will to tame complexity, to make the flows of a network society traceable. It could be more interesting, then, to not simply look at the map but at what desires network mapping is trying to satisfy. If in the past cartography has been linked to imperial conquests of space, what space is there left to conquer today? The space between the nodes or even the space of all potential connections and links? Just as network formations are indications that an unstable reshuffle of the categories for understanding the social is playing itself out, mapping this rearranging sociality indicates an aesthetic at work to order more rampant and mutant forms of emergent social relations. It is not surprising that the impetus for network mapping arrives today from the social sciences on the one hand and from the analysis, tracking, and tracing of crime on the other.[13] We ought to be suspicious of the pervasive will to network mapping as well. For Brian Holmes, on the other hand, there is no reason to downgrade the importance of making maps. For Bureau d'Etudes, their maps are tools among others, used within workshops on specific topics.[14]

The Fou Code

Over the past two decades, aesthetics has been extended, stretched, and turned upside down from a discipline dealing with the interpretation of the meaning and structure of the object of beauty into a philosophical praxis investigating the very conditions of contemporary life. Aesthetics is not the science of eye-candy, in which taste is reduced to a matter of mere statistics and samples of information. Instead, we must investigate the "aesthesia" of today's networked experience. How do we perceive the socially invisible, yet all too real, relationships that are accumulating around us? Distributed aesthetics, as a project, needs to be understood as a participatory journey of network users, aiming to capture the not-yet-described and the not-yet-visualized, and to go beyond poles such as real–virtual, new–old, offline–online, and global–local. We should forget about exposing the links that are already there and, with our capacity to engage a networked logic, forge links to what is *in* the network but not yet *of* the network. By this we mean to invoke a project more akin to social aesthetics or aesthesia in which we engage in and with the collective experiences of being embroiled in networks and being actively part of their making. We can contrast this with the abstracted activity of simply mapping quantities of data such as social network maps, which is a form of production already captured by the codes and conventions of connectivity.

We do not need allegorical readings of networks. Networks are not proposals, constructions, metaphors, or even alternatives for existing social formations such as the church, the corporation, the school, the NGO, or the political party. Instead, we should analyze the rise of networks as an all too human endeavor, a tragic fall, and not as posthuman machines automating connections for us. Networks are not the answer to global problems nor are they a substitute for forgotten religions or disintegrated communities. Networks are not models to be transposed from one social or political situation or conflagration to another. It is certainly the case that technology provokes networking. But then this provocation is not the be all and end all of the network. We should be wary of techno-contradictions like social software that suggest technology will glue us humans together (again).[15] Instead, we should read—and enjoy—networks as info-clouds that cover the sun and disperse the bright light of broadcasting media.

Networks act as "fragmentators." They break up strong signs and experiences into countless threads. These info-bits might in themselves be meaningless but their overall sum provides enough distraction to topple the attention monopoly of newspapers and television. This is not done through the classic activist strategy of building up parallel counterworlds. Lists, blogs, chat rooms, and social networks sites are the "long tail" of the media landscape.[16] Networks do not burn off the media, take center stage, and continue to provide the background noise of the chattering classes. It doesn't matter how big they grow. Instead of anticipating a takeover by the corporate sphere and attempting to protect networked and locative media from demise, it is more than likely that business interests will integrate selected parts of the blogosphere. The rest of the online noise will likely fade away into digital oblivion. In the meantime, blogs, wiki, podcasting, and whatever comes next will continue to run under the rubric of media diversification. Nothing is as fluid, fragile—and unsustainable—as today's network landscape.

In the meantime, we could treat the info-bits that flow our way as short-term solutions to the environmental crises brought about by the breakdown of both massified media outlets and dedicated high-end digital aesthetics. Data flows from peer to peer, in networks hardly noticed by authorities. But before the law moves in—and with it, the academics—the crowds will have already moved on to cooler pastures. Let's not invest some salvation in all of this distribution. Distributed media are both too loose and too large upon which to build a new utopia. Their fragmentary nature will have effects but we cannot link them to a cause. We may be unable to house the endless link lists, unanswered calls and e-mails, cute blogs, and stagnant conversations under the banner of complete social and media transformation. However, we will nonetheless have to find a mode of comprehending their everyday perceptual accretions—the ways in which they make small changes to our social relations with others and with broader groupings such as mainstream media.

What network theory, and with it, distributed aesthetics, needs to tackle first is the myth of seamless and perpetual growth. Once upon a time during the golden dotcom days it was an insight to present networks as dynamic, ever-growing entities. These days, we have moved to obsessively focusing upon the micro-politics of networks within networks. It is impressive but useless to know that your social network puts you in connection with 371,558 "friends." At that point, friends are simply an effect of a network, not its constituent relations.[17] The social scientists almost reveal the desires that shape their own trajectories around "social and organizational network analysis" with their talk of egocentric networks. The micro has become awash with the atomized individuals and we waste our capacity on comprehending the shapes or shaping of networks by plotting out the link lines of one node to another. In actuality, the lines that appear so connected, seamless, and smooth on network maps can never account for the human labor required to create and maintain the link or the sudden death and change of direction for a network in which strong lines give way. Rhizomes, in fact, have odd shapes and are actually small roots that die off at some point in their lifeline. So do trees. The problem with a naïve cloning of Deleuze and Guattari's botany in the networked context lies with an unreconstructed commitment to growth. This involves a blinding by the potentialities that the network-as-dream-machine would seem to offer. Here the network and info-capital converge rather than produce friction, complications, or even poisonings. Instead, we could say that growing could mean not simply expansion but maturing. There is plenty of quantity in the mediascape and so to grow without changing or dying only multiplies or clones more networks of connected atomized units. Networks need ideas and aesthetic projects directing how they might mature and transform. The distribution concept, for instance, does not automatically imply seamless expansion.

Let's draw a difference here between growth and persistence. Growth feeds the lifecycle of capital and capital loves any kind of growth—upward, downward, or outward. Persistence, on the other hand, comprehends that something doggedly survives but that its growth or decay depends on other forces, conditions, and effort. Bits of the network break off and wither and it may be that something can endure elsewhere because of this little death. But maybe the whole damn patch of grass just up and dies one day, and there is no longer a network in your backyard. Online social formations are more like these small tendrils of growth that shoot and die— the list, for example, lives for a while as its members try to feed it. They work to shape and develop it, providing it with new impetus while the overall form just lumbers along. But then its energy burns out and there is no more growing left to do. Something endures between some of the participants or another effort starts up elsewhere but then that something, that network, has changed too. These processes are not all part of the same growing organism or self-organizing system. Attempts to homogenize or sustain processes as a singular drive toward growth are endemic to capital. The processes are instead lateral, cumulative, and de-energized modes of laboring; also endemic to capital but, for the most part, the unpaid arc of its cycle.

Against Biologism

Networks do not simply emerge. They are cybernetic constructs that, once founded and installed, erupt and then slumber, decline, go on and on, fall asleep and wake up again before they die a sudden death or face an entropic decline. Networks do not follow the simplistic models of linear mechanics or of evolutionary growth. A critical theory of scalability and sustainability has to go beyond the biological metaphors that speak of contagion, copy-paste epidemics and memes. We have to make a distinction between real existing patterns, behaviors within technical networks, and the wet dreams (or nightmares) of marketing departments trying to give a positive spin on the unpredictable moves of their blogging customers.

Complexity—of data, of connectivity—has been rolled out as an excuse for technical and cultural phenomena being too hard to comprehend. Subsequently, it figures that we have to feed all of this complexity back into the machine to be analyzed. Numbers are too hard so we get a picture instead. Complexity should not be an excuse for deferring the work of human thought and human creation—theoretical and aesthetic—to network software. Complexity is difficult and arduous but not aesthetically unmanageable. Let's not cede the complexity of networked life to procedures. If we want suggestions as to how this complex networked aesthetics might be rendered, then let us look less to maps and more to sketches and roughs that infer a category of "the relational" comprised of potentialities. This would be somewhat different from framing relations within reductive models of utility or connectivity. Let's look instead to work such as Graham Harwood's software research NetMonster.[18] Here variable keywords related to a user's current image interests or obsessions are used to initialize a crawl for sites that contain text or images related to the keywords. The crawl returns these sites as stripped text and pictures, rearranging them around an image mask based upon the user's current image obsession, collaging and redrawing the information so that it butts up in convoluted lines of connection against itself.

The links that connect the text and image together in NetMonster's collage of information arise out of a differential between what is prelinked online—the image's "mediated causes of its own existence"—and the variables a user introduces into these connections via the mask and the keywords. There are other aspects to this software in which the crawler automatically attempts to spam the phone numbers and e-mails from the garnered sites, alerting people to ways in which their information has participated in a link or connection against common sense. There is an antinavigational and irresolvable aesthetic oscillation that results from this work. Its informatic rendering is monstrous, rampant, and pathological rather than friendly or sociable. As Harwood suggests, the image functions in the unimaginable spaces and indeterminate relations of distributed information. "The picture acts as a proposition—frustrated—oscillating between a picture's ability to say and show."[19]

We need a more complex conception of network sociality than the concept of social software that is currently attached to descriptions of networks of friends or lovers in an online dating database. We need a more complex understanding of the visual plane of information than the pictorial map of the network. Networks are not glued together by software and software does not make us social. Networks are not resolvable into zoomable details of landscapes that must fit the window of a browser. But equally we cannot take the social out of software; in fact, what we need is to be more specific about how the social and its myriad aesthetics are operating through and in software. How is a network really being sustained—computationally and through creative labor? How is the network experience to be thought and felt? Whose labor—creative, manual, skilled, disorganized—keeps it moving along? What intrusions of rhetoric from other images of neo-liberal democratic theory and its dreams of customized participation, for example, break into and intrude upon the fragile links that tentatively form within networked experience?

Where Are You Going?

Networks should not be defined by the visible links they place on display. Getting "linked in" a network is not materialized through (digital) information. This is what makes it so fake to ask a computer to visualize a network or to believe in link lists. Putting a link in is work, a tedious activity that requires precision and dedication. Only a few of us develop a routine that leads us to the "felt experience" of actual linking in the network. Today's networked existence hops from one medium to the next and then demands that we return back to our links in order to put in the work of connecting again and again.

What constitutes linking and how could we describe its mirror phantom, or rather, its shadow? The link as a reference to another informational object only comes into being as a conscious act. There is no automated process of putting links. And there is no unconscious or subliminal linking either. These could all be worthy scientific propositions but as of yet they do not exist. Linking is tedious work. It is an effort and should be considered extra work. There is no routine in linking. It is a precise job that needs constant control. The opposite of the conscious link is not the broken but the absent link.

We are in search, instead, of an aesthetic that comes to terms with conflict, boredom, confusion, and stagnation—one that includes social complexity (as opposed to biocomplexity). At the same time, we are dealing with a nonvisual aesthetic with respect to networks or at least a visual that is not pictorial and cannot be depicted as such. What kind of aesthetics then does the network herald? We should not forget that our debates are not entirely out of the blue and respond to certain software configurations, which can be changed. A future generation of blogs may not have the option to externally respond to postings. Due to spam, wikis could lose their capacity to alter texts. At the same time, we could see impressive new incorporations of data flow now circling around inside mobile communication space. These configurations are not merely technical innovations or developments. Software-wise they are easy to write and implement. Their innovative power is not in the complexity of code but in the simplicity of their techno-social implementations. This simplicity comes from many directions and forces at once—efficiency, standardization, and commercial viability, and from user circumvention and invention. We are not merely reflecting, imaging, or imagining when we engage distributed aesthetics. We are configuring and remaking.

Social networks should not be seen as separate entities that float out there, as a parallel reality. Rather, they reflect—and accelerate—tendencies that already exist. This is important to keep in mind if we discuss the narcotic and depressive culture of social networks like Orkut, Friendster, and MySpace. Sadness management is a key activity in this Prozac society. Social anxiety, gadget addiction, and attention deficit disorder have to be seen as one complex set of phenomena. Electronic solitude and frantic networking are nowhere near opposite phenomena. Networks can bring us down and should by no means be presented as a solution for the ruling state of mind. In that sense, distributed aesthetics can also be seen as a medicine to cheer us up. Concepts should not just cover but create tensions. What distributed aesthetics has proven is its ability to overcome suburban isolation. Let's overcome the sorrows of the young blogger. Instead of pinning down people by asking, "Where are you?" we may as well map out desired directions: "Where are you going?" Let's draw matrices of the possible and get into a "state of readiness" as Jordan Crandall described it: "It is a state that operates at the level of both perception and corporeality, where one is not only cognitively but affectively engaged. A form of alertness on the edge of action, where the vigilant and optimized machine-body is roused and poised to act."[20]

Technologically informed network theory needs to overcome the limited canon found in popular network literature. How the Medici ran their empire and how certain school groups later turned out to rule powerful corporations are all interesting examples, but they tell surprisingly little how the contemporary online world functions. In brief, the stability of the old boys network stands in contrast to the instability of large social networks that migrate from one service to the next in no time. It is easy to blame American culture for the extraordinary inflation of the term *friends*. Against the manic collection of friends on Orkut and MySpace (but also the business network LinkedIn), we can talk about what real friendship is and quote Foucault. We may as well leave such obvious responses and admit that in that Internet context friendship lacks any romantic connotation. What the friends option does is design one's social environment and homogenize relationships. The social is not a given, defined by family, school, church, work, or society, but is something that has to be constructed in a personal manner.

Distributed aesthetics can be a catchword, critical concept, and project. Repeatedly it has proven productive to use philosophical terms and put them to work as metaphors, assisting us in the journey from here to there. It is high time to invite art historians, art critics, and many others into the field and confront them with the networked condition. It may be depressing that many of the efforts are not going beyond appropriation of commodities and services that were developed many years ago. Even for those taking up the most advanced positions, it must be a sober realization that all we do is investigate yesterday's consumer products. The gap between innovative applications in use by business and government on the one side, and the cultural rearguard on the other is wider than ever. Distributed aesthetics is one among many projects calling for a radical investigation of today's technology platforms. The least we can do is catchup.

CHAPTER 11

Introducing Organized Networks[1]
The Quest for Sustainable Concepts

At first glance, the concept of "organized networks" seems self-evident. In technical terms, all networks are organized. There are founders, administrators, moderators, and active members who all take up specific roles. Networks consist of mobile relations whose arrangement at any particular time is shaped by the "constitutive outside" of feedback or noise.[2] The order of networks is made up of a continuum of relations governed by interests, passions, effects, and pragmatic necessities of different actors. The network of relations is never static and not to be mistaken for some kind of perpetual fluidity. The quest for practical and conceptual probes into organized networks originates from the contradiction between the emergence of a network society (Castells) and the secondary and invisible status that networks still have in society.

Then why should networks get organized? Isn't their chaotic, disorganized nature a good thing that needs to be preserved? Why should the *informelle Öffentlichkeit* of a network be disturbed? Networks should be organized for the simple fact that their size, importance, and potential power is growing by the day. But don't worry. Organized networks do not yet exist. This concept that I developed with my friend, the Australian theorist Ned Rossiter, is to be read as a proposal, a draft in the process of becoming that needs active steering through disagreement and collective elaboration.[3] Needless to say, organized networks have existed for centuries. Just think of the Jesuits, the Italian mafia, drugs-smuggling rings, or global terrorist networks. Various subjective states of mind can be organized, such as "organized innocence" as described by Adilkno in their

239

collection of unidentified theoretical objects called Media Archive.[4] The archeology of organized networks can and will be written, but that does not advance our inquiry for now.

The networks we are talking about are specific in that they are situated within digital media. They can be characterized by their moving irrelevance and invisibility for old media and the powers that be. General network theory as performed by Duncan Watts and Albert-László Barabási might be useful for enlightenment purposes, but will not answer the issues that next-media-based social networks face. The issue here is one of fermentation: how can networks mutate into something else as they integrate into society? Will networks by default remain on the outside or will they consolidate? Seen from the perspective of organized networks, Yochai Benkler should have renamed *The Wealth of Networks* as *The Poverty of Networks* as there is, at least thus far, hardly any wealth (measured in hard currencies) floating around within Internet-based networks that is accessible for the individual member. The suggested richness, as I already indicated in the Introduction, is a meme designed to create ever more default amateurs. A possible connection with Bruno Latour's Actor-Network Theory has yet to be investigated and is not self-evident either. Does it satisfy you to know that molecules and DNA patterns also network? Today's analogy industry that compares nature with culture and art with science provides a boost for the reputation of the writers involved, but is of little use in this context. In fact, it distracts attention away from the urgent question: how can networks become organized and generate visibility and income?

There are no networks outside of society. Like all human-techno entities, they are infected by power. Networks are ideal Foucault machines. They undermine power as they produce it. The networks with which we are dealing are a product of command and control logic, and yet they undermine it at the same time. At the moment, the networks that are Internet-related seem to, more than anything else, break down traditional power structures. It is too early to know if they will take over or take up classic forms of power, but we have to presume so. For the time being, they celebrate their own failure (such as the Howard Dean campaign as told in Chapter 1) in the political realm and portray themselves as emerging agents of change inside the old media realm. It is easy to break careers and election campaigns. But can blogs also initiate social processes beyond a supporting role? The outcome may be uncertain, but, not to miss the boat, Hugh Hewitt's warning has a clear authoritarian undertone: "Most folks know who Luther is. Not many people know who Leo X is. Because Luther overwhelmed Leo. Don't be a Leo."[5]

The opposite of organized networks is not a random field of chaos. Organized networks routinely intervene in the radical temporality of today's media sphere. Acting on short-term interests is the prevailing condition that infects governments, corporations, and everyday life. We constantly respond in a permanent mode of panic and crisis management and, as Bifo indicated, psychopharmacology is the bio-technical supplement of this condition.[6] Organized networks express the desire to move up, away from the 1990s bio-social metaphors, such as mobs and swarms, toward a higher order in which the extraordinary power of networks is recognized and rewarded. Networks do not need more informality (there will always be plenty of that), but rather a transformation toward more formal relationships.

Network users do not see their circle of peers as a closed sect. Users are not like lifelong political party members. Quite the opposite. Ties are loose, up to the point of breaking up. To understand networks, we have to study slackness and the pleasure of resignation. The default user is the lurker. Engagement is the state of exception and, as in political philosophy, an interesting one indeed. Exception is neither rare nor the rule. Instead of overvaluing or underestimating, it is better to take an amoral approach to the question of signal/noise ratios and see the mind and figure of the prosumer as it is, namely, ideology.

Delete Innocence

The ontology of the user mirrors the logic of capital in so many ways. The user is the identity par excellence of capital that seeks to extract itself from rigid systems of regulation and control. Increasingly the user has become a term that corresponds with the auto-configuration of self-invention. Some would say the user is just a consumer, silent and satisfied—at least until something fails and all hell breaks loose. The user is the identity of control by other means. In this respect, the user is the empty vessel awaiting the spectral allure of digital commodity cultures and their promise of mobility and openness. Let us harbor no fantasies. Sociality is bound intimately within the dynamic array of techniques exerted by the force of capital. Networks are everywhere. The challenge for the foreseeable future is to create the next openings, the possibilities, the temporalities and spaces within which life may assert its insistence for an ethic-aesthetic existence.

The organized network should be read as a radical proposal aimed to replace the problematic term *virtual community.* Organized networks also supersede the level of individual blogging, whose logic of networks does not correspond with the concept developed here. It is with some urgency that internal power relations within networks are placed on the agenda. Only then can we make a clear break with the invisible workings of electronic networks that defined the consensus era. Organized networks are clouds of social relationships in which disengagement is pushed to the limit. Community is an idealistic construct and suggests bonding and harmony, which often is simply not there. The same could be said of the call for trust. Networks cry out for imaginary forms of insecurity.

Networks long for peaks in traffic and rhetoric yet are fully geared to survive long, dull periods of radio silence and never-ending streams of banality. Networks thrive on diversity and conflict (the "notworking" aspect), not on unity, and this is what community theorists have been unable to reflect upon. For community advocates, disagreement equals a disruption of the constructive flow of dialogue. It takes effort to reflect on distrust as a productive principle. Indifference between networks is one of the main reasons not to get organized, so this aspect has to be taken seriously. Interaction and involvement are idealistic constructs. Organized networks also question the presumed innocence of the chattering and gossiping networks. Networks are not the opposite of organizations in the same way the real is not opposed to the virtual. Instead, we should analyze networks as an emerging social and cultural form. Networks are precarious and this vulnerability should be seen as both its strength and its weakness.

Beyond Intervention

According to Henk Oosterling, in the information society interpassivity rules.[7] Browsing, watching, reading, waiting, thinking, deleting, chatting, skipping, and surfing are the default conditions of online life. Total involvement implies insanity. Instead, we remain cool. Networks are categorized by a shared sense of a potentiality that does not have to be realized. Millions of replies from all to all would cause every network, no matter what its architecture, to implode. Within every network, there are prolonged periods of passivity interrupted by outbursts of activity. Networks foster and reproduce loose relationships—and it is better to look this fact straight in the eye. Networks are hedonistic machines of promiscuous contacts. Networked multitudes create temporary and voluntary forms of collaboration that transcend but do not necessarily disrupt the Age of Disengagement.

The concept of organized networks is useful to enlist for strategic purposes. After a decade of tactical media, the time has come to scale up the operations of radical media practices and deal with the knotty issue of organization. We should all have emerged from the retro fantasy of the benevolent welfare state with its opulent funding for media, education, culture, and the arts. Networks will never be rewarded and "embedded" in well-funded structures. Just as the modernist avant-garde saw itself punctuating the fringes of society, so has tactical media taken comfort in the idea of targeted micro-interventions. The *fort-da* game that the communication guerilla is playing with old media heavily depends on the ups and downs of social movements. Tactical media too often reproduces the curious spatio-temporal dynamic and structural logic of the modern state and industrial capital: difference and renewal from the peripheries. But there is a paradox at work here. Disruptive as its actions may often be, tactical media corroborates the temporal mode of post-Fordist capital — short-termism. In essence, it does not break with the strategies of disappearance.

It is retrograde that tactical media in a post-Fordist era continues to operate in terms of ephemerality and the logic of tactics. Since the punctuated attack model is the dominant condition, tactical media has a fatal affinity with that which it seeks to oppose. This is why tactical media is treated with a kind of benign tolerance. There is a neurotic tendency to disappear. Anything that solidifies is lost in the system. The ideal is to be little more than a temporary glitch, a brief instance of noise or interference. Tactical media sets itself up for exploitation in the same manner that "modders" do in the game industry: both dispense with their knowledge of loopholes in the system for free. They intervene, point out the problem, and then run away. Capital is delighted, and thanks the tactical media outfit and the nerd-modder for the home improvement. The paradigm of neo-liberalism is extensive throughout the apparatus of social life. This situation is immanent to the operation of radical media cultures, regardless of whether they are willing to admit it. The alarm bells will only start ringing when tactical media cranks up its operations. When this happens, the organized network emerges as the modus operandi. Radical media projects will then escape the bemused paternalism of the state-as-corporation.

But make no mistake, the emergence of organized networks amounts to an articulation of info-war. This battle currently revolves around the theme of sustainability. It is no accident that sustainability is the meme of the moment because it offers the discursive and structural advantage required by neo-liberal governments and institutions wishing to extricate themselves from responsibility to annoying constituencies. Organized networks are required to invent models of sustainability that go beyond the latest plan of action update, which is only then inserted into paper shredders of member states and citizen-friendly businesses. The empty center of neo-liberalism is sociality. The organized network is part of a larger scramble to fill that void. One has only to cast an eye toward the new legitimacy granted to the church as a provider of social services. Civil society, in short, is replacing the ground of the social. But the assertion of the social is underpinned by ongoing antagonisms. The rise of right-wing populism is an example of how open the empty center is to a tolerance of fundamentalism.

Organized networks compete with established institutions in terms of branding and identity building, but it is as sites of knowledge production and concept development that primarily defines the competitive edge of organized networks. These days, most "brick and mortar" institutions can only subtract value from networks. They are not merely unwilling but in fact incapable of giving anything back. Virtual networks are not represented in negotiations over budgets, grants, investments, and job hiring. At best, they are seen as sources of inspiration among peers. This is the real potential of virtual networks—they are enhancement engines. When they work well, they can inspire new expressions, new socialities, new techniques. The organized network grows out of a hybrid formation: part tactical media, part institutional formation. There are benefits to be obtained from both lineages. The clear distinction of the organized network is that its institutional logic is internal to the socio-technical dimensions of the media of communication. This means there is no universal formula for how an organized network might invent its conditions of existence. There will be no "internationalism" for networks.

Mirroring the Organization

Eventually organized networks will be mirrored against the networked organization. But we are not there yet. There will be no easy synthesis. Roughly speaking, one can witness a convergence between the informality of virtual networks and the formality of institutions. However, this process is anything but harmonious. Clashes between networks and organizations are occurring before our very eyes. Disputes condition, and are internal to, the creation of new institutional forms. Debris spreads in every possible direction, depending on the locality. One could say that the organized multitude is constituted—and crushed—as a part of this process. In this sense, a new political subject is required, one that emerges from the current state of disorganization that defines the multitude. It is naïve to believe that, under the current circumstances, networks will win this battle (if, indeed, it is even useful to still think in those terms). This is precisely why networks need their own form of organization. In this process, they will have to deal with the following three aspects: (1) accountability, (2) sustainability, and (3) scalability.

Let's start with the question of whom networks represent or if indeed they hold such a capacity and what form of internal democracy they envision. Formal networks have members but most online initiatives do not. Let's face it; networks disintegrate traditional forms of representation. This is what makes the question "Did blogs affect the 2004 U.S. election?" so irrelevant. The blogosphere at best influenced a handful of television and newspaper editors. Instead of spreading the word, the Internet has questioned authority—any authority—and therefore was not useful for pushing this or that candidate up the rating scale of electoral appeal. The role of blogs is interesting, but is limited to that of catalyst. Networks that thrive higher up will eventually fail because they will be incorporated and co-opted, and will degenerate into the capitalist mainstream. No matter what you think of Derrida, networks do not deconstruct society. Distributed media models undermine, correct if you like, but have no capacity as of yet to overcome capitalism. It is deep linkage that matters, not some symbolic coup d'état. If there were an aim, it would be to parallel hegemony, which can only be achieved if underlying premises are constantly put under scrutiny by the initiators of the next techno-social wave of innovations.

The rise of community informatics as a field of research and project building could be seen as an exemplary platform to deal with the issues treated here.[8] Yet for all the interest community informatics has in building projects from below, a substantial amount of research within this field is directed toward e-democracy issues. It is time to abandon the illusion that the myths of representational democracy might somehow be transferred and realized within networked settings. That is not going to happen. After all, the people benefiting from such endeavours are, for the most part, those on the speaking and funding circuits, not the grassroots initiatives that are supposedly represented in such a process. Funding for informal and invisible networks that practice new logics of politics is needed. It is a dead-end street to go only for a handpicked collection of NGOs that have identified themselves as global civil society and that strategically use this term to exclude those that do not subscribe to the NGO-model of organization—a form of friendly exclusion as it is done without evil intentions.

Mapping the Post-Democratic

Networks are not institutions of representative democracy, despite the frequency with which they are expected to model themselves on such failed institutions. Instead, there is a search for non-representational democratic models of decision making that avoid classical models of representation and related identity politics. The emerging theme of non-representative democracies places an emphasis on process over its after-effect, consensus. Certainly, there is something attractive in process-oriented forms of governance. Ultimately the process model is about as sustainable as an earthworks sculpture burrowed into a patch of dirt called the 1970s. Process is fine as far as it integrates a plurality of forces into the network. But the primary questions remain: Where does it go? How long does it last? Why do it in the first place? Who is speaking? Why bother? A focus on the vital forces that constitute socio-technical life is thus required. Herein lay the variability and wildcards of organized networks. The persistence of dispute and disagreement can be taken as a given. Rational consensus models of democracy have proven, in their failure, that such underlying conditions of social-political life cannot be eradicated.

Organized networks have to be concerned with their own sustainability. Networks are not hypes. Networks emerge after the orgy. We have passed the 1990s and that potlatch era will not return. Networks may look temporary but their impact on society remains, despite their constant transformations. Individual cells might die off sooner rather than later, but there is a will to connect that is hard to suppress. Links may be dead at some point but that is not the end of the data itself. Nonetheless, networks are extremely fragile. This may all sound obvious, but let us not forget that pragmatism is built upon the passions, joys, and thrills of invention. Time has come for cautious planning. There is a self-destructive tendency of networks faced with the challenge of organization. Organized networks have to feel confident about defining their value systems in ways that are meaningful and relevant to the internal operations of their social-technical complex. That is actually not so difficult. The danger is ghettoization and deadening routine. The trick is to work out a collaborative value system able to deal with issues such as funding, internal power plays, and the demand for accountability and transparency as they scale up and transform their operations.

Get Monetary

Organized networks first have to keep their virtual house in order. It is of strategic importance to use a non-profit provider (ISP) and have backups made, or even run a mirror in another country. Also, it is wise not to make use of commercial services such as Yahoo!Groups, Hotmail, Geocities, or Google, as they are unreliable and suffer from regular security breaches. If you believe there is something to hide, visit NGO-in-a-Box and get your act together.[9] Be aware of the (minimal) costs for domain names, e-mail addresses, storage, and bandwidth, even if they are relatively small. Often conflicts arise because passwords and ownership of the domain name are in the hands of one person who is leaving the group in a conflict situation. This can literally mean the end of the project, as happened with Digital City Amsterdam, where, in the end, it resulted in a conflict over who owned the domain name (www.dds.nl).

Networks are never one hundred percent virtual and are always connected at some point to the monetary economy. This is where the story of organized networks begins. Perhaps incorporation is necessary. If you do not want to bother the network with legal matters, keep in mind what the costs of not going there will be. Funding for online activities, meetings, editorial work, coding, design, research, or publications can be channelled through allied institutions. Remember that the more online activities you unfold, the more likely it is that you will have to pay for design, editorial work, and a network administrator.

The inward-looking free software world only uses its paradise-like voluntary work rules for its own coding projects. Cultural, artistic, and activist projects easily fit into this logic and all have a long history of free work. The same goes for content editors and Web designers. Ideally, online projects are high on communitarian spirits and are able to access the necessary skills. But the further we leave behind the moment of initiation, the more likely it will be that the work will have to be paid. Organized networks have to face this economic reality or find themselves marginalized, no matter how advanced their dialogues and network use might be. Talking about the rise of immaterial labor and precarious work is useful but could run out of steam, as it remains incapable of making the jump from speculative reflection to a political agenda that outlines how networks can be both funded and mobilized over time.

Organized networks are always going to face great difficulty in raising financial resources through the traditional monetary system. It is not easy to attract funding from any of the traditional sectors of government, private philanthropy, or business. Alternatives need to be created. Arguably, the greatest asset of organized networks consists of what they do: exchanging information and conducting debates on mailing lists; running public education programs and archiving education resources; open publishing of magazines, journals, and books; hosting individual Web sites, wikis, and blogs; organizing workshops, meetings, exhibitions, and conferences; and providing an infrastructure that lends itself to rapid connections and collaborations among participants and potential partners.

If there is a decision to be made, and an antagonistic challenge to be singled out, it is the techno-libertarian religion of the free. As I have already pointed out in the Introduction, it is high time to openly attack the cynical logic of do-good vulture capitalists that preach giving or taking content for no money while making millions of dollars with software, hardware, and telco-infrastructure that the masses of amateur-idiots need in order to give or take content for free. Organized networks are wary of the gurus who inspire others to make a living out of selling t-shirts: "You poor bugger, fool around with your funky free content, while we make millions with the requirements." It is time to unveil this logic and publicly resist it. Knowledge as such, in this case, is not enough. Civil courage to speak out, particularly when opponents are friends, is needed. It is with the best of intentions that good people do wrong. The time when we identify the capitalist merely as an exploiter with a black hat and a cigar in his mouth is over.

If we know that we can get a piece of software, music, or book for free through our social network, why would we bother to buy it? Why pay for *Britannica* if Wikipedia has a comparable yet free offer? We are willing to live with (and work on) the many problems of this free encyclopedia and shed no tears for those pipe-smoking *Britannica* editors. They are out-collaborated by the free cooperation multitude. But how graceful should we be about this short-term victory? To what extent can collectively created content repositories challenge or parallel the content hegemonies of traditional institutions? Howard Rheingold describes how knowledge collectives hunt and gather information.[10] These accumulative collaborations are inspiring. They also fire up corporate sharks who want to sink their teeth into all of these centralized, user-created content silos. They also love all that distributed creativity, all these geeks who leave traces of their ideas on blogs and wikis. The biggest deal about these practices is the fact that massive amounts of knowledge are moved into the unregulated commons, as Yochai Benkler calls it. Here it is free and available to those who have an Internet connection and the necessary media literacy. Here, these files live on a different turf. For the most part, they can be changed or creatively improved upon. Often this content cannot be commodified. However, it remains to be seen if these licenses really stick legally. The property issues of collaborative practices in the commons matter a great deal. They are a more complex affair than the traditional scheme of the individual author "selling out" to the System. We could state, for instance, that Google Incorporated sucks off profit from the thousands of unpaid Wikipedians. Equally, the cadres of free software scripters are arguably turned into cash cows for the young Google czars who cash in through ads, not software (let alone content).

Mass amateurization as promoted by Lawrence Lessig, Joi Ito, and countless other cyber-libertarians is a seductive, empowering ideology that appeals to a broad spectrum. It is a meme that was designed to give a positive spin to a depressing picture. The thousands of volunteer contributors to Wikipedia simply out-collaborated commercial efforts. So what is the problem with "extreme democracy" (as Ratcliffe and Lebkowsky called their anthology) in a time when there is only loss of individual liberties, mass deception, and spin? For this, we need to transcend good intentions and look at the long-term economic implications of the worthy ideology-of-the-free. Sustainable cooperation, of course, aims at mass professionalization. People want to make a living doing the work they love. The question then becomes how can we turn the cynical logic of the liberal communists who repeatedly set the Internet agenda?

The key point of networks is not so much their form of organization but the fact that their business model is now on the agenda. Business for all, that is. The networked organization is setting the terms for entry into economic sustainability. Precursors to the organized network—lists, collaborative blogs, and alternative media—are used to being on the vanguard of inquiry and practice. At the same time, there is an undeniable distrust of the business-for-us mentality of networked organizations. For too long the ghetto of Usenet and list cultures resulted in a self-affirmation that is now a major obstacle to the possibility of scalability. What is required for the organized network to break open and scale up? A transparency of formalization and shift in the division of labor? It is well known that formal networked organizations are the darlings of funding bodies, whereas real existing networks miss out because they fail to undertake the proper lobby work and cannot adequately represent themselves. It is ironic that it is exactly the global nature of networks that makes it next to impossible to fund them. There are no global funds for global networks, despite all the 1990s rhetoric.

Let's turn to perhaps the least investigated aspect of scalability. Why is it so difficult for networks to scale up? There seems to be a tendency to split up in a thousand micro-conversations. This even counts for social networks like Orkut, Friendster, LinkedIn, and MySpace in which millions from all over the globe participate. For the time being, it is only the geeky Slashdot that manages to centralize conversations, assisted by a number of professional (paid) editors among the tens of thousands of its online users. Electronic mailing lists do not seem to get above a few thousand before the conversation actually slows down, heavily moderated as it often is. The ideal size for an in-depth, open discussion still seems to be somewhere between 50 and 500 participants. What does this mean for the networked multitudes? To what extent are these access and software issues? Could the necessary protocols be written up by literally anyone? What protocols would be adopted in such a case? Can we imagine very large-scale conversations that do not only make sense but also have an impact? Which types of network cultures can become large transformative institutions?

Perhaps organized networks will always indulge in their pure potentiality. This option should never be dropped. Even if resilient fluidity and eternal metamorphosis are too good to be true, they simply may never even happen. Networks often stall and collapse into profound resentment. There is no inherent necessity to institutionalize in the brick-and-mortar world. Maybe organized networks cannot work in collaboration with existing institutional structures. If so, how might the virtual be formalized? By this, I do not mean formalization in the old sense, whereby the network takes on a hierarchical structure made up of a director, an elected secretariat, and so forth. Such a model was adopted by the grass-roots movements of the 1960s and 1970s, and is now the primary reason why such entities are unable to deal with the demands and realities of net-worked sociality. Against this mode of formalization, how might infor-mality acquire an organized response to the unpredictability of needs and crisis and the rhythms of global capital?

As unstable as this model may sound, perhaps it is the form best suited to the habitus of networks, as sketched out previously. It is necessary, after all, to identify the characteristics, tendencies, and limits, that is to say, the short history of the network, and develop a plan from there. There is no point assuming that established patterns of communication and prac-tice will somehow evaporate and entirely new projects start afresh. To do so would mean the invention of a new network and that would mean undertaking that time-consuming task of defining practices and protocols through experimentation, trial and error. By all means, let's see new net-works emerge—they will in any case. But the solution is not to abandon the hard labor, accumulated resources, and curious network personas—or brands, if you like—that have already been cultivated.

While it seems that we are forever in some perpetual crisis and phase of transition, now really is the time for the organized network to establish the ground upon which new politics, new economies, and new cultures may emerge within the dynamics of the social-technical system. In this way, the network opens up to an entirely new range of external variables that, in turn, function to transform the internal operation of the network. Such is the work of the constitutive outside—a process of postnegativity in which rupture and antagonism affirm the future life of the network. The tension between internal dynamics and external forces comprises new ground for the political.

Democracy theorists are still slow and far from recognizing this new field of techno-sociality. Where they posit a negation of social antagonisms within ideologies such as the Third Way, and thus identify the disintegra-tion of liberal democratic principles, the emergence of organized networks is constituted, by contrast, precisely in this denial of antagonisms by the culture of liberal democracy. The institutional structures of liberal democ-racy have become disconnected from the field of sociality, and in so doing are unable to address the antagonisms of the political. Antagonisms do not evacuate the scene so much as take flight into new terrains of communi-cation. The organized network is open to the antagonisms that comprise social-technical relations. For this reason, it is urgent that organized net-works confront the demands of scale and sustainability in order to create new institutional horizons where conflicts might find a space for expres-sion and a capacity for invention.

Accompanying such a transformation is the recognition of power structures and the fact that organized networks will always be shut out of them. There are also internal informal power structures—and to recognize them as such is the first step toward transparency. Too often the denial of existing structures prevents a discussion of how new forms of organization could emerge. The prevailing assumption of decentralization shuts down debate and imagination of how things could be done differently. Moreover, it reproduces the absolute and central power of the geeks for whom it is not an issue because they can safely continue their engineering class without having to confront the urgency of translation that accompanies networks seeking to deal with the turmoil of new socialities.

Similarly, the structures that call themselves networks deny how centralized they are. Consider the proliferation of research networks within higher education. There is an amazing amount of confusion over what networks are within these settings, and in many ways, such obfuscation is quite deliberate. It is no wonder that we see this latest attempt at window dressing, for the institution of the university—a networked organization—is beyond repair and is chronically unable to deal with the complexities of an informatized society. There is a bizarre assumption that if governments and funding bodies throw money at projects that demonstrate a correspondence with networks—whatever that means—then, by some peculiar magical process, innovation will spontaneously emerge. And what do you know? The procedure for submitting proposals, developing research partners, justifying budgets, outlining time schedules, undertaking research, and so on is *exactly* the same as the previous year of harvesting. The result: existing elites are rewarded and power is consolidated through the much more accurate model of the cluster (a rather ugly word that finds its birthplace in the schoolyard playground). There is no chance for these so-called networks to encounter infection. Quarantined inquiry is what these research networks are all about. Why? Because there is a complete failure to engage the technics of communications media in the first instance, to say nothing of the dependency model of funding which simply functions to reproduce the same thing, over and over and over.

Leaving institutional blues aside, organized networks have their own problems to confront. Because of the lack of transparency regarding who is in charge of operations and project development they are slowed down considerably. This is in part a question of software architecture; for instance, the fact that we cannot vote every month for the moderator for the month or the owner of the domain name for that matter. Imagine Google rotating or sharing the ownership of www.google.com among its users or even its workers. There is no technical reason why we don't have this. Rather, it points again to the culture of networks—they can change fast in terms of applications but not in terms of ideologies. To illustrate these issues, we turn now to a discussion of blogs, wikis, and Creative Commons.

The blog is another technology of networks, one whose logic is that of the link. The link enhances visibility through a ranking system. This is how the blogger tackles the question of scale. However, the question of scale cannot be reduced here to one of scarcity. The technics of the blog do not add up to what we are calling organized networks. The blogger does not have infinite possibility but is governed by a moment of decision. This does not arise out of scarcity because there is the ability of machines to read other machines. Rather, there are limits that arise out of the attention economy and out of affinity: I share your culture, I don't share you culture; I like you, I don't like you. Here we see a new cartography of power that is peculiar to a symbolic economy of networks.

Quite importantly, the "decisionism" of the link constitutes a new field of the political. This is where schizo-production comes to an end. Deleuzomaniacs would say, "Everything connects with everything." Technically speaking, there is no reason why you cannot include all the links in the world—this is what the Internet Archive does. The blog, however, is unable to do this—not because of a lack of space, though, because space is endlessly extensive through the logic of the link. Nor is this really an issue of resources. Instead, it is an issue that attends the enclave culture of blogs. They are zones of affinity with their own protectionist policies. If you are high up on the blog-scale of desirable association, the political is articulated by the endless requests for linkage. These cannot all be met, however, and resentment if not enemies is born. The enemy is always kept on the outside. It remains invisible. As such, the blog is closed to change. Blogs can thus be understood as incestuous networks of auto-reproduction.

Since organized networks comprise new institutional forms whose relations are immanent to the media of communication, we can say that ultimately the blog does not correspond with the organized network. The outside for organized networks always plays a constitutive role in determining the direction, shape, and actions of the network. This is not the case for the blog, where the enemy is never present and never visible because the network of the blog is the link, and the link is the friend.

Having said this, why is the blog visible in the mainstream media in a way that the organized network is not? Blogging started as a commentary on the mainstream media: television, newspapers, and their Web sites. At a discursive level, the blog was operating internally to mainstream media. In a genealogical sense, the blog was part of the news industry. The main controversy within the news industry has been whether bloggers can be considered as qualified journalists. This is part of a broader problem of categorization of bloggers: they are not poets, writers, or scholars. Nowadays, blogging has become a profession with a professional code of ethics and job description, yet bloggers are still working in conditions we associate with post-Fordist flexible labor. Paradoxically, the blogger is currently expunged and questioned by the networked organization in the same way corporations feel threatened that social network software might unleash cooperation between workers beyond the rigid tasks inside the team.

The deep necessity or precondition of the blogger/social networker is not so much its networking capacity, since it is performing the self. Networking is secondary. But if you had a "notworker" who is self-performing without linking, you would remain invisible. Without the right links and tags, you are nonexistent. Thus, your self-performance is identical to linking. However, there is a difference between networking and linking. There is a strong social network among Web workers, one that is highly intimate and highly disclosing of personal details. In that sense, there is a correspondence between the blog and reality television—the latter, of course, is opposite the logic of networks. So, in terms of remediation, to what extent does this anti-networking character of reality TV carry over to blogs?

This is where the idea of the political needs to be readdressed. As noted with the blog, the political corresponds with the moment of linking, which is technically facilitated by the software, how it works, and the decisions that need to be made. Just as the blog is a self-performance so too is the instantiation of the political. Both are invisible undertakings. The fact that I do *not* link to you remains invisible. The unanswered e-mail is the most significant one. So while the blog has some characteristics of the network, it is not open and it cannot change because it closes itself to the potential for change and intervention. With the blog, you can comment but you cannot post. Your comments might even be taken down. The blog, along with social networks, is finally characterized in terms of the software that refuses antagonism. The early version of Orkut had a software interface that cut straight to the issue: "Are you my friend? Yes/No". Only a very few have the courage to tell someone straight in the face: "No." Seriously, what choice is there except to create an inflation of friends? We all want them. We find ourselves back at the seventeen stages of joy and enter Nirvana. This is New Age revivalism at work, desperately insecure, in search of a "friend."

Wikis offer another example of organized networks with their own specific social-technical characteristics. Here a collective intelligence is created, produced as a resource immanent to the media form. Yet it is important to understand that the wiki model will not work in all cultures and countries. The wiki is a specific collaborative operation. You can have as many ideas as you want, but this does not mean they will translate into a resource. On their own, the technical facilities will not explain the story. Japanese and Chinese cultures, for example, do not like full visibility and rather prefer not to be seen, heard, or read in public. Instead, they create intimate spaces outside of the official public domain. Paradoxically, these private enclosures can be inside Web-based blogs, chatrooms, or social networks as long as they do not have an official image. So why join collaborative projects? Then think of the political histories of the countries. The wiki presumes there is a willingness to work in the public and share knowledge. These are not universal values or aspirations.

The key to networks is the tension between open and closed systems of communication, ideas, and action. For the most part, e-democracy folk are unreconstructed techno-libertarians. The Creative Commons movement is also caught up in this persona, as if it is still 1999. Increasingly, we are seeing advocates of the Creative Commons license claiming they are not political, as if this gesture will somehow enamor them to old-style institutions and publishing industries they are seeking to coax over to the other side. There is a naïve assumption that if Creative Commons can dissociate itself from leftist movements in particular, then they will have greater success in promoting Creative Commons as a dominant alternative to the strictures of IP regimes. There is, however, no escape from politics, and the libertarian ethos of Lessig and his colleagues would do well to be clearer about this.

The rhetoric of openness, shared by the advocates of Creative Commons and libertarians, has purchase on governments who also trade in political populism. Yet it disguises the political motivations and economic interests at work in these projects. The libertarian geek elite have thus far effectively stopped networks from mobilizing their own financial resources. Most famously, there is the inability of networks to work effectively with micropayment systems in the form of, for example, membership fees. The libertarian geek option gives you one choice: give everything of yours away for nothing and we will take the money. Academic databases are an exception, where content (business data, reports, and articles) can be accessed for substantial subscription fees. Libraries have thus far not protested enough and are forced to continue subsidizing money-hungry information services and publishing industries such as ElsevierReed. The open access movement of peer-reviewed scientific and scholarly journal articles is facing similar issues as discussed here of how to scale up and enforce a general policy.[11] The telcos and hardware manufacturers also do okay—it is the researchers, activists, artists, and free-floating intellectuals who get burned.

The provocation of organized networks is to unveil these mechanisms of control and contradiction, to discuss the power of money flows, and to redirect funds. The organized network struggles with its own informality. This is not a case of wanting a piece of the pie—organized networks don't even get a taste. Organized networks want to open source the whole bakery!

They are not examples for the network economy. Even in the case of Creative Commons, which do have a beta model of redistributing finance, this is retrograde because it multiplies the necessity of intermediaries—a function eradicated in post-Fordist economies. You cannot earn money from content; you can only provide services around it. In this 1990s model of an information economy, the thing itself borders on being an untouchable sacred object despite its banality. Organized networks will break with the "information wants to be free" logic and move toward sustainability.

Since organized networks are seemingly in a condition of perpetual exclusion from conventional, institutional modes of financing, then there is really only one option left: to leave the network or, alternatively, to understand the logic of crime. There is not much to obtain from the open source gurus. At least they have not totally captured the attention of so-called Internet culture and research. Instead, they have migrated over to traditional cultural institutions, which now consider open source as the primary model. This will be an interesting experiment to observe because the open source model goes against the border controls of the traditional institution. Whether such institutions are able fully to embrace the logic of open distribution and retain both their brand and funding capacity remains to be seen.

Networks represent themselves and not an external constituency whose interests require distillation within a party-political form. There is always the temptation to present networks as constituencies that are somehow obliged to be capable of articulating the needs and interests of what is, by definition at the social-technical level, a mutable formation. There is no permanency here. People come and go according to what holds a passing affinity and interest for them. This, perhaps above all else, is the primary condition networks must address if they are to undertake the passage to organization. What is commitment and how can it grow from a one-off engagement in a time when politics is event-driven and long-term dedication is a rare commodity?

Given that the organized networks do not yet have a financial basis for their activities, why, then, is accountability an issue here? This, of course, relates back to the question of transparency, governance, and control, and thus the structural dynamics of networks. Making visible the capacities of the network to undergo transformation may reveal as much as accountability reveals limits. What does accountability mean outside the framework of representation? What does representation mean within a postrepresentative political system? These questions go far beyond Internet research and will sooner, rather than later, be on the agenda of democracy theory.

Notes

Introduction

1. Instead of a definition of Web 2.0, for instance the one from Wikipedia, I would like to suggest this Listible entry: http://www.listible.com/list/complete-list-of-web-2-0-products-and-services.
2. Christopher Allen, "Tracing the Evolution of Social Software," October 2004, http://www.lifewithalacrity.com/2004/10/index.html.
3. Jo Twist, "The Year of the Digital Citizen," http://news.bbc.co.uk/go/em/-/2/hi/technology/4566712.stm.
4. Nicholas Carr, "The Amorality of Web 2.0," October 3, 2005, http://www.roughtype.com/archives/2005/10/the_amorality_o.php.
5. Ian Davis, comment on The Ian Davis Blog, http://iandavis.com/blog/2005/07/talis-web-20-and-all-that.
6. See Ethan Zuckerman, "Ten – or Maybe a Dozen – Things That Will Be Free," October 6, 2005, http://www.worldchanging.com/archives/003593.html.
7. Ross McKibben, "The Destruction of the Public Sphere," *London Review of Books*, 28, no. 1 (January 5, 2006). http://www.lrb.co.uk/v28/n01/mcki01_.html.
8. Slavoj Žižek, "Nobody Has to be Vile," *London Review of Books*, 28, no. 7 (April 6, 2006). http://www.lrb.co.uk/v28/n07/print/zize01_.html.
9. Konrad Becker and Felix Stalder, "IP and the City,", http://world-information.org/wio/readme/992003309/1135254214 (accessed October 22, 2005).
10. In the MSN group 5434 of April 2004, Aboe Qataadah explained how to act when taking shooting lessons. In the MSN group tawheedwljihad, Aboe Qataadah answered the question whether he who abuses the prophet should be killed. His answer: "It is an obligation to kill he who abuses the Prophet whether he is Muslim or Kaafir. And Hirsi Ali and Theo van Gogh, these pigs who have abused the prophet their punishment is death and their day will come with Allah's will..!" (from Benschop's report).

11. Hans Magnus Enzensberger, Der radikale Verlierer, *Der Spiegel*, 45/2005.

12. Albert Benschop, "Kroniek van een Aangekondige Politieke Moord, Jihad in Nederland," Forum, Utrecht, the Netherlands, October 2004. http://www.sociosite.org/jihad_nl_en.php (English translation).

13. According to Benschop's report in September 2001, Leefbaar Nederland (Liveable Holland) decided to close its discussion forum because of the many discriminatory contributions. Leefbaar Nederland had insufficient volunteers to steer the derailed discussion in the right direction. After the murder of Pim Fortuyn on May 6, 2002, the tone in many public discussion forums became much more violent and vicious. They were flooded with vitriolic brawls, racist statements, and provocative death threats. Daily newspaper Algemeen Dagblad could not cope with such a massive form of forum vandalism and closed her open forum, in order to open again afterward with a mandatory registration of visitors who wanted to participate in the discussion.

14. See Gerard Goggin, "SMS Riot: Transmitting Race on a Sydney Beach, December 2005," *M/C Journal*, 9, (1) (March 2006), http://journal.mediaculture.org.au/0603/02-goggin.php. See also Angela Mitropoulos, "Under the Beach, the Barbed Wire," Metamute, February 7, 2006. http://www.metamute.org/?q=en/Under-the-Beach-the-Barbed-Wire.

15. Global Voices, May 22, 2006.

16. The text was originally published by the Chaos Computer Club in *Die Datenschleuder* #89, Berlin, 2005, 2–9. The author, Frank Riedel, gave a talk based on this text at the 22nd CCC Conference late December 2005 together with Hacktic and Xs4all founder Rop Grongrijp. http://frank.geekheim.de/?page_id=128. The nettime debate about this text continued from January 7 to January 17, 2006.

17. This is a reference to the famous phrase from the Cluetrain Manifesto: "Markets are getting smarter — and getting smarter faster than most companies. These markets are conversations." http://www.cluetrain.com.

18. Trebor Scholz, "Against Web 2.0," discussion on the IDC mailinglist, May 26, 2006. The following quotes are all from the same thread.

19. See the static archive of the project: www.discordia.us and *My First Recession*, NAi-V2, Rotterdam, 2003, pp. 244–248.

20. Internal Discordia e-mail, October 7, 2004.

21. Whereas I do believe that it is too early to come up with a General Theory of the Internet, I do think it is possible, and necessary, to formulate larger statements about the workings of certain applications such as blogs, wikis, social bookmarking, and tagging. Bifo, in response to a lecture I gave in Milan on March 16, 2006: "The theoretical Lovink's contribution (radical pragmatism and Net criticism) can be viewed as a critique of the cynicism of the European (vanishing) intellectual life. Geert says that it's not yet the moment for a general Theory of the Net. Well, it will never be the moment for a general Theory of the Net. The Net is the end of any possible General Theory because it is ever expanding, and the most essential thing (in the Net) is the last one, the just emerging one, the not-yet happened, the happening just now." (nettime, March 22, 2006.)

22. This estimate comes from Blogherald.com (October 10, 2005). There is no Web site yet that has taken up the challenge to do a blog count on a global level. One problem is the blogs that are no longer in use. Blogs are so "haut-nahe," so close to life that you can praise yourself lucky to read them as most of them disappear overnight. Internet providers that offer blog services or the makers themselves have taken down the disappeared diaries. Some blog services take down blogs after three months of inactivity. A test done in the Netherlands in 2005 showed that the infamous archive.org did not store the vanished blogs of www.web-log.nl, which, at that point, claimed to host over 100,000 blogs.

23. Saul Hansell, "Convergence, As Gadgets Get It Together, Media Makers Fall Behind," *The New York Times*, January 25, 2006.

24. A worrisome trend is the demand of some film festivals to have artists pay in order to get their work screened. Eva Drangsholt, in a letter to the River's Edge Film Festival: "I am very disappointed that you have presented me with a screening fee-bill at the same time as you are informing me that a film of mine has been accepted for screening at the River's Edge Film Festival. Your initial call for submissions did not mention any entry fees. In luring me into sending my films to you under the pretense that you do not charge money for films that are submitted, you have made me spend money on postage, the bubble envelope, and the DVD." Posted to Spectre, January 6, 2006.

25. For more info, take this tour: http://www.google.com/services/adsense_tour/.

26. Nicholas Carr, "A Year in the 'Sphere," April 15, 2006, http://www.roughtype.com/archives/2006/04/a_year_in_the_s.php.

27. http://chitika.com/mm_overview.php?refid=livingroom

28. http://slashdot.org/article.pl?sid=06/05/16/2013205&from=rss

29. Seth Goldstein, "Media Futures: From Theory to Practice," posted November 17, 2005, http://majestic.typepad.com/seth/2005/11/media_futures_t.html.

30. Nicholas Carr, "Hypermediation 2.0," November 25, 2005, http://www.roughtype.com/archives/2005/11/hypermediation.php.

31. Chris Anderson, "VC Advice on Finding Money in the Long Tail," posted December 15, 2005, http://www.thelongtail.com/the_long_tail/2005/12/vc_advice_on_fi.html.

32. http://el-oso.net/blog/archives/2006/07/14/amateurism-individualism-and-collectivism/.

33. Charles Arthur, "What is the 1% rule?" *The Guardian*, July 20, 2006. "Each day there are 100 million downloads and 65,000 uploads—which as Antony Mayfield (at http://open.typepad.com/open) points out, is 1538 downloads per upload—and 20 million unique users per month. Wikipedia: 50% of all Wikipedia article edits are done by 0.7% of users, and more than 70% of all articles have been written by just 1.8% of all users. That puts the 'creator to consumer' ratio at just 0.5%." Nick Carr mentions the example of social bookmarking site Digg: "Data reveal that of Digg's 445,000 registered users, only 2,287 contributed any stories to the site during the last six weeks. But here are the real eye-openers: The top 100 users contributed fully 55% of the stories that appeared on the site's front page, and the top 10 users contributed a whopping 30% of the front page stories." (Roughtype.com, August 2, 2006)

34. Chris Gaither and Dawn C. Chmielewski, "Is the Bubble about to Burst Again?" *Los Angeles Times*, July 16, 2006.
35. "Credit card payments rule the Internet today. An obvious question, then, is why try to invent something new. The short answer is credit cards are unprofitable for the *seller* at purchases below $5.00" (Steve Crocker, "The Siren Song of Internet Micropayments," http://www.merchantseek.com/article9.htm).
36. Allan de Botton's notions on status anxiety have thus far not yet been transferred to conceptual levels and institutional power politics. "There are few more powerful desires than to be treated with respect. We long for status and dread humiliation. But such an aspiration is rarely spoken about, or at least not without sarcasm, embarrassment or condemnation." The "we" could very well be new media or Internet culture (quote from http://www.channel4.com/life/microsites/S/status_anxiety/alain.html). For instance, translate this warning: "From failure will flow humiliation: a corroding awareness that we have been unable to convince the world of our value and are henceforth condemned to consider the successful with bitterness and ourselves with shame."

Chapter 1

1. Research by the Pew Internet Project, published in July 2006, gives empirical evidence for my central thesis that too much attention has been focused on a small number of U.S. high-traffic, A-list bloggers. "A national phone survey of bloggers finds that most are focused on describing their personal experiences to a relatively small audience of readers and that only a small proportion focus their coverage on politics, media, government, or technology. Blogs, the survey finds, are as individual as the people who keep them. However, most bloggers are primarily interested in creative, personal expression—documenting individual experiences, sharing practical knowledge, or just keeping in touch with friends and family." http://www.pewinternet.org/PPF/r/186/report_display.asp.
2. How such communities are created by founders of sites such as Craig's list, Flickr, and MySpace is described by Danah Boyd in a talk she gave at O'Reilly Emerging Technology Conference, March 6, 2006, "G/localization: When Global Information and Local Interaction Collide," http://www.danah.org/papers/Etech2006.html.
3. Variation of "I work here, but I am cool," the marketing phrase of Alan Liu's *The Laws of Cool* (Chicago, IL: University of Chicago Press), 2004.
4. http://blogs.washingtonpost.com/earlywarning/2006/01/good_news_the_a.html.
5. Information taken from Michael Massing, "The End of the News?", *The New York Review of Books*, 52, no. 19, December 1, 2005. http://www.nybooks.com/articles/18516.
6. Clay Shirky, "Power Laws, Weblogs, and Inequalities," http://www.shirky.com/writings/powerlaw_weblog.html. Chris Anderson, http://longtail.typepad.com/the_long_tail/.
7. Taken from Wikipedia's blog definition, http://en.wikipedia.org/wiki/Blog (accessed December 21, 2005).

8. David Kline and Dan Burstein, *Blog!: How the Newest Media Revolution Is Changing Politics, Business, and Culture* (New York: CDS Books, 2005), 130.

9. "Ten Tips for Writing a Blog Post," posted at problogger.net, December 30, 2005, http://www.problogger.net/archives/2005/12/30/tens-tips-for-writing-a-blog-post/

10. See Rebecca Blood's history of blogs, written September 7, 2000: http://www.rebeccablood.net /essays/weblog_history.html.

11. Jean Baudrillard, *The Intelligence of Evil or the Lucidity Pact* (Oxford/New York: Berg Publishers, 2005), 25.

12. For regular updates on this figure, go to www.blogherald.com. All researchers involved in blogcounting admit how arbitrary and unreliable the available statistics are as closed and abandoned blogs are not taken into account.

13. Adilkno, Media Archive, Brooklyn, Autonomedia, 1998, http://thing.desk.nl/bilwet/adilkno/TheMediaArchive/04.txt. "Vague media do not respond to success. They do not achieve their goals. Their models are not argumentative, but contaminative. Once you tune in to them, you get the attitude."

14. Axel Bruns, *Gatewatching*, Collaborative Online News Production (New York: Peter Lang, 2005), 23.

15. Thomas Mallon, *A Book of One's Own, People and Their Diaries* (New York: Ticknor & Fields, 1984), xiii.

16. Ibid., p. xvii.

17. Ibid., p. 31 and p. 34.

18. http://www.zephoria.org/thoughts/archives/2006/05/20/erosion_of_yout.html.

19. Ed Phillips from San Francisco reports that "unit testing is now de rigueur in the software world and just as it would be hard to imagine a major software effort without unit testing, it is now hard to imagine big media without the blogosphere." e-mail, March 27, 2006.

20. Geert Lovink, Interview with Cecile Landman, January 17, 2006, http://www.networkcultures.org/weblog/archives/2006/01/support_iraqi_b.html.

21. See his Master's thesis (in Dutch): http://www.networkcultures.org/weblog/archives/2005/08/bloggen_is_zo_2.html. Sjoerd van der Helm's personal blog: http://www.sjoerdvanderhelm.nl/weblog/index.php.

22. Peter Johnson, "Increasingly the News 'Scoop' is Found Online," *USA Today*, March 19, 2006, http://www.usatoday.com/life/columnist/mediamix/2006-03-19-media-mix_x.htm.

23. See the report of University of Amsterdam researcher Albert Benschop, "Chronicle of a Political Murder Foretold, Jihad in the Netherlands," November 2005, http://www.sociosite.org/jihad_nl_en.php.

24. http://www.sourcewatch.org/index.php?title=Viral_marketing.

25. Bobbie Johnson, "Cleaner Caught Playing Dirty on the Net," *The Guardian*, October 6, 2005. Constantin Basurea has compiled a list of blogs that focus on public relations (http://www.sourcewatch.org/index.php?title=Public_relations). See also www.spinwatch.org.

26. O'Dwyer's PR Daily, September 21, 2005.

27. http://www.prwatch.org/taxonomy/term/6?from=80

28. Adapted from the article of Jim George, "Leo Strauss, Neo-Conservatism, U.S. Foreign Policy: Esoteric Nihilism and the Bush Doctrine," in *International Politics*, 2005, 24, pp. 174–202.
29. Joe Trippi, *The Revolution Will Not Be Televised*, ReganBooks, New York, 2004, p. xviii.
30. Nick Gall: "A lot of the media are thinking about blogs as a new form of publishing but it's really a new form of conversation and a new form of community" in David Kline and Dan Burstein, *Blog!: How the Newest Media Revolution is Changing Politics, Business, and Culture* (New York: CDC Books, 2005), 150.
31. "'Journalism,' James W. Carey tells us, 'takes its name from the French word for day. It is our day book, our collective diary, which records our common life.' To record the events of the day is equally the aim of the newsroom and the diary writer." Jay Rosen, "The Weblog: An Extremely Democratic Form in Journalism," March 8, 2004, http://journalism.nyu.edu/pubzone/weblogs/pressthink/2004/03/08/weblog_demos.html.
32. Wolf-Dieter Roth, "Mein blog liest ja sowieso kein Schwein." December 27, 2005, http://www.heise.de/tp/r4/artikel/21/21643/1.html.
33. Glenn Reynolds, *An Army of Davids, How Markets and Technology Empower Ordinary People to Beat Big Media, Big Government, and Other Goliaths* (Nashville, TN: Nelson Current, 2006).
34. Ibid.93.
35. Greg Sherwin and Emily Avila, January 12, 2001, http://www.clickz.com/experts/archives/ebiz/ecom_comm/article.php/835141.
36. A random rant, found on the Internet, that deals with the cynical nature of society, in this case in the United States: "Lies have transformed a once good people into the most frightened, insecure and bewildered unrugged individualists on the planet. Sure, they think they 'have it all' — all the stupid shit that they can't afford — but they sleep through their lives — and they do so cynically. Oscar Wilde said that a cynic knows the price of everything and the value of nothing. That's why Las Vegas is as popular as it is." http://www.americanidealism.com/articles/some-guesses-about-american-mass-psychology.html
37. Dictionary for the Study of the Works of Michel Foucault, http://users.california.com/~rathbone/foucau10.htm
38. http://www.cynical-c.com/
39. Found in Quote-o-Rama, http://www.otd.com/~paul/Quote/sa.html.
40. http://www.poconorecord.com/2001/local/exd81858.htm
41. Interview with Jean Baudrillard by Deborah Solomon, *The New York Times Magazine*, November 20, 2005.
42. Michèle Roberts , quoted by Maya Jaggi in *The Guardian*, November 5, 2005, http://books.guardian.co.uk/departments/generalfiction/story/0,,1627808,00.html.
43. Paulo Virno, *A Grammar of the Multitude* (Los Angeles, CA: Semiotext(e), 2004), 86–88.
44. As Terry Eagleton writes: "Hermeneutics, as the art of deciphering language, taught us to be suspicious of the glaringly self-evident." (Terry Eagleton, *After Theory*, New York: Basic Books, 2003), 53. This is precisely what bloggers do.

45. Peter Sloterdijk, *Critique of the Cynical Reason* (Minneapolis, MN: University of Minnesota Press, 1987), 5.

46. See Stefan Lorenz Sorgner, "In Search of Lost Cheekiness, An Introduction to Peter Sloterdijk's 'Critique of Cynical Reason'", http://www.petersloter-dijk.net/international/texts/en_texts/en_texts_lost_cheekiness.html.

47. http://www.petersloterdijk.net/international/texts/en_texts/en_texts_lost_cheekiness.html.

48. http://www.livejournal.com/users/imomus/121980.html, described to a U.K. friend as a "semi-legendary post-new–wave ironic-ish experimental pop music guy with intellectualoid bits and bobs thrown into the mix."

49. David Weinberger, "The Virtue of Engineering Cynicism," *Darwin*, September 25, 2002. http://www.darwinmag.com/read/swiftkick/column.html?ArticleID=531.

50. Cornel West, *Race Matters* (Boston, MA: Beacon Press, 1993), 14.

51. David Kline and Dan Burstein, *Blog!: How the Newest Media Revolution is Changing Politics, Business, and Culture* (New York: CDS Books, 2005), xix.

52. Justin Clemens, *The Romanticism of Contemporary Theory: Institution, Aesthetics, Nihilism* (Hants, England: Ashgate, 2003), 93.

53. Branden W. Joseph, "Interview with Paolo Virno," *Grey Room*, no. 21 (Fall 2005), 26–37. Also available at http://mitpress.mit.edu/catalog/item/default.asp?ttype=4&tid=2 (posted March 13, 2006).

54. Clemens, 88.

55. Karen Carr, *The Banalization of Nihilism* (Ithaca, NY: State University of New York Press, 1992).

56. Interview with Andre Gluckmann, in *Frankfurter Rundschau*, November 11, 2005, http://www.fr-aktuell.de/ressorts/kultur_und_medien/feuilleton/?cnt=754264.

57. See Renato Poggioli, *The Theory of the Avant-Garde* (Cambridge, MA: Harvard University Press, 1968), 61.

58. Florian Cramer, "Notizen zu Blogs," *Rohrpost*, October 13, 2005.

59. Reynolds, 99.

60. Kline and Burstein, 144.

61. Clemens, 77.

62. Ibid., 89.

63. Carr, 3.

64. Ibid., 7.

65. Kline and Burstein, p. xxv.

66. A typical blog as agenda setting theory would be Aaron Delwiche, "Agenda-Setting, Opinion Leadership, and the World of Web Logs," *First Monday*, vol. 10, no. 12, December 2005, http://www.firstmonday.org/issues/issue10_12/delwiche/index.html. See also the work of Kaye Trammell (http://kaye.trammell.com/).

67. Kline and Burstein, 249.

68. Ibid., 21.

69. Ibid., 131.

70. Trippi, xv.

71. Ibid.,xix.

72. http://www.edge.org/3rd_culture/foreman05/foreman05_index.html.

73. Kline and Burstein, 159.

74. Masserat Amir Ebrahimi, "Emergence of the Iranian Cyberspace and the Production of the Self in Weblogestan," Pages #4, Rotterdam, July 2005, 119–125.

75. Annabelle Sreberny, "From Mouth to Mouth: Problems of Truth in an Information Society," Pages #4, July 2005, Rotterdam, 129.

76. Personal e-mail correspondence, January 12, 2006.

77. Kline and Burstein, 249.

78. See Terje Rasmussen's paper, "Media of the Self," http://www.media.uio.no/personer/terjer/.

79. See Dominic Pettman, *After the Orgy, Toward a Politics of Exhaustion* (Albany, NY: State University of New York Press, 2002).

80. Carl Trueman, "The Theatre of the Absurd," Reformation 21, 6, January 2006, http://www.reformation21.org/

81. Caire E. Write, "The Author's Dilemma: To Blog or Not to Blog," The Internet Writing Journal, November 2005, http://www.internetwritingjournal.com/nov05/cew4.htm.

82. Summary of David Weinberger's lecture "The Shape of Knowledge," Helsinki School of Economics, December 1, 2005.

83. Peter and Trudy Johnson-Lenz, "Groupware: Coining and Defining It," 1994, http://www.awakentech.com/.

84. http://many.corante.com/archives/authors/danah.php.

85. http://www.shirky.com/writings/group_politics.html.

86. See www.fuckedcompany.com.

87. Cornel West, *Democracy Matters* (New York: The Penguin Press, 2004), 3.

88. The chapter mirrors a chapter with the same name, "Nihilism in Black America" in Cornel West's **Race Matters** (Boston: Beacon Press, 1993), 11–20.

89. West, 39.

90. Ibid., 176

91. Ibid., 29.

92. Ibid., 216.

93. Chris Garrett, "Maximise Your Income with Common Sense," January 12, 2006, http://performancing.com/node/830.

94. See Jacques Derrida, *The Post Card* (Chicago, IL: University of Chicago Press, 1987); Bernhard Siegert, Relays, Literature as an Epoch of the Postal System, Stanford University Press, Palo Alto, CA, 1999.

95. Alex Halavias, "Blogs and Archiving," September 16, 2004, http://alex.halavais.net/?p=825.

96. Of course, there are blogs dedicated to MMORPGs (such as embedded journalist Wagner James Au, whose New World Notes blog reports about the Second Life game, http://secondlife.blogs.com/), but that's not the point. A MMORPG that feeds off the daily buzz in the blogosphere would perhaps be a start.

97. Phil Windley blogging Matthew Berk's presentation at the June 10, 2003 Jupitermedia ClickZ Weblog Business Strategies Conference, http://www.windley.com/archives/2003/06/10.shtml.

98. http://www.roughtype.com/archives/2005/10/the_amorality_o.php.

99. Nicholas Carr, "The New Narcissism," February 17, 2006, http://www.roughtype.com/archives/2006/02/the_new_narciss.php.

100. AlwaysOn Summit, July 20, 2005. http://www.alwayson-network.com/comments.php?id=12328_0_1_0_C.
101. Friedrich Kittler, "What's New about the New Media?" in Mutations, Rem Koolhaas et al., Actar, Barcelona, 2000, 64–65.
102. http://www.zephoria.org/thoughts/archives/2004/02/23/echochambers_and_homophily.html. All links to Weblogs that were relevant in the debate, compiled by Danah Boyd: http://www.zephoria.org/cgi-bin/mt/mt-tb.cgi?_mode=view&entry_id=4041.
103. http://weblog.burningbird.net/archives/2004/02/11/community-member-or-writer.
104. Glenn Reynolds emphasizes that bloggers "tend to link to original sources wherever possible. The result, as Lileks says, is that you can follow the link and make up your mind for yourself. The best links, usually, are to things the reader would never have found otherwise." Reynolds, 118.
105. Hugh Hewitt, *Blog: Understanding the Information Revolution That's Changing Your World* (Nashville, TN: Thomas Nelson Books, 2005), 1.
106. From http://www.urbandictionary.com/define.php?term=snarky.
107. http://snarkiness.typepad.com/.
108. http://pitsch.wordpress.com/.
109. http://scobleizer.wordpress.com/2006/03/05/the-john-dvorakification-of-the-blogosphere-im-signing-off-of-memeorandum/.
110. Erich Fromm, *The Fear of Freedom* (London: Routledge, 1942), x.
111. Ibid.,207.
112. Geoff Parker's bio (Toowoonba, QLD/AUS) is an absolute read for those into contemporary nihilism. http://home.iprimus.com.au/laurapalmer/aboutme.htm.
113. Trevor Butterworth, "Blogged Off," *The Financial Times Weekend*, February 18–19, 2006.
114. http://scripting.wordpress.com/2006/03/19/scripting-news-for-3192006/.
115. See Clive Thompson, "Blogs to Riches, The Haves and Have-Nots of the Blogging Boom," *New York Magazine*, February 13, 2006.
116. Butterworth.

Chapter 2

1. Peter Sloterdijk, *Im Weltinnenraum des Kapitals*, Suhrkamp Verlag, Frankfurt, 2005, p. 18.
2. Armin Medosch, "Good Bye Reality! How Media Art Died But Nobody Noticed," February 7, 2006, Mazine, http://www.mazine.ws/node/230.
3. I would like to thank Richard de Boer, Anna Munster, Scott McQuire, Nikos Papastergiadis, Henry Warrick, Linda Wallace, and Warren Neidich for their critical comments and editorial work.
4. Armin Medosh, in his review of the ISEA 2004 floating conference on the Baltic Sea, asks: "What is this media arts scene about then? Escapism? Are we going anywhere, or are we just drifting? Is there anyone still at the helm of this ship? The well-known accusations about the self-reflexive nature of media arts discourse, of media art living in its own ghetto, in a comfortable sort of bubble, are not going away. The suspicion grows, watching the circus

travel from station to station, from Transmediale to Futuresonica to ISEA, that the notion of 'new' in new media allows us to continue in some state of historical amnesia, hopping from one theme to the next. What comes after the wireless-generative-locative hyperventilation? It appears to me that the real developments are dictated by successive commercial and technical 'revolutions' and media art just surfs on those waves." http://www.metamute. org/?q=en/The-Wireless-Loveboat-ISEA-2004.

5. Renato Poggioli, *The Theory of the Avant-Garde* (Cambridge, MA: Harvard University Press, 1968), 3.

6. An early fragment of this chapter appeared online: http://www.media-culture.org.au/0308/10-fragments.html. In 2004/2005 I wrote a first draft that appeared in *Empire, Ruines and Networks*, edited by Scott McQuire and Nikos Papastergiades (Melbourne University Press, 2005). I also used a text on the same topic, focusing on the Australian Fibreculture debate, published in the Basque art magazine Transition (no. 57, 2005) called "New Media, Technology and the Arts, Unhappy Marriage or Perfect Synthesis." Thanks to Ned Rossiter, Trebor Scholz, Andres Raminez Gaviria, Henry Warwick, Anna Munster, and Scott McQuire for critical comments.

7. For an extensive debate on the merits of the new media term, see Lev Manovich, *The Language of New Media* (Cambridge, MA: MIT Press, 2001), 27–61.

8. See www.mediaarthistory.org. Books of individual authors include, among others, Dieter Daniels, *Kunst als Sendung. Von der Telegrafie zum Interne,* (München: Beck Verlag, 2002); Charles Gere, *Digital Culture* (London: Reaktion Books, 2002); Oliver Grau, *From Illusion to Emersion* (Cambridge, MA: MIT Press, 2003); Siegfried Zielinski, *Audiovisions: Cinema and Television as Entr'actes in History* (Amsterdam: Amsterdam University Press, 1999).

9. http://www.banffcentre.ca/bnmi/events/refresh/.

10. http://www.cultureandrecreation.gov.au/articles/newmedia/.

11. Boris Groys, *Topologie der Kunst* (Munich: Hanser Verlag, 2003), 59. "Je mehr die neue Medienkunst, also die Kunst, die mit bewegten Bildern operiert, Eingang in die Museen findet. Desto mehr verbreitet sich das Gefühl, daß die Institution Museum dadurch in eine Krise gerät."

12. Charlie Finch (Artnet) about Chris Kraus' book on the Los Angeles art scene, *Video Green* (Cambridge, MA: Semiotexte, 2004).

13. Wikipedia: "Intermedia was a concept employed in the mid-sixties by Fluxus artist Dick Higgins to describe the ineffable, often confusing, interdisciplinary activities that occur between genres that became prevalent in the 1960s. Thus, the areas such as those between drawing and poetry, or between painting and theater could be described as intermedia. With repeated occurrences, these new genres between genres could develop their own names (e.g. visual poetry or performance art).

14. Additional comment made by Jon Ippolito, email correspondence, July 21, 2006.

15. Jon Ippolito: "Plenty of contemporary paintings and installations include obscure philosophical or historical references. The difference is that the curators know more about these allusions than the vast majority of their gallery visitors, whereas references to new media are often better understood by a museum's audience than its resident experts. For example, art-

history trained curators at the Guggenheim were at a loss to understand the context for a Cory Arcangel game mod, while the guards were like, 'Hey, a light gun! I remember these....'"

16. Hans Ulrich Reck, *Mythos Medienkunst* (Köln: Verlag der Buchhandlung Walther König, 2002), quoted from the translated manuscript, May 2005.

17. Kanarinka, "Interactive City: Irrelevant Mobile Entertainment," *iDC*, August 13, 2006.

18. Anna Munster, "Re: Interactive City: irrelevant mobile entertainment?," *iDC*, August 21, 2006.

19. Paul Brown, Danny Butt, Anna Munster, and Melinda Rackham all responded in the New Media Arts Board Axed thread, Fibreculture, December 10, 2004.

20. Lucy Cameron, Fibreculture, December 12, 2004.

21. Simon Biggs, "Letter to Jennifer Bott," Fibreculture-announce, January 23, 2005.

22. See Rick Poynor's http://www.undesign.org/tiborocity/.

23. Andreas Broeckmann, Spectre, August 16, 2005. The Spectre list archive can be found here: http://coredump.buug.de/pipermail/spectre/. Other contributors to the debate were Shulea Chang, Yukiko Shikata, John Hopkins, and Eric Kluitenberg.

24. Tom Holley, Spectre, August 18, 2005.

25. Andreas Broeckmann, Spectre, August 26, 2005.

26. For instance, Eric Kluitenberg, "Media Without an Audience," *nettime*, October 19, 2000. See also http://subsol.c3.hu/subsol_2/contributors0/kluitenbergtext.html.

27. Georgina Born, *Rationalizing Culture, IRCAM, Boulez and the Institutionalization of the Musical Avant-Garde* (Berkeley: University of California Press, 1995), 4. Thanks to Timothey Druckrey for the reference.

28. Ibid., 314.

29. Anna Munster, Spectre list, February 18, 2006.

30. Paul Brown, Spectre list, March 14, 2006.

31. Anna Munster, Spectre list, March 15, 2006.

32. Chris Crawford, *Interactive Storytelling*, New Riders Press, Berkeley, CA, 2004, p. 73. Thanks to Richard de Boer for this quote.

33. Ibid., 75.

34. Poggioli, 138.

35. See C.P. Snow, *The Two Cultures* (Cambridge: Canto Books, 1993 [1959]).

36. See John Brockmann, *The Third Culture* (New York: Simon & Schuster, 1995) and his website http://www.edge.org/.

37. See www.creativecommons.org and www.lessig.com/blog.

38. In a private correspondence, Melbourne art theorist Charles Green points at the "power of the boom, that is continuing in contemporary art, especially the US and Europe and now China. Art follows money. Both are more connected with mainstream media than with new media. There's lots of money, and art adapts. The sheer scale of the market in contemporary art simply is beyond belief, though no doubt there will be a crash some point coming, the size of the sector still means the survivors will be numerous and big." (April 27, 2006)

39. See www.caedefencefund.org.

40. Jean Baudrillard, *The Conspiracy of Art* (Cambridge, MA: Semiotexte, 2005), 55.

41. Sylvère Lotringer and Paul Virilio, *The Accident of Art* (Cambridge, MA: MIT Press, 2005), 70.

42. See www.kether.com.

43. Ellen Dissanayake, "The Core of Art: Making Special," in *Homo Aestheticus: Where Art Comes From and Why* (New York: The Free Press, 1995).

44. Eric Kluitenberg, Spectre, August 27, 2005.

45. Timothey Druckrey, Spectre, September 15, 2005.

46. Judith Rodenbeck, iDC mailinglist, October 5, 2005.

47. Interpretation from Giacco Schiesser's essay "Arbeit am und mit Eigensinn." http://www.xcult.org/texte/schiesser/eigensinn_d.pdf. An English translation was published on the Piet Zwart Institute Web site: http://pzwart.wdka.hro.nl/mdr/pubsfolder/Eigensinn/view.

48. http://pzwart.wdka.hro.nl/mdr/pubsfolder/Eigensinn/

49. This and the following quote taken from Charles Green, "The Visual Arts: an Aesthetic of Labyrinthine Form," in *Innovation in Australian Arts, Media and Design: Fresh Challenges for the Tertiary Sector*, R. Wissler, ed. (Sydney, Australia: Flaxton Press, 2004).

50. See www.artbrain.org. Neidich about his work: "Neuroaesthetics as a methodology, which is now about neurobiopolitics and post phenomenology, imports neoroscience into aesthetics and uses it as a ready made." Quotes from e-mail exchange with the artist, May 20, 2006.

51. Quoted in Michael Naimark, "Truth, Beauty, Freedom and Money-Technology-Based Art and the Dynamics of Sustainable." Downloadable at www.artslab.net.

52. Peter Lunenfeld, ed., *The Digital Dialecti* (Cambridge, MA: MIT Press, 1999), 7; quoted by Frieder Nake, "Und wann nun endlich 'Kunst'-oder doch lieber nicht," in Claus Pias (Hrg.), *Zukünfte des Comptuters* (Zürich and Berlin: Diaphanes, 2005), 51.

53. Poggioli, 37.

54. Jon Ippolito: "VR's original promise—to construct a ghostly realm where consciousness could roam free of the constraints of flesh—became *socially* obsolete. The archetypal user of 1990s-era virtual reality was a white 'data cowboy' with no social life; the archetypal user of 2000s-era augmented reality is a Japanese teenage girl with too much social life. Gawky VR helmets have given way to burnished Palms and scarlet Nokia phones—and people use these stylish wireless devices not to escape bodies but to find them."

55. Fred Camper, "End of Avant-Garde Film," *Millennium Film Journal*, no. 16/17/18, (Fall/Winter 1986–1987), 100–101. The parallels between Camper's description and the crisis of new media are significant. Camper complains about academicism. He rejects teaching "avant-garde" or "experimental" film making. Increased opportunities through teaching jobs, grants, and lecture tours "have not been accompanied by a greater social impact for the work." By the 1980s, public audience had fallen drastically. Works of the newer generation "lack the authentic power of the original," which, in my

view, is not the case in new media arts. The problem is not the fall of a movement but the voluntary closure that arguably prevents new media arts from becoming a movement.

Chapter 3

1. The two books are Alice Lagaay and David Lauer (Hg.), *Medientheorien, Eine philosophische Einführung* (Frankfurt am Main: Campus Verlag, 2004) and Stefan Weber (Hrsg.), *Von der Kulturkritik bis zum Konstruktivismus* (Konstanz: UVK, 2003). Stephen Weber discusses four distinguished discourses that rarely interact: postmodern media theories, system theory and radical constructivism, historical and ethnological research, and the philosophical–linguistic focus on the medial turn.
2. Pit Schulz, Rohrpost, October 15, 2004.
3. According to Wikipedia, "anti-German" is a generic term applied to a variety of theoretical and political tendencies within the German radical left. Rooted in the militant anti-fascist milieu, the anti-Germans emerged as a response to the rise in racist pogroms and nationalism in the wake of the German reunification. A position commonly associated with the anti-Germans is that of solidarity with the state of Israel.
4. See Adilkno's review of Klaus Theweleit's first and second *Book of Kings* in *The Media Archive* (Brooklyn, NY: Autonomedia, 1998), 129–140. http://thing.desk.nl/bilwet/adilkno/TheMediaArchive/34.txt.
5. From http://www.petersloterdijk.net/.
6. Another reference is the Old Boys Network initiative (www.obn.org). Some of the ideas were presented at the 2001 Future Bodies conference in Cologne. http://gender.khm.de/futurebodies/.
7. See my interview with Norbert Bolz in *Uncanny Networks* (Cambridge, MA: MIT Press, 2002), 18–27.
8. Florian Cramer's explanation of why German media studies have not embraced Anglo-American cultural studies has to do with the Marxist legacy of cultural studies, and the fact that it took off in the early 1990s when Germany experienced the fall of the Berlin Wall, a period during which academics cut off their last remaining ties to Marxist thinking. "For most German academics, cultural studies were a relapse into the 1970s. This explains what might appear as the politically conservative tendency of German humanities. The German concept of 'Kulturwissenschaft' is mostly unrelated to cultural studies, but draws from Aby Warburg's homonymous concept from the 1920s, and refers to transdisciplinary humanities research instead of a politicized concept of 'culture'. In this context, one should mention Ernst Cassirer as an important media philosopher avant-la-lettre, teacher of among others Warburg and Panofsky. Lev Manovich's concept of 'database as symbolic forms' draws from Panofsky (without knowing that Panofsky took the concept of 'symbol forms' from Cassirer's Philosophy of Symbolic Forms)." (From a private e-mail correspondence, July 26, 2006.)

9. I used this material for a short essay on German media philosophy, which was published in *Lettre,* 63, Spring, 2004. Available online, written in German: http://laudanum.net/geert/files/1077786752/.
10. Stefan Münker u.a. (Hrg.), *Medienphilosophie. Beiträge zur Klärung eines Begriffs* (Frankfurt am Main: Fischer Taschenbuch Verlag, 2003), 53.
11. Ibid., 172.
12. Interview with Frank Hartmann, posted on nettime, June 16, 2000. http://amsterdam.nettime.org/Lists-Archives/nettime-l-0006/msg00093.html. The interview was published in my collection of interviews *Uncanny Networks* (Cambridge, MA: MIT Press, 2002), 294.
13. Iconic turn is a concept that was mentioned first by Gottfried Boehm in 1994, pointing to the cultural transformation away from printed matter to visual culture. Other authors associated with the mostly German *Bildwissenschaften* are Horst Bredekamp, Vilem Flusser, and W.J.T. Mitchell, whose pictorial turn from 1992 is an influential text. See also http://www.iconic-turn.de/.

Chapter 4

1. Bob the Builder game, Design a House with Mr. Bentley: http://www.bob-thebuilder.com/uk/bentley.html.
2. The other writers and speakers at this mini-conference were NAI director Aaron Betsky, landscape architect Wouter Reh, art historian Jeroen Boomgaard, the writer Dirk van Weelden, Flemish photography theoretician Steven Jacobs, and artist Hans van Houwelingen. A shorter version of this chapter was originally written in Dutch and translated by Bart Plantinga. Thanks to Bastiaan Gribling, Steffen Lehmann, Rob Annable, Wim Nijenhuis, Lars Spuybroek, Marisa Yiu, and Jennifer W. Leung for critical comments and responses.
3. Rob Annable pointed out a similar plan in the U.K. for the north of England in which Liverpool and Manchester would be one urban sprawl, spreading to Hull on the Eastern coast. See Will Alsop's Supercity: http://news.bbc.co.uk/1/hi/england/4187409.stm.
4. Blogs may turn out to be a fad, taken over by the next wave of Web applications, but that is not the point here. I use blogs as an example to point out the massive uptake in Internet use.
5. It is interesting, as Rob Annable suggests, to counterbalance this thesis with the case of Second Life (www.secondlife.com) where we see a conscious reintroduction of scarcity. Within large and crowded virtual environments, game developers are creating a dynamic in which real life economics, such as real estate prices, are being duplicated.
6. Random examples of this would be the (Japanese) Toyota houses based on the "Skeleton & Infill" approach. http://www.toyota.co.jp/en/more_than_cars/housing/index.html.
7. See, among others, Saskia Sassen, *The Global City* (Princeton, NJ: New York, London, Tokyo: Princeton University Press, 1990).
8. See the research of telecommunications work by the Amsterdamse Internet sociologist Albert Benschop, http://www2.fmg.uva.nl/sociosite/telewerk/.

9. http://www.haycock.fsbusiness.co.uk/diss4.htm.
10. I am consciously mixing up the two different meanings of "virtual" here, not because I am ill-informed, but because I strongly believe that 1990s cyberculture can only be properly understood if we blend the Deleuzian meaning (which emphasizes the potential) with the one coming from computer science that usually refers to 3D environments.
11. A nice example of the old-fashioned top–down view of the Internet by architects can be found at the German site http://www.internet-fuer-architekten.de/. The site covers subjects such as "marketing with the help of digital media" and the question "Web site or brochure?"
12. Stefan Iglhaut, Florian Roetzer, and Armin Medosch (Hrg.) *Stadt am Netz: Ansichten von Telepolis* (Mannheim: Bollmann Verlag, 1996).
13. Jennifer W. Leung, private e-mail correspondence, August 10, 2006.
14. Scott McQuire, private e-mail correspondence, July 6, 2006.
15. Lars Spuybroek, *NOX: Machining Architecture* (London: Thames & Hudson, 2004), 4.
16. Lars Spuybroek, private e-mail correspondence, June 14, 2006.
17. See Chris Anderson's "The Long Tail," a theory that tries to explain the fact that most blogs are visited only by a dozen or so friends and family members. http://www.wired.com/wired/archive/12.10/tail.html
18. *Dark Fiber* (Cambridge, MA: MIT Press, 2003), 42–67 and Reinder Rustema's masters thesis, http://reinder.rustema.nl/dds/.
19. See Sjoerd van der Helm's masters thesis (in Dutch), Bloggen is zo 2004!, een onderzoek naar de Nederlandse weblogwereld, scriptie Universiteit van Amsterdam, http://www.networkcultures.org/weblog/archives/2005/08/bloggen_is_zo_2.html.
20. Of course there are exceptions, for instance the Architect Web site, which aims to bring together designers from around the world to introduce new ideas from all disciplines, mainly focused on students. www.archinect.com/ (remark of Steffen Lehmann).
21. This material and the following quotes are from a private e-mail exchange in June 2006 with Wim Nijenhuis, who approved the text and translation into English.
22. Increased interest in *real* and *reality* goes back to Hal Foster's *The Return of the Real* from 1996 and ends with Slavoj Žižek's *Interrogating the Real*, published in 2005. The 2006 Berlin Transmediale festival was titled "Reality Addicts."
23. Bernard Huisman, *NRC-Handelsblad*, June 16, 2006.
24. Winy Maas of MVRDV: "There are different approaches to a global market. You can brand your style, as, say, Zaha is doing in a very super manner, or you can brand your approach. And I think our approach is very practical and dialectical; there is a desire to build the outstanding out of a dialogue." *Icon Magazine*, Summer 2006. http://www.icon-magazine.co.uk/issues/036/mvrdv.htm (thanks to Rob Annable for the reference).
25. See, for instance, the work of Urban Tapestries: http://urbantapestries.net. "Urban Tapestries is an experimental software platform for knowledge mapping and sharing—public authoring. It combines mobile and internet technologies with geographic information systems to allow people to build relationships between places and to associate stories, information, pictures,

sounds and videos with them. Urban Tapestries aims to enable people to become authors of the environment around them—Mass Observation for the 21st Century" (reference from Rob Annable).

26. IJburg is an artificial island, east of Amsterdam, constructed around 2000–2002, with thousands of residential houses, offices, a harbor, and a newly constructed beach.

27. From a private e-mail correspondence, August 10, 2006.

28. Willem van Toorn, NRC-Handelsblad, September 24, 2005.

29. Currently Job Goedhart is employed by his largest client Tom Postma Design (http://www.destandbouwer.nl/).

30. Marisa Yiu, private e-mail correspondence, July 29, 2006. www.eskyiu.com.

31. Steffen Lehmann, private e-mail correspondence, July 8, 2006.

32. Private e-mail correspondence, August 10, 2006.

33. See http://www.architectenwerk.nl/wiwo/index/achtergrond.htm.

Chapter 5

1. An earlier version of this chapter was submitted to Robert Hassen and Ron Purser, Eds., *On Time: Essays on Temporality in the Network Society* (Palo Alto, CA: Stanford University Press, 2006). Thanks to Robert Hassan for his comments and editorial assistance.

2. Paul Virilio in conversation with Carlos Oliveira, "Global Algorithm 1.7: The Silence of the Lambs: Paul Virilio in Conversation," June 12, 1996, *CTheory*, http://ctheory.net/articles.aspx?id=38.

3. Stefan Heidenreich, "Datenstroeme oder: >>Zeit im Netz.<<," *Berliner Gazette* 351, March 14, 2006, www.berlinergazette.de.

4. Douglas Kellner, "Virilio on Vision Machines," http://www.film-philosophy.com/vol2-1998/n30kellner.

5. Franco Berardi, "Biopolitics and Connective Mutation," Culture Machine 7, 2005, http://culturemachine.tees.ac.uk/Cmach/Backissues/j007/Articles/bifo.htm.

6. Timi Stoop-Alcala, "Thoughts on Internettime," private e-mail to the author, July 12, 2005.

7. Wolfgang Hagen, *Gegenwartsvergessenheit* (Berlin: Merve Verlag, 2003), 11.

8. Term coined by the Dutch sociologist Kees Schuyt.

9. Rachel Konrad, "For Some Techies, an Interminable Workday," *India Daily*, May 9, 2005, http://indiadaily.com/breaking_news/34689.asp.

10. Andrew Ross, *Fast Boat to China, Lessons from Shanghai, Corporate Flight and the Consequences of Free Trade* (New York: Pantheon Books, 2006), 97.

11. See Geert Lovink, "Net.Times, Not Swatch Time: 21st-Century Global Time Wars," in *Dark Fiber* (Cambridge, MA: MIT Press, 2002), 142–159.

12. http://www.swatch.com/internettime/.

13. See for instance www.clocklink.com. "Clocklink provides fashionable clocks that you can easily embed in your web page. All you need to do is simply paste the tag on your web page. Our clock will display the city name of your choice if you choose. You can also choose a time zone for your clock so it will show the correct time."

14. For a cultural history of satellites and the first real-time global broadcasts, see Lisa Parks, *Cultures in Orbit, Satellites and the Televisual* (Durham, NC: Duke University Press, 2005) and my interview with Lisa Parks, posted on the nettime mailinglist, November 1, 2005.
15. http://www.stevepavlina.com/blog/2006/02/time-management/. The site also gives tips on how to become an early riser.
16. Concept developed by Dutch sociologist Kees Schuyt. See Robert Henry Cox, "The Social Construction of an Imperative: Why Welfare Reform Happened in Denmark and the Netherlands but Not in Germany," in *World Politics*, 53, no. 3 (2001), 463–498.
17. http://www.alamut.com/subj/economics/attention/frank_discussion.html.
18. http://www.well.com/user/mgoldh/principles.html. See also his essay on First Monday, http://www.firstmonday.dk/issues/issue2_4/goldhaber/.
19. http://www.socialcustomer.com/2005/11/on_time_attenti.html. See also the work of the Austrian author Georg Franck, who in 1998 published a book called *Attention Economy* (*Ökonomie der Aufmerksamkeit*). A 1996 debate in English with Georg Franck can be found at http://www.alamut.com/subj/economics/attention/frank_discussion.html.
20. "When you pay attention to something (and when you ignore something), data is created. This 'attention data' is a valuable resource that reflects your interests, your activities and your values, and it serves as a proxy for your attention." www.attentiontrust.org. The four principles that are fundamental to Attention Trust are property, mobility, economy, and transparency.
21. Joi Ito, "Will More Moblog Help?", December 12, 2005, http://joi.ito.com/archives/2005/12/12/will_more_moblog_help.html
22. I have written more about this in my inaugural speech, *The Principle of Notworking* (The Netherlands: Amsterdam University Press, 2004).
23. Jean Baudrillard, *The Intelligence of Evil or the Lucidity Pact* (Oxford: Berg, 2005), 27.
24. John Holloway, "Time to Revolt—Reflections on Empire," http://libcom.org/library/time-to-revolt-empire-john-holloway (2002).
25. E-mail to the author, December 14, 2005.
26. See Bruce Sterling, *Shaping Things* (Cambridge, MA: MIT Press, 2005).
27. As a mirror project of the attention economy, a similar group of technorati around Stuart Brand developed the Long Now project, a clock that ticks every 10,000 years. http://www.longnow.org/. "The Long Now Foundation hopes to provide counterpoint to today's 'faster/cheaper' mind set and promote 'slower/better' thinking."
28. http://nomediakings.org/vidz/time_management_for_anarchists_the_movie.html.

Chapter 6

1. See http://waagsarai.waag.org/.
2. See http://www.RaqsmediacollectiveNet/.
3. Private e-mail conversation with Ravi Sundaram, May 18, 2006.

4. Johny and Mrinal, "Why Indian Boys Like to Shit in Western Toilets?" http://artindia.net/johny/art1.html. Raqs Media Collective co-founder Jeebesh Bagchi writes that this was a response to a work done by Raqs in 2000 called the Global Village Health Manual (GVHM), shown in exhibition print.com in Delhi. "Assessment of work within India has since being much more complex. The critical dialogue within the art scene in India has moved much ahead."

5. A report of my visit to Sarai was posted to nettime, March 23, 2001. A slightly different version can be found in *Dark Fiber* (Cambridge, MA: MIT Press, 2002), Sarai's Web site: www.sarai.net.

6. Supreet, one of the Sarai programmers, explained: "We have a PII 400 Mhz with 56 kbps dialup which I think is pretty decent config for a machine connected to net. It requires 333.916 secs this particular page to load which is AFAIK is graphics which shows all the projects inside the OPUS database." See http://www.opuscommons.net/templates/doc/index.htm. A few more numbers are available at http://www.opuscommons.net/usage/.

7. More than 180 million people in India regard Hindi as their native language. Another 300 million use it as a second language. Source: http://www.cs.colostate.edu/~malaiya/hindiint.html.

8. See, for instance, http://www.indlinux.org/wiki/index.php/Hindi.

9. See www.indic-computing.sourceforge.net.

10. See also Wikipedia entry, http://en.wikipedia.org/wiki/Cybermohalla.

11. Shveta Sarda, private correspondence, June 11, 2006.

12. Online version available at http://www.sarai.net/community/cybermohalla/book01/bylanes.htm.

13. URLs of the Cybermohalla Ibarat newsletter: http://www.sarai.net/community/cybermohalla/ibarat01/page1.html
http://www.sarai.net/community/cybermohalla/ibarat02/pages/page01.html
http://www.sarai.net/community/cybermohalla/ibarat03/PAGES/page01.html

14. See: http://www.documenta.de/data/english/artists/RAQS_media/txt_kurz-text.html.

15. The platform took place from May 7–12, 2001. See report at http://mail.sarai.net/pipermail/reader-list/2001-May/000069.html.

16. www.opuscommons.net. Silvan Zurbruegg and Pankaj Kaushal did the coding. See also Sarai's posting to nettime, July 2, 2002.

17. RAQS Media Collective @ Sarai: The New Media Initiative, Emoção Art. ficial Exhibition, Itau Cultural Center Sao Paulo, Brazil, August 2002, http://www.itaucultural.org.br/index.cfm?cd_pagina=1415.

18. http://lap.linux-delhi.org/cgi-bin/view/Main/LapHome.

19. http://www.linux-delhi.org/.

20. Taken from a posting on the Reader list in which the winning fellowships were announced, January 5, 2006. Throughout the year fellows post their research outcomes, theses, questions, and remarks to the Reader list, https://mail.sarai.net/pipermail/reader-list/.

21. The Web site of the Crisis Media workshop: http://www.sarai.net/events/crisis_media/crisis_media.htm and http://swj.waag.org/crisis.

22. See: http://www.sarai.net/cybermohalla/works/scratch_book/scratchbook. htm. "This is a book of suggestions. It contains a set of inscriptions that map the journeys and lines of flight of different people who have been working collaboratively in media labs for over thirty-two months. It embodies their process of work, experimentation, inventiveness and play. It is a register of notes, annals, journals, manuals, annotations, commentaries, conversations, suggestions, reflections, indexes and scrap books. It is a map of different projects undertaken, without defining final destinations. Instead it offers suggestions for alternative routes, and considerations on the possibilities that might lie in roads 'not yet taken'. It details everyday practical experiences, while creating something new in the process. It is an invitation to inscribe, and so to participate in this process of creating."
23. See http://broadsheet.var.cc/blog/archive/2005/06/13/letter-to-the-reader. html.
24. See http://www.sarai.net/cybermohalla/cybermohalla.htm.
25. Online diary of the Delhi–Liverpool exchange: http://cm-bootle-diary.var. cc/.
26. http://nangla.freeflux.net/.
27. E-mail interview, May 20, 2006.
28. To get a feel for Nehru Place, go to http://www.npithub.com/, a portal for computer parts that calls itself the "soul of the Indian IT Industry." See also the Satyam Cineplex at Nehru Place and the Intercontinental Hotel Eros.
29. Personal e-mail exchange, April 28, 2004.
30. For a workshop report see http://www.sarai.net/events/ipl/ipl.htm.
31. See also Taha Mehmood's story: "Three Men and a Tenant Verification Form," Reader-list, December 31, 2004.
32. The website http://waag.sarai.net/ is documenting the collaboration.
33. ALF homepage: http://www.altlawforum.org/. The Web site of the platform is slightly conceptual: http://www.opencultures.net/.
34. http://www.altlawforum.org/LITIGATION/litigation.
35. See http://world-information.org/wio/program/bangalore.
36. David Garcia wrote a background report on Autolabs in *Mute* 29 (London, 2005), 28–30. In it he asks "Do Autolabs simply appear critical, at best providing a few jobs for the most cooperative members of the excluded classes?" And: "Can a project originating from "outside" a community become the property of that community?"
37. See http://culturadigital.converse.org.br/tiki-index.php.
38. http://nangla.freeflux.net/blog/archive/2006/04/07/a-welcome-to-those-who-come-by-jaanu.html. "This dream would sit among us while we talked and did our own things, his eyes closed, but ears listening intently. Off and on, some word we said would sting him like a mosquito bite, and he would say, 'Where did you bring that word from?' The mosquitoes would buzz for a while, and then become quiet. Then the dream would open a notebook and scribble something in it."
39. http://blog.sarai.net/users/cartographicity/.
40. Shveta Sarda, private e-mail correspondence, June 11, 2006.
41. From a private e-mail conversation, May 18, 2006.
42. Ibid.

43. The Delhi Declaration of a New Context for New Media, http://www.vir-tueelplatform.nl/article-533-en.html (2005).

Chapter 7

1. Thanks to Michael Gurstein and Steve Cisler for useful comments on the draft. Some parts of this chapter were written with Soenke Zehle, co-moderator of the Incommunicado list and Web site. For more information, visit www.incommunicado.net. See also the proceedings of the Incommunicado '05 conference, published by the Institute of Network Cultures, *Incommunicado Reader*, Geert Lovink and Soenke Zehle, eds., (Amsterdam: INC, 2005), http://www.networkcultures.org/incommunicado/.
2. IICD is an independent non-profit foundation established by the Netherlands Minister for Development Cooperation in 1997. Its sources of core funding are the Dutch Directorate-General for Development Cooperation (DGIS), the U.K. Department for International Development (DFID), and the Swiss Agency for Development Cooperation (SDC).
3. http://www.itu.int/osg/spu/sfo/missinglink/index.html. During WSIS 2005, a book was published that looked into the history of The Missing Link report and its impact 20 years later. Gerard Milward-Oliver, Ed., *Maitland +20, Fixing the Missing Link* (Wiltshire: The Anima Centre Limited, 2005).
4. http://www.ips.org/. See also Cees J. Hamelink, *Cultural Autonomy in Global Communications* (New York: Longman, 1983).
5. Cees J. Hamelink, "Human Rights for the Information Society," in *Communicating in the Information Society*, Bruce Girard and Seán Ó Siochrú, eds., UNRISD, Geneva, 2003, 123.
6. For further information, see the ppp-l mailinglist and related Web site on public-private partnerships in ICT, an outcome of the Incommunicado 05 conference, www.pppwatch.org.
7. Gbenga Sesan, Ed., *Global Process, Local Reality; Nigerian Youth Lead Action in Information Society*, Paradigm Initiative Nigeria, *Lagos*, 2005, 17.
8. Sylvestre Ouédraogo, *L'ordinateur et le djembé* (*The Computer and the Jembe*) (Paris: L'Harmattan, 2004).
9. As part of the INC ICT4D research group, Roy Pullens wrote a report on border control as ICT for Development and the role of the International Organization for Migration (IOM) in the management of global migration. http://www.networkcultures.org/weblog/archives/2005/06/migration_manag.html.
10. Arturo Escobar, *Encountering Development, The Making and Unmaking of the Third World* (Princeton, NJ: Princeton University Press, 1995), 217.
11. Ibid., p. 221.
12. Ibid., p. 224. For Escobar's recent position, listen to his March 2006 speech "Information beyond Modernity: Globalization and Difference," http://broadcast.iu.edu/lectures/escobar/index.html.
13. See list archive: http://mail.sarai.net/pipermail/solaris/.
14. Writer Paul Theroux had a similar experience when he criticized the development work he observed in Malawi during his overland track from Alexandria to Cape Town. In *The Times* (January 1, 2006), Theroux wrote: "I got

a dusty reception lecturing at the Bill & Melinda Gates Foundation when I pointed out the successes of responsible policies in Botswana compared with the kleptomania of its neighbors. Donors enable embezzlement by turning a blind eye to bad governance, rigged elections and the deeper reasons why these countries are failing. Gates has said candidly that he wants to rid himself of his burden of billions. Bono is one of his trusted advisers. Gates wants to send computers to Africa—an unproductive not to say insane idea. I would offer pencils and paper, mops and brooms: the schools I have seen in Malawi need them badly."

15. Announcement of the Solaris Electronic Mailinglist, Initiative for Critical Issues of Internet and Development, nettime-lat, April 21, 2002.
16. An exception would be Roberto Verzola, *Towards a Political Economy of Information, Studies on the Information Economy* (Quezon City, Philippines: Foundation for Nationalist Studies, Inc., 2004).
17. Global Voices: http://www.globalvoicesonline.org/.
18. Thanks to Gerbrand Oudenaarden, who, as a tactical media activist, witnessed the protests in The Hague and Bonn from nearby.
19. An informed insider's account comes from Jonathan Peizer, who ran the Internet Program of the Soros Foundation for fifteen years. Jonathan Peizer, *The Dynamics of Technology for Social Change, Understanding the Factors That Influence Results: Lessons Learned from the Field* (New York: iUniverse, Inc., 2006).
20. See the SSRC Information Technology and International Cooperation (ITIC) program. http://www.ssrc.org/programs/itic/. I was on the Steering Committee of the IT & Civil Society section and, together with Jodi Dean and Jon Anderson, co-edited the anthology *Reformatting Politics: Information Technology and Global Civil Society* (New York: Routledge, 2006) in which some of the findings were collected.

Chapter 8

1. For this chapter I used and rewrote fragments from the following texts: Introduction to *Brazilian Tactical Media Reader*, Sao Paolo, 2006; "Another World is Possible" (with Florian Schneider), in makeworld paper #3, September 2002; "Review of the Age of Consent," nettime, September 30, 2003; and "Notes on the State of Networking" (with Florian Schneider), in makeworld paper #4, February 2004.
2. Geert Lovink and David Garcia, "The ABC of Tactical Media," netttime, May 16, 1997.
3. http://mediafilter.org/.
4. Alex Galloway, *Protocol* (Cambridge, MA: MIT Press, 2004), 175–206.
5. http://waag.sarai.net/display.php?id=2.
6. The argument is a rewrite, a tribute to Saskia Sassen, in an interview with *The Guardian*, July 4, 2006, http://www.guardian.co.uk/globalisation/story/0,,1812148,00.html.
7. George Monbiot, *The Age of Consent: A Manifesto for a New World Order*, Flamingo, London, 2003 (New York: The New Press, 2004). Reviews of *The Age of Consent*: Morag Fraser, *Sydney Morning Herald*, July 11, 2003; Peter

Taaffe, *The Socialist*, July 14, 2003; Michael Meacher, *The Guardian*, June 21, 2003; *The Economist*, June 26, 2003. See also George Monbiot's homepage, www.monbiot.com.

8. See Thomas Kuhn, *The Structure of Scientific Revolutions* (Chicago, IL: University of Chicago Press, 1962).

9. This changed in June 2006 when 11 heads of leading NGOs signed a global accountability charter for the non-profit sector. See http://news.amnesty.org/index/ENGPOL306062006.

10. ATTAC stands for Association pour la Taxation des Transactions pour l'Aide aux Citoyens, the Association for the Taxation of Financial Transactions for the Aid of Citizens that favors a tax on foreign exchange transactions. Its slogan is "The world is not for sale." See www.attac.org.

11. See the debates on the Oekonux mailinglists about the "germanition" of free software into a free society (www.oekonux.org) and the related chapter in my latest book, *My First Recession* (V2_Publishers, 2003).

12. http://www.ideasatthepowerhouse.com.au (Brisbane), http://www.adelaidefestival.org.au/ideas/2003/index.asp (Adelaide).

13. Fareed Zakaria, *The Future of Freedom* (New York: WW Norton, 2003).

14. Alex Foti, "Demoradical vs Demoliberal Regulation," nettime, July 6, 2006. Co-inventor of the tactical media concept, David Garcia comes to a similar conclusion in his essay "Learning the Right Lessons," posted to the Mute Web site on January 25, 2006, where he presents feminism as an "essential legacy of cultural politics." http://www.metamute.org/?q=en/Learning-the-Right-Lessons.

15. http://www.networkcultures.org/weblog/archives/2006/06/from_lists_to_b.html. See also my exchange with Kenneth Wirbin, "Critique of Ranking and Listing," nettime, August 24, 2006.

16. See Joseph Heath and Andrew Potter, *The Rebel Sell, Why Culture Can't Be Jammed* (Toronto: HarperCollins, 2004).

Chapter 9

1. In this chapter, I do not distinguish between the dark term *collaboration* and the somewhat idealistic term *cooperation*. In his text *Collaboration: The Dark Side of the Multitude*, Florian Schneider does make the distinction and explains that "in contrast to cooperation, collaboration is driven by complex realities rather than romantic notions of a common ground or commonality. It is an ambivalent process constituted by a set of paradoxical relationships between co-producers who affect each others. ...Collaboration as a traitorous cooperation with the enemy provides a counter to what management theory since the 80s has been promoting as team-work." Schneider defines collaborations as "black holes within knowledge regimes. Collaboration produces nothingness, opulence or ill-behavior. It does not happen for sentimental reasons, charity nor for the sake of efficiency, but for pure self interest." http://contre-conference.net/dp/?q=taxonomy/term/2 (French trans.). English version to be published in Sarai Reader 6 (New Delhi: Turbulence, 2006).

2. Rudy Hoeboer from the consultancy company Crossing Signals once explained to me why Europeans hesitated to talk about "the social" in a commercial context. Whereas U.S.-American business discourse has no problem plugging concepts such as social networks and pointing at their (technical) capability to facilitate people making connections with one another, Europeans would (unconsciously) associate "social" with weakness and the decline of the (failed) social welfare state. This is a remarkable turn as one would expect the U.S. management gurus to not make any references to "socialism," as opposed to Europeans, at least those who defend the Rhineland model and its post-World War II social achievements.

3. See the conference Web site www.freecooperation.org for the archive of the mailinglist and the program. Also a pdf of the free newspaper, which was produced at the eve of the event in a circulation of ten thousand can be downloaded from this site.

4. Brian Holmes, "Free Cooperation and After," extended text, unpublished text, written in October 2005, initial version posted to nettime, May 3, 2004.

5. The Third Mind is the title of a common publication of Gysin and Burroughs, published in 1978 by Viking Press. Jon Cates: "The Third Mind is s a compilation of fragments, texts and experiments that Gysin and Burroughs worked on at various points during their friendship. Naming Gysin, as well as Burroughs, is important because The Third Mind was a compilation of collaborative efforts rather than being an individual project about collaboration." *Empyre*, February 16, 2004.

6. One out of many examples that could be listed is the documentary of Willem Tyler Smith about the collaboration between the writers/musicians Michael McClure and Ray Manzarek. http://mcclure-manzarek.com/third-mind.html.

7. The list archive, pdf of the newspaper, and individual contributed quoted material can all be found on www.freecooperation.org.

8. Brian Holmes, "Artistic Autonomy and the Communication Society," nettime, October 26, 2003.

9. Christoph Spehr, (Hrsg.), *Gleicher als anderes* (Berlin: Dietz Verlag, 2003). The essay was written as a contribution to a competition set up by the Rosa Luxemburg Foundation, Berlin in 2000 as an answer to the question "Under which conditions can social equality and political freedom be compatible?" To his astonishment, Christoph Spehr won the prize. For Spehr, freedom and equality coincide in the concept of free cooperation. The essay was translated into English and published in the Buffalo 2004 proceedings, Trebor Scholz and Geert Lovink, eds., *The Art of Online Collaboration* (Brooklyn, NY: Autonomedia, 2006).

10. "Science Fiction for the Multitudes," Nettime, June 6, 2003, www.nettime. org.

11. The 2004 Buffalo conference resulted in a common effort to get Christoph Spehr's essay translated into English. It will be published in *Free Cooperation*, Geert Lovink and Trebor Scholz, eds. (Brooklyn, NY: Autonomedia, 2006), which also contains other material related to the Buffalo event.

12. See the chapter on the German Oekonux community in my book *My First Recession* (2003).

13. Quoted from the English translation manuscript of *Gleicher als andere*.
14. Online exchange between Christoph Spehr and Geert Lovink, April–June 2006.
15. Christoph Spehr, "Free Cooperation," transcript of a video made by O. Ressler, 2003, http://www.republicart.net/disc/aeas/spehr01_en.htm.
16. https://mail.cofa.unsw.edu.au/pipermail/empyre/2004-February/thread.html.
17. See the review by Adilkno of Klaus Theweleit's Book of Kings series, in Adilkno, *The Media Archive* (Brooklyn, NY: Autonomedia, 1998), http://thing.desk.nl/bilwet/adilkno/TheMediaArchive/33.txt.
18. Anna Munster, Empyre, February 17, 2004.
19. More on team and teamwork in Alan Liu, *The Laws of Cool, Knowledge Work and the Culture of Information* (Chicago, IL: University of Chicago Press, 2004), 47. Liu refers to the positive definition of the team as "the unit of ephemeral identity that most flexibly fuses technology and techniques into skill sets, adapted to the changefulness of the global economy." A negative definition is more compelling: "By definition a team is not an identity group, and it is assuredly not a class formation."
20. Private e-mail exchange with Matteo Pasquinelli, June 30, 2006.
21. Barry Wellman and Keith Frampton, "Neighboring in Netville: How the Internet Supports Community in a Wired Suburb," *City & Community* 2,4 (December 2003), 277–311. See also http://www.chass.utoronto.ca/~wellman/publications/index.html.
22. http://www.shirky.com/writings/situated_software.html. First published March 30, 2004 on the Networks, Economics, and Culture mailing list.
23. http://www.kolabora.com/news/2006/01/04/the_year_of_collaboration.htm.
24. See, for instance, http://www.medienkunstnetz.de/themes/overview_of_media_art/communication/14/.
25. Geert Lovink, "The Art of Collaboration, Interview with Charles Green," nettime, December 8, 2001.

Chapter 10

1. See *Fibreculture Journal*, no. 7, Distributed Aesthetics, http://journal.fibreculture.org/issue7/issue7_munster_lovink.html. The term "distributed aesthetics" came into being during the preparations of the Distributed Difference day that the Fibreculture network convened as part of the BEAP conference in Perth, Australia on September 10, 2004. See Ingrid Richardson's report on Fibreculture list, posted on September 14, 2004. This one-day event and the following *Fibreculture Journal* issue were organized by Lisa Gye, Anna Munster, and Ingrid Richardson.
2. The workshop was organized by Geert Lovink and Anna Munster. Participants: Giselle Beiguelmann, Brian Holmes, Richard Rogers, Warren Sack, Mercedes Bunz, Sebastian Lütgert, Nils Röller, Judith Rodenbeck, Clara Völker, Sabine Niederer, Linda Wallace, Trebor Scholz, and Olga Goriunova. See Trebor Scholz's report of the seminar, http://www.collectivate.net/journalisms/2006/5/16/distributed-aesthetics.html.

3. Warren Sack, "Aesthetics of Information Visualization," in *Context Providers*, Christiane Paul, Victoria Vesna, and Margot Lovejoy, eds.(Cambridge, MA: The MIT Press, forthcoming).
4. Taken from Trebor Scholz's seminar report.
5. Warren Sack, "What Does A Very Large-Scale Conversation Look Like?" *Leonardo: Journal of the International Society for Arts, Sciences, and Technology*, 35, 4 (2002), 417–426.
6. The most complete contribution of a formalist analysis of new media is made by the work of Lev Manovich. This is evident in his book *The Language of New Media* (Cambridge, MA: MIT Press, 2001) where he proposes a set of formal principles for the analysis of new media, but also in more recent texts, such as "The Shape of Information" (http://www.manovich.net, 2005). Although Manovich does not maintain that new media can be analyzed through a universal form or aesthetics, the question of emerging forms of culture driven by information as process and flow drive the theoretical trajectory of his work. The medium specificity approach is best exemplified in a text such as Janet Murray's essay "Inventing the Medium," her introduction to *The New Media Reader*, Noah Wardruip-Fruin and Nick Montfort, Eds. (Cambridge, MA: MIT Press, 2003), 3–29.
7. Pit Schultz, "The Producer as Power User," nettime, June 20, 2006. In this essay, Schultz describes the power user as someone who is "neither professional nor amateur, neither hobbyist nor self-employed, between sofa and kitchen table, sometimes expert, sometimes dilettante, leaving the suburbs and moving to the city centers or the countryside, using trains and airplanes but not owning a car. Living from project to project and shifting between unemployment and immediate wealth, the power user has left the factories and office buildings long ago to stay home and be the post-industrial anti-hero."
8. For further debates on this issue, see Janet Abrams and Peter Hall, Eds., *Else/where: Mapping New Cartographies of Networks and Territories* (Minneapolis, MN: University of Minnesota Design Institute, 2006).
9. PatternTracer is a software package for professional crime investigators that analyses and maps telephone call data to "quickly and automatically uncover clusters and underlying patterns," Product Overview–i2: Investigative Analysis Software, http://www.i2inc.com/Products/Pattern_Tracer/default.asp. Valdis Krebs is the most obvious example of recent work being conducted in the field of social network analysis and was responsible for mapping the network of pilots and hijackers involved in the World Trade Center attacks on September 11th. The Web site for the map of the Internet is at http://mapoftheinternet.com/.
10. Richard Rogers, "Why Map? The Techno-Epistemological Outlook", https://pzwart.wdka.hro.nl/mdr/pubsfolder/whymap/.
11. Ibid.
12. M. Dodge and R. Kitchin, *Atlas of Cyberspace* (London: Routledge, 2000), 107–128.
13. See Mark Granovetter, "The Strength of Weak Ties," *The American Journal of Sociology* 78.6m, 1360–1380, 1973 and Phil Williams, "Transnational Criminal Networks," in *Networks and Netwars: The Future of Terror, Crime, and Militancy*, J. Arquilla and D. Ronfeldt, eds. (Santa Monica, CA: RAND Corporation, 2001).

14. More on networks and maps, see Janet Abrams and Peter Hall, Eds., *Else/where: Mapping, New Cartographies of Territories* (Minneapolis, MN: University of Minnesota Design Institute, 2006).
15. There is no standardized usage or understanding of the term "social software." It is deployed by marketing executives and radical software analysts to categorize two polarized vectors in networks—the social and collective understanding and production of distributed software and the deployment of software to produce social ties between individualized subjects. Our concern with a use and elaboration of the socio-technical is with this latter deployment. See, for example, the article by Stowe Boyd, "Are You Ready for Social Software?" *Darwin: Information for Executives*, May 2003, http://www.darwinmag.com/read/050103/social.html.
16. Chris Anderson, "The Long Tail," *Wired*, 12.10, October 2004, http://www.wired.com/wired/archive/12.10/tail.html.
17. See particularly the Friendster network, which aims to "make the world a smaller place by bringing the power of social networking to every aspect of life, one friend at a time." "About Friendster," http://www.friendster.com/info/index.php?statpos=footer.
18. http://www.scotoma.org/notes/index.cgi?NetMonster.
19. Graham Harwood, Net Monster research site: HowItWorks, wiki located at http://www.scotoma.org/notes/index.cgi?HowItWorks. Plus research site Description, wiki located at http://www.scotoma.org/notes/index.cgi?NetMonsterDescription.
20. Jordan Crandall, "War, Desire, and the 'State of Readiness'," nettime, June 21, 2005.

Chapter 11

1. This chapter is a remix of an essay that I wrote with Ned Rossiter, published as "The Dawn of Organized Networks," *Fibreculture Journal* 05, 2005, http://journal.fibreculture.org/issue5/lovink_rossiter.html. An Italian translation is available at http://www.cybercultura.it/blog/?p=28. See also Ned Rossiter, *Organized Networks, Media Theory, Creative Labor* (Rotterdam: New Institutions, Netherlands Architecture Institute, 2006).
2. For elaboration on the concept of the constitutive outside as it relates to media theory and the politics of information, see Ned Rossiter, "Creative Industries, Comparative Media Theory, and the Limits of Critique from Within," *Topia: A Canadian Journal of Cultural Studies* 11 (Spring 2004): 21–48.
3. See the discussion on the Fibreculture mailing list about list governance, censorship, and organized networks in November/December 2004, www.fibreculture.org. More recently, discussions on the Spectre mailing list on media art and culture in Europe have broached the topic of new institutional forms and models of organization in the field of media art. See the thread on "ICC and for the media art center of 21C", August 2005 and Chapter 2 in this book on the crisis of new media arts.
4. Adilkno, *Media Archiv* (Brooklyn, NY: Autonomedia, 1998). http://thing.desk.nl/bilwet/adilkno/TheMediaArchive/40.txt.

5. Hugh Hewett, *Blog: Understanding the Information Reformation That's Changing Your World* (Nashville, TN: Thomas Nelson, Inc., 2005): xi.
6. See Bifo, "Biopolitics and Connective Mutation," *Culture Machine* 7, (2005), http://culturemachine.tees.ac.uk/Articles/bifo.htm.
7. See http://www.henkoosterling.nl.
8. One of the many crossovers between computer science and humanities, as proposed by Michael Gurstein and others. Some of their texts can be found at http://www.netzwissenschaft.de/sem/pool.htm.
9. Visit www.ngoinabox.org or www.frontlinedefenders.org.
10. Andrea Saveri, Howard Rheingold, and Kathy Vian, *Technologies of Cooperation* (Palo Alto, CA: Institute for the Future, 2005). http://www.rheingold.com/cooperation/Technology_of_cooperation.pdf.
11. See, for instance, the Directory of Open Access Journals, http://www.doaj.org/. For definitions, go to http://www.earlham.edu/~peters/fos/overview.htm.

Bibliography

Frequently Used Mailing Lists, Blogs, and Online Journals:

Nettime-l, International mailing list for net criticism, www.nettime.org.

Nettime-nl, Dutch list for Internet culture and criticism, www.nettime.org.

Syndicate, European list for new media arts and culture, www.v2.nl/syndicate.

Rohrpost, German language list for new media culture, www.nettime.org/rohrpost.

Fibreculture, Australian list for critical Internet research and culture, www.fibre-culture.org.

Fibreculture Journal, Australian-based peer reviewed publication related to the Fibreculture communitiy, http://journal.fibreculture.org/.

Oekonux, German (and parallel English) discussion list about free software and society, www.oekonux.org.

LINK, Australian discussion list for IT policy, http://sunsite.anu.edu.au/link/.

JUST-WATCH-L, international list for human rights and media, http://listserv.acsu.buffalo.edu/archives/justwatch-l.html.

LBO-talk, Left Business Observer discussion list, http://www.panix.com/~dhenwood/lbo-talk.html.

IDC, mailinglist of the Institute for Distributed Creativity, http://mailman.thing.net/cgi-bin/mailman/listinfo/idc.

Air-l, list of the Association of Internet Researchers, www.aoir.org.

Reader-list, discussion list of the New Delhi-based Sarai new media center, www.sarai.net.

Bytes for All list, ICT for development discussion list, www.bytesforall.org.

iMomus, blog and diary-journal of electronic musician and critic Momus (Nick Currie), http://imomus.livejournal.com/.

Streamtime, Web site of the international support campaign for Iraqi bloggers, http://www.streamtime.org/.

Always On, social network and collective blog of the Silicon Valley corporate culture, http://www.alwayson.goingon.com/.

Rough Type, blog of ICT critic Nicholas Carr, http://www.roughtype.com/index.php.
ProBlogger, "helping bloggers earn money" by Melbourne-based Darren Rowse, http://www.problogger.net/.
Global Voices, collaborative blog filtering, "The World is Talking, Are You Listening?"
http://www.globalvoicesonline.org/.
Datenströme, blog from Pit Schultz and Stefan Heidenreich (in German), http://www.datenstroeme.de/
World Changing, "another world is here," collaborative site on ecology and new technology, http://www.worldchanging.com/.
Joi Ito's personal Weblog, http://joi.ito.com/.
Chris Anderson's Web site on his Long Tail theory and related book, *The Long Tail*, Hyperion, 2006, http://longtail.typepad.com/.

Books and Articles:

Adilkno, *The Media Archive*, Brooklyn, NY: Autonomedia, 1998.
Agamben, Giorgio, *Die kommende Gesellschaft*, trans. Berlin: Merve Verlag, 2003.
Alavi, Nasrin, *We Are Iran, The Persian Blogs*, Brooklyn, NY: Soft Skull Press, 2005.
Barabási, Albert-László, *Linked, How Everything Is Connected to Everything Else and What It Means for Business, Science and Everyday Life*, London: Penguin Books, 2003.
Barkhoff, Jürgen/Böhme, and Hartmut/Riou, Jeanne, *Netzwerke, Eine Kulturtechnik der Moderne*, Köln: Böhlau Verlag, 2004.
Baudrillard, Jean, *The Intelligence of Evil or the Lucidity Pact*, trans. Oxford: Berg Publishers, 2005.
Baudrillard, Jean, *The Conspiracy of Art*, trans. Cambridge, MA: Semiotext(e), 2005.
Becker, Konrad, *Tactical Reality Dictionary*, Vienna: Edition Selene, 2002.
Benkler, Yochai, *The Wealth of Networks*, New Haven, CT: Yale University Press, 2006.
Benschop, Albert, *Kroniek van een Aangekondige Politieke Moord, Jihad in Nederland*, Utrecht: Forum, October 2004.
Bense, Max, *Ausgewählte Schriften 3, Ästhetik und Texttheorie*, Stuttgart: Verlag, J.B. Metzler, 1998.
Bifo (Franco Beradi), "Biopolitics and Connective Mutation," trans. *Culture Machine* 7, 2005, http://culturemachine.tees.ac.uk/frm_f1.htm.
Blood, Rebecca, Ed., *We've Got Blog, How Weblogs Are Changing Our Culture*, Cambridge, MA: Perseus Books, 2002.
Born, Georgina, *Rationalizing Culture: IRCAM, Boulez and the Institutionalization of the Musical Avant-Garde*, Cambridge , MA: MIT Press, 1995.
Brunnengräber, Achim, Klein Ansgar, and Walk, Heike, *NGOs im Prozess der Globalisierung, Mächtige Zwerge—Umstittene Riesen*, Bonn: Bundeszentrale für politische Bildung, 2005.
Bruns, Axel, *Gatewatching, Collaborative Online News Production*, New York: Peter Lang, 2005.
Bürger, Peter, *Theory of the Avant-Garde*, trans. Minneapolis, MN: Minnesota Press, 1984.
Cacciari, Massimo, *Zeit ohne Chronos*, trans. Klagenfurt: Ritter Verlag, 1988.

Carr, Karen, *The Banalization of Nihilism*, Albany, NY: SUNY Press, 1992.

Carr, Nicholas G., *Does IT Matter? Information Technology and the Corrosion of Competitive Advantage*, Boston, MA: Harvard Business School Press, 2004.

Chadwick, Whitney, and de Courtivron, Isabelle, Eds., *Significant Others, Creativity and Intimate Relationship*, London: Thames and Hudson, 1993.

Chatterjee, Partha, *The Politics of the Governed, Reflections on Popular Politics in Most of the World*, Delhi: Permanent Black, 2004.

Chorus, Jutta, and Olgun, Ahmet, *In Godsnaam, Het Jaar van Theo van Gogh*, Amsterdam: Contact, 2005.

Cioran, E.M., *On the Heights of Despair*, trans. Chicago, IL: Chicago University Press, 1992.

Citythoughts Architects (red.), Citythoughts #9, *Suburban Scenario's*, Stichting Citythoughts, Amsterdam, 2006.

Clemens, Justin, *The Romanticism of Contemporary Theory: Institution, Aesthetics, Nihilism*, Ashgate: Aldershot, 2003.

Clifford, James, *The Predicament of Culture*, Cambridge, MA: Harvard University Press, 1988.

Cox, Geoff, Krysa, Joasia, and Lewin, Anya, *Economising Culture, On 'The (Digital) Culture Industry'*, Brooklyn, NY: Autonomedia, 2004.

Dawkins, Kristin, *Global Governance, The Battle over Planetary Power*, New York: Seven Stories Press, 2003.

Decostere, Stefaan (red.), *Weak Media—Dit Is Als Of Dat*, Oostende: Cargo, 2006.

Eagleton, Terry, *After Theory*, Cambridge, MA: Basic Books, 2003.

Eliade, Mircea, *Ewige Bilder und Sinnbilder*, Frankfurt am Main: Insel Verlag, 1986.

Escobar, Arturo, *Encountering Development, The Making and Unmaking of the Third World*, Princeton, NJ: Princeton University Press, 1995.

Feenberg, A., and Bakardjieva M., Eds., *Community in the Digital Age: Philosophy and Practice*, Lanham: Rowman and Littlefield, 2004.

Foucault, Michel, *Aesthetics, Method, and Epistemology*, London: Penguin Press, 1998.

Fromm, Erich, *Fear of Freedom*, London: Routledge & Kegan Paul, 1942.

Furedi, Frank, *Politics of Fear, Beyond Left and Right*, New York: Continuum, 2005.

Galloway, Alexander R., *Protocol, How Control Exists After Decentralization*, Cambridge, MA: MIT Press, 2004.

Gillmor, Dan, *We the Media*, Sebastopol: O'Reilly, 2004.

Gilroy, Paul, *After Empire*, London: Routledge, 2004.

Girard, Bruce, and Ó Siochrú, Seán, *Communicating in the Information Society*, Geneva: UNRISD, 2003.

Gladwell, Malcolm, *The Tipping Point, How Little Things Can Make a Big Difference*, New York: Little, Brown and Company, 2002.

Goudsblom, J., *Nihilisme en cultuur*, Amsterdam: De Arbeiderspers, 1960.

Greenblatt, Stephan, *Renaissance Self-Fashioning, From More to Shakespeare*, Chicago, IL: Chicago University Press, 1980.

Greenspan, Anna, *India and the IT Revolution*, New York: Palgrave Macmillan, 2004.

Groys, Boris, *Topologie der Kunst*, München: Hanser Verlag, 2003.

Hagen, Wolfgang Hagen, *Gegenwartsvergessenheit*, Berlin: Merwe Verlag, 2003.

Hamelink, Cees J., *Cultural Autonomy in Global Communications*, New York: Longman, 1983.

Hardt, Michael, and Negri, Antonio, *Multitude, War and Democracy in the Age of Empire*, New York: Penguin Press, 2004.

Hartmann, Frank, *Medienphilosophie*, Wien: WUV, 2000.

Hartmann, Frank, *Mediologie, Ansätze einer Medientheorie der Kulturwissenschaften*, Wien: WUV, 2003.

Heath, Joseph, and Potter, Andrew, *The Rebel Sell, Why Culture Can't Be Jammed*, Toronto: HarperCollins, 2005.

Helm, Sjoerd van der, *Bloggen is zó 2004!, een onderzoek naar de Nederlandse weblogwereld*, afstudeerscriptie, Universiteit van Amsterdam, Media & Cultuur, juni 2005.

Hewitt, Hugh, *Blog: Understanding the Information Reformation*, Nashville, TN: Nelson Books, 2005.

Hoffer, Eric, *The True Believer, Thoughts on the Nature of Mass Movements*, New York: Harper & Row, 1951.

Houellebeq, Michel, *Whatever*, London: Serpent's Tail, 1998.

Kaene, John, *Global Civil Society?* Cambridge: Cambridge University Press, 2003.

Kaldor, Mary, *Global Civil Society, An Answer to War*, Cambridge: Polity Press, 2003.

Karatani, Kojin, *Transcritique: On Kant and Marx*, Cambridge, MA: MIT Press, 2003.

Kennedy, David, *The Dark Sides of Virtue, Reassessing International Humanitarianism*, Princeton, NJ: Princeton University Press, 2004.

Kingsnorth, Paul, *One No, Many Yeses, A Journey to the Heart of the Global Resistance Movement*, London: Simon & Schuster, 2003.

Kline, David, and Burstein, Dan, *Blog!, How the Newest Media Revolution is Changing Politics, Business, and Culture*, New York: CDS Books, 2005.

Kroker, Arthur, *The Will to Technology & The Culture of Nihilism*, Toronto: University of Toronto Press, 2004.

Lagaay, Alice, and Lauer, David, *Medientheorien, Eine philosophische Einführung*, Frankfurt am Main: Campus Verlag, 2004.

Latour, Bruno, *Reassambling the Social, An Introduction to Actor-Network-Theory*, New York: Oxford University Press, 2005.

Leadbeater, Charles, *Up the Down Escalator: Why the Global Pessimists are Wrong*, London: Viking, 2002.

Leadbeater, Charles, and Miller, Paul, *The Pro-Am Revolution, How Enthusiasts are Changing our Economy and Society*, London: Demos, November 2004, http://www.demos.co.uk/publications/proameconomy.

Lessig, Lawrence, *Free Culture, How Big Media Uses Technology and the Law to Lock Down Culture and Control Creativity*, New York: Penguin Books, 2004.

Liu, Alan, *The Laws of Cool, Knowledge and the Culture of Information*, Chicago, IL: University of Chicago Press, 2004.

Locke, Christopher, *The Bombast Transcripts*, Cambridge, MA: Perseus Books, 2002.

Lotringer, Sylvère, and Virilio, Paul, *The Accident of Art*, Cambridge, MA: Semiotext(e), 2005.

Löwith, Karl, *Martin Heidegger and European Nihilism*, New York: Columbia University Press, 1998.

Lovink, Geert, *Uncanny Networks, Dialogues with the Virtual Intelligentia*, Cambridge, MA: MIT Press, 2002.

Lovink, Geert, *Dark Fiber, Tracking Critical Internet Culture*, Cambridge, MA: MIT Press, 2002.

Lovink, Geert. *My First Recession, Critical Internet Culture in Transition*, Rotterdam: V2_/NAi Publishers, 2003.

Lovink, Geert, *The Principle of Notworking* (brochure), Amsterdam: University of Amsterdam Press, 2005.

Lovink, Geert, and Zehle, Soenke, eds., *Incommunicado Reader*, Amsterdam: Institute of Network Cultures, 2005.

Lunenfeld, Peter, *User, InfoTechnoDemo*, Cambridge, MA: MIT Press, 2005.

Mallon, Thomas, *A Book of One's Own, People and Their Diaries*, St. Paul, MN: Hungry Mind, 1984.

McCaughey, Martha, and Ayers, Michael D., *Cyberactivism, Online Activism in Theory and Practice*, New York: Routledge, 2003.

McQuire, Scott, and Papatergiadis, Nikos, *Empires, Ruins + Networks, The Transcultural Agenda in Art*, Melbourne: Melbourne University Press, 2005.

Meikle, Graham, *Future Active, Media Activism and the Internet*, Annandale: Pluto Press Australia, 2002.

Monbiot, George, *The Age of Consent, A Manifesto for a New World Order*, London: HarperCollins, 2003.

Mouffe, Chantal, *On The Political*, New York: Routledge, 2005.

Münker, Stefan, Roesler, Alexander, and Sandbothe, Mike, *Medienphilosophie, Beiträge zur Klärung eines Begriffes*, Frankfurt am Main: Fischer Verlag, 2003.

Munroe, Jim, *Time Management for Anarchists*, No Media Kings (blog), April 27, 2005, http://nomediakings.org/vidz/time_management_for_anarchists_the_movie.html.

Nandy, Ashis, *The Romance of the State, And the Fate of Dissent in the Tropics*, New Delhi: Oxford University Press, 2003.

Narula, Monica, Ed., "The Public Domain," *Sarai Reader* 01, Delhi: Sarai/CSDS, 2001.

Narula, Monica, Ed., "The Cities of Everyday Life," *Sarai Reader* 02, Delhi: Sarai/CSDS, 2002.

Narula, Monica, Ed., "Shaping Technologies," *Sarai Reader* 03, Delhi: Sarai/CSDS, 2003.

Narula, Monica, Ed., "Crisis/Media," *Sarai Reader* 04, Delhi: Sarai/CSDS, 2004.

Narula, Monica, Ed., "Bare Acts," *Sarai Reader* 05, Delhi: Sarai/CSDS, 2005.

Nederveen Pieterse, Jan, *Development Theory, Deconstructions/Reconstructions*, London: Sage, 2001.

Nederveen Pieterse, Jan, *Globalization or Empire?* New York: Routledge, 2004.

Notes From Nowhere, *We Are Everywhere, The Irresistable Rise of Global Anticapitalism*, London: Verso, 2003.

Oosterling, Henk, *Radicale Middelmatigheid*, Amsterdam: Boom, 2000.

Ouédraogo, Sylvestre, *The Computer and the Jembe, Between Dreams and Realities*, Paris: L'Harmattan, 2003.

Parks, Lisa, *Cultures in Orbit, Satellites and the Televisual*, Durham, NC: Duke University Press, 2005.

Parfitt, Trevor, *The End of Development, Modernity, Post-Modernity and Development*, London: Pluto Press, 2002.

Pax, Salam, *The Clandestine Diary of an Ordinary Iraqi*, New York: Grove Press, 2003.

Peizer, Jonathan, *The Dynamics of Technology for Social Change*, New York: iUniverse, Inc., 2006.

Perniola, Mario, *Wider die Kommunikation*, trans. Berlin: Merwe Verlag, 2005.

Peters, Tom, *Reimagine!* London: Dorling Kindersley Limited, 2003.

Pettman, Dominic, *After the Orgy, Towards a Politics of Exhaustion*, Albany, NY: SUNY Press, 2002.

Pias, Claus (Hg.), *Zukünfte des Computers*, Zürich: diaphanes, 2005.

Poggioli, Renato, *The Theory of the Avant-Garde*, trans. Cambridge, MA: Harvard University Press, 1968.

Postrel, Virginia, *The Substance of Style, How the Rise of Aesthetic Value is Remaking Commerce, Culture and Consciousness*, New York: HarperCollins, 2003.

Ratcliffe, Mitch, and Lebknowsky, Jon, *Extreme Democracy*, print on demand, www.extremedemocracy.com, 2005.

Reck, Hans-Ulrich, *Mythos Medienkunst*, Köln: Verlag der Buchhandlung Walther König, 2002.

Reynolds, Glenn, *An Army of Davids, How Markets and Technology Empower Ordinary People to Beat Big Media, Big Government and Other Goliaths*, Nashville, TN: Nelson Current, 2006.

Rheingold, Howard, *Smart Mobs, The Next Social Revolution*, Cambridge, MA: Perseus Books, 2002.

Rieff, David, *A Bed for the Night, Humanitarianism in Crisis*, New York: Simon & Schuster, 2003.

Ronell, Avital, *Stupidity*, Urbana, IL: University of Illinois Press, 2003.

Rosa, Hartmut, *Beschleunigung, Die Veränderung der Zeitstruktur in der Moderne*, Frankfurt am Main: Suhrkamp, 2005.

Rose, Eugene, *Nihilism: The Root of the Revolution of the Modern Age*, Platina: St. Herman of Alaska Brotherhood, 1994.

Ross, Andrew, *Fast Boat to China, Lessons from Shanghai*, New York: Pantheon Books, 2006.

Rossiter, Ned, "Creative Industries, Comparative Media Theory, and the Limits of Critique from Within," *Topia: A Canadian Journal of Cultural Studies* 11, 21–48, 2004.

Sassen, Saskia, *Globalization and Its Discontents, Essays on the New Mobility of People and Money*, New York: The New Press, 1998.

Scott, Jill, *Artists in Labs, Processes of Inquiry*, Wien: Springer Verlag, 2006.

Sen, Amartya, *Development as Freedom*, New York: Anchor Books, 2000.

Siegert, Bernhard, *Relays, Literature as an Epoch of the Postal System*, trans. Palo Alto, CA: Stanford University Press, 1999.

Sloterdijk, Peter, *Im Weltinnenraum des Kapitals*, Frankfurt am Main: Suhrkamp, 2005.

Smith, Neil, *The New Urban Frontier, Gentrification and the Revanchist City*, New York: Routledge, 1996.

Snow, C.P., *The Two Cultures*, Cambridge: Cambridge University Press, 1993.

Spehr, Christoph, *Die Aliens sind unter uns! – Herrschaft und Befreiung im Demokratischen Zeitalter*, München: Goldmann Verlag, 1999.

Spehr, Christoph (Hrsg.), *Gleicher als andere, Eine Grundlegung der freien Kooperation*, Berlin: Dietz Verlag, 2003.

Spuybroek, Lars, *NOX: Machining Architecture*, London: Thames & Hudson, 2004.

Stalder, Felix, *Open Cultures and the Nature of Networks*, Novi Sad; kuda.read, 2005.

Strauss, Leo, *Persecution and the Art of Writing*, Chicago, IL: The University of Chicago Press, 1952.

Surowiecki, James, *The Wisdom of Crowds, Why the Many Are Smarter Than the Few*, New York: Doubleday, 2004.

Terraova, Tiziana, *Network Culture, Politics for the Information Age*, London: Pluto Press, 2004.

Tholen, Georg Christoph, Scholl, Michael, and Heller, Martin, *Zeitreise, Bilder/Maschinen/Strategien/Rätsel*, Zürich: Stroemfeld/Roter Stern, 1993.

Trippi, Joe, *The Revolution Will Not Be Televised, Democracy, the Internet, and the Overthrow of Everything*, New York: HarperCollins, 2004.

Vattimo, Gianni, *Nihilism and Emancipation: Ethics, Politics and Law*, New York: Columbia University Press, 2004.

Verzola, Roberto, *Towards a Political Economy of Information*, Quezon City, the Philippines: Foundation for Nationalist Studies, Inc., 2004.

Virno, Paul, *A Grammer of the Multitude*, Cambridge, MA: Semiotext(e), 2004.

Vishmidt, Marina, Ed., *Media Mutandis: a NODE.London Reader*, London: open-mute.org, 2006.

Watts, Duncan J., *Six Degrees, The Science of a Connected Age*, New York: W.W. Norton, 2003.

Weber, Stefan, *Medien—Systeme—Netze, Elemente einer Theorie der Cyber-Netzwerke*, Bielefeld: transcript Verlag, 2001.

Weber, Stefan (Hrsg.), *Theorie der Medien, Von der Kulturkritik bis zum Konstruktivismus*, Konstanz: UVK, 2003.

Weigel, Gerolf, and Waldburger, Daniele, *ICT4D—Connecting People for a Better World*, Berne: SDC/GKP, 2004.

Weinberger, David, *Small Piece Loosely Joined, a Unified Theory of the Web*, Cambridge, MA: Perseus Books, 2002.

Weinrich, Harald, *Knappe Zeit, Kunst und Ökonomie des befristeten Lebens*, Hamburg: C.H. Beck, 2004.

West, Cornel, *Race Matters*, New York: Vintage, 1994.

West, Cornel, *Democracy Matters, Winning the Fight Against Imperialism*, New York: Penguin Books, 2004.

Winkler, Hartmut, *Versuch über die innere Ökonomie der Medien*, Frankfurt am Main: Suhrkamp, 2004.

Winthrop-Young, Geoffrey, *Friedrich Kittler zur Einführung*, Hamburg: Junius Verlag, 2005.

Wolfson, Rutger (red.), *Kunst in Crisis*, Amsterdam: Prometheus, 2003.

Yúdice, George, *The Expediency of Culture, Uses of Culture in the Global Era*, Durham, NC: Duke University Press, 2003.

Zakaria, Fareed, *The Future of Freedom: Illiberal Democracy at Home and Abroad*, New York: WW Norton, 2003.

Index

Local events, as foundation of global justice movement, 200
Local Internet systems, collapse in Netherlands, 105
Local radio, role in relation to Internet, 172
Local time
end of, 117
Internet site postings of, 122
Locality labs
loyalty to neighborhoods, 156
open *vs.* closed nature of Sarai's, 155
at Sarai, 145, 146
Localized content, 175
Lost time, 126–127
as rule not exception, 128
Luhmann, Niklas, 84

M

Mahajan, Ashish, 132
Mapping software, 229, 281
Maquis, as synonym for multitudes, 211
Market-managerialism, xiv
Massively Multiplayer Online Role-Playing Games (MMORPGs), 33
McLuhan, Marshall, 95
Meaningless art, as future luxury, 72
Media archeology, 41
Media freedom
fear of, 36
undermining of listening by, 27
Media philosophy, 91, 94, 96
Marshall McLuhan and origins of, 95
Mediocrity, association with Germany, 84
Medium, relationship to electronic arts, 45
Mental capitalism, 129
Michellemalkin.com, 2
Micro-identities, 191
Micropayment systems, network inability to work with, 254
Microsoft
engagement in ICT4D, 163
involvement in global telecenter support effort, 163
product use in India, 142, 143
Microsoft Windows, support for Hindi Unicode, 135
Middlemen, elimination by amateurs, 111, 116
Migrant labor, impact in hardware/software industries, 182
Military
and origins of new media arts, 83
relationship to media and literature, 83
role in infotainment, 93
Miniaturization, failure of new media arts to exploit, 79
Ministerio de Industria de España, viii
MIT Media Lab
closure of, 52
One Laptop per Child initiative, 162, 168
Mobs, ix
Modernity, subverting hegemony of, 171
Monbiot, George, 193–199
Monetary economy, network connections to, 246–247
Monopolies, xx
Moronic cynicism, 16
Motivational art, 51–52
Multiple-purpose National Identification Card (MNIC), introduction in India, 149–150
Multitudes, 186
and crisis of society of labor, 216
digital, 193
fluidity and becoming of, 216
power to constitute world, 196
and precarity, 215
Spehr's maquis as, 211
Munster, Anna, 48, 225
Museums, nonacceptance of new media by, 66
Mutual aid initiatives, 209
difficulties of, 159
MVRDV, 109
My First Recession, vii, xxi, 12
MySpace.com, 3, 203